FRENCH
LITERATURE

FRENCH LITERATURE

ITS HISTORY AND ITS MEANING

WALLACE FOWLIE

Duke University

PRENTICE-HALL, INC.   *Englewood Cliffs, New Jersey*

Library of Congress Cataloging in Publication Data

Fowlie, Wallace
  French literature.

  Bibliography: p.
  1. French literature—History and criticism.
I. Title.
PQ103.F6 1973   840'.9   72-3960
ISBN 0-13-331181-3
ISBN 0-13-331173-2 (pbk.)

10 9 8 7 6 5 4 3 2 1

Printed in the United States of America

PRENTICE-HALL INTERNATIONAL, INC., London
PRENTICE-HALL OF AUSTRALIA, PTY. LTD., Sydney
PRENTICE-HALL OF CANADA, LTD., Toronto
PRENTICE-HALL OF INDIA PRIVATE LIMITED, New Delhi
PRENTICE-HALL OF JAPAN, INC., Tokyo

CONTENTS

SEVENTEENTH CENTURY   57

EIGHTEENTH CENTURY   99

NINETEENTH CENTURY 131

TWENTIETH CENTURY   215

INTRODUCTION

FRANCE SEEN THROUGH HER LITERATURE

All of France's achievements in ideas and culture, in art and political thought and science, are contained in her literature. The history of Paris as well as the particular customs of the provinces are reflected in the novels, the essays, and the poetry of French writers. This is to say that the culture of France is essentially the cultivation, practice and sensitivity of her language.

The extraordinary respect the French feel for their language is a key to the achievements of France. The continuity of the French language, which is as clearly identifiable in the 15th century poetry of François Villon as it is today, is synonymous with the continuity of French culture. The awareness and pride in this continuity has colored the French mind century after century. The great professors of France, from Pierre Abélard of the 12th century to Jean-Paul Sartre of the 20th, have fashioned the French language in such a way that it can express theological and metaphysical complexities. At the same time their thought was controlled and shaped by the language they had inherited. Medieval students in the drinking houses of Paris debated the great issues of thought and life in the same language and with the same animation that students today, in the Latin Quarter, discuss the same issues.

The very elegance of the language, its sharpness and flexibility, has kept alive the desire to debate and record debates as they have occurred throughout history—we find them in the *essais* of Montaigne, the *pensées* of Pascal, and the *journal* of Gide. The skill of argument serves both to delight and scandalize, but the language comes first and provides the delicate means for the debate. And the language has been formed by every generation and every class—by students and teachers in the university, by lawyers of the king, by merchants, by nobles and by peasants.

Although Abélard was one of the first internationally known teachers and philosophers of France, he is probably better remembered today for his love affair with his pupil Héloïse, for love and philosophy easily cohabit in France. In the fifteenth century Villon celebrated the beauty of Héloïse in his *Ballade des dames du temps jadis*, and in the

18th century Rousseau, in his autobiographical novel *La Nouvelle Héloïse*, saw himself as a new Abélard, perhaps more romantic and passionate than philosophical. Abélard actually wrote his love letters in Latin, but this is the same language, in the etymological sense, as the language of the letters of Rousseau's Abélard. The continuity of the language and the sentiment make these works seem almost contemporaneous.

So the language is the literature, and the literature is the awareness France has had of herself through the centuries. No other country places such high importance on its literature as being the fullest and truest expression of its destiny. And yet no one writer represents France or the French mind in the way that Dante represents Italy and Shakespeare represents England. The less great voices of France—the minority voices—never allow a single voice to dominate. Racine was put down in his age; Molière was constantly opposed during his career as dramatist and theater director. Voltaire, Mme de Staël and Victor Hugo lived in exile during a part of their careers.

The civilization of ancient Rome is the basis of French civilization, and the ancient Romans were initiated into the cult of thought and beauty by the Greeks. Thus the humanist tradition of France is both Roman and Greek in origin. It is to be found not only in architecture, literature, and philosophy but also in the institutions, laws, and customs of the French, in their habits and their education. The Roman temple in Nîmes called *la maison carrée* was so much admired by Thomas Jefferson that he made it the model for the Virginia state capitol in Richmond. The Romanesque churches of Burgundy and Languedoc were built before the days of Gothic architecture.

However, the best record of the tradition by which Gaul was romanized is to be found in the literature. The Roman sense of law and order is seen in Montesquieu; the Roman cult for man's reason and his sense of greatness are found in Corneille and Bossuet. The Greek spirit has had less extensive impact on the French mind, but it is apparent in the tragedies of Racine, the fables of La Fontaine, and the poetry of André Chénier. Victor Hugo oversimplified this double heritage when he claimed that France is Athenian in its worship of beauty and Roman in its cult of greatness.

The sense of a literary culture and tradition is stronger in France than in other countries. When Cardinal Richelieu, the 17th-century prime minister, consolidated the power of the feudal lords, the last powerful barons resembling feudal lords, he founded L'Académie Française, which still functions today and which for more than three hundred years has put down anarchy in language and style and favored obedience to the rules of good taste. The Académie was the creation of the French monarchy, and one thinks of it as a force that helped to develop and sustain the movement in art and letters that is called classicism. Its forty members, called *les quarante immortels*, are the official representatives of literature. Throughout its history the Académie has elicited irony, wit, and sarcasm from the French, and today is still criticized for its tendency toward ossification. Yet some of the ablest men still rival one another in their efforts to be elected an academician.

In our day some of the greatest writers, such as Malraux, Sartre and Char, are not in the Académie and have not gone to the trouble of placing their candidacy. When Jean Cocteau was elected to the Académie in 1955, it seemed incredible to most

Frenchmen that he had solicited such an election and that he was elected. When questioned about this, Cocteau merely replied that he did it because it was unpredictable and therefore in keeping with his legend of *enfant terrible*. With the election in 1960 of René Clair, the French Academy finally recognized the art of the cinema.

Louis XIV, as sun king and absolute monarch, reigned during the second half of the seventeenth century when France set the standards for the civilized world. At that time French became the first foreign language learned in other countries, and this tradition still continues today. Louis was the embodiment of classicism—the protector of all the arts, literature in particular. The literary forms and the literary aesthetics of classicism remain more alive today than the painting, architecture, music, or politics of *le grand siècle*.

After Louis XIV, literature separated from the king, the state, and the Church. Voltaire became in the 18th century the supreme example of the independent writer critical of the institutions of his age. But no writer from that time, including Voltaire himself, ever forgot or disclaimed his roots in classicism.

During the latter part of his lifetime Voltaire enjoyed universal glory. The prestige the French language had won under Louis XIV was enhanced by the example Voltaire gave the world of his wit and the clarity of his writing—that kind of clarity that was looked upon as an intellectual virtue.

Voltaire became the notorious enemy of orthodox Christianity; even today in France believers tend to be militantly intellectual. A large part of the population appears indifferent to Christianity, and there is considerable evidence, especially in *la classe ouvrière*, of hostility.

Prose is the dominant medium in French literature, and seems to give more power to the French language than does poetry. There have been few really great poets in France: Villon, Ronsard, Baudelaire, Mallarmé, and very few others. Rivarol called poetry a luxury object: "C'est la prose qui donne l'empire à une langue." Flaubert, in one of his letters, pointed out that poetry is detested in France and has to be disguised: "Il faut déguiser la poésie en France, on la déteste." The poet André Chénier said that of all the European nations, the French like poetry the least. And Jean Cocteau, in one of his essays, restated the same thought, asking, "Qui fait la grandeur de la France? C'est Villon, c'est Rimbaud, c'est Verlaine, c'est Baudelaire."

The ordinary French reader wants to read everything and believes he should be able to read everything easily. He finds he cannot read Rimbaud and Mallarmé and Valéry without study, so they are merely names for him associated with obscure poetry. He is often surprised that foreigners, Americans in particular, have more time than he does for the reading of such esoteric poets. The Frenchman is by nature sceptical, especially sceptical of what he does not comprehend readily. He prefers to give up lyrical effusions for contemporary realities. In fact, he has given as a title to one of his popular magazines the word *Réalités*.

The problem of poetry and its limited audience is a subject of enduring inquiry in France. Molière and La Fontaine are still known and admired by a wide segment of the population. Balzac became a fairly popular novelist in his day—as popular as

Dickens in England or Mark Twain in America. But the best poetry from the time of Baudelaire on has been difficult and baffling for the majority of French readers. Even Louis Aragon, a luminary and key literary figure in the French communist party, was not read by the people who knew his name and applauded him at public meetings.

Baudelaire was the first of the modern poets in terms of his sensibility and his understanding of poetry. He best exemplifies the artist in conflict with society—the type of poet who asks of poetry the solution to the mysteries of man and his destiny. By joining poetry with metaphysics, he founded a lineage, almost a dynasty, of poets: Mallarmé, Rimbaud, Valéry, Claudel, Jouve and Bonnefoy, all of whom have acknowledged their debt to him. No other age in the history of French poetry equals in richness and brilliance the sixty-five years between *Les Fleurs du Mal* of Baudelaire and *Charmes* of Valéry.

If France has shown great boldness in her political revolutions and aesthetic innovations, the fundamental conservatism of French taste has always tempered the boldness. The French public is slow to accept the new in art and literature. Protected and patronized by the king and his court, a poet such as Ronsard in the 16th century and dramatists such as Molière and Racine in the 17th received full recognition in their day, but only by a public of connoisseurs.

The case of Stendhal is exemplary. Looked upon today as one of the four or five great French novelists, he himself predicted in 1830 that he would not be read and recognized until 1880. It was an accurate prophecy. Flaubert, another of the major novelists, was slow to be recognized, and he constantly berated and vilified the bourgeois public for its stupidity and lack of good taste. Mallarmé probably never expected to be recognized by more than a few ardent disciples, but he bemoaned the fate of his good friend Edouard Manet, whose masterpieces remained year after year in the studio. In the twentieth century, the surrealists were scorned by the general public during their active years in the 20s and 30s, but since that time their importance has grown, and today their influence on poetry, painting and the cinema is recognized.

The average Frenchman speaks better than the average citizen of other countries. But though he has more respect for the prestige of literature, he does not necessarily read it. Marcel Proust is a name in France. His life and excentricities are somewhat known, but he is not read, save possibly for a few passages on hawthorns and linden tea from the beginning of *Du côté de chez Swann*.

If poetry does not represent the most eminent achievement in French literature, what does? The votes are usually cast in favor of classical tragedy and the modern novel. These two forms, each belonging to a different age, have permitted the French writer to demonstrate and indulge his skill in the analysis of passion. French literature could be described in its totality as the analysis of man, or even the analysis of the effect of love in man, if by love is meant both love for woman and love for God.

The primary reason for the importance of these forms seems to be the absence of myths in French culture. There have been no indigenous myths in France—there is no Prometheus and no Orpheus, no Trojan War, no Odyssey, no Narcissus—although the French have used these classical myths in every age, Ronsard in his odes, Racine in *Phèdre*, Voltaire in *Oedipe*, Camus in *Le Mythe de Sisyphe*.

In the absence of any native French myths, dramatists and novelists have concentrated their efforts on a search for answers to such questions as: What elevates man? What depresses him? What motives explain his life? These are some of the questions asked by writers in prose and verse—by Chrétien de Troyes in the *roman courtois* of the 12th century, by Rutebeuf in his poems of the 13th century, by the Lyon poet Maurice Scève in the 16th, by La Bruyère and La Rochefoucauld in the classical age. How can one explain man's thirst for power? What are the various forms that man's vanity takes?

We could make the claim here that the most searching and compelling analyst of them all is Marcel Proust. He studies in his long novel *A la recherche du temps perdu*, not once but many times, how love is born, how it grows, how it dies. Only Stendhal competes with him for first place among the analysts of love. But after these two there are countless French writers who have taught the world something about the experience of love, which remains the most important and tantalizing of all of man's experiences: Mme de Lafayette in *La Princesse de Clèves*, Constant in *Adolphe*, Mauriac in *Le Désert de l'amour*, Gide in *La Porte Etroite*. These are deliberately mentioned as representative of four very different kinds of love story.

In order to be read in France, philosophy, history and theology must be literary. Some critics believe that the greatest prose writer of France is the historian Jules Michelet. Here again we touch on the mystique of language. There is perhaps no other country in which a major writer would make such a statement as Stéphane Mallarmé once made: "Everything exists in the world in order to end in a book [Tout existe au monde pour aboutir à un livre]."

The problems of spirituality are explored in French literature by means of a dialogue that seems to be perpetuated from century to century. With two voices, one offsetting or even contradicting the other, the problem at hand can appear richer and more meaningful. When the critic Charles Du Bos spoke of this form of dialogue in France, he cited as first example the dialogue between Montaigne and Pascal—the dialogue between doubt and certainty. He called it the major French dialogue, the one that still fascinates and disturbs the French mind.

In America we tend to take sides in questions of taste and belief, and we express our preferences and usually abide by them. We might prefer, for example, either the literary style of Henry James or Hemingway; we might prefer the dithyrambic poetry of Whitman or the intellectualized controlled poetry of Wallace Stevens. The French do not take sides easily. They enjoy defending each side in turn. If one day a Frenchman argues in favor of Montaigne, and persuasively, he might argue the next day in favor of Pascal with equal persuasiveness.

Many able critics have tried to explain the intelligence of the French mind and the charm of the French character. Some have dealt quite profoundly with this difficult subject, as Henry Adams in America, for example, Ernst-Robert Curtius in Germany, and Dennis Brogan in our own time in England. Such men are well aware of the contradictions in the French temperament that make definitions almost impossible or unworkable. Although the clarity of French thought has often been extolled, studied obscurity is also decidedly French.

It has been claimed that the French have no sense of the infinite—no visionary power such as can be found in Spanish literature, in a Saint John of the Cross, for example. It is true that the religious poetry of Racine and Claudel is not primarily mystical, but there are passages in D'Aubigné, Hugo, Péguy, Bernanos, and even in Rimbaud's *Saison en enfer* that are difficult to characterize in any other way than mystical. After all, France is as much the country of Jeanne d'Arc and Teilhard de Chardin as she is the country of Voltaire and Sartre. Attempts at generalized definitions are unsatisfactory and even futile, and the reason is fairly simple to explain. In the case of French writers, literature is much more than a reflection of life—it is a reordering of life, the creation of a new life.

When the Gauls adopted Rome, they did it quite quickly, and therewith adopted and assimilated a very mature civilization. This adoption is still visible in monuments— for example in Le Pont du Gard, the Roman aqueduct near Nîmes. The Roman heritage is also present in the judicative French mind, in which is rooted a sense of history, an awareness of this legacy of Rome, and the achievement of each century since the beginning of what can be called French history. *La Chanson de Roland* is at the head of these achievements, and the phrase *la douce France* occurs for the first time in that work.

In France, the present is never allowed to obliterate the past. At appropriate moments the French deliberately recall the past and celebrate it by reexamination, by a process of reevaluation. Thus in 1971, the French celebrated both the centenary anniversary of the Commune and the birth of Marcel Proust.

Without morbidity, the French remember the dead as if they were still living. Whenever Baudelaire's monument in the Cimetière Montparnasse is visited, there is almost certain to be a small bunch of fresh flowers placed there on the stone. There are many societies organized in the names of writers of the past to perpetuate the study of their work and to relate it to the present. The reasons are not pietistic or chauvinistic; these societies exist to make the past present. Each May the *Société des amis de Marcel Proust* meets in Illiers, now called Illiers-Combray, where, in addition to the reading of papers, they pick hawthorns in memory of Proust's novel. This is not a purely sentimental act, but an almost sacred testimony to the aesthetic joy and intellectual stimulation that Proust has given the world.

In the foyer of the Comédie Française there is on permanent exhibit the chair used by Molière when he played *Le Malade Imaginaire*. During the last performance he was to give, he was seated on that chair when he had an attack that caused his death a few hours later. This chair is not so much a sentimental relic as a testimonial to the writer who combined perhaps the greatest number of French traits—the writer who is undoubtedly the most universally loved French genius. Louis XIV once asked Boileau, the foremost critic of his time, who, of all the writers of his kingdom, would be remembered the longest. Boileau's answer came quickly: "Molière, Sire."

In 1969, soon after General de Gaulle had withdrawn as president of the Fifth Republic, *Time Magazine* published a long controversial article entitled "The French Face Mediocrity." The editors of *Time* wondered how France could survive after losing the lofty spirit of the man who had ruled over the French for so long, after the silencing of the speeches that had incited in the French dreams of greatness and glory. The general had made a sustained effort to place France once again among the powerful nations of the world. Like the novelists Balzac and Zola, he was both realist and visionary. After his withdrawal and after his death, the French have reexamined their cultural as well as their economic and social problems, and the *Time* editors, aware of the new wave of industrialism in France since World War II, questioned whether or not such an emphasis has led the French to neglect the resources of the imagination and the intelligence. They applied the word "mediocrity" especially to the literary and artistic output in recent years. "Is not the artistic center of the world today New York rather than Paris?" they asked. In a purely commercial sense, this is probably true, for New York has certainly become the selling center of art.

De Gaulle made André Malraux minister of culture, giving him power to stimulate and strengthen a new creativity in the arts. Malraux' most important work seems to have been the museum shows he organized, such as the big retrospective exhibitions of Picasso and Vermeer. In recent years young painters from other countries have continued to go to Paris in large numbers to work with such masters as André Lhôte, Zadkine and Gromaire, and it is estimated that today there are more young painters in Montparnasse than there were in the time of Modigliani. French pop artists like Martial Raysse have attracted as much attention as American pop artists.

One of the leading questions in the *Time* report was, "Have there been any successors to Sartre and Camus?" and the implication was that there have not been any. It is true that those two writers, who had far-reaching influence, especially on the young in the 1950s, were not referred to by the students in the May 1968 revolt. A similar question could be asked in our own country: "Who are the successors to Faulkner and Hemingway?" The problem of a writer's communication with his public is not solely a French problem. A much bigger question is being asked today in every country by a few critics: Will literature survive anywhere?

The *Time* article claimed that the theaters in Paris are languishing, and we hear similar reports every year about New York theaters. No nation can produce a new genius every theatrical season. A good dramatist needs several seasons before he is accepted. It took ten years of strong opposition before Ionesco was fully accepted. Genet today is a universally known figure, but it is safe to claim that his work is not well known.

A fairer judgment of the contemporary scene in Paris would point out that the quality of intellectual creative works has diminished less than it has changed direction. The most recent output of poetry is perhaps less impressive than the critical writings on the meaning of poetry we can read in the pages of Maurice Blanchot and Georges Poulet. The most recent novels contain less imaginative creative power than the personal experiences in thought and criticism we find in the writings of Barthes, Starobinski, Jacques Derrida, and of the most universal of contemporary French thinkers, Claude Lévi-Strauss.

The French literary milieu does represent a unique phenomenon in its geographical and social concentration. Unlike London, New York, Milan (not to mention Rome), the literary scene in France is totally concentrated in Paris. A recent census showed that in a list of the 170 leading French writers, only 16 live outside Paris. Moreover, French writers know one another. They meet regularly. They talk with one another, argue and fight with one another. All the publishers are in Paris, and most of them are in three *arrondissements*. All the leading magazines are published in Paris. All the leading critics exercise their power and influence by publishing regularly in Paris newspapers.

We remember great moments in literature because they have become part of our lives: the first meeting between Manon and Des Grieux; the moonlit night when Julien Sorel climbed up to Mathilde's window with the intention of seducing her; the picture of the young girls on the beach at Balbec. There is a ceaseless traffic going on between ideas and books, between thought and action—a movement, a circulation constantly going on between literature and life by which great writers lead men more subtly than politicians. There exists a relationship between the enigmatic prose of Samuel Beckett and our contemporary problems, between Camus' myth of the absurd and our modern wars, between the resurrection of the past in the novels of François Mauriac and our efforts today to prepare the future.

FRENCH
LITERATURE

MIDDLE AGES

HISTORY		LITERATURE	
778	Charlemagne's defeat at Roncevaux		
800	Charlemagne's coronation	842	Serments de Strasbourg
1095–1099	First Crusade	c. 1080–1100	Chanson de Roland
		1100–1200	Chansons de geste
		1150–1200	Romans courtois
		c. 1165	Tristan et Iseut
		1165–1190	Chrétien de Troyes
1226–1270	reign of Saint Louis	c. 1230	Roman de la Rose I
		c. 1280	Roman de la Rose II
1337	beginning of Hundred Years War	1309	Joinville, Vie de Saint Louis
		1370–1400	Froissart, Chroniques
1431	death of Joan of Arc	1450	Gréban, le vrai mystère de la Passion
1453	end of Hundred Years War	1461	Villon, Grand Testament
1461–83	reign of Louis XI	1465	Pathelin

antiquity = quality v 6. ancient

The Earliest Texts

The expression *moyen-âge*, "Middle Age" or "Middle Ages," as it is usually called in English, was invented by 16th-century humanists to designate the transitional period between classical antiquity and the Renaissance. They scorned the Middle Ages as dark times of ignorance and superstition. They forgot that medieval monks had copied the manuscripts of antiquity and were responsible for the transmission of literary and philosophical masterpieces from the Greco-Latin world. The virtues of classical antiquity were not reborn in the 16th century, as the humanists claimed, and were not defunct in the Middle Ages. It is true, however, that they became better known and were more ardently studied in the Renaissance.

In the strict French literary sense, the Middle Ages extended from the end of the 11th century (*La Chanson de Roland*) to the end of the 15th century (Villon's *Le Grand Testament*). There are very few texts in French prior to the year 1100. The 12th and 13th centuries were great ages of literary creation, as evidenced by *chansons de geste, romans courtois*, lyric poetry, *Le Roman de la Rose, fabliaux*, and dramatic works. The 14th and 15th centuries appear less brilliant, probably because they were so upset by wars.

Literary study of the Middle Ages was neglected and even scorned by the humanists of the 16th century, by the so-called classical writers of the 17th century, and by the *philosophes* of the 18th century. The rehabilitation of the Middle Ages did not begin until the 19th century; first by Chateaubriand, who in his *Génie du Christianisme* initiated a new attitude toward the beauty and power of Gothic art. Many of the later romantics, influenced by Chateaubriand, were attracted to the Middle Ages—Victor Hugo, especially, who made dramatic use of the violent contrasts of that period.

Thanks to excellent scholars at the end of the 19th century and beginning

2

of the 20th century, many erroneous ideas concerning the Middle Ages have been dispelled. Now seen as far more than a mere transitional period, that era stands today in its own greatness—an age in which the major problems of man were faced and almost all the literary genres flourished. The anonymous medieval works, literary and plastic, are today looked upon as works created by authentic and fully conscious artists. On the whole, those men were *clercs,* a word that today corresponds to *lettrés. Clercs,* in opposition to *laïcs,* enjoyed ecclesiastical privileges and were under the jurisdiction of the Church. When Jean-Paul Sartre speaks of the Middle Ages he uses the word *clercs* to designate writers.

Between the 4th and the 9th centuries, Latin or "vulgar" Latin (used by Roman soldiers), which had been spoken in Gaul since the Roman conquest, was altered and enriched by foreign elements, Germanic in particular. In the north, Latin became French, *la langue d'oïl,* and in the south, it became Provençal, *la langue d'oc.* (The affirmative *oui* was pronounced *oïl* in the northern dialects, and *oc* in the dialects of the south.) Throughout the Roman Empire, the varied use of Vulgar Latin developed into what is today called Romance languages (*langues romanes*): French, Provençal, Italian, Spanish and Rumanian. In France the linguistic frontier separating French and Provençal ran approximately from La Rochelle in the west through Limoges, Clermont-Ferrand, Lyon and Grenoble.

The earliest French text, *Les Serments de Strasbourg,* dates from the year 842, and is actually a political treaty dividing the Carolingian Empire. The earliest literary text is a thirty-line fragment of the *Cantilène de Sainte Eulalie,* written at the end of the 9th century. Other stories of the lives of saints followed *Eulalie,* especially the *Vie de Saint Léger* and the *Vie de Saint Alexis* (dating from about 1040). These works are examples of hagiography, texts of a purely religious nature written to inform and inspire the faithful. The Council of Tours (812) had advocated that sermons be preached in the language of the people, and stories of the saints were probably associated with church services.

LA CHANSON DE ROLAND
and other *chansons de geste*

The oldest version of the legend of Roland was discovered in the 19th century. It is known today as the "Oxford manuscript" and is kept in the Bodleian Library. The editor gave to the text the title *La Chanson de Roland*. It is made up of 4002 ten-syllable lines and is organized into 291 *laisses*, or uneven stanzas, each one of which is written in assonance. This assonance, the repetition of the same vowel sound at the end of each line, gives a technical unity to the *laisse*.

The date of the Oxford manuscript is approximately 1170, but it is generally believed that the poem is older, and contemporary with the first crusade, at the end of the 11th century. It has been the most enduring of all the old French epics (*chansons de geste*). German and Norwegian versions date from the 12th and 13th centuries; Pulci and Boiardo in the 15th century, and Ariosto in the 16th century, wrote their Italian versions of the *Roland*. But not until the 19th century was *La Chanson de Roland* studied and admired as a work of art composed in accordance with a definite plan and providing an accurate picture of the medieval literary hero.

The poem is clearly divided into three major actions: the plot or betrayal destined to defeat Charlemagne; the battle; and the punishment of the enemy.

1. *laisses* 1–79. The pagan leader Marsile holds court in Saragossa, the only part of Spain that has not been conquered by Charlemagne. The traitor Blancandrin proposes that promises be made to Charlemagne so that he will leave the country. Once he is out of Spain, the promises will not have to be kept. In a similar council scene, in Cordua, the traitor Ganelon proposes to Charlemagne a politics of conciliation. Roland opposes the plan for peace; Blancandrin and Ganelon together plot the death of Roland. The rear guard of Charlemagne's army is placed under the command of Roland, and the emperor returns to France.

2. *laisses* 80–176. The battle takes place at Roncevaux in the Pyrenees. After the initial attack of the Saracens, Olivier, Roland's friend and companion-in-arms, urges Roland to blow his horn (*olifant*) for help, but Roland refuses because of his *gloire*, his honor. *Roland est preux, et Olivier est sage.* Provocations and individual fights announce the major conflict. Not until the French warriors know they are doomed and the martyrdom of the twelve peers begins, does Roland blow his horn. Charlemagne replies, and the battle continues. Olivier is killed, and then Turpin the archbishop, and finally Roland.

3. *laisses* 177–291. Charlemagne reaches Roncevaux too late to save his

own army, but he destroys the Saracen army. As he pays honor to the dead, more Saracens appear and another heavy battle begins, ending with Charlemagne's victory over Baligant thanks to the intervention of the archangel Gabriel. In the city of Blaye (near Bordeaux), in the church of Saint-Romain, the bodies of Olivier, Roland and Turpin are buried. Ganelon is put to death, and Charlemagne dreams of setting out on a new mission.

The historical data concerning the battle of Roncevaux in 778 were radically altered by the poet who composed the *Chanson* three hundred years later. Out of a local incident in which the Basques, Christians themselves, attacked the army of the young king Charles, the poet created the story of a war with a religious and political significance and exalted the figure of Emperor Charlemagne. Roland's fidelity to Charlemagne and his bravery were feudal concepts that had grown with the power of the Church and with the founding of sanctuaries containing religious relics. The first crusade (1096–1099), in which Godefroi de Bouillon and French *seigneurs* set out to free the Holy Land, coincided with the writing of the epic. Since Charlemagne had once intervened in Moslem Spain, he was looked upon as the forerunner of the crusades. *La Chanson de Roland* is a transfiguration of that war in Spain and a poem of praise to the mystical aspect of feudalism; namely the conviction that the bearing of arms will open up the gates of heaven.

The author of the *Roland* is unknown. The last line, "Ci falt la geste que Turoldus declinet [Here stops the *geste* that Turoldus exposes]" is ambiguous. Turoldus might be the poet who composed the work, the scribe who copied the text, or the *jongleur* who recited it.

Chanson de geste is the genre name of the medieval French epic. *Geste* would seem to mean "accomplishments" or even "history." The work is a narrative poem destined to be recited or chanted and accompanied by a primitive harp called *une vielle*. The popularity of *la geste* is attested to by the proliferation of the genre extending to the 14th century. This proliferation grew around cycles— the one concerning Charlemagne (*Berthe au grand pied, Huon de Bordeaux, Le couronnement de Louis*), the cycle of Garin de Monglane (in celebration of Guillaume d'Orange), and the cycle of Doon de Mayence, in which the themes are more purely feudal than Christian.

Scholars have paid more attention to theories concerning the origins of the *chansons de geste* than to the texts themselves, many of which appear crude and monotonous. When *La Chanson de Roland* was first published in 1837, it was looked upon as an arrangement of popular songs that had been composed by various generations of *trouvères*. (*Un trouvère* is a poet of northern France as opposed to *un troubadour of the south.*) This is called the theory of the *cantilènes*, the hypothesis suggesting that lyric poems existed before the longer narrative or epic poem. Gaston Paris, in particular, favored the *cantilène* theory.

Other scholars, Pio Raysia, for example, believed that the origin of *La Chanson de Roland* was an epic composed at approximately the same time of the event it celebrated and that it was constantly modified in successive generations, eventually becoming the Oxford manuscript of the *Roland*. Still other scholars assign to it a Germanic mythic origin.

Joseph Bédier, in his *Légendes épiques* of 1912, refuted these theories by attempting to prove that *La Chanson de Roland* could not have been written before the end of the 11th century. Bédier developed the theory that pilgrimages encouraged the birth of legends associated with heroes, and thus the *Roland* was associated with the famous pilgrimage to Saint Jacques de Compostelle, which passed through Blaye, Bordeaux, Roncevaux and Pampelune. The abbey church of Roncevaux was, according to this theory, the center of the growth of the Roland legend, and the *Chanson* was the work of an excellent poet who put together various legends that were attached to the long itinerary.

Pauphilet goes farther than Bédier in his interpretation of the genesis of the epic poems by crediting the poet himself with the full invention of the legend. New theories continue to revise or correct earlier theories, and no one theory today seems fully justifiable.

The artistic effects in the *Roland* were certainly achieved through conscious effort: these include the logical succession of episodes, the presentation of characters in action, and the marked sobriety of the narrative. Each major character has clearly delineated traits: Turpin, the archbishop, is also a courageous soldier; Ganelon, the traitor, is filled with hate but is also courageous; Olivier, the prudent knight, *le sage*, is valorous in battle and a devoted friend; *Roland le preux* is headstrong and proud and needs the fury of battle to achieve satisfaction; Charlemagne, the chosen of God, is pictured as a superhuman character pursuing a sacred mission.

The organization of the poem is simple. The poet never intervenes to explain the behavior and the action of the characters. He describes objectively the gestures that they made. The epic universe is unreal. All the battles are colossal, the fighters have extraordinary strength, their horses are magnificent, and their swords are incomparable! These men seek out heroic adventures and means of demonstrating their valor. Love has no place in their lives. Their exaltation comes from danger; their motives are human and religious because the spirit of the early epics coincides with the spirit of the crusaders and the spirit of adventurers. The knight's *gloire* is the same as that of his lord (*seigneur*, or *suzerain*). Roland incarnates the exemplary devotion of the vassal to his lord. The medieval *paladin* (as he was called, the word *paladin* coming from *palais*) became an international literary type.

COURTLY LOVE IN THE 12TH CENTURY:
les romans courtois of Chrétien de Troyes

By the middle of the 12th century another kind of narrative literature had come into prominence, addressed essentially to the aristocratic class and destined to spread throughout Europe. "Courtly romance" is the translation of this new form, *le roman courtois*. The word *roman* originally meant the "vulgar tongue"; that is, French as opposed to Latin. It was applied so vigorously to the new literature that it finally came to designate the narrative form and "novel." After eight centuries (c. 1150–1970), it still is the most permanent and stalwart literary form.

The adjective *courtois* comes from *la cour*, the "court," and designates the spirit that prevails in the stories. *Le roman courtois* represented, first, a social ideal that flourished in the second half of the 12th century, when the power of woman in both the royal court and the baronial courts grew rapidly. Thus the second feudal age saw the codifying of rules of moral conduct of the knights (*chevaliers*) and the creation of social etiquette in the two kinds of courts (*la cour royale* and *la cour seigneuriale*) when the subject of conversation and inquiry became an examination of the problem of love—a discussion of how both man and woman behave during the experience of love. *L'amour courtois*, as it is called, is the submission of the knight to the lady (*le chevalier–la dame*), a submission that strongly resembled the submission of the vassal to his lord (*le vassal–le suzerain*).

From the south (*le midi*) where it had its origins, *l'esprit courtois* spread to the north, largely through the influence of the two daughters of Aliénor d'Aquitaine: Marie de Champagne, in her court at Troyes, and Aélis de Blois, in her court in Touraine. These two courts were typical centers of literary activity in which a code of behavior was developed that was to resemble preciosity of the 17th century.

The genesis of the *romans courtois* was in such works classified as *romans antiques* (*le roman de Thèbes, le roman d'Enéas, le roman de Troie*) and the Breton material (*la matière de Bretagne*). *Brut*, by the Anglo-Norman poet Robert Wace, canon of Bayeux, was the verse translation of the *Historia Regum Britanniae* by Geoffrey of Monmouth. This Latin chronicle described the reigns of British kings, Celtic heroes, and Arthur and the knights of the Round Table. The date of the French translation was 1155. The "novel" as written by Chrétien de Troyes grew out of the classical and celtic themes to which were added Christian themes.

The second half of the 12th century was fairly peaceful. Bishop Maurice de Sully laid the first stone of Notre Dame de Paris in 1163, and the cathedral was completed a century later. Latin liturgical dramas, to which stanzas in French were added, were sung at Christmas and Easter. *Chansons de geste* were still sung in public squares, and another public began reading for pleasure works written in Latin and in French. In addition to the fictional works of Chrétien de Troyes, there were *lais*, short poems by Marie de France, *fables*, and the novel of *Tristan et Iseut*, written by Béroul and Thomas independently of one another.

Chrétien de Troyes was concerned with his literary reputation and his desire for fame. He names himself in several places in his writings, either Chrétien or Chrétien de Troyes, which may mean that he came from the northern province of Champagne or that Troyes, famous for its fairs, was the center of his activity.

His first novel, *Erec et Enide*, written about 1162, introduces Arthur and his knights. *Cligès* came probably two years later. *Lancelot ou le chevalier à la charrette* was written about 1168 at the suggestion (or the command) of Marie de Champagne, and illustrates more vividly than other *romans* the significance of courtly love. The hero owes to the lady total devotion, and she owes nothing in return. When Lancelot hesitates for even a few seconds before climbing into a cart, a dishonorable act for a knight but one that would help him in a mission to deliver Queen Guenivere, he errs in his devotion and must pay for it by fighting as a coward in a tournament.

Yvain ou le chevalier au lion, written about 1170, became well known, along with the earlier *romans*, throughout 13th-century Europe. These are "thesis novels" in the sense that they develop theories about passion and love, about the problems raised by a hero's conscience. *Yvain*, for example, deals with the danger of sacrificing love to the temptations of heroic adventure. Chrétien constructs elaborate plots in which feats of chivalry vie with magical enchantments, and sword fights follow love scenes. He enjoys the analysis of motives and discussion of ideas related to love. He is, moreover, an able versifier. All of his *romans* are written in octosyllabic lines with rhyming couplets.

Tristan

The earliest literary version of the Tristan legend has been lost, but the two existing versions, written in about 1170, are doubtless derived from it. Béroul's version of 4,500 lines contains the major episodes of the story and was written for a wide public. It has some of the simplicity and pathos of the *chansons de geste*. Thomas' version is shorter—3,000 lines—and is often referred to as the courtly version. It is the complete story and is more refined in its treatment of the love story. One of the *lais* of Marie de France is the Tristan subject, *Le Chèvrefeuille*. Gottfried de Strasbourg's adaptation in German follows the Thomas version. Wagner's opera in the 19th century and Cocteau's 20th-century film, *L'Eternel Retour*, were inspired by the Tristan story. In the early 20th century, Joseph Bédier reconstructed *Le roman de Tristan* in modern French prose, drawing upon all the existing versions and translations.

Tristan is raised by his uncle Marc, king of Cornwall, and as a valiant knight frees the country of the giant Morholt. Wounded by the poisoned sword of Morholt, he is cured by the mother of Iseut-la-blonde. On his return to Cornwall, King Marc shows him a golden hair and vows he would marry the girl to whom it belongs. Tristan finds *la belle aux cheveux d'or*, who is Iseut. On the ship taking them home, they drink from a magic potion (*le philtre d'amour*) destined for Marc and Iseut, and fall in love. Marc marries Iseut and does not learn of the love between Tristan and Iseut for some time. When they are discovered they flee the castle and enter the forest of Morois. Marc comes upon them asleep, a sword between them, and does not kill them; although their remorse forces them to separate, they never recover from their love.

Tristan and Iseut were guilty of adultery and victimized by love. Tristan betrayed his king (or his second father) and Iseut betrayed her husband. Love is a "passion" (in the sense of suffering), inspired by the magic potion, and stronger than moral and religious laws. *Tristan* is preeminently the novel of fate, and is recapitulated in the tragedies of Racine and *La Princesse de Clèves* of the 17th century and in Wagner's opera in the 19th. *Roland*, the epic of will-power and honor, is recast by Corneille in his tragedies in the 17th century. It is not possible to give the Tristan legend a Christian interpretation (see Denis de Rougemont's *L'Amour et l'Occident*) and it is difficult to make it fit the code of chivalry. Today it stands out as one of the most tragic love stories in world literature, and remains closely associated with the Celtic tradition of savagery and melancholy, with its appropriate setting of the sea and the forest of Morois and the heathland.

When a recent French scholar was asked the meaning of love, he replied, "Love? You mean that invention of the 12th century?"

Perceval (12th–13th centuries)

In Chrétien de Troyes' last work, *Perceval*, the myth of the Holy Grail is introduced into the Arthurian legends. Since Chrétien died before completing the *roman*, it is impossible to know how far he would have developed it in the direction of Christian mysticism. He completed 10,000 octosyllabic lines. Four other poets completed the work, which has 60,000 lines in all (the longest *chanson de geste* was 20,000 lines). In the next century, the elaborate Lancelot-Grail material, recast by several writers, appeared in a long prose work. Whereas Chrétien's *Perceval* is a moving narration of poetic charm, the prose *Lancelot* is the legend of the quest of the Holy Grail, representing the soul's search for God. The contemplation of the Grail would seem to be man's happiness in God, a happiness that can be known only by the pure in heart and body.

Young Perceval, in the Chrétien version, wants to be a knight (*chevalier*) despite the precautions his mother takes to keep him from such a career. One day in his wanderings he finds himself in the castle of the Fisher-King (*le roi pêcheur*) and observes a procession in which a vase is carried. He does not dare ask for an explanation. If he had, the suffering king would have been cured, and all the inhabitants of the castle and the kingdom would have profited. The next day nothing remains of his vision. Later, when he learns that what he saw was the Holy Grail (the cup used by Christ in the last supper and in which Joseph of Arimathea received the blood of Christ on the cross), he sets out to find it.

In the prose *Lancelot* of the 13th century, the complete legend is developed, including the story of the Holy Grail, Merlin, Lancelot of the Lake, the quest of the Grail, and the death of King Arthur. The sacred vessel is kept in the castle of la Terre Foraine (the castle in which young Perceval had once seen the Grail). Even the most courageous knights fail in the quest because they are impure and have lived in sin: Gauwain, Parsifal and Lancelot (lover of Queen Guenivère). But the son of Lancelot, Galahad (Galaad), accomplishes the mission, and his purity enables him to behold the mysteries of the Grail. At Galahad's death, the Arthurian world vanishes in a vast conflagration. It is the "twilight of the gods."

The word *grail* (*graal*) has given as much trouble to philologists as the Grail itself gave to the knights of the Round Table. Its history is an example of the mysteries attached to the origins of the important symbols of mankind. It might have come from the Latin words *gratus* and *gradus*, which mean a plate with food piled upon it, but it more likely comes from the Vulgar Latin *cratalem* (and the Greek *kratêe*), close to the English word *crater*. The Greek word designated a hollow dish in which wine was diluted. Pilgrims in the Middle Ages were anxious to procure relics from the Holy Land, so the chalice of the Last Supper was naturally a very revered and sought-after object.

In the prose *Lancelot*, it is learned that the Grail is in the castle of Corbenic, in Great Britain, in *terre foraine* (foreign land). Galahad sees the vase but does not hold it. The "gods" who vanish at that moment had been the Breton knights of Arthur. Since that time the Grail had been associated with the Cathari who had placed it in Rocamadour (in Montégur, in Montsalvat, in Montserrat). It was shown to the faithful in the cathedral of Genoa, in the cathedral of Toulouse, and other places.

By a softening of the final c, the castle of Corbenic in Cornwall became *corps-béni* (the blessed body), and thus the quest of the Grail became a symbol of Christian communion.

Rabelais, in the 16th century, gives an interesting parody of the Grail in *Pantagruel*. When, on the island of Cassade, Pantagruel asks to see the Grail, he is shown *un visage de connin rôti*—a rabbit's head. The inhabitants of Cassade, going farther than the grail symbol, also show the head of the roasted lamb as the remnants of the Last Supper. The quest of the Grail is the symbol of man's highest aspirations, the secret for the key that will open Paradise, sought after even today in the aspirations of hippies and flower-children and of all those who seek to purify the world.

OTHER MEDIEVAL FICTION IN VERSE AND PROSE: 12TH–15TH CENTURIES

Marie de France, writing in the second half of the 12th century, was an author of tales rather than a poet. The subjects of her *lais* (short stories in verse) were probably borrowed from Breton stories. Their theme is chivalric love, which she describes as a <u>melancholy tender passion.</u> Although not much is known about her, she probably lived in England and knew the writings of Chrétien de Troyes. She is the first woman poet to write in northern French.

The unknown author of *Aucassin et Nicolette* was a successor to Chrétien de Troyes in the early 13th century. The work, still famous today, is an idyllic love story, a *chantefable*, with prose passages alternating with verse. The prose was probably recited and the verse sung. It is the story of two lovers, separated by their parents, who overcome obstacles and adventures and are reunited at the story's end.

Story-telling in prose does not become significant in France until the Renaissance, with the short stories of Marguerite de Navarre and the long narrative of Rabelais. The word *roman* in French means first "romance" and then "novel." The word is used from the 12th to the 20th centuries, but there is no work before the 17th century corresponding to the 20th-century concept of a novel. During the course of the 15th century, however, at least three works of fiction were written that begin to show a literary form which will be perfected in later centuries.

Soon after the middle of the 15th century, Antoine de la Salle, a prolific writer who ended his career in the service of Louis XI, published a kind of novel, *Le Petit Jehan de Saintré*, which contains an appealing characterization of a pageboy. In order to become a perfect knight and thus deserve the love of his lady, the boy leaves for war in a distant land, but he is disillusioned on his return because the lady has betrayed him with a rather coarse *clerc*. The book is, to some degree, a story of the degeneration of the courtly ideal. Beaumarchais' page Chérubin in *Le Mariage de Figaro* later revives the character of Jehan de Saintré.

The other two important collections of the 15th century are anonymous. *Les Quinze Joyes de Mariage* recalls the antifeminism of the second part of *Le Roman de la Rose*. The "joys" are in reality the torments of a young husband who is set upon by all the women in his house. *Les Cent Nouvelles Nouvelles* (c. 1460) is reminiscent of the *fabliaux*, and follows quite closely the form of the one hundred stories of Boccaccio's *Il Decamerone*. The French stories were written for the court of Burgundy and presented as if they were being told by nobles. Humorous and licentious, they announce the style of stories that will be written in the 16th century.

THE 13TH CENTURY:
didacticism and *Le Roman de la Rose*

used for teaching; intended for instruction

If the first half of the 12th century was dominated by the *chanson de geste* and the second half by the *roman courtois,* the 13th century was essentially an age of study and philosophical inquiry, when "Gothic" art flourished and the universities, especially *l'université de Paris,* were attended by large numbers of young men. It was the age of Saint Thomas Aquinas and scholasticism. One major literary work, *Le Roman de la Rose,* was destined to have an extensive influence in Europe. This long didactic poem is in two parts, written by two authors, one of whom continues to explore the meaning of courtly love and the other who offers a summation of medieval knowledge.

Half of the century, 1220–1270, corresponds to the reign of Louis IX (Saint Louis). Before his reign began, at the beginning of the century, the word "university" was used for the first time to apply to institutions providing higher education. The origins of those schools were in the great abbeys of France (*écoles abbatiales*), organized as early as the 9th century. By the 13th century, grants for the universities were given by the king; a concession to the university of Paris was given in 1200. One of the *collèges* in the university was founded in 1252 by Robert de Sorbon for students of theology. "La Sorbonne" today designates the humanities section of the University of Paris. From the beginning, a university was a professional corporation made up of masters (*magister* or *maître*) and students (*écoliers*). There were four faculties (or departments): *la faculté des arts* (literature and science), *théologie, médecine* and *décret* (law), each placed under the authority of a dean (*doyen*).

The great development in learning in the 13th century was philosophy. Aristotle had become, during the 12th century, an object of controversy. Arabic scholars had translated Aristotle into Latin, and at first the Church had condemned the Greek philosopher because of seeming contradictions with Christian dogma. Soon after the middle of the century, Thomas Aquinas (Thomas d'Aquin) undertook his massive work of attempting to reconcile Aristotle's works with the Bible. This work, *Summa Theologica* (*la Somme théologique*) still represents the authoritative Roman Catholic philosophy. The philosophy of Aquinas and of other medieval philosophers is called scholasticism (*la scolastique*) or even thomism (*le thomisme*). The goal of Aquinas' teaching was to prove that truth can be reached by reason; that there is no conflict between reason and Christian revelation.

During the same years the Gothic cathedrals were being built in the north of France and Aquinas was formulating and demonstrating his philosophy,

Le Roman de la Rose was being written. The first part, by Guillaume de Lorris, in 4,058 octosyllabic lines, was composed between 1225 and 1240 and the second part, by Jean de Meung, in 17,722 octosyllabic lines, between 1275 and 1280.

The two parts of the poem are very different. Guillaume de Lorris was inspired by Ovid's *Art of Loving* and wrote his own *art d'aimer* in the form of a narrative poem in conformity with the rules of courtly love. He tells the story of a dream and allegorizes abstract ideas and moral qualities. Such literary practices were traditional in the Middle Ages and extend back to antiquity. His writing has elegance of expression, and above all, demonstrates a deep respect for woman and the experience of love. The hero of the narrative, L'Amant (the lover), represents the poet himself and is at the same time the prototype of all lovers. His love is an exclusive passion and directs all his actions.

Guillaume tells his readers that his story is a dream he had when he was twenty, in which he is in a garden surrounded by such characters as *Médisance* (slander), *Danger*, *Doux Regard* (soft looks), *Beauté*. He is helped by some and hindered by others in his attempt to pick a Rose symbolizing the Beloved, who is passive, perfect, and carefully guarded.

Guillaume de Lorris has considerable insight into the characters he allegorizes, and because of this insight, avoids the tediousness of allegory. The search for the Rose is on one level of interpretation a refined social duty, but on a mystical level, it is not unlike the quest for the Grail.

The second and longer part of *Le Roman de la Rose* is a learned didactic work which, while continuing the story of the search in its main action, is an exhibition of theory, philosophy and encyclopedic knowledge. Among Jean de Meung's many digressions are discussions concerning the origin of the world, the disagreeable aspects of marriage, the dangerous cunning of women, the meaning of charity and the arrogance of nobles. He varies the tone as well as the themes of his poem. He is enthusiastic as a philosopher and cynical as an observer of human nature, in one passage attacking the parasiticism of the mendicant orders of his day and in another eloquently describing the struggle between Death, as it makes its harvest of lives, and Nature, in its everlasting power of creation.

Jean de Meung holds a position close to that of a philosopher in his cult for nature. He scorns the courtly ideal and the worship of woman. In his poem, *l'esprit gaulois* (realistic, gallic and sensual) replaces *l'esprit courtois*. Love is not the end in itself, as it is for Guillaume de Lorris, but a means by which nature perpetuates life. (Love as a force of nature is also found in the *Tristan* poems.) His philosophy of human nature announces the attitude and the thought of Rabelais, Molière and Voltaire.

REALISTIC OR BOURGEOIS LITERATURE:
les fabliaux and *Le Roman de Renart*

The 13th century saw the emergence of a rich middle class which, as the aristocracy had done, especially in the 12th century, engaged professional writers to compose works for their entertainment. Societies, called *puys* or *confréries*, organized theatrical performances and poetry competitions. This literature, far less refined than that of Chrétien de Troyes and Guillaume de Lorris, was addressed to a wider public and is very diversified, with narrative works that are humorous and realistic, such as the *fabliaux* and *Le Roman de Renart*, or semi-religious works in such dramas as the *Jeu d'Adam* and the *Jeu de Saint Nicolas*, or more purely lyrical writing, as in the poems of Rutebeuf. During the course of the century, the two literary publics of the aristocracy and the bourgeoisie tended to merge. The nobles were amused by the *fabliaux*, and the bourgeoisie began to pay attention to poetry.

The word *fabliaux* is the Picard form for *fableaux*, or "short fables." These amusing popular stories, written in verse, were composed between the end of the 12th century and the beginning of the 14th. They depict and satirize actual customs of the day. They attack women for their traits of fickleness and stupidity and egoism, and they attack priests for their malice, selfishness and lasciviousness. Some *fabliaux* are very brief, organized around a play on words, and others have a more elaborate action with episodes resembling a play. One of the most famous is *Le vilain mire (le paysan médecin)*, a farcical text which later inspired Molière in writing *Le Médecin malgré lui*. The caustic wit and eroticism of the *fabliaux* also reappear in the writing of La Fontaine. *L'esprit gaulois*, for the first time, found a literary form in the *fabliaux*. Rutebeuf was one of the many authors of the stories.

Le Roman de Renart

The Renart stories have a literary ancestry going back to Aesop's fables, which had been translated into Latin and French (see Marie de France's *Isopet*). Animals illustrating their own characteristics but acting as if they were human beings form the tradition of *Le Roman de Renart*, a work which tends to moralize less than did the ancient fables.

The work in French, written in the traditional eight-syllable couplets, is in two cycles, the first written between 1175 and 1205 and the second between 1205 and 1255. New versions and additions were written in the 13th and 14th centuries. The spirit of the earlier cycle is malicious and humorous; that of the later cycle is in the form of a more serious, more virulent social satire.

The various episodes or poems of the long work are called *branches*. The principal theme is the war waged by Renart the *goupil* (fox) on Isengrin (the wolf). This animal epic is a parody of the *chansons de geste*. The characters who reappear remain true to type: Renart is sly and resourceful, Isengrin is stupid. Tibert the cat and Chantecler the cock are often able to outwit Renart.

The purpose of the poem, as written by the early *clercs*, was certainly to provoke laughter. All social conditions and types are made fun of in the early *branches*. Renart and the others are both animals and feudal barons. They appear on horseback, they own castles, they plead in law courts. Everything in the *chansons de geste* is parodied in *Le Roman de Renart*. The tone is transformed in the later *branches*, in which there is more satire and more didacticism, where mendicant orders are taken to task. The Church is blatantly satirized in passages that deal with miracles and pilgrimages.

Renart enjoyed tremendous success in every level of society. Adaptations were made throughout Europe. Disney films today and movie animal cartoons (Bugs Bunny, Micky Mouse) maintain the Renart tradition of violence and satire and cunning resourcefulness. Such was the success in France of *Renart* that by the 15th century the common noun for fox, *goupil*, was replaced by the proper name *renard*.

RUTEBEUF

The greatest poet of the 13th century was Rutebeuf (died in 1280), a *trouvère* of Paris and contemporary of Saint Louis and Philippe III le Hardi. He wrote in almost all the genres: hagiography, drama, *fabliau*, pious poetry, satiric poetry, the poetry of complaint (*la complainte*). He was impoverished and wrote freely about himself and his suffering. He was indeed the first modern poet in the sense we give to a poet who reveals himself in his poems, who sings of his life and his feelings and distress. Rutebeuf was proud to be a poet and claimed dignity for the calling of a poet.

He was *engagé* in the existentialist sense—a committed poet who was primarily a satirist. The controversies of his age are reflected in his work, which he addressed to the bourgeoisie. He denounced, for example, those monks who coveted wealth and tried to evict secular teachers from the university. He pointed out the decadence of chivalry. The new type of knight and the new type of monk represented for Rutebeuf examples of spiritual degradation.

He was a militant Christian, longing to correct the abuses of the Church, vituperating against the growing religious skepticism of his age. His strongest religious theme was praise of the Blessed Virgin. His lyric and dramatic skills are both present in his play, *Le Miracle de Théophile*. In this Faust-like story, the priest Théophile signs a pact with Satan so that he will acquire land and fortune. His repentance and his prayer to Notre Dame for help form the most dramatic scene of the play. Our Lady intervenes and the diabolical pact is broken. The play, revived in the 20th century at the Sorbonne by Gustave Cohen and his "Théophiliens," is one of the best of the century—particularly the seduction scene of Théophile, his hesitations, and his role of sinner imploring the Virgin. *Théophile* is one of the few miracle plays that can be called dramatic.

Rutebeuf's most personal poems, *La Pauvreté Rutebeuf* and *La Griesche d'hiver* (*la malchance d'hiver*) touch on some of the themes that Villon, two centuries later, developed with greater craftsmanship and depth of feeling. Rutebeuf prefigures Verlaine, the *poète maudit* in the 19th century and even, to some extent, Jean Genet in the 20th.

represents beforehand

MEDIEVAL THEATER

The French theater had its beginnings in religious ceremonies and therefore had an origin comparable to that of the Greek theater. By the 10th century, at the time of the most solemn feast days, Christmas and Easter, the liturgy was enlarged by processions before the altar and by characters in costume who exchanged questions and answers related to the feasts. In the Easter liturgy, for example, the three holy women come to the empty tomb and question the angel about Jesus. In the Christmas ritual, the visit of the shepherds to the manger is acted out (although "acted" is too strong a word).

pre-scribed forms u rituals

Drames Liturgiques

During the 11th and 12th centuries, such dialogues were extended and most of the large churches used them. The settings became more complex, the number of characters increased, and the lives of the saints as well as the life of Christ were drawn upon. These dialogues, or *drames liturgiques,* moved from the inside of the church to the church steps outside (*le parvis*), and from there to platforms (*tréteaux*) erected in the city squares. French replaced Latin, and the actors were recruited not from the priesthood but from lay *confréries.* Theatrical productions, in a somewhat primitive form, were taking place by the middle of the 12th century.

The first important text dates from the end of the 12th century: *Le Jeu d'Adam.* By this time scenery was being used in the squares to depict heaven, on the public's left, and hell, on the right, in the form of a dragon's mouth. Between the two extremes were the "mansions" (*décors*), settings for the action. A few of the scenes in *Le Jeu d'Adam* give a feeling of theater—for example the temptation scene, in which the Devil persuades Eve by the use of flattery.

Mystères

Le Jeu d'Adam is half liturgical drama and half mystery play (*mystère*). In fact, it is the earliest mystery play in any language other than Latin. The word *mystère* comes from the medieval Latin *misterium,* meaning "ceremony." The full development of this form was reached in the 15th century, and its subject matter was derived from the Bible and the lives of the saints. The religious or edifying intention of the *drames liturgiques* eventually gave way to the concept of a spectacle, of a performance which used hundreds of characters and lasted for days, and the mystery plays moved away from the cathedral or church. An entire town was often given over to the performance. About sixty texts still exist today, most of which are very long, ranging from 30,000 to 65,000 eight-syllable lines.

The principal subject of the *mystères* was Christ's Passion. It is surprising that there is no really good dramatic version of this tragedy in any language. The mysteries were composed (by adapting and rewriting then existing versions) for specific cities. The most famous, *La Passion* of Arnoul Gréban, was performed in Le Mans in about 1450. In this text of 35,000 lines, we see: 1) the life of Adam; 2) the life of Jesus; 3) the Passion; and 4) the Resurrection and Pentecost. Each of the four parts took a day for performance. There are good dialogues between Jesus and Mary, but the work is generally over-long and monotonous.

Jean Michel's *Passion* (45,000 lines) was a prolongation of Gréban's. It added realistic and farcical scenes, including a love affair of Judas. This *Passion* was performed in Angers in 1486. The mixture of genres, as is found in Jean Michel, led finally to scandal, and the *mystères* were condemned in 1548 by the Parliament of Paris. At that time, a troupe of actors called *les confrères de la Passion* were playing in the Hôtel de Bourgogne in Paris. The fraternity itself, which had been organized at the end of the 14th century for the direction and performance of the *mystères*, was not actually dispersed until 1671, by an edict of Louis XIV.

Miracles

The miracle play was well represented in the 13th century by Rutebeuf's *Miracle de Théophile*, but this genre, the third type of religious play, was particularly popular in the 14th century. The *miracles* differed from the *mystères* in being quite short and in using subjects not biblical. They depicted miracles performed by saints and especially by the Virgin, and usually consisted of rapid successions of tableaux, ending in a miraculous dénouement in which the Virgin intervened and saved a repentant sinner.

The earliest miracle play in French is the *Jeu de Saint Nicolas*, written in about 1200 by Jean Bodel of Arras. The plot involves a crusader captured by the Saracens and saved by his patron saint. This play, as well as the forty or so *miracles* of the 14th century, combines varied dramatic tones: tragic, comic, serious, pathetic, coarse and farcical. Such *jeux* as *Le Jeu de Saint Nicolas* originated in the abbey schools of the 12th century and were dramatic performances usually played in Latin. Gradually the plays moved away from the jurisdiction of the church schools and passed to urban centers. Saint Nicolas was the patron saint of students. Bodel's play was traditionally performed on December 5, vigil of the saint's feast day.

Comédie

The earliest comic scenes were attached to the liturgical drama, but by the middle of the 13th century the separate genre of comedy was clearly represented in two plays (*jeux*) by Adam de la Halle, called le Bossu, a *clerc* from

Arras. *Le Jeu de la Feuillée* was written in about 1275 for the town of Arras. *Le Jeu de Robin et Marion*, ten years later, was written for the French court of the Count of Artois, residing in Italy.

Le Jeu de la Feuillée contains scenes of contemporary life. Adam and his wife and other characters appear in them, and the tone is a mixture of satire and fantasy. *Le Jeu de Robin et Marion* is a pastoral play, with dialogues, songs and dances that culminate in a comic-opera finale. Molière's *comédie-ballet* later used and enlarged this genre. The English Robin Hood and Maid Marian may be descendents of Robin and Marion.

The 14th century, fertile in *miracles*, left no comedies, but the 15th century had a variety of forms, probably because of the growth and success of societies of actors. *Les Confréries de la Passion* were responsible for performances of the mystères, but the newer groups, called *Sots* (fools), made up of *clercs*, bourgeois, and students, performed comedies. *La Basoche* (from *basilica*) was a guild of clerks in the Parliament of Paris instituted in the 14th century. The plays of the *basochiens* were forerunners of French comedies; *Les Enfants sans souci* were students and bohemians (today's hippies).

Two genres in particular were important: *la sotie*, first a satiric parade with political overtones and usually played by *Les Enfants sans souci* disguised as *sots*. The satire of the *soties* was directed against mankind in general, or sometimes against one well-known personality. Pierre Gringoire's *Sotie du Prince des Sots* (1512) was a satire of the pope. (In the 20th century, André Gide will call his *Caves du Vatican* a *sotie*.)

La farce, the second important genre of 15th century comedy, was destined to have a long life in the history of the French theater. Unlike the *sotie*, the *farce* was not satirical. It was originally a burlesque slapstick, serving as an interruption in a *mystère*—a pause or *intermède* for the purpose of arousing laughter. The word itself, coming from Vulgar Latin, means stuffing for fowl or pastry. (*Une tomate farcie* today means a stuffed tomato.)

Themes and characters in the *farces* resemble those of the *fabliaux*. *La farce du cuvier* is still played today in schools, and even more popular today is *La farce de Maître Pathelin*, written in about 1465. The principal theme of *Pathelin* is knavery and deceit. Every character is tricking some other character. The characters are well drawn and the scenes are lively, especially the lawsuit scene, during which the judge keeps calling out, "*Revenons à ces moutons*" (cloth and sheep are involved in the suit), a phrase which has become a French proverb. The parody of legal cunning in *Pathelin* is later remembered by Racine in his one comedy, *Les Plaideurs*, and the word itself, *pathelin*, is still used to designate a suave hypocrite.

On the whole, the language of medieval plays is weak and monotonous. Other genres are much stronger in a purely literary sense. Medieval theater was essentially a popular theater, and was replaced in the 16th century by other more literary forms.

PROSE CHRONICLES: 13TH–15TH CENTURIES

Hostilities between France and England began openly in 1337 and lasted a century, until Jeanne d'Arc succeeded in liberating her country and restoring a king's power to Charles VII. The Hundred Years War, as it is called, was not only a period of intermittent battles but one of growing discontent and suffering for the masses. By the middle of the 15th century France was devastated and exhausted. Louis XI's reign (1461–1483) restored France economically, but recovery for the country as a whole was not achieved until the beginning of the 16th century when, once again, a brilliant culture flourished, comparable to the best years of the 12th and 13th centuries.

With the exception of a few works, the literature of the 14th and 15th centuries was poor by comparison with that of the 12th and 13th. There was an effort on the part of Charles V (who reigned from 1360 to 1380) to maintain and enlarge the cultural heritage. He established in the Louvre *la librairie royale,* which was the origin of *La Bibliothèque Nationale.* The encouragement he gave for efforts to translate texts of antiquity was a sign of what soon was to be called the movement of "humanism."

Rhymed chronicles recording real events were written down during the 11th and 12th centuries, and were usually commissioned by a wealthy patron. The chronicle in prose is exemplified by four writers of the Middle Ages who made a marked contribution to the art of prose writing and at the same time laid the foundation of the art of writing history.

Geoffroi de Villehardouin, the first of these chroniclers, was maréchal de Champagne and one of the leaders of the Fourth Crusade (1202–1204). His *Histoire de la Conquête de Constantinople* seems to be an effort to justify the fourth crusade, which never reached the Holy Land but which sacked the Christian city of Byzantium. Villehardouin never returned to France, and wrote his history in a castle in Macedonia where he died in 1213. He addressed his history to friends in France and tried to explain the reasons for the diverting of the crusade. He often relied on the theory that what happened was God's will. He related deeds and battles soberly, like a good soldier who is tired of fighting.

Joinville's *Histoire de Saint Louis* is almost a *légende dorée*, but reveals sufficient care for accuracy and detail to be classified as history. Jean de Joinville (1225–1317) came from Champagne, as did Villehardouin. He participated in the Egyptian crusade in 1248 during which he became an intimate of Louis IX. He then returned to France with the king and spent considerable time at court. He disapproved of the crusade of 1270, in which Louis lost his life at Tunis, and from then on the object of his life was to commemorate the life of his king and friend. He testified to the holiness of Louis, which eventually helped bring about the canonization of that king.

At the age of eighty, Joinville began writing the biography which was completed in 1309. It is disjointed and anecdotal, but contains two beautifully sketched portraits of Louis IX and himself. The king is depicted in his ordinary daily life, a man characterized especially by his virtue and his remarkable sense of charity. Joinville gives a candid self-analysis. We see him as soldier, Christian and vassal. He described his personal experience with the utmost sincerity.

The third major chronicler, Jean Froissart, from Valenciennes in Flanders, was not a participant in the history he records, as Villehardouin and Joinville had been, but a reporter, a man who sought information and travelled extensively in England, Scotland, Aquitania, Italy.

At the age of thirty-three, in 1370, he began the writing of his *Chroniques*, today the principal document on the Hundred Years War. The work, in four parts, was completed in 1400. His very non-objective history covers the period from 1325 to 1400. In his early writings, Froissart appeared to be an anglophile, but when he was enrolled in the service of Guy de Châtillon, a French noble who was hostile to the English, he became a defender of the French and even altered somewhat his first book. He was primarily a courtly writer, and sought out refined aspects of a civilization that was no longer essentially refined. He was at his best when describing court festivities and battles—the exploits, for example, of the admirable soldier Bertrand Duguesclin. On the other hand, he paid little attention to the efforts of Charles V to bring about some kind of national unity.

Philippe de Commynes, from a noble Flemish family, is closer to an historian in the modern sense than were the other medieval chroniclers. He was a diplomat and politician who developed theories about the ideal ruler. In the early part of his career he served the man who was to become the powerful Burgundian duke, Charles le Téméraire. In 1472, Commynes changed sides and entered the service of King Louis XI. He served the king well and was rewarded with ambassadorships in Italy and Germany. After the death of Louis, he fell out of favor for a time but made a comeback under Charles VIII. His *Mémoires*, written between 1489 and 1498, were published posthumously.

Of the eight books in the *Mémoires*, six deal with the reign of Louis XI and his struggle with Charles VIII and the expedition into Italy. The *Mémoires* end with the coronation of Louis XII.

Commynes was the confidant of both Louis XI and Charles VIII. He gives very astute portraits of these kings and of Charles le Téméraire. His reporting seems to be impartial, although he took sides with the king against the feudal lords. Louis XI was the king who came closest to his ideal of a strong and moderate political ruler. Commynes' style is uneven and at times very flat, but he is the first historian in France to be interested in cause and effect.

THE DEVELOPMENT OF MEDIEVAL POETRY

12th Century

The earliest French poems of the north, written in *la langue d'oïl*, were contemporary with the *chansons de geste*. They were decasyllabic assonanced couplets called *chansons de toile*, brief love stories sung as women did their weaving or sewing. The poets of the north who wrote them were *trouvères*.

At the same time, in the south (*le midi*), the Provençal poets, those writing in *la langue d'oc*, were composing a richer poetry which had its origins probably in Arabic and Latin models. Provençal was spoken in at least four provinces: la Provence, le Languedoc, l'Auvergne and le Limousin. These poets were the *troubadours* (from *trobar*, to find), and their theme was courtly love in the form of a love song, *canso d'amor*. In these poems the poet's mistress appeared as the guide of his life. Human love was seen as akin to religious faith. The typical Provençal *canso d'amor* is like a hymn to the Virgin. In the 13th and 14th centuries this theme reached its highest form in Dante's story of his love for

Beatrice, in _La Vita Nuova_ and _La Divina Commedia_, and in Petrarch's love for Laura, as expressed in his sonnets.

13th Century

As poetry developed in the north, it was strongly influenced by Provençal poetry. Several genres flourished in the 12th and 13th centuries: _la chanson d'amour_ (on the humbleness of the lover and the inaccessibility of the lady); _l'aube_ (the separation of the lovers at dawn); _la pastourelle_ (the meeting of a _chevalier_ and a shepherdess); _le débat_ and _le jeu-parti_ (debates on love); _la reverdie_ (a May song); _le serventois_ (a political poem); _la chanson de croisade_; and _la chanson pieuse_ (on the glory of God or in praise of the Virgin). The _trouvères_ were either poets in the service of a count (Gace Brulé, Blondel de Nesle), or wandering poets (_trouvères errants_), or powerful barons themselves, such as Conon de Béthune and the Châtelain de Coucy.

The most gifted of the _trouvères_, sometimes called _le prince des trouvères_, was Thibaud, comte de Champagne et de Brie, who died in 1253, and whose surviving work comprises about sixty poems. Jean Bodel of Arras, ill with leprosy, wrote a moving _congé_, a farewell to his friends and his age. It is a forerunner of Villon's _Testament_. Colin Muset, like Rutebeuf, wrote during the reign of Saint Louis and sang also of his difficult life and the need for a poet to find a patron.

14th Century

The word _rhétorique_ in the Middle Ages meant the art of writing in verse. It was used in this way beginning with the career and the example of Guillaume de Machaut (1300–1377) and extending through the period of the Pléiade in the 16th century. It represents a movement away from the popular poet, the wandering _jongleur_, to the more professional _ménestrel_, who was quite literally "hired" by a lord and attached to his court. The formal patterns of poetry became more fixed and more difficult to execute. Two forms in particular were approved of by the new _rhétorique_: _la ballade_ and _le rondeau_ (or _rondel_). _La ballade_ is not a narrative poem like the English ballad. It has three stanzas and an _envoi_ or half-stanza at the end. Each stanza ends with the same line, called _un refrain_. The same three rhymes are used in each stanza. The _rondeau_ is shorter and has only two rhymes.

person under care of another

Machaut was the protégé of several lords, and he was also a *chanoine* of Notre-Dame-de-Reims. He was a gifted musician who composed the music for his own poems, and who is usually considered the inventor of polyphonic music. He wrote *ballades, rondeaux, dits* (debates on gallantry) and *le Voir dit*, a personal novel in verse. He was the founder of the new school of poetry which continued through the 15th century.

15th Century

Machaut's principal disciple was Eustache Deschamps (1346–1406?) who wrote the first poetics in French: *Art de dictier* (1392). His work is voluminous, varied and uneven.

Christine de Pisan (1364–1430), daughter of an Italian astrologer, was attached to the court of Charles V. An ardent feminist, she praised Jeanne d'Arc and vituperated against Jean de Meung. Her best poems are personal laments on the themes of solitude and mourning and the need to write in order to live.

Alain Chartier died probably the same year as Christine de Pisan. He was primarily a political orator, but left one poem that is still famous today, *La belle dame sans merci*, about a lady whose insensitivity caused her lover to die of despair.

Charles d'Orléans (1394–1465) became the leader of the Armagnacs after the murder of his father (brother of King Charles VI). He fought at Azincourt and was held prisoner in England between 1415 and 1440. The outcome of a battle and a twenty-five year exile in England helped to decide this nobleman's vocation of poet. In brief poems, usually *rondeaux*, he sang of his melancholy and his disappointments. He used the fixed form of the *rondeau* more easily and skillfully than other medieval poets.

After his liberation, he returned to France where he lived twenty-five more years, principally in the castle at Blois, where he presided over a court of great elegance, where he welcomed poets, and established poetry competitions. Blois became *une cour de poésie*. One of the competitions was for the writing of *ballades* on the theme *Je meurs de soif auprès de la fontaine*. It is believed that François Villon, from Paris, participated in this *concours*. An invalid and sufferer during his last years, Charles d'Orléans died in Amboise.

By his style of living, and his devotion to the cause of poetry, Charles d'Orléans was the last of the great feudal lords in France and the last of the courtly poets such as the Middle Ages knew. When a prisoner in England and writing from Dover Beach, *en regardant vers le pays de France*, the vivid memories of his country softened his sense of exile. (The experience of prison was quite different for such poets as Villon, Verlaine, Apollinaire and Genet.) In the poems written after his exile, he speaks more of the pleasures of life and his impressions of nature: *Le temps a laissé son manteau* (his best-known poem), or *Hiver, vous n'êtes qu'un vilain*. Nature, solitude, and the passing of time are among the themes that reveal his deepest emotions. He often used allegory, in the tradition of *Le Roman de la Rose*, but this practice never seemed to deaden or stultify the delicacy of his imagination: *La Nef d'Espérance*, for example, and *Le puits profond de mélancolie*.

Les Grands Rhétoriqueurs

After Charles d'Orléans and François Villon, the group of poets known as *les grands rhétoriqueurs* (their name came from the practice of *la rhétorique*) bridged the 15th and 16th centuries. Only one of them, Jean Lemaire de Belges, stands out as a poet who has something to say. The others, court poets, several of whom were attached to the court of Burgundy, were erudite versifiers. The early *rhétoriqueurs* seemed to look upon Alain Chartier as their guide. They developed in verse the long complex Latin periodic sentence. They incorporated dreams, allegories, and mythology into their poems, and they enriched (or overburdened) the French language with diminutives and derivatives. Rhymes were often puns or riddles in their poems (*Louange/loup ange*). They stressed the use of difficult forms and the need to learn the craft of poetry (*le métier*).

At the court of Burgundy under Charles le Téméraire were *rhétoriqueurs* such as Georges Chastellain and Jean Molinet. At the court of France the most distinguished was Jean Marot, father of Clément.

Jean Lemaire (1473–1525), born in Belges, in the Belgian department of Le Hainaut, was the nephew and disciple of Molinet. He travelled extensively and lived in some of the most cultivated centers of the day—Flanders, Lyon, Venice and Rome. He had studied not only many of the ancient writers, Homer in particular, but also Dante and Petrarch. Reminiscences of the Italian poets are in his poems. He attempted to use the *terza rima* of Dante and the twelve-syllable alexandrine line. The simple sensuality of some of his lines announces Ronsard and the Pléiade.

VILLON (1431–?)*

The 20th century has elevated François Villon to a very high position and placed him among the five or six greatest French poets. He ranks now with Baudelaire and Rimbaud, not only because of his art of lyricism but also because, like them, he is a *poète maudit*—a poet cursed by society. Almost all the critical writing about Villon has been biographical. He was thief, pimp, hard drinker, whoremonger, murderer. His poetry, great as it is, is less well known than is his legend.

"Legend" is a safer word to use than "life," because little is known of Villon's life. He speaks of himself constantly in his verse but not everything can be read literally. What has been learned about Villon and the people he names, thanks to the historical research done at the end of the 19th century, does not help us either understand the poems or why they are great poems. With the new critical approach to poetry developing in the 20th century, the meaning of Villon's poetry is entering a new phase.

Villon was born François Montcorbier, in Paris, and used the name of his guardian, Guillaume de Villon, who was chaplain of the church of Saint-Benoît-le-Bétourné. He studied at the University of Paris, where he received his *baccalauréat* in 1449 and his *licence* and *maître ès arts* in 1452. He was pardoned for killing a priest (an act probably done in self-defense) and participated in a theft from the Collège de Navarre in 1452. That year he wrote *Les Lais* (The Legacies) which is sometimes called *Le Petit Testament*, a burlesque poem of 320 lines. *Le Testament*, a much longer poem of 2,023 lines, was written in 1461. There are some separate poems, such as *Epitaphe Villon*, known as *La Ballade des pendus*, and other *ballades*, written in the jargon of the famous thieves of the 15th century, *Les Coquillards*.

According to *Le Testament*, Villon spent the summer of 1461 in the prison of Meung-sur-Loire. In October, Louis XI, passing through the city, set him free. In 1463, at the age of thirty-two, Villon was banished from Paris for ten years. There are apocryphal stories about the rest of his life, but nothing is known for certain.

The earliest editor of Villon's poems, Clément Marot, claimed in 1533, one hundred years after they were written, that they could not be understood because of the places and people and events alluded to, but when historical research was done, the poems still seemed inexplicable. Today, in such critical studies as those of G. A. Brunelli and David Kuhn, the poems are looked upon as self-contained works of art.

---

*At the age of thirty-two, Villon disappeared from history.

The mock testament used by Villon as his form of poetry was a well known medieval genre. Villon's *Testament* is richer and more personal than others. He changes the comic intention of a testament into a form that is serious and even tragic. *Les Lais* begin with a *congé d'amour*, a picture of the poet martyred by a cruel mistress. (One thinks of *La belle dame sans merci* of Alain Chartier.)

> Veult et ordonne que j'endure
> La mort et que plus je ne dure

> [She wills and commands that I endure
> Death and that I cease to live]

Then the poem continues with the giving away of goods. In the last section, the poet speaks of the Sorbonne bell and Aristotle and the small amount of change he has!

At the beginning of *Le Testament*, Villon speaks of the poverty-stricken years behind him and about a vision he has of a beautiful city (*une bonne ville*) that might well be the city of God. Many of the opening lines are on death, evoked with a firm sense of reality. The *ubi sunt* theme is everywhere but is not treated conventionally. The beauty that has gone, the famous people who have died—all that is really over. There is lament over the brevity of life, but there is also a tone of humor. Villon dictates his will, and the will is the poem. The bequests have both literal and sexual meanings. David Kuhn has pointed out the symbolism of the sexual parts (testament and testicle come from the same root) and aphrodisiacs. Life is destroyed through living (Villon is love's martyr), but life is also renewed in art.

RENAISSANCE

HISTORY		LITERATURE	
1498–1515	reign of Louis XII		
1515–47	reign of François premier	1518–42	Marot, official court poet
		1530	founding of Collège des lecteurs royaux (to become Collège de France)
		1532	Rabelais, *Pantagruel*
1534	Affaire des Placards	1534	Rabelais, *Gargantua*
		1536	Calvin, *Institution chrétienne*
		1544	Scève, *Délie*
1547–59	reign of Henri II	1549	Du Bellay, *Défense et illustration de la langue française*
		1550	Ronsard, *Odes*
		1552	Ronsard, *Amours*
		1558	Du Bellay, *Les Regrets*
1559–60	reign of François II	1559	Amyot, *Vies de Plutarque*
1560–74	reign of Charles IX	1560–74	Ronsard, official court poet
1572	Massacre of St. Bartholomew		
1574–89	reign of Henri III	1577	D'Aubigné, *Les Tragiques* (begins composition)
1589–1610	reign of Henri IV	1580	Montaigne, *Essais* I, II
		1588	Montaigne, *Essais* I, II, III
1593	Henri IV enters Paris		
1598	Edit de Nantes		

There is no clear-cut demarcation between the Middle Ages and the Renaissance. Humanism was a characteristic of the 12th century as well as of the 16th. The Renaissance represents a development of medieval humanism, and new influences helped to transform it.

The last-quarter of the 15th century was a dry and infertile period for literature and culture in general. Religious faith was undergoing a crisis. Theological quarrels had replaced a direct study of Holy Scripture. The University of Paris had failed to rejuvenate its methods, and students were dissatisfied with the heavy pedantic practices of their teachers. The mystery plays (*les mystères*) had become primarily commercial enterprises, and the poems of the *rhétoriqueurs* demonstrated verbal acrobatics and gave no sense of poetry.

A new life, coming from several different sources, gradually penetrated all aspects of French culture: the first printing of books, the stories of new world explorers, and above all the study of Greco-Roman civilization that had been going on in Italy for more than a century. Martin Luther's campaign in Germany against papal authority culminated in the founding of a reformed church in about 1520.

The fact of the Italian Renaissance was discovered by three French kings who invaded Italy in order to establish their rights especially over Milan and Naples: Charles VIII at the end of the 15th century, Louis XII at the beginning of the 16th, followed by Francis I. In several Italian courts, Florence and Ferrara in particular, they came upon a cultivated worldly society that had not existed in France since the "bourgeois" reign of Louis XI.

Italian painters, scholars and writers so impressed these French kings that French civilization soon became permeated with Italianism. Gothic art was replaced by Italian art. *The Divine Comedy* of Dante, the 300 sonnets of Petrarch, and the political writings (especially *Il Principe*)! of Machiavelli became key texts. But even more than had the Italian works of the 14th and 15th centuries, the Italian Renaissance encouraged the French to rediscover or discover for the first time the great Latin and Greek writers: the philosophy of Plato, the epic poems of Homer, the tragedies of Sophocles, the odes of Pindar, the history of Herodotus, the moral treatises of Plutarch.

At the very beginning of the century, the Dutch thinker Erasmus, who lived many years in France, laid the basis for the Reformation not only by his writings but also by the exchange of ideas he held with French humanists. In his *Adages*, Erasmus extracted essential ideas from philosophers and writers of classical antiquity. He emphasized the direct use of the Bible as the principal source for moral guidance. He tended to deprecate theological disputes promoted by the Sorbonne (which was the theological faculty of the University of Paris in the 16th century), and certain devotional practices of the Church, such as fasting and abstinence. Erasmus did not reject the authority of Rome, as Luther had, but he helped institute a new spirit having its source in the direct study of the Gospels and the stressing of the moral example of the life of Jesus. This spirit and practice were to be called, as developed by the French humanists, *l'évangélisme*.

François Ier reigned over France between 1515 and 1547. During the first twenty years of his reign, he showed sympathy for the "reformers," and encouraged the new life in art and letters that came from Italy. In 1530 he founded, with the help of the eminent philologist Guillaume Budé, *le collège des lecteurs royaux*, which was later called *le Collège de France*, a free university with three chairs, at the beginning: Greek, Latin and Hebrew. These three professorships themselves represent the new spirit of both the Renaissance and the Reformation. Budé (1467–1540) was the type of humanist scholar who sought to reconcile the study of Greek thought and literature with Christianity. Lefèvre d'Etaples was another type of humanist who translated the Epistles and the Gospels of the New Testament.

A change of attitude was apparent during the last years of François' reign and during the reign of Henri II (1547–1559). *L'Affaire des Placards*, a protest in 1534 against the Catholic mass, made public in many places and even in the king's quarters in Amboise, changed François' opinion, and he instituted measures of repression. Marot, Rabelais and Calvin were all affected by the new severity of the king. Most writers abandoned the movement of the Reformation (*la Réforme*). The Pléiade poets revived the study of the ancient poets. They remained Christian, but did not, on the whole, participate in the religious disputes.

A third phase of the Renaissance took place in the reigns of Charles IX (1560–1574), Henri III (1574–1589), and the beginning of the reign of Henri

IV. This was the period of the religious wars which began in 1560, at the time of the very brief reign of François II, and which ended with the Edict of Nantes in 1598, in the reign of Henri IV. Literature was very much affected by the violence of these wars. A few writers openly took sides: Agrippa d'Aubigné, for example, took the side of the Protestants, and Ronsard, the side of the Catholics. Montaigne, the greatest French writer in the latter half of the century, avoided any expression of religious fanaticism. His attitude of sage and thinker made it difficult for him to find truth in any one political or religious opinion.

The Renaissance, then, was not so much a century of revolution (as the romantics will call it) as a century of intellectual renewal in the reign of François Ier, and an aesthetic renewal in about 1550. The richest literary period began after *l'Affaire des Placards*, about 1535, and ended in 1560, at the beginning of the wars of religion. During that generation (roughly during the reigns of François Ier and Henri II), there was such fervor and joy in the creative work of the imagination that the 19th century historian Michelet felt justified in calling that part of the Renaissance *le rire des dieux* (the laughter of the gods.)

No one illustrates the rich varied aspects of the French Renaissance spirit better than Marguerite d'Angoulême, queen of Navarre. She was the sister of François Ier, who married, first, the duc d'Alençon, and in her second marriage, Henri d'Albret, king of Navarre. She possessed the Renaissance fervor for study and knew Latin, Greek, German, Italian and Spanish. Like her brother, she was a patron of the arts and encouraged humanists, such as Amyot and Lefèvre d'Etaples, and writers, such as Clément Marot, who was for a while her secretary at court, and Rabelais, who dedicated *Le Tiers Livre* to her.

Marguerite de Navarre played an important political role at the court of France and elsewhere. As a writer, her importance was not studied and not apparent until the 20th century. She was not an innovator of genres, but followed quite closely several of the medieval forms: stories, plays, poetry, most of which was published posthumously. Her correspondence is also significant.

In literary history her best known work is a collection of seventy-two stories, *L'Heptaméron* (a title not chosen by her), whose general plan is based on Boccaccio's *Decameron*. A group of nobles, men and women, are forced, because of floods, to stay in an abbey in the Pyrenees. As a diversion they begin an elaborate story-telling program. Ten stories each day for seven days are told (hence the title *Heptaméron*), and two stories for the eighth day. The collection is unfinished. The stories are fairly original, probably based on experiences at court. They are love stories that often have licentious elements, and represent a curious mixture of sensuality and courtliness (*courtoisie*). The subject of love is treated quite seriously, especially in the commentaries that follow each story. Here the religious and moral preoccupations of Marguerite are apparent in her frequent quotations from Saint Paul and the Gospels. Examples of the medieval *esprit gaulois* are in the *contes* as well as the greater refinement of sentiment from Italian models and the personal mystical fervor of Marguerite herself.

Her mystical writings and her poetry may in time be seen to be more important than *L'Heptaméron*. *Le Miroir de l'âme pécheresse*, published in 1531; the long poem *Les Prisons*, strongly influenced by Dante; and, at the end of her life, in 1547, *La Marguerite de la marguerite des Princesses* (*marguerite* with the Greek meaning of *margarita*, "pearl") are metaphysical poems on the subject of love, which for Marguerite meant the love for God as well as love for her brother the king and for all things of the earth. Her deep attachment to the Gospels, her constant study of platonism, and her attraction to the more simple faith of what will be called calvinism, help explain her ever-present fear that the love she experienced in so many different ways is not pure enough.

CLÉMENT MAROT (1496-1544)

Marot's father, the *rhétoriqueur* Jean Marot, had taught Clément the art of writing poetry according to the medieval forms such as the *rondeau* and the *ballade*. He had taught his son how to use allegory and how to celebrate courtly love. (Later, Clément Marot published an edition of *Le Roman de la Rose*.) He was first with his father at the court of Louis XII. Then, in 1515, he served as a page at the court of the new king François. Three years later Marguerite de Navarre appointed him her secretary and thus gave him an official position. From then on he was in every sense a court poet (*poète de cour*).

Marot was sensitive to the new influences from Italy, the Petrarchan in particular, apparent in his love poems written to Anne d'Alençon, a niece of Marguerite. But Marot was more simple, more direct, and more clear than Petrarch and the *pétrarquistes*. The other major influence, one that was to endanger his life, came from the Reformation. Influenced in this by Marguerite de Navarre herself, he discovered a great joy in reading the Old Testament and the Gospels. Boldness in religious matters was easier for a queen in the early 16th century than for a queen's secretary. Marot was imprisoned twice, in 1521 and 1527, and liberated both times thanks to the king.

His first collection of poems, *L'Adolescence Clémentine*, of 1532, brought him fame. Two years later, l'Affaire des Placards brought about a change of attitude in François Ier, and Marot went into exile in Italy at the court of Ferrara. After two years in Italy, he abjured protestantism and returned to France. Again, in 1542, François gave up his support of Marot. This time the poet went to Geneva, where he finished a translation of the Psalms. There he quarrelled with Calvin. He died, a lonely man, in Turin.

His best poems narrate the adventures and changes of fortune in his life. His *Epître à Lyon Jamet* (1526) is a request to his friend to have him released from the Châtelet where he had been imprisoned for eating meat (*lard*) during Lent. *L'Enfer* (1527) is a long satirical and emotional poem about his coming to the Châtelet. His poems are often addressed to the king for various favors: *Epître au Roy pour sa délivrance* (1527), *Epître au Roy pour Marot étant malade à Paris* (1531), a request for money, and *Epître au Roy du temps de son exil à Ferrare* (1534).

Clément Marot wrote no great poems. They were occasional verses, petitions for help, or episodes in his life. But he created a style, a graceful seemingly spontaneous kind of writing that contrasts with the heaviness of the *rhétoriqueurs*. The pun poem (*calembour*) and the discontinuous *coq-à-l'âne* (cock and bull) poem remained light and witty. Marot forged a new suppleness for the decasyllabic line.

RENAISSANCE POETRY AFTER MAROT:
platonism, petrarchism, *l'école lyonnaise* (Scève, Labé)

The 16th century is the first great century of French poetry. It was later surpassed by the 19th and 20th in richness and variety, but was never surpassed in the innovations and achievements of individual poets.

The doctrine about love usually associated with platonism in France is called *amour pur*. The *chevalier* of the courtly romances of the 12th century was often called the perfect lover (*le parfait amant*)—he was fervent in his worship of his lady, and he was submissive to her. Satisfied with her slightest favors, her slightest recognition, in his *amour pur* he was resigned not to hope for any real favor. This characteristic of the *chevalier courtois* was later remembered by the Renaissance poets.

In the 13th century, the discussion concerning *Le Roman de la Rose* took on the aspect of a debate for or against woman and the love she inspired. This debate reached considerable proportions in the 16th century, just before Rabelais began writing *Pantagruel*. One side, headed by André Tiraqueau, stressed the weakness and corruption of woman, and the other side, headed by Amaury Bouchard, wrote an apology for the female sex.

Platonism, as taught in Italy in the 15th century, especially by Marsilio Ficino, translator and commentator of Plato, in France took on the forcefulness of a movement in ideas. Ficino became one of the favorite authors of the king's sister. Scève was probably presented to her when she stopped in Lyon between April and July 1536. Antoine Héroët, one of the assiduous poets of Marguerite's court, defined the cause of platonism in *La Parfaite Amie*, a poem in three cantos, published in 1543.

Ficino derived the platonic theory of love from *The Symposium* (*Le Banquet*) and other works of Plato. According to this theory, when on earth, the soul retains memories of the world of perfect beauty from which it comes. The sight of physical beauty stirs these memories. The soul of a man then realizes that the body is but the envelope or the prison of the soul. By contemplation of increasingly higher forms of beauty, the soul is able to rise to union with God. In God beauty, love and goodness are the same. So earthly or physical love is in the platonic sense one step in the direction of love for God. In Marguerite de Navarre's poetry these platonic concepts easily harmonize with Christian mysticism.

The poems of the 14th century Italian poet Petrarch (Pétrarque) show the detailed development of his love for Laura. There is at first for Petrarch a conflict between the body and the spirit, but after Laura's death his love becomes more strongly spiritual. The final poem of the *Rime* is spoken to the Virgin and not to Laura. Petrarch refined the tradition of the Provençal troubadours and extensively used the sonnet form. The attentive study of Petrarch and other Italian poets was first introduced in Lyon, which had a cultivated society and had become an important publishing center.

The poetry of Ronsard and the other poets of the Pléiade was to be accepted by the 19th century as the great poetry of the French Renaissance. But a new canon of poetry, having its origins in Baudelaire and the symbolists, was developed in the 20th century that has called particular attention to Maurice Scève and the Lyonnaise school.

Maurice Scève (1500?–1562?)

Maurice Scève probably grew up in the wealthy society of Lyon where his father was either a nobleman or a high civil servant. In 1533 he was studying archeology and literature at Avignon, and played a part in the discovery of the supposed tomb of Petrarch's Laura.

The use to which he put poetry, a use largely metaphysical, has endeared him to 20th-century readers of poetry. To be a poet for Scève was to grow in an awareness of self, to become more and more conscious of one's subconscious and one's total being.

Délie, his principal work, was published in Lyon in 1544. It was approved of by his small circle of friends in Lyon and by those elsewhere who had been initiated into the art of poetry. The year after the death of François Ier, in 1548, Scève helped organize the festivities in honor of Henri II's entrance into Lyon. His last work, *Le Microcosme*, a long philosophical poem, appeared in 1562. Soon after that year his name is not found in any historical records.

Scholars have tried to assign to Délie a real name, that of Pernette du Guillet, a celebrity in Lyon and a poet herself. *Délie* is actually an anagram of the word *l'idée*, and is the fictitious name given to the lady Maurice Scève loved and with whom all his poems are concerned. There are 449 *dizains* or poems of ten decasyllabic lines (100 syllables therefore in each poem!) Five *dizains* serve as introduction and three as conclusion. The other 441 *dizains* are divided into 49 groups of 9 *dizains* each. There is obviously a number symbolism, since 49 is the square of 7, and 9 the square of 3. Three could be the symbol of divine love (Trinity) and 7 the symbol of human love, since it represents human factors: 7 sins, 7 days of the week, 7 liberal arts, 7 notes of the scale. Each of the groups is preceded by an emblem which is usually inspired by the last line of the following *dizain*, and a frontispiece emblem brings the total number of groups in the work to fifty.

Since each of the *dizains* relates one aspect or one moment of the same experience, there is an organic composition throughout the work. The 449 *dizains* are really one long poem on love, composed of 4,490 lines. After the poet's first vision of the lady, his life is transformed and he lives as in a spell, tormented by all his senses. Many of the *dizains* describe the particular beauty of Délie's countenance and body, but others analyze the impossibility of Scève being loved as he loves, and these poems describe a progress in self-knowledge and self-torment that gives the work its unity.

The real domain of Scève is that of human suffering, and there he differs from Dante and Petrarch. The poems of *Délie* are firm condensed units (similar in this aspect to the sonnets of Shakespeare and John Donne), but they contain an energy that is mortal and suicidal. In the most intense and tragic forms of literature, the goal of the writer is casting a passion destined to annihilate into a permanent form.

Platonism and petrarchism are dim backgrounds for Scève; they exert none of the compelling attraction and conviction that Christian theology does for Donne and Milton. The same themes of life and death in love summarize in each *dizain* the one subject that preoccupies Scève: the knowledge of sensuality. The study of this experience appears to be the subject of *Délie*. The poet resembles the lover—in giving himself, he fecundates himself. It is a fatal process of identification: the lover becoming poet and the poet becoming lover.

Louise Labé (1524?–1565)

The *école lyonnaise* was very much dominated by women, and of those women the best poet and the most striking character was Louise Labé. Whereas the metaphysics of love interested Scève, the reality of love, physical love in particular, interested Labé. Legend has it that, disguised as a soldier, she followed one of her lovers to the siege of Perpignan.

She came from the rich merchant class of Lyon where she held court and received such literary figures as Scève, Pernette du Guillet, Bonaventure des Périers, Pontus de Tyard, and Olivier de Magny, who was in love with her. Her work, published in 1555, is brief: three elegies and twenty-four sonnets. They are love poems, poems of longing for a passion that will never completely satisfy the woman. Louise was known as *la belle cordière* (her husband was a *cordier*, a merchant dealing in cordages.) She was courted by many men, and in her sonnets tried to answer accusations of promiscuity made against her by other ladies in Lyon (see the 3rd and 24th sonnets, for example).

JEAN CALVIN (1509-1564)

During the first part of his life Calvin, like his contemporary Rabelais, was a humanist and a student of antiquity, taking delight in the new discoveries of the age. When the king, after 1534, took sides with the Sorbonne against the reformers, Rabelais began exercising great prudence, but Jean Calvin gave up his humanistic studies in order to devote his life to the Protestant movement. When he settled for good in Geneva in 1541, he founded a new reformed Church.

Settling in Bâle first, Calvin published in Latin, in 1536, *L'Institution de la religion chrétienne*, which has as a preface a letter to François Ier, in which the theologian defends the Reformation and pleads for royal support. His remarkable sermons, given especially in Geneva, helped make him the foremost authority on Protestantism. In 1541 he published a French edition of *L'Institution*, and in 1560, a revised edition. A comparison of these two editions shows the painstaking care Calvin took to write in simple clear French. In his choice of vocabulary he avoided pedantic Latin words as often as possible. His syntax is simplified and more purely analytical. The French of Calvin, later developed by Pascal in his method of argumentation and by Bossuet in his oratorical eloquence, was as revolutionary as was his theology.

Calvin is best known, of course, for his interpretation of the Bible and Christian thought. Two major concepts are at the basis of his doctrine: first the omnipotence of God. Everything in the universe is controlled by the Providence of God. Evil and sin exist through the fault of man. Irrevocably pessimistic about the nature of man, Calvin believed him basically corrupt because of original sin. Thus he was opposed to Saint Thomas Aquinas, who sought to demonstrate the great resources of human reason. He was opposed also to that aspect of Rabelais' philosophy that adhered to the naturalism of antiquity.

The predestination of man was Calvin's second major tenet. Jesus Christ, the incarnation of God, came to save mankind, but no creature has the power to save himself. Only the chosen (*les élus*) are saved, and God knows through all time and all eternity who the chosen are. Each man is therefore predestined to salvation or damnation.

FRANÇOIS RABELAIS (1490?–1553)

Born in about 1490 in La Devinière near Chinon, Rabelais was for a time a Franciscan monk in Fontenay-le-Comte. Too much a humanist for the Franciscans, he soon changed orders (a very infrequent happening) and entered the Benedictine Order first in the Abbey of Maillezais and then in the Abbey of Ligugé near Poitiers. He studied medicine in Montpellier between 1530 and 1532. As a physician, he was attached to the Hôtel-Dieu de Lyon in 1532. Later he served as secretary and physician to Cardinal Jean du Bellay (cousin of the poet) and accompanied him to Italy on several occasions. Despite constant troubles with the Sorbonne because of his writings, he received at the end of his life two *cures* or parish livings. He died in Paris in 1553.

Rabelais was the most gifted and brilliant prose writer of the Renaissance. He was also a humanist in the fullest sense, as is shown by his enthusiasm for the ancients, his broadmindedness in religious matters, and his critical attitude toward Catholicism, the Sorbonne, and the legal and educational systems of his day. The spirit of the Renaissance was incarnated in Rabelais, and at times it must have been difficult for him to reconcile the humanist and the monk in himself.

At the August fair of 1532, in Lyon, there appeared an adventure-romance book destined to enjoy an immense success called *Les grandes et inestimables chroniques du grand et énorme géant Gargantua*. The story involved not only the giant Gargantua but the sorcerer Merlin and King Arthur. Rabelais, in writing his first book, *Pantagruel* (son of Gargantua), which he published in Lyon at the autumn fair in the same year, continued the popularization of romance and myth. Legend has it that he wrote this story about the son of Gargantua in order to amuse his patients. It would probably be closer to the truth to say that he wrote it to amuse himself and amuse and impress his peers and patrons. He signed the book "Maistre Alcofribas Nasier," an almost exact anagram of François Rabelais.

Two years later, he published *Gargantua*, probably at the time of the August fair in Lyon. (James Joyce, who has many traits in common with Rabelais, also wrote first the story of the son, Stephen Dedalus in *Portrait of the Artist as Young Man*, and then related the story of the father-figure Leopold Bloom, in *Ulysses*.) The Sorbonne had censured *Pantagruel*, and in the preface to *Gargantua*, Rabelais argued that his book had a profound meaning. He compares it to little boxes called *silènes*, grotesque on the outside but containing precious drugs. Such boxes are like Socrates, a philosopher with an ugly physical exterior and a noble soul. (The image is borrowed from Alcibiades in Plato's *Symposium*.)

Rabelais' full story begins, therefore, with *Gargantua* (1534). Chapters 1–13 trace the birth and childhood of the giant. At his birth, which takes place through the left ear of his mother, Gargantua cries out, "*A boire* [Give me a drink]." This episode unfolds during a lively, realistically described country scene (*propos des bien-ivres*). The education of the boy (in chapters 14–24) satirizes the outdated scholastic method of the Sorbonne in favor of the new kind of teaching of Ponocratès. This experimenter teaches by having his pupil do and experience directly. The body must be trained as well as the mind. In this method, much has to be memorized, but the pupil's powers to judge and criticize are trained as well. The war with Picrochole (chapters 25–51) takes place in Touraine. The beginning of the war is a stupid quarrel between *vignerons* (vinegrowers) and *fouaciers* (markers of *fouaces*, a kind of cake). In the fight, Gargantua is helped by the monk Jean des Entommeures. The last section of the book (chapters 52–57) is devoted to the Abbaye de Thélème, a Renaissance castle built by Gargantua as a reward for Frère Jean. This is a utopia in which lords and ladies live together in an atmosphere of politeness and culture and luxury. The only rule guiding this new kind of monastery is "*Fais ce que voudras* [Do as you wish]."

Gargantua has almost no role in books II, III, IV, and V. Pantagruel and his companion Panurge, a complex scoundrel, are the heroes of the last four books. *Pantagruel* (book II) relates the childhood of the giant, his appetite and strength, his studies in Poitiers, Toulouse, Montpellier, Valence, Angers, Bourges, Orléans, and especially in Paris, where he meets the rascal Panurge. On returning home to Utopie, he finds that the Dipsodes have invaded it. With the help of his friends (his "apostles"), he routs them. In many ways *Pantagruel* is a parody of the *romans de chevalerie*. The name Pantagruel probably comes from the name of a small sea demon, found in the *mystères* of the Middle Ages, who had the magic power of provoking thirst in other people.

The *Tiers Livre*, published in 1546, is quite different from *Pantagruel* and *Gargantua* both in style of composition and in subject matter. Its erudition is heavier and the attacks on the Sorbonne doctors more determined and more serious. The principal theme, however, is the status and psychology of women. Panurge wonders whether he should get married. He consults many different people on this question, and by means of these consultations, Rabelais' anti-feminism becomes clear. (Like Molière in the next century, Rabelais seemed to believe that woman's place is in the home. This problem was discussed in *Le ·Roman de la Rose* in the 13th century, by Rabelais in *Le Tiers Livre*, by the Platonists and anti-Platonists in the Renaissance, by Molière at the time of Louis XIV, and still in the 20th century, as the Woman's new liberation movement.) Receiving no satisfactory answer, Panurge (and Pantagruel) decide to consult *l'oracle de la Dive Bouteille* (Holy Bottle).

Their voyage is the subject of *Le Quart Livre* (1552) and *Le Cinquième Livre* (published in 1564, eleven years after the death of Rabelais, and the authenticity of which is a subject of controversy). The travellers stop at symbolic islands: Les Chicanous, for example, representing justice; Les Papefigues, or Protestants; Les Papimanes, or Catholic fanatics; Messer Gaster, representing the stomach, or Epicureans. The intention of *Le Quart Livre* is steadily satire, especially satire of the power of Rome and the politics of persecution.

Many scholars today believe *Le Cinquième Livre* a rewriting of a Rabelais manuscript. The sea voyage continues, and at the end Panurge and Pantagruel reach the oracle and hear the one word: "*Trinck* [Drink]." Satire, chaotic ordering and quantity of material, obscenity and fantasy characterize the last two books. The five books, taken together, epitomize an age of critical investigations and great learning, but they also epitomize the very enigmatical character of a single man. The quest for discovery is in Rabelais and also the havoc that often comes from extensive study and discovery.

LA PLÉIADE:
Du Bellay, Ronsard, other poets

By the middle of the century, thanks to the stimulation of humanistic studies and thanks to the prestige that Maurice Scève and others had brought to poetry, a few ambitious and talented young men founded a school of poetry called La Pléiade (at one time there were seven members, hence the name of the seven constellations, the Pleiades) in order to win for themselves the immortality of poets, with the examples before them of Homer, Pindar, Virgil, Horace. Deadly serious about the cause of poetry, they exalted and imitated the major genres of antiquity and at the same time wrote of their own emotions, of the joys and tragedies of life in the 16th century. The prestige of the Pléiade under the leadership of Ronsard endured until the beginning of the 17th century. For two centuries thereafter the Pléiade was forgotten until the new romantic movement in the 19th century revived interest and admiration.

In Paris, the collège de Coqueret, in the Latin Quarter, was the first rallying point of the young poets, many of whom, especially Ronsard, Du Bellay and Baïf, were taught by Jean Dorat. This gifted teacher initiated his pupils to the culture of antiquity, to the Greek and Latin poets, to the sense of beauty extolled by the ancients, and shared with them abundant enthusiasm for such study.

The poetic doctrine which the group evolved, annotated, and defended, was incorporated in a manifesto, the first significant book of literary theory in France, *Défense et illustration de la langue française* (1549) by Joachim Du Bellay. The purpose of the treatise was to prove the dignity of the French language equal to the dignity of Greek and Latin. The young poet Du Bellay advised a break with medieval tradition and a deliberate effort to imitate the genres of the classical authors. He denounced *ballades*, *virelais*, and *rondeaux*, and praised the major forms *ode*, *épopée*, *comédie*, *tragédie*, and the shorter forms: *épigramme*, *élégie*, *épître*, *églogue*, *satire* and *sonnet* (a nonclassical genre.) Du Bellay was somewhat responsible for the love sonnet that was to have such success in the 16th and 17th centuries, and for the Horatian and Pindaric odes. One of the achievements of the Pléiade poets was their elevation of the alexandrine verse (*le vers alexandrin*), the twelve-syllable rhyming couplet, to the place of superiority over all other meters—a position it still holds in French poetry.

As students, the group called themselves by the military term La Brigade. The seven Pléiade poets were Ronsard, Du Bellay, Antoine de Baïf, Jodelle, Pontus de Tyard, Remy Belleau and Dorat, but many others also belonged to the school.

‿Joachim Du Bellay (1522–1560)

Du Bellay celebrated in verse his native province of Anjou. Less well trained as a youth than the others of La Brigade, he studied hard in Paris after his meeting with Ronsard, a distant relative, and soon became their equal, despite constant ill health and semi-deafness. In the same year of *Défense et illustration*, he published a sonnet sequence, *L'Olive* (anagram of Viole, the name of the girl he celebrated), a work close to Petrarch's in style, vocabulary, and theme.

In 1553, he accompanied his cousin, the cardinal Jean Du Bellay, to Rome, on a voyage from which he hoped to gain ecclesiastical benefits and an introduction to the world of diplomacy and Roman society. The experience, lasting three years, proved a deep disappointment.

The cardinal's mission to the pope on behalf of Henri II failed, and the duties of running the vast household of the cardinal's palace turned the visit into an exile for Du Bellay. Two collections of sonnets came from this experience. *Les Antiquités de Rome*, published in 1558, evokes the grandeur of Rome, but the personal note is uppermost when Du Bellay meditates on the vicissitudes of human fate. *Les Regrets* (also 1558) is a more bitter and personal series of sonnets in which the poet laments his exile, his homesickness for Anjou, and the vices of the papal court, the life of courtiers, flatterers and financiers that he observes.

Du Bellay remains in French poetry one of the masters of the sonnet. In Rome he matured as a poet, despite his unhappiness there (or perhaps because of his unhappiness). His nostalgia for France and for his province was deeply felt and expressed in a variety of tones. His is the kind of melancholy the romantics later appreciate. His poems on pastoral subjects, *Jeux Rustiques* (1558), are lighter and demonstrate his technical agility. In *Les Antiquités de Rome* there is a resonance, almost a pompousness, in his verse that had not been present in French poetry before. His Petrarchan love sonnets in *L'Olive* open up the way to similar sonnet sequences in the poetry of Ronsard, Tyard, Baïf, Magny and Jodelle. Some of the satirical sonnets in *Les Regrets* caused a break with his cousin the cardinal. At the end of his life, Du Bellay felt abandoned and desperate because of his lack of financial stability and his increasing deafness. He was writing a poem when he died of apoplexy on January 1, 1560, at the age of thirty-seven.

✓ Pierre de Ronsard (1524–1585)

Born in an Italianate château in Le Vendômois, Ronsard was destined to be the French Orpheus, the professional poet attached to the king, and the humanist. He was, like Du Bellay, the man of his province, the Vendômois singing of love, wine, and the natural beauty of La Touraine, the voluptuary who used the brief ode of Horace and the sonnet. But he was also the Renaissance scholar, attracted to the elaborate ode of Pindar with its strophes, antistrophes and epodes, who sang of the king, the queen, of cardinals and statesmen. As a writer he had two fairly distinct careers, that of the natural love poet, almost the *chansonnier*, and the learned court poet, almost the *engagé*.

As a pageboy from a noble family, Pierre de Ronsard first planned a military diplomatic career. Early deafness may have counted to some extent in his change of plans. He studied with Dorat at the collège de Coqueret and fell in love with antiquity. The first part of his career coincided with the reign of Henri II (1550–1559). He published his first *Odes* in 1550, and in them he followed the patterns of Pindar and Horace. The Pindaric odes seem cold and forbidding today, with some exceptions, such as the brilliant *Ode à .Michel de l'Hôpital*. The Horatian odes are lighter and more epicurean with their themes of the passage of time, the need to enjoy life and profit from immediate and passing pleasures (*Mignonne, allons voir si la rose*).

The first collection of love sonnets to Cassandre Salviati, daughter of an Italian banker whom Ronsard had met at the château of Blois when she was only thirteen and he twenty, *Les Amours de Cassandre* (1552), are close to Petrarch in form, and complex in metaphors and mythological allusions. *Les Amours de Marie*, sonnets addressed to a peasant girl, Marie Dupin, are more simple, more moving. In the Marie sequence, Ronsard found his most congenial themes: love for a young girl, the beauty of spring and roses.

By this time Ronsard was famous, and turned to heavier subjects in *Les Hymnes*. His *Hymne à Henri II*, for example, compares the king to Jupiter. During the reign of Charles IX (1560–1574), Ronsard was the official court poet. He continued to write poetry about the beauty of nature and the pleasures of love, but also composed *poèmes de circonstance* to celebrate royal events.

Les Discours (1560–1563) are long poems on the wars of religion in which Ronsard defends his king and the Catholic side. Passionate and oratorical, the *Discours* are among Ronsard's greatest achievements: see, *Discours sur les misères de ce temps*, and especially his last *Discours*: *Réponse aux injures et calomnies*, in which he answers attacks made on him and on his poetry.

His epic poem, *La Franciade* (1574), is generally considered a failure. In it he narrates the legend of the founding of Paris by Francus, a descendent of the Trojans (in imitation of Virgil's *Aeneid*, which narrates the founding of Rome).

At the death of Charles IX, Ronsard lost his position at court. Henri III (who reigned from 1574–1585) had his own favorite poet, Desportes. Living away from court in various priories, Ronsard returned in his poems to the more purely lyric themes: the death of Marie, for example (*Comme on voit sur la branche au mois de mai la rose*), an attack on the woodcutters in his forest of Gastine (*Ecoute, bûcheron, arrête un peu le bras*), and especially the celebration of his last love, for a proud young lady-in-waiting (*demoiselle d'honneur*) of Queen Catherine de Médicis, Hélène de Surgères (*Les Amours d'Hélène*, 1578). Hélène was something of a prude and a bluestocking. These numerous sonnets often express the melancholy of an older man in love with a young girl (*Quand vous serez bien vieille*), and Ronsard reasons with himself that it is high time to give up his useless courtship: "J'ai honte de ma honte, il est temps de me taire."

Ronsard was revered by all of Europe. He was invited to every country: Holland, Germany, Poland, Sweden. The Italians read him more avidly than their own favorite poets. But his poetry was condemned by the two major arbiters of poetic taste in the 17th century: Malherbe and Boileau. Not until Sainte-Beuve published his *Tableau de la poésie française au 16e siècle*, in 1828, was Ronsard's greatness rediscovered. The Parnassian poets in the middle of the 19th century admired and imitated him. In the domain of French love poetry, Ronsard is one of the greatest, with Baudelaire, and possibly Apollinaire and Eluard.

Other Lyric Poets of the 16th Century

The other poets of the Pléiade did not add to the achievements of Du Bellay and Ronsard—Pontus de Tyard was a friend of Scève and was strongly influenced by him; Jodelle is better known as a dramatist. Remy Belleau's *Bergeries* are mainly nature poems. Baïf was an innovator in metrics, an erudite poet who closely imitated the ancients.

Philippe Desportes (1547–1606) was the official court poet (of Henri III) after Ronsard. He wrote a mannered poetry, almost more Italian than French. He was a priest and made, as successor to Marot, a new translation of the Psalms.

After a long period of neglect, two poets who wrote at the end of the century have been rediscovered in recent years. Jean de Sponde (1557–1595), a Protestant who abjured his faith, as did Henri IV, left a brief work—sonnets on death and other religious poems—that the English scholar Alan Boase reedited in the 20th century. Because of the rich qualities in his poems, the abundance of metaphor and antithesis, Jean de Sponde's name is today associated with "baroque" poetry and the poetry of John Donne.

The second discovery was of Jean de La Ceppède (1550–1622), a more prolific poet than Sponde, in his five hundred sonnets called *Théorèmes sur le sacré mystère de notre rédemption*. As the triangle was used in the Middle Ages to designate the mystery of the Trinity, so the theorem was used by 16th-century French poets to represent the mystery of the Redemption. The symbolism and beauty of many of La Ceppède's sonnets seem strikingly modern. The title *Teorema*, a film (1968) of Pier Paolo Pasolini, was probably taken from La Ceppède.

Of all the disciples of Ronsard, Guillaume du Bartas (1544–1590), a militant Protestant, was probably the most gifted and the most creative. His plan was to compose an epic poem, giving in successive tableaux the history of the universe. There were to be two *Semaines* of which only the first was written (1578). This first *Semaine* narrates the creation of the world. The tone of the poem is exuberant but the style is heavy with moral sermons and linguistic exaggerations. The English have given Du Bartas a higher place than have the French; Milton probably knew and borrowed from *Semaine*.

WRITERS and the WARS OF RELIGION

Between the "conjuration d'Amboise" of 1560, when the Huguenots tried unsuccessfully to separate the king, François II, from the Catholic influence of the Guise family, and the "Edit de Nantes" of 1598, which granted religious freedom to Protestants and Jews, France was torn by religious wars. Many literary works were inspired by the strife, but two writers in particular, both soldiers and representing the two sides, composed works of high literary value: the Protestant Agrippa d'Aubigné and the Catholic Blaise de Montluc.

At the age of fifteen, d'Aubigné was fighting on the side of the Huguenot partisans. He became companion-adviser and squire (*écuyer*) of Henri de Navarre, and helped him to conquer the kingdom of France. His long poem,

Les Tragiques, was written in order to serve his intransigent faith. Having been seriously wounded in 1577 in the battle of Casteljaloux, and believing himself doomed, he dictated the first part of his work. But he recovered, fought again, and continued writing his poem during the military campaigns.

Les Tragiques is divided into seven cantos (*chants*). *Les Misères* describes France ravaged by civil war; *Les Princes* denounces the favorites (*les mignons*) of Henri III and the homosexual activities of the king; *La Chambre Dorée* is an attack on the lawcourts and their injustices; *Les Feux* depicts the martyrdom and torture by fire of the Protestants; *Les Fers* describes the military achievements of the Huguenots and contains a violent passage on Saint Bartholomew's Day massacre; *Les Vengeances* lists the punishments meted out by God, beginning with Cain, throughout history. *Le Jugement* is an apocalyptic vision of the resurrection of the bodies that precedes the Last Judgment.

Les Tragiques was not published until 1616, an unfortunate date for such a work, because by that time Malherbe was imposing a different ideal of poetry. Like Ronsard, d'Aubigné was forgotten for two hundred years. Again, it was Sainte-Beuve who rehabilitated him, with the Pléiade, in the 19th century. His poetic gifts of satire and epic richness, which are fairly unique in the history of French poetry, are fully recognized today. Passages of Milton's *Lycidas* are not unlike the style of d'Aubigné.

At first, d'Aubigné resented Henri de Navarre's conversion to Catholicism, which made him Henri IV and which brought peace to France, but he did forgive the king at the end of his life. His son Constant was a reprobate, whose daughter Françoise married first the writer Scarron, and then Louis XIV, by whom she was named Marquise de Maintenon. It is ironic indeed that Mme. de Maintenon was largely responsible for the revocation of the Edict of Nantes that ended the toleration of Protestants in France.

Blaise de Montluc (1502?–1577) was an even more fanatical soldier than d'Aubigné. He served under three kings: François Ier, Henri II, and Charles IX. Henri III honored him with the title *maréchal de France*. Courageous in battle and brutal in ordering endless executions of Protestants, he acted always as the devoted agent of the king. At the end of his life, he dictated the story of his military campaigns. The title of these memoirs, *Commentaires*, is justified because Montluc, endowed with a remarkable memory of places and events, gave not only a vivid picture of battles, but also moral reflections and a self-portrait of a ruthless but honest soldier.

✓ Tragedy

Medieval plays, *mystères* and *farces*, continued to be performed through the first half of the 16th century. But the research of the humanists who helped to bring about a change in the development of poetry was instrumental in promoting a similar change in theatrical forms. The first tragedies in French were translations from Greek. Lazare de Baïf (father of Antoine), for example, adapted *Electre* of Sophocles.

Such experiments led to the writing of the first original French tragedy in 1552: *Cléopâtre captive*, by Etienne Jodelle, a member of the Pléiade. This play is the ancestor of the genre that was to culminate in the art of Racine a century later. It has five acts and choruses. The alexandrine verse is used in only two acts. The violent action in the play (such as the suicide of Cleopatra) does not take place on the stage. Much of the dialogue is in the form of a debate, such as Corneille used later. Ronsard and his friends looked upon *Cléopâtre captive* as an important literary event.

The first attempt to fix the rules of tragedy was made by J. C. Scaliger in 1561, in a work in Latin that was primarily a commentary on Aristotle's *Poetics*, defining tragedy as "the fate of a famous person, with an unhappy *dénouement*, and written in verse, in a serious style." Other commentators followed Scaliger, and by the end of the century a doctrine for French tragedy, including the three unities of place, time, and action, was established that was to be only slightly revised by Boileau and best illustrated in the works of Racine.

One dramatist of considerable talent did emerge in the second half of the 16th century: Robert Garnier (1544–1590). He was a lawyer and judge skilled in argumentation who reveals in many of the lyric scenes of his plays a moving treatment of pathos. He wrote seven tragedies and one tragicomedy. Of these, his one Biblical tragedy is his best: *Les Juives*, of 1583, which narrates the massacre of the royal family of Judah by Nebuchadnezzar. The spiritual drama unfolds on the stage and the scenes of physical horror take place offstage.

Bradamante (1582), Garnier's tragicomedy, is one of the first of a genre that was destined to have great success in France. The action of the play, with its happy ending, takes place at the time of Charlemagne. The subject is taken from Ariosto's *Orlando furioso* rather than from *La Chanson de Roland*. In his plays based on Greek tragedies (*Hippolyte* (1573) and *Antigone* (1580), for example), Garnier depicts fate as a divine force ultimately crushing man.

Comedy

In addition to being the author of the first French tragedy, Jodelle was also the initiator of a new type of comedy based on models of antiquity and on Italian comedy. *Eugène* (1552), by Jodelle, technically the first French comedy, was usually played with *Cléopâtre captive*.

Pierre Larivey was by far the most able writer and adapter of comedies in the new style of the 16th century. This Florentine who lived in France, in Troyes, left nine comedies in prose. His best play, *Les Esprits*, is drawn from a play of Lorenzino de Médicis, which had imitated Latin plays of Terence and Plautus. In the next century, Molière borrowed from Larivey's play when he wrote *L'Ecole des Maris* and *L'Avare*. It is not known whether the comedies of Larivey were actually performed. He favored always the Italian type of *imbroglio*, or complicated situation, with many disguises, recognitions and substitutions.

The Italian *commedia dell'arte* was a more entertaining form than the purely French comedy. It was particularly popular during the reign of Henri III (1574–1589), and its presence at court was encouraged by Henri's Italian mother, Catherine de Médicis. The Italian company had first come to France earlier in the century and their style of improvisations in dialogue and vigorous clowning was already familiar. Their stock characters became well known in France: the pedant, the conniving valet (Arlecchino or Arlequin), the comic old man (Pantalone), the young lovers, and the maid Colombine. The *commedia dell'arte* which later influenced Molière and Marivaux, with ballets and mascarades, delighted the court of France as well as poets, musicians and painters who were mobilized to provide scenarios, music, costumes and settings, where rulers and nobles, princesses and mignons danced in a spectacle-like manner that today is faintly recalled in the Folies-Bergère performances and the American musical comedy.

TRANSLATORS, STORYTELLERS,
MORALISTS, POLITICAL THEORISTS

Jacques Amyot (1513–1593) was both translator and masterful prose stylist. The vigor of his French is as important as that of Calvin and Rabelais in the development of the French language. His erudition as Hellenist explains why Marguerite de Navarre gave him a professorship (*une chaire*) at the University of Bourges. He was also honored by Henri II, who gave him a bishopric, by Charles IX, who appointed him *grand aumonier de France*, and by Henri III, who elevated him *Commandeur de l'Ordre du Saint-Esprit*.

But it was François Ier who commissioned the work destined to make Amyot famous: the translation of the *Lives* of Plutarch (*Vies des hommes illustres*). He labored on this translation for seventeen years (1542–1559), and later translated also the *Morals* (*Oeuvres morales*). On all sides this translation of the Greek moralist was admired, and the moral code derived from the *Lives* of Plutarch replaced the earlier code of chivalry. Montaigne's *Essais* are imbued with the spirit of Plutarch, and the French essayist often mentions his debt to Amyot's translation: *C'est notre bréviaire*. Although Corneille did not read Plutarch directly, he owed a great deal to the concept of *gloire* as emanating from the lives of Cicero, Scipio and Caesar.

As translator, Amyot took tremendous liberties; he rearranged some passages, skipped others, and misunderstood precise meanings. He rewrote Plutarch in his own style and added a large number of words to the French language: *enthousiasme, misanthrope, horizon, mage, panégyrique*, and even *atome*. North's English translation of Amyot's French made Plutarch's *Lives* a favorite book among Elizabethans. Shakespeare's *Coriolanus, Julius Caesar, Antony and Cleopatra*, as well as Racine's *Mithridate*, come from this translation of Plutarch.

Bonaventure des Périers (1510–1544) was an atheist, a satirist (his *Cymbalum mundi* is a dialogue attacking religion), a short-story writer (*Nouvelles récréations et joyeux devis*, derived from the *fabliaux* and Boccaccio, and broadly humorous), and a protégé of Marguerite de Navarre, who was courageous in supporting him. The *Cymbalum* was seized by Parliament. Périers committed suicide.

Noël du Fail (1520–1591) was a more gifted storyteller than des Périers. His *Propos rustiques et facétieux* and his *Baliverneries* reproduced the speech of peasants and portrayed the stock characters of the doctor, the priest and the notary. Noël du Fail would have fared better had he not been overshadowed by Rabelais.

Pierre Charron (1541–1603) was a priest who in his first book, *Les Trois Verités* (1593), attempted to prove that God exists, that Christianity is the true religion, and that the true Church is Catholic. Therein he was addressing himself first to atheists, then to Jews, Moslems, and deists, and thirdly to Protestants.

His second book, *De la Sagesse* (1601), was closer to his philosophy, which was that of Montaigne. In terms of orthodox theology, the book was subversive because its principal goal was to prove, in keeping with much of Renaissance thought, the excellence of man as man. Charron illustrated the major dilemma of the Renaissance in that he was both a Catholic priest and an ardent disciple of Montaigne. He was later read by the libertines of the 17th century and the deists of the 18th.

Guillaume du Vair (1556–1621), one of the truly noble spirits of the 16th century, was undoubtedly a major ancestor of the great moralists of the 17th century. He was first a priest, then a magistrate and orator, and finally a champion of Henri de Navarre, whom he persuaded to convert to the Catholic Church and thereby bring peace to France. After Henri's triumphant entrance into Paris, the king appointed du Vair president of the Parlement d'Aix and thus the pacifier of Provence. In his old age, he returned to the priesthood, and was bishop of Lisieux at his death.

He simplified the art of oratory, both political and judicial, as much as Malherbe simplified the art of poetry. In the domain of philosophy, he went very far in harmonizing the morality of the stoics with Christian teaching. *La Sainte Philosophie* is his translation of Epictetus. His principal thesis stated that the virtuous life is based on a control of the passions. This is the subject of his *Philosophie morale des stoïques*.

Between the two extreme parties, Catholic and Protestant, was a third, *les Politiques*, composed of more moderate men who as writers emphasized the need for peace: Jean Bodin (*La République*), and François de la Noue (*Discours politiques et militaires*) were two of these men. After Henri de Navarre's (Henri IV) entrance into Paris in 1593, there appeared in the following year a pamphlet written by several authors called *La Satire Ménippée* (named after the cynical Greek philosopher Ménippe), which was an example of clandestine political literature that celebrated the new king's victory.

MONTAIGNE (1533–1592)

The most mature work of the French Renaissance, *Essais* of Michel de Montaigne, were written during the years of war and fanaticism in order to give a lesson of wisdom not only to France but to the world.

Michel Eyquem was born in 1533 in the château of Montaigne, a medieval fief or domain that had been purchased by his great-grandfather Ramon Eyquem. It is in the province of Périgord, near the town of Bergerac (Dordogne). His father, of Portuguese ancestry, had made a fortune on salted fish, pastel and wine. His mother came from a family (de Louppes) of Spanish Jewish merchants who had become Protestant.

The boy was brought up a Catholic in an atmosphere of freedom, and allowed to mingle with peasant children. Pierre Eyquem had broadminded educational theories. Michel learned Latin as a living language. His tutor and servants had to speak Latin in his presence. He resented the rigors of the collège de Guyenne in Bordeaux which he attended between the ages of six and thirteen, but was allowed to read *en cachette* Ovid, Virgil, Plautus and Italian comedies.

He studied law in Périgueux and Toulouse. After his first appointment as *conseiller* at the Cour des Aides de Périgueux, he served in the Bordeaux parliament where he was often shocked by the sentences given to criminals. There in parliament he met another counsellor, Etienne de La Boétie, three years his elder, for whom he felt immediately an intense kind of friendship, which he considered stronger than the love for a woman.

In the style of a young humanist, La Boétie wrote a tract against tyrants, *Discours de la Servitude Volontaire*, which was published later by the Protestants under the forthright title *Contre-Un*. The two young men, Montaigne and La Boétie, tried to emulate the life of Roman stoics. Later, in one of his essays, Montaigne analyzed this friendship in detail and explained it in sentences that have become famous: "Parce que c'était lui, parce que c'était moi. . . Nous nous cherchions avant que de nous être vus. . . Nous nous embrassions par nos noms." The fatality of love has never been more vividly expressed. La Boétie's death, at the age of thirty-three, was a lofty example of Socratic stoicism. This death was Montaigne's greatest personal loss, but it moved him closer to the vocation of writer, in which he found solace and salvation.

He married a dowry rather than the woman Françoise de la Chassaigne. A negligent husband, he fathered six daughters, only one of whom survived him, but always pretended he could not remember the exact number of his children. His father urged him to translate the *Theologia naturalis* of a Toulouse theologian, Raymond Sebond. After his father's death, in 1568, Montaigne published in Paris the posthumous writings of La Boétie, and then gave up his post of *conseiller* in Bordeaux and retired to his estate of Montaigne. Held in high esteem by Henri III, Catherine de Médecis and Henri de Navarre, he accomplished for them several diplomatic missions, but barely mentioned them in the *Essais*.

Most of his time was spent in his *librairie*, his library of one thousand books, in a tower of his château. There he read, annotated his readings, and gradually organized the annotations into chapters of personal meditations. (Montaigne's writing habits closely resemble those of Marcel Proust in the 20th century, who isolated himself in a cork-lined room in his Paris apartment for the writing of his novel.) On the beams of his library ceiling, he painted and engraved maxims of antiquity. The room was a fortress that cut him off from civic and conjugal duties—there Michel Eyquem became Montaigne.

His meditations on death, with the example of the deaths of La Boétie and his father, were at first stoical. With arguments from Seneca, Lucan and Cato, he praised man's will, able to triumph over suffering and death. (*Que philosopher, c'est apprendre à mourir*, I. 26) Then gradually more sceptical philosophers held his attention: Sextus Empiricus, the interpreter of Pyrrho, for example. He began to feel a kinship with such writers, and cultivated, almost ecstatically, the attitude of uncertainty about everything. In 1576, he had a medal cast in bronze with a motto from Sextus Empiricus: "*Que sais-je?*"

The first two books of Montaigne appeared in Bordeaux, in 1580, with the mysterious title *Essais*. This word had never been used before in such a way. By testing himself (*s'essayer*) or experimenting with himself in these pages, with quotations and reflections on the quotations, Montaigne invented a genre of writing that was immediately appropriated by Francis Bacon in England, and that was destined, in England and France, especially, to proliferate and almost rival that more popular literary form, the novel.

In testing himself, Montaigne grew more and more interested in himself—in his person, his habits and his reactions. The purpose of his writing was to present a self-portrait—"Je n'ai d'autre objet que de me peindre moi-même." His excuse was his conviction that each man is universal, that each man bears in himself *la forme entière de l'humaine condition*.

After the 1580 publication of the *Essais*, Montaigne left Périgord for an extensive voyage. Since 1578, he had been suffering from *la pierre* (the "stone," a concretion or calculus in the kidney or bladder or gallbladder), which served as another form of self-testing. In the company of four youths, sons of noblemen, he left his château, his wife and children, his vineyards, his neighbors, and the civil war. Going first to Paris, he presented his *Essais* to Henri III.

After crossing Lorraine and Alsace, he stopped at Plombières-les-Bains, in the Vosges, for the mineral waters, went through Switzerland, stopping at Baden for the waters, Germany, and finally Italy, where in Rome he was given the title of Roman citizen.

The plague (*la peste*) broke out in Bordeaux two months before the end of his term of office. At that time he was in his château, and he simply decided to stay there rather than risk death in Bordeaux. It seemed more reasonable to Montaigne to continue writing his essays than to play the martyr at his post of mayor, as. it had always seemed more reasonable to him to remain a Catholic and accept the mysteries of religion rather than denounce them in the raucous manner of the Renaissance.

He retouched the essays of the first two books, composed thirteen new essays which he grouped together as the third book, and published the new edition in 1588. In the new essays he wrote of his life (*Du repentir*, III. 2), of his pleasure in friends, love, and reading (*Des trois commerces*, III. 3), and of the role he played in the civil war and the plague (*De la physionomie*, III. 12).

Between 1588 and his death in 1592, Montaigne was comforted by an admiring young lady, Marie de Gournay, whom he called his *fille d'alliance*. He continued revising old essays and wrote new ones. Marie de Gournay published in 1595 the third edition of the *Essais* that contains corrections and additions.

Among the many themes and subjects of the essays, the moral character of Montaigne, his own self-assessment, is the most dominant, revealing a man of independence, jealous of his freedom, refusing to live at court, a man enjoying life and cultivating his mind in an almost voluptuous way. He was a humanist who read widely, especially Latin writers, historians, and Plutarch's *Lives* in Amyot's translation. He was also something of a dilettante in his scorn of pedants and specializations. He loved and needed solitude, but he was also social-minded and enjoyed seeing his neighbors or receiving his friends in his château —on one occasion he received the king of Navarre and all his suite. He was a gifted conversationalist (see *De l'art de conférer*, III. 8). Conversation was a mental exercise for him, a sharpening of his wits, rather than an exhibition of knowledge. In every way, he prefigured the *honnête homme* of the 17th century.

Montaigne was not, in a strict sense, a philosopher, but he faced and discussed many philosophical problems. He was concerned with the meaning of happiness and the way of reaching it. From nature he learned the lesson that death is not terrifying, but simply the ending of life. His great principle includes a submission to nature and the natural forces of the universe and one's own body. Self-knowledge helps in this submission. He felt that there are countless ways of living, and that each individual must find a way that is in keeping with his own temperament. In politics, Montaigne was a conservative, believing that there is no ideal form of government and therefore it is useless to overthrow the existing regime and traditional religion. He protested against cruel verdicts of justice, against torture, and against all the odious forms of colonization. With equal vehemence, he attacked scholastic pedantry. The best lessons for a young student, he felt, are those that lead him into direct contact with the subject matter, through conversations, reading and travel—everything, in other words, that will train the critical mind.

The general picture of man that the *Essais* give reappear later in the writings of Pascal, La Fontaine, La Rochefoucauld and La Bruyère. All these writers owed a debt to Montaigne. His familiar conversational style, far less heavy than that of Rabelais, makes him readable today. His independent thinking and his freedom of judgment mark him as that kind of French writer (ancestor of Montesquieu and Voltaire) who accepted the relativity of knowledge and the impossibility of reaching absolute truth.

SEVENTEENTH CENTURY

HISTORY		LITERATURE	
1610–43	reign of Louis XIII	1628	death of Malherbe
		1630–45	major period of Hôtel de Rambouillet
1624–42	ministry of Richelieu	1635	founding of Académie Française
		1636	Corneille, *Le Cid*
		1637	Descartes, *Discours de la méthode*
1643	Louis XIV king; regency of Anne d'Autriche·		
1643–61	ministry of Mazarin		
1648–52	La Fronde	1656–57	Pascal, *Lettres Provinciales*
		1659	Molière, *Précieuses Ridicules*
1661–1715	reign of Louis XIV	1665	La Rochefoucauld, *Maximes*
1665–1700	building of Versailles	1666	Molière, *Le Misanthrope*
		1667	Racine, *Andromaque*
		1668	La Fontaines, *Fables* I–VI
		1670	Pascal, *Pensées*, éd. Port-Royal
		1677	Racine, *Phèdre*
		1678	La Fayette, *Princesse de Clèves*
1685	Révocation de l'Edit de Nantes	1688	La Bruyère, *Caractères*
		1695	Fénelon, *Télémaque*
		1697	Bayle, *Dictionnaire*

Pre-Classicism, or the Age of the "Baroque": 1600–1660

Henri IV reigned over France from 1589 to 1610. Louis XIII, son of Henri IV and Marie de Médicis, was king between 1610 and 1643. He reigned first under the regency of his mother, and then, for approximately twenty years, France was ruled by its prime minister, Cardinal Richelieu. Louis XIV, son of Louis XIII and Anne d'Autriche, was king of France from 1643 to 1715, but did not rule directly until 1661. His mother was regent and the government was largely in the hands of Cardinal Mazarin between 1643 and 1661.

The half-century saw the development of an absolute monarchy. Richelieu, in the name of the king and centralized power, opposed the nobles of France, and Mazarin suppressed the Fronde, the civil war between the nobles and the king. In 1661, Louis XIV was twenty-three, and from then until his death, fifty-four years later, he ruled as an absolute sovereign, *le roi soleil*.

At the close of the wars of religion, the power of the Catholic Church was restored and the Jesuits, in particular, as educators and confessors, led in a counter-reformation of conversion and evangelization. François de Sales (1562–1622), a priest but not a Jesuit, illustrates by the example of his life and his writings (*Introduction à la vie dévote* and *Traité de l'amour de Dieu*) an effort to show a more charitable aspect of the Catholic Church.

The doctrine of classicism was elaborated on by Malherbe, especially in regard to poetry, by Richelieu in his founding of the Académie Française in 1635, by the movement of preciosity, initiated in the Hôtel de Rambouillet, and even by the lessons in grammar and syntax of Vaugelas. Descartes' philosophy contributed to the classical ideals. Malherbe and his disciples fixed the rules of poetry, Descartes laid the basis of rationalism, and Corneille applied, for the first time with artistic success, the rules of tragedy.

During the half-century, the rigors of classical art were offset by baroque tendencies, already visible in the 16th century. The word "baroque," more applicable to a style of architecture and sculpture than to literature, suggests a rich, almost extravagant form, with ornate and intricate flourishes. In literature, baroque applies to metaphorical writing, writing with elements of fantasy and irrationality, and to forms that translate the anguish of man in elaborate language. It is found in the poetry of Sponde, early Malherbe, and the plays of Corneille. The term applies to the Italian writing of Marino and the Spanish writing of Gongora. Classical art was, by definition, sober, measured and clear. The baroque taste was its opposite, and was everywhere in evidence during the years when classical art was coming into its own.

The Age of Classicism: 1661–1685

   These arbitrary dates of the classical generation stand for the year in which Louis XIV began his personal reign, at the death of Mazarin, and the year of the Revocation of the Edict of Nantes. A sense of order reigned everywhere. Louis XIV was responsible only to God. In the political domain, the power of the Church and of Parliament was considerably restricted. The king chose and dismissed at will his ministers and artists. The correctness of tone and behavior (*les bienséances*) came from the royal court in Paris and Versailles, and no longer from the Hôtel de Rambouillet. Politeness and ceremony seemed more important than virtue. The new type of courtier was the *honnête homme* who was sufficiently cultivated to sustain conversation on any topic. He was elegant in speech, manner and dress, and somewhat knowledgeable about many subjects. The king opposed the Jansenist movement within the Church, and he directed a veritable campaign against the Calvinists, which culminated in his revoking the Edict of Nantes.

   Classicism was first a set of rules for writing, but it represented principally "taste" in the art of writing, and in the subject matter of the writing. It was the effort of the artist to please the cultivated public of Paris and Versailles. Molière has one of his characters say, "La grande règle de toutes les règles est de plaire." The miracle of classicism was the astuteness with which the *public de connaisseurs* of the classical age recognized and applauded the really fine authors: Racine in tragedy, Molière in comedy, La Fontaine in his fables and *contes*, Bossuet in his sermons, La Rochefoucauld in his *Maximes*, Boileau in his theory and satires.

**First Signs of the *esprit philosophique:*
1685–1715**

Here again, the arbitrary dates (the Revocation of the Edict of Nantes and the death of Louis XIV) conveniently frame a generation in which free thinking (*la libre pensée*) began to be expressed more openly than in the earlier part of the century. The prestige and the power of the king were diminishing. At his death, France was exhausted with wars, defeats, and excessive financial expenditures. Discreet opposition to the king's absolutism was being articulated. In literature a violent quarrel between the two factions of the Ancients and Moderns helped to initiate a new age of literary expression. Such men as Bayle and Fontenelle, forerunners of the 18th century *philosophes*, began openly to oppose religious orthodoxy and political institutions.

MALHERBE (1555–1628)

Born in Caen, François de Malherbe had traits of character that are often associated with the typical Norman: petulance and even anger, and a relentlessness in work and ambition. He was often vindictive, and developed into a tyrant in linguistic and poetic matters. His power became such that he could easily depose opponents and rivals. Desportes, favorite poet of Henri III, having invited Malherbe to dinner, wanted to show him his translation of the Psalms, but Malherbe stopped him and gruffly said, "I prefer your soup to your Psalms [Votre potage vaut mieux que vos Psaumes]."

During the first part of his career, when he wrote poetry full of the defects he eventually criticized in others (see, for example, his inflated translation of *Les larmes de saint Pierre* of Tansillo, a work he dedicated to Henri III). Malherbe lived in Caen and in Provence, and was always looking for a suitable patron. When, in 1600, Marie de Médicis spent two days in Aix-en-Provence on her way from Italy to Paris to be married to Henri IV, Malherbe presented her with a carefully written ode of welcome:

Peuples, qu'on mette sur la tête
Tout ce que la terre a de fleurs . . .

Finally, in 1605, the anxious poet was introduced to the king, in the Louvre. Henri IV was on the point of leaving Paris to visit the province of Le Limousin (which he was to annex to the crown) and suggested that Malherbe write something about it. On his return, Malherbe presented him with *Prière pour le roi Henri le Grand allant en Limousin.* Henri was satisfied with the ode. Although not particularly keen on poetry, he gave Malherbe a valet, a horse and a pension (*mille livres d'appointements*). The poet was fifty years old. He had been working a long time for such a recognition. He remained at court the rest of his life.

Like Descartes, a few years later, Malherbe began clearing the way for a new beginning of poetry. He attacked Ronsard and the Pléiade poets for their belief in the divine mission of poets and for the excessive ornaments of their poetry. He deleted half the contents of a book of poems of Desportes. He condemned all provincialisms ("Je veux dégasconner la langue"), all hellenisms, latinisms, italianisms. When asked what remained for vocabulary, he advised (in blatant exaggeration) "the speech of porters [les crocheteurs du Port-au-Foin]." He wrote a large number of command pieces and *poèmes de circonstance* (such as his often-anthologized *stances: Consolation à Du Périer*, written in 1600), and sonnets on Henri IV's love affairs. His last highly disciplined poems have measured and elevated general metaphors: see his *Ode au roi Louis XIII allant châtier la rébellion des Rochelois* (1628).

Malherbe avoided personal emotional themes in his poetry in order to write of universal matters: the disasters of war, the fragility of life. He imposed his type of classical writing on many poets. His theories are found in his *Commentaires sur Desportes*, marginal notes in the works of Desportes. Poetry for Malherbe was a craft (*métier*) based on a well-defined technique. He denounced hiatus, cacophony, the filling out of a line with unimportant words (*cheville*), the overflow of one line to the next (*enjambement*). In a sonnet to Louis XIII, he had the audacity to write:

Ce que Malherbe écrit dure éternellement.

Malherbe's Disciples

Two disciples in particular have survived, and deservedly. François Maynard (1582–1646) used the forms recommended by Malherbe: *stances, odes, sonnets, chansons, épigrammes.* Such a close discipleship probably limited Maynard. The epigram, with its precision and brevity, became, at the end of his life, his most congenial form. Racan (Honorat de Bueil, marquis de Racan, 1589–1670) wrote a dramatic pastoral poem, *Les Bergeries.* He was a more simple, more elegiac poet than Maynard or Malherbe. Although he lived to the age of eighty-one, he wrote his famous retirement poem, *Stances sur la retraite,* at the age of twenty-nine:

Tircis, il faut penser à faire la retraite.

Malherbe's Adversaries

Malherbe's theories on poetry and the tyranny of his régime were contested by many poets, but especially by two very able ones: Mathurin Régnier (1573–1613) and Théophile de Viau (1590–1626).

Régnier was the nephew of Desportes, and wrote a satire (*Satire IX à Rapin*) in order to avenge his uncle. He was one of the early *libertins* (freethinkers) in the century. Almost every aspect of the art of his *Satires* is opposed to Malherbe: his digressions, rich vocabulary, bold imagery, freedom from rules of syntax, and the general ebullience of the writing. Poetry comes from inspiration, according to Régnier, and this belief alone was enough to place him in the opposite camp. His poems are studies in customs and types: the hypocrite, for example, in *Satire XIII sur Macette*. Because of the keenness of his observations, Boileau, later in the century, hailed Régnier as a precursor of Molière.

Théophile de Viau, also a *libertin*, was the son of a Huguenot lawyer. He wrote odes, elegies, satires and one tragicomedy: *Pyrame et Thisbé*. Like Régnier, he supported the rights of free inspiration, but acknowledged his debt to Malherbe's technique. He has been ridiculed for two bad lines in his play, in which a bloody dagger is said to be blushing! Not quite a bohemian poet, not quite a *poète maudit*, Théophile was a popular poet of his day. His love poems and his poems about his love of nature were esteemed by young readers who often idolized him. He sang of the poet's freedom:

> J'approuve que chacun écrive à sa façon.

Théophile was accused of *libertinage* and pornography by the Jesuits. At one point he was exiled from France. On his return, he was pardoned by Louis XIII, but eventually the Jesuit priest Garasse had him seized for obscene poems he had not written. The Paris Parliament condemned him to be burned alive. For twenty-five months he was jailed in the Conciergerie. Young Parisians clamored for his release, and he was finally liberated, but died soon after, at the age of thirty-six, from a malignant fever contracted in the cell.

PRECIOSITY

Before Richelieu founded the Académie Française, by which he hoped to control and direct literary activity, the Hôtel de Rambouillet exerted a strong influence on literature during the first third of the century. Preciosity, as a form of literary taste and practice, came into prominence in the Hôtel de Rambouillet and spread to other salons. It was, and still is, an idealism that exalted love and heroism.

La marquise de Rambouillet, Catherine de Vivonne, was an intelligent and gifted woman. In about 1608 she reacted against the coarseness of behavior and language of the court of Henri IV, when she began receiving writers and members of the aristocracy in her own home. Her *chambre bleue* where, often reclining on her bed, she received her guests, was famous for half a century. Between 1608 and 1630, among the writers who paid homage to Mme de Rambouillet in the *ruelle*, the space beside her bed, were Malherbe, Racan, Vaugelas, Chapelain and Voiture. The years between 1630 and 1645 were the most brilliant, with La Rochefoucauld, Scudéry, Mairet, Benserade, Cotin, Rotrou, Corneille, Scarron, Balzac, and especially Voiture, the favorite figure in the salon. After 1645 two new habituées attended: Mme de Sévigné and Mme de Lafayette. But by then the importance of the salon was declining.

Conversation was the great pleasure of the *précieux* salons. Every topic and every tone were permitted, provided the rules of *bienséance* were observed. Corneille read his tragedies there and Voiture his letters. Poems were composed for the daughter of Mme de Rambouillet, Julie d'Angennes, and collected into *La Guirlande de Julie*. The term *précieuses* designated those ladies who opposed anything vulgar in language and behavior, who insisted on using elegant phrases or words for ordinary objects. Preciosity became "ridiculous" (*les précieuses ridicules*, Molière later says) when refinement in manners, language and sentiment became extravagant.

Preciosity, in its literary connotation, has flourished in different centuries and countries. In England it is called *euphuism* (after Lyly's *Euphues*); in Italy, *marinismo* (after Marino) or *concetticism*; in Spain, *gongorismo* (after Gongora). Elegance of dress and manners were obvious signs. More important was the preciosity of sentiment, the refinement of love, not unrelated to platonism. The *Carte de Tendre*, traced in Mlle de Scudéry's salon, was the game of love, the blueprint of obstacles encountered by lovers.

Almost an entire language was forged for and by the *précieuses* and the *précieux*. Sommaize in 1661 published his *Grand dictionnaire des précieuses*. The cheeks of a lady were called not *les joues*, but *les trônes de la pudeur*. A wig was not *une perruque* but *la jeunesse des vieillards*. A looking glass, *un miroir*, became *le conseiller des grâces*. The *précieuses* favored long adverbs such as *furieusement* and *épouvantablement*, and plays on words and witticisms. In addition to the aristocratic salons of Mme de Rambouillet and Mme de Sablé, there were bourgeois salons, those of Mlle de Scudéry and Mme Scarron, the future Mme de Maintenon. The new language and the new sentiments, before their appearance in literature, were practiced in the salons, veritable laboratories in which lords and ladies rivaled one another in wit and graciousness and, at times, maliciousness.

Honoré d'Urfé (1567-1625)

Three genres in particular were influenced by preciosity—the novel, the letter and poetry.

D'Urfé came from a learned noble family. He spent part of his life in the service of his relative, the duc de Savoie. His long novel, *L'Astrée*, came from many sources: Spanish pastorals (*Galatée* of Cervantes), Italian pastorals (*Aminta* of Tasso and *Pastor Fido* of Guarini), courtly romances, and the atmosphere and ideals of preciosity.

The setting is d'Urfé's native province, Le Forez, a region west of Lyon, with its small river, the Lignon. The action takes place at the time of the Druids. The principals are the shepherdess Astrée and the shepherd Céladon. The story is that of a faithful love between the two, and is undoubtedly an idealization of D'Urfé's own youthful experiences. This long work, of five volumes and 5,500 pages, published at intervals over twenty years, had a tremendous success in the 17th century. D'Urfé's method of narrative encouraged such length because adventures and episodes are able to prolong such a story indefinitely.

D'Urfé led the life of a cosmopolitan *seigneur*. In studying the doctrines of love in Plato, Ficino, and Pico de la Mirandola, he reached the conviction that love is the supreme experience leading man to God. In the perfect union of the soul and body, he thought, man aspires to total love. D'Urfé added military scenes to his somewhat insipid pastoral themes. Shepherd's crooks mingle with swords in his novel. Each of his characters is a moralist, analyzing why he loves and why he suffers. The doctrine on which D'Urfé built *L'Astrée* came from the Renaissance, and by emphasizing love as the expression of will and sacrifice, he pointed the way to the writings of Descartes and Corneille.

D'Urfé delighted his wide public by presenting them with a mode of behavior, a *savoir-vivre*. The idealism of the doctrine enchanted such different writers as Corneille and La Fontaine, and later, Rousseau in Geneva.

Other Novelists

Novels of adventure, as they appeared in the 17th century, tended to drop the pastoral elements of *L'Astrée* and emphasize historical settings. La Calprenède wrote adventure stories (*romans de cape et d'épée*) and Mlle de Scudéry developed especially moral disquisitions and analyses of love in high circles: *Artamène ou le Grand Cyrus* (1648–1653) and *Clélie*, with its *Carte de Tendre* (1654–1661). Helped by her brother Georges de Scudéry, she was a rival of La Calprenède, who is caricatured in *Le Grand Cyrus*. *Clélie* is a novel about women's rights, especially the rights of passion.

Such idealistic novels were parodied and caricatured by more realistic-minded novelists who depicted the world of the *cabarets* rather than the world of the *ruelles*. Charles Sorel (1599–1674) in *L'Histoire comique de Francion* (1622) portrayed an adventurer in a bohemian world. The picaresque hero, Francion, was not unlike Théophile de Viau in his real life. In its philosophy, the novel praised the reign of reason and advoçated a new kind of life, with sexual freedom, that will destroy the false conventions of life.

The best representative of the burlesque novel was Paul Scarron (1610–1660) who, after a carefree life as a *chanoine*, suffered a serious paralysis. A paralytic at forty-two, he married Françoise d'Aubigné, granddaughter of the poet, who was seventeen. He wrote burlesque poetry, but is best known for his *Roman comique* (1651–1657), the adventures of travelling players in and around the city of Le Mans, where Scarron himself had lived.

In *Le Roman Bourgeois* (1666), Antoine Furetière (1619–1688) parodied the heroic novel. With Swift-like humor, and with considerable coarseness, he depicted the French bourgeoisie of the 17th century. Balzac and Jules Romains used the same subject matter in the 19th and 20th centuries and went much farther than Furetière in documentation and analysis.

Epistolary Art

The first half of the century took great delight in the *Lettres* of Jean-Louis Guez de Balzac (1597–1654). Their first publication in 1624 consecrated him a hero of the salons, a kind of oracle of the *ruelles*, a master in the art of prose-writing. The letters were addressed to celebrities of the day and to numerous writers: Corneille, Voiture, Scudéry, Saint-Amant. The largest number went to Chapelain and Conrart. These last two, with Balzac, were the most powerful arbiters of literature under Richelieu.

The letters, destined to be read publicly and to be printed, treat various moral and philosophical subjects (Balzac was a combination of stoic and fervent Catholic), develop critical judgments on new literary works (he defended *Le Cid*, for example, in a letter to Scudéry, and discussed *Cinna* in a letter to Corneille himself), and comment on contemporary events, such as the scandalous life of Théophile de Viau. But the real importance of the *Lettres* was their style, fully representative of *précieux* taste and refinement. The clear articulation of Balzac's elegant periodic sentence was decidedly classical, and was later perfected by Pascal and Bossuet. Guez de Balzac pleased the young with his modernistic outlook, with his tendency to relegate the humanists and the ancients to their historical position.

Like Guez de Balzac, the poet Vincent Voiture (1598–1648) was a favorite of the Hôtel de Rambouillet. His letters too were intended to be read and commented on. They were often written to habitués of the Hôtel—to the marquise herself, to Julie d'Angennes and to Mme de Sablé. His precious style is lighter than Balzac's, more witty, more given to exaggeration and an excessive use of metaphor. Voiture narrates social events and describes himself in an obvious desire to please. A style of banter (*badinage*) characterizes these letters. They are affected in many ways, but their gracefulness saves them. Boileau ranked Voiture with Horace. La Fontaine equated him with Rabelais and Marot.

Poetry and Preciosity

Poetry written for the salons tended to use the briefer forms (*petits genres*) such as *sonnets, stances, chansons, épigrammes,* and *madrigaux* (complimentary gallant poems.) Voiture was the most successful poet of this category. As in his letters, he was witty, graceful and ingenious in his poems. Of the many poets who wrote in similar fashion, Benserade was perhaps the least conventional (he wrote poems for Lully's ballets) and Gilles de Ménage, who was also a philologist.

Many poets in the heyday of preciosity attempted to compose epic poems, the most pretentious works of the period. Chapelain (1595–1674), official critic of the Académie Française, in charge of royal grants (*pensions*) to writers, published his epic on Jeanne d'Arc, *La Pucelle d'Orléans,* in 1656. It had a brief success before its fundamental mediocrity was realized. Chapelain's pompousness, opportunism and servility to Richelieu were later satirized by Boileau in his *Satire IX.*

The epic poem on *Clovis* by Desmarets de Saint-Sorlin was also an artistic failure. The literary public of the 17th century counted on seeing French epic poems produced that would equal *The Iliad* and *The Aeneid* and Tasso's *Gerusalemme liberata.* But each effort (and there were many) failed. The temptation was to use *le merveilleux chrétien* and surpass the *chansons de geste.* Finally, in 1672, Bussy-Rabutin ordained: "Un poeme épique ne peut réussir en notre langue."

Fantasy-Grotesque Lyricism

The term *grotesque* was used especially by Théophile Gautier in the 19th century to designate an unusual fantasylike poetry.

After a military career, Cyrano de Bergerac came to Paris to study with the philosopher Gassendi. He became known for his free thinking (*libertinage*) and his humor. As a writer, he used many forms: a tragedy (*Mort d'Agrippine*); a comedy (*Le pédant joué*); two prose fantasies, *Le voyage dans la lune* and *L'Histoire comique des Etats et empires du Soleil*; letters and maxims. Cyrano's moon trip is both fantasy and ingenious scientific hypotheses. His political-religious views were bold for his day. In 1897, the play of Edmond Rostand romanticized and falsified a good deal of the character and the achievements of the real Cyrano.

The reputation of Tristan L'Hermite (1601–1655) was that of dramatist and poet. He used the favorite forms of his century: *stances, odes, sonnets, chansons, épigrammes*, and *madrigaux*. When his poetry is *précieux* (he made every effort to be the French Marino), it is far less successful than when it is burlesque. In his picaresque novel, *Le page disgracié*, he narrates his own adventurous adolescence.

The Norman writer Saint-Amant (1594–1661) was a free-thinker like his friends Théophile de Viau and Cyrano de Bergerac—a traveller, a soldier, and a rather famous drinker. He frequented cabarets as well as throne-rooms in Paris, Madrid, Rome, London, Warsaw. His work is so varied that it defies any classification. *Les Visions* and *La Solitude* are poems on nightmares and ghosts. There is no malice but considerable humor in his works on English and Roman customs: *Albion* and *Rome ridicule*. In this latter work he shows none of the reverence with which Du Bellay approached Rome. Saint-Amant's verbal opulence was not in harmony with the new sober classical style as it was developing, and before his death he seemed already out of date. Boileau was harsh in his judgment of Saint-Amant.

RENÉ DESCARTES (1596–1650)

The philosophical writing of Descartes has been vastly over-simplified by literary historians and interpreters of French classicism. "Cartesianism," a term based on the philosopher's Latin name Cartesius, is synonymous with rationalism because he was the founder of the philosophical thinking known as rationalism in the 17th and 18th centuries. But Descartes was not a rationalist in the sense of opposing reason to faith. However it is true that later, in the 18th and 19th centuries, his work did encourage this tendency to oppose science to revelation. Throughout all of his writings, Descartes gave evidence of believing the universe ordered by laws of a Creator whose existence he never doubted.

Reason, with which man is endowed, is a natural faculty, according to Descartes, and man uses his reason in the pursuit of truth. The practice of reason is a discipline that cannot lead to error. Man is a microcosm of the universe—all qualities are in him, but especially the will and ability to find truth.

Descartes' "method" is the aspect of his work that has been the most exploited by literature. This "method," or the idea of it, probably appeared to him as an "illumination" on the night of November 10, 1619. When the book itself was first published in 1637, it listed and explained four rules for the search of truth in the sciences.

1. Never accept anything unless it can be proved. This would seem to be an expression of universal doubt. One must judge everything scrupulously without having recourse to earlier authority.

2. Divide the difficulties into as many parts as is necessary. This procedure is called analysis.

3. The procedure of synthesis, by which the parts of the difficulty are put together in an orderly fashion, then follows logically.

4. Recapitulate and reexamine all the steps. This represents the need to revise and check.

The formula, then, is: evidence, analysis, synthesis, and a careful checking (dénombrement).

Descartes' is a purely intellectual process that makes no reference to God or to Christian doctrine. By comparison with medieval scholasticism, his method is totally simple. It also appears very different from the speculations of the 16th century humanists. His Discours de la méthode (1637) is a work of French prose unprecedented in its clarity. Later works, Méditations métaphysiques (1641) and Principes de la philosophie (1644), were originally written in Latin. Most of his work was done in Holland. He died in his first winter in Stockholm, where he had been invited to reside by Queen Christina.

Descartes' writings are really for philosophers, despite the allegations made through the centuries that his philosophy can be read by the average reader, or by that reader called *l'honnête homme* in the 17th century. Because of the example of Descartes, the French have often claimed that every philosophical idea can be expressed in simple language. This is as far from accurate as is the statement that Descartes' philosophy is an example of *la clarté française*.

Literary figures such as Péguy in the 20th century have tended to exaggerate the influence of Descartes on other writers and to oversimplify his philosophy. His is not the philosophy of common sense that is found in every French peasant! He did not deliver French thought from the dogmas of authority. It is erroneous to say that French philosophy is rationalistic because of Descartes. His *Discours* is only one of the masterpieces of French philosophy. The bulk of his work is directed toward the specialists, as is the work of Henri Bergson in the 20th century.

CORNEILLE (1606–1684)

The Theater in Corneille's Time

During the course of the century, the theater became a permanent institution in France, and a cultivated public applauded the masterpieces that were written and produced for it.

In the large fairs, groups of actors and acrobatic performers (*bateleurs* such as Tabarin) played on improvised stages (*tréteaux*). Such groups after the Paris season often went to the provinces, where they performed pastoral plays and tragicomedies, usually in a *jeu de paume* (tennis court).

At the end of the 16th century, there was only one real theater in Paris, the Hôtel de Bourgogne, which belonged to the *confrères de la passion* and which had full monopoly. Another troop of actors took over the Hôtel in 1628. They were authorized by Louis XIII to use the name *Troupe Royale*. At first they played farces (with the popular clowns Gros Guillaume and Turlupin) and then specialized in tragedies.

Another rival company occupied a *jeu de paume* in the rue Vieille-du-temple, le théâtre du Marais (le Marais was the section of the city). This theater closed down in 1673 and the actors went either to the Hôtel de Bourgogne or to Molière's company.

The history of this company was written by the actor La Grange in *le registre* he kept week by week of the performances and receipts. After twelve years in the provinces, the company occupied in Paris first *la salle* du Petit Bourbon and then *la salle*, more spacious and elegant, of the Palais-Royal, built by Richelieu. Several of Molière's actors became favorites of the public: La Grange in roles of the lover; du Croisy, a comic; the tragedian Mlle du Parc; and Baron, a boy trained by Molière who developed into the best actor of the century. Molière favored naturalness in acting and opposed the declamatory style of the Hôtel de Bourgogne.

After Molière's death there were dissensions among the actors, and at about the same time similar dissensions troubled the Hôtel de Bourgogne. The two companies decided to amalgamate, and the king in 1680 gave the sole authorization to the *comédiens français* to perform comedies in Paris. It was the birth of La Comédie Française. An *académie d'opéra* had already been authorized by the king in 1669. From 1680 on, Italian players occupied the Hôtel de Bourgogne. Italian was a familiar language in the city and many of the actors were popular—Trivelin and Scaramouche, in particular. In accordance with the *commedia dell'arte* tradition, each actor played one stock character, Pierrot, Arlequin, Polichinelle, Pantalone.

Performances in these theaters were always given in the afternoon. The boxes (*les loges*) were reserved for ladies, and the orchestra (*le parterre*) for men. On each side of the stage there were often benches reserved for *les petits marquis* (fops) who applauded or hissed the actors. The settings were rudimentary at first, but by the end of the century sumptuous decorations were used. Elaborate stage costumes were in vogue, but no attempt was made to use costumes in keeping with the historical period of the play's action.

The strict form of classical tragedy as developed in the 16th century lost out at the beginning of the 17th to two very popular forms: *la tragi-comédie* and *la pastorale*. Tragicomedy was a melodramatic tragedy with a happy ending. The pastoral play involved shepherds and lengthy analyses of love. In about 1630, these two genres were replaced by the stricter forms of tragedy and comedy.

The extremely prolific Alexandre Hardy (1570–1631) was the most success-ful playwright during the first thirty years of the century. He wrote tragedies, comedies, and a large number of tragicomedies. He had a sense of dramatic action which was perfected by Corneille in later years. He pleased his public by giving them complex plots, unpredictable changes of fortune in the action and melodrama—battles, rape and banditry were plentiful in his plays.

Then, as a reaction to Hardy's theater, critics, especially Richelieu and Chapelain, began calling for a more ordered, more sober, more classical type of play. Jean Mairet (1604–1686) answered this need. After writing baroque melodramatic plays, he gave, in 1634, the first regular French tragedy, *Sophonisbe*, in which the rules of tragedy were applied. The success of this play helped to determine the French formula of tragedy. Hardy brought movement and life into serious theater, and Mairet a sense of order and reasonableness. Corneille surpassed both dramatists by means of what may legitimately be called genius.

Pierre Corneille

Born in Rouen, Corneille was taught by Jesuits in their *collège*, where he developed a love for Latin writers. In keeping with his family's tradition, he studied law and pleaded at least one case. He led a carefree existence for a few years, during which time he often attended performances of Hardy's plays in the *jeu de paume* of Rouen. He wrote a comedy, *Mélite ou les fausses lettres*, based somewhat on his first romantic adventure, and this was performed at the Théâtre du Marais in 1629. The success of this play encouraged him to continue writing for the stage. His comedies that followed *Mélite*, though better than those being written by other playwrights at the same time, were not com-parable to the comedies of Molière.

At thirty, Corneille suddenly became famous with the success of his tragi-comedy *Le Cid*. He had read the Spanish play of Guilhem de Castro, *Las Mocedades del Cid* [*The Youth of the Cid*] (1621) and was fired by this tense dramatic story of a knight of Burgos marrying the daughter of a man he had killed. Corneille wrote *Le Cid* in 1636, and it was probably first performed in early 1637 in the Théâtre du Marais. The success was phenomenal.

Its youthfulness and romantic idealism stirred the public. The remarkable diversity of movements and colors—lyric passages, epic narration, swift-moving scenes—evoked a sense of tragedy and pathos. The newness of the play was in

Corneille's understanding of his characters: Chimène's love for her father and for Rodrigue; Rodrigue's love for Chimène and his almost feudal sense of honor (*gloire*); the unbending pride of the count, Chimène's father; and the more humble sense of honor in Don Diègue, Rodrigue's father. *Le Cid* is the first of a large number of 17th century plays noteworthy for well-developed psychological studies of character. The agon of the play, the principal psychological struggle, is that between honor and passion. Corneille's thesis is clear: love cannot exist and continue without honor. The very strength necessary to preserve honor comes from love.

Le Cid's success called forth stalwart adversaries. Georges Scudéry, in his pedantic *Observations sur le Cid*, criticized the subject of the play, the playwright's infidelity to the rules of tragedy, and the elements he claimed were plagiarisms. Guez de Balzac defended Corneille in an open letter to Scudéry, and called for the Académie to arbitrate. *Les Sentiments de l'Académie sur le Cid*, drawn up principally by Chapelain, judged that both the rules of tragedy and the laws of *la bienséance* had been broken in *Le Cid*. This condemnation interfered in no way with the continuing success of the play.

Corneille, irritable by nature, retired to Rouen where after three years he finished *Horace*, a tragedy observing closely the three unities of time, place, and action, and the play was performed in 1640. The subject is drawn from Livy's history of Rome. This tragedy is an even greater exaltation of the theme of honor and the powerful play of will in the leading characters. But the exposition is overlong, as are also the oratorical passages. *Cinna* of 1642 was more successful in the 17th century, and still seems today more human than *Horace*. Its subject comes from a chapter of Seneca's *De Clementia*. It is the analysis of a willful act on the part of Emperor Augustus, who, by a sublime gesture of clemency, proves that his character has been regenerated. But this tragedy too, like *Horace*, lacks the vitality and exuberance of *Le Cid*.

After his marriage, Corneille retired again to Rouen, but often went to Paris, where he frequented the Hôtel de Rambouillet. There, in 1642, he read to the assembled salon a new tragedy, *Polyeucte*, taken from the *Lives of the Saints*. The reception in the salon was not favorable, but when the tragedy was put on at the Hôtel de Bourgogne in 1643, the public was moved by the nobility of the play and its success was assured. *Polyeucte* is both a love story (Polyeucte loves his wife Pauline) and the story of a Christian martyrdom. The will of self-sacrifice, on a human level in *Le Cid*, is on a supernatural level in *Polyeucte*.

After *Rodogune* of 1644, Corneille wrote almost twenty other plays, which did not have the success of his first works. The Cornelian hero, both in his psychological makeup and in the eloquence with which he analyzes his dramas and dilemmas, remains one of the major figures of French literature. The dignity of man is in his freedom, and he retains and uses this freedom in whatever situation he faces. It is a power and a privilege not given to everyone. The Cornelian hero is both clairvoyant and sufficiently energetic to accomplish what it is his duty to accomplish. His very willpower allows him to accomplish his duty. The tragedies of Corneille created a universe of human greatness, in which the typical hero forges his own destiny, and in many instances reaches a happy ending: *Le Cid*, *Cinna* and *Polyeucte* (because martyrdom is a prelude to supernatural happiness.)

In a preface to one of his plays, Corneille claims that a tragedy does not have to be "likely" (*vraisemblable*). The situation he usually creates is extraordinary and demanding. In many of his tragedies, he draws on Roman history and this gives an aspect of authenticity to his *invraisemblance*: the beginning of Rome in *Horace*; Roman conquests in *Nicomède*; the collapse of the Republic in *La Mort de Pompée*; the reign of Augustus in *Cinna*; the Empire's struggle with Christianity in *Polyeucte*.

Two Contemporaries of Corneille

Jean Rotrou (1601–1650) was probably the best of the many playwrights of Corneille's time. Almost as prolific as Hardy, he wrote regularly for the Hôtel de Bourgogne. His style of writing was not unlike that of his friend Corneille. His religious tragedy, taken from Polish history and from Lope de Vega, *Saint Genest*, is an imitation of *Polyeucte*. (Jean-Paul Sartre also used this title when he wrote his long study of Jean Genet.)

Nineteen years younger than his brother Pierre, Thomas Corneille (1625–1709) had some of the outstanding commercial successes of the century. He first imitated the tragedies of his brother and then, after Molière's death, wrote comedies, opera libretti, and lavish spectacle plays.

Port-Royal

The abbey of Port-Royal, in the Chevreuse valley, was built in the Middle Ages and housed in the 17th century a religious community of women. The mother superior of the order, Angélique Arnauld, had instituted in 1608 a very rigorous rule, which represented a reform in Catholic religious life that attracted attention to Port-Royal. When a large number of nuns joined the order, a part of the community was transferred to Paris in 1626, and a part remained at Port-Royal under the direction of la mère Angélique.

A group of pious laymen, theologians, and scholars joined the community. They were called *les messieurs* or *les solitaires* of Port-Royal: one of these was Antoine Arnauld, brother of la mère Angélique and known as le grand Arnauld; others were the philosopher Nicole and the humanist Lancelot. A school was founded in 1643 where the teaching was done in French (not in Latin, as was the custom) and the study of Greek was emphasized. The most illustrious friend of Port-Royal was Blaise Pascal, and its most illustrious pupil was Jean Racine.

Port-Royal became the center of a movement of reform within the Catholic Church known as Jansenism. The abbot Saint-Cyran directed the religious life of the nuns and the studies of the *solitaires* of Port-Royal-de-Paris and Port-Royal-des-Champs. He was a friend of Jansénius, the bishop of Ypres, who wrote a long work on the doctrine of grace in the writings of Saint Augustine, *L'Augustinus*. This work, both a compilation of texts of Saint Augustine and a commentary by Jansénius, was introduced to Port-Royal by Saint-Cyran and served as the theological basis of the reform. Eventually, by order of Richelieu, Saint-Cyran was imprisoned, *L'Augustinus* was eventually condemned by Rome, the religious of Port-Royal were dispersed, and the buildings in the vallée de Chevreuse were destroyed by order of Louis XIV at the end of his reign.

Pascal

Blaise Pascal was born in Clermont-Ferrand in the province of Auvergne, the son of a magistrate who moved to Paris after his wife's death and brought up his children, one boy and two girls, in scholarly surroundings in which Blaise was introduced to science and became a precocious scientific genius.

At sixteen, he wrote a *Traité sur les sections coniques*. At nineteen, he built an adding machine.

Through friends of his father, Pascal learned of the new Jansenist ideas and avidly read Jansénius and Saint-Cyran. He converted his father and his two sisters Gilberte and Jacqueline to these ideas, and Jacqueline later became a nun at Port-Royal. His scientific research and his religious crises aggravated his ill health, but he frequented aristocratic society after his father's death, especially the salon of Mme de Sablé where he met La Rochefoucauld.

He underwent a religious experience the night of November 23, 1654, during which he wrote a *mémorial* of what was happening to him, a parchment that was found sewed in the lining of his doublet on the day of his death. This mystical experience was what convinced Pascal to devote all his strength to the cause of religion.

The principal theological problem separating Jansenists and Jesuits was the doctrine of grace. The orthodox formula, given by Saint Augustine in the 5th century, states that no man can be saved without grace which is given or denied by God in accordance with his divine will. The Spanish theologian Molina, in the 16th century, softened this doctrine by affirming the possibility that a repentent sinner could call down "efficacious" grace by his own merit, which comes to him from "sufficient" grace given by God to every man. The Jansenists had returned to the harsher doctrine of Augustine. The Jesuits were disciples of Molina. The pope, urged by the Jesuits, condemned in 1653 five propositions falsely accredited to Jansénius. At this point the controversy became so acute and intense that the Jansenists solicited the help of Pascal.

Between 1656 and 1657, Pascal published eighteen letters that were collected under the title *Provinciales ou lettres écrites par Louis de Montalte à un provincial de ses amis et aux RR.PP. Jésuites sur la morale et la politique de ces pères*. In these anonymous letters, in which Pascal is more philosopher than theologian and more polemicist than philosopher, he tried to justify the position of Arnauld and the Jansenists. He attacked the indulgence of the Jesuits in matters of morals, and condemned the practice of casuistry, by which sin is judged by a confessor in terms of the circumstances surrounding the sin. *Les Lettres Provinciales* was a polemical work attacking the Jesuits, and a forerunner of the apologetic work called *Les Pensées*, in which Pascal attacked nonbelievers (*libertins*).

During the last four years of his life (1658–1662), suffering from serious ill health, Pascal attempted the writing of a huge project—a defense of the Christian religion. At the time of his death, he had written only scattered notes which, grouped together, are referred to as *Les Pensées*. The first classification or edition of these notes was made at Port-Royal in 1670. Much later,

Brunschvicg's edition regrouped the *Pensées* in a logical sequence. Today a new edition by Louis Lafuma follows a copy of Pascal's notes prepared by himself and discovered in 1944.

In order to convince the nonbeliever that he should think about his salvation, Pascal appeared to begin with a discussion of the nature of man and the worried restlessness (*inquiétude*) of man. He believed that the teaching of the Bible alone, and especially of the Gospels, is able to quiet this restlessness. Pascal spoke first of the wretchedness of man without God: *Misère de l'homme sans Dieu*. In this part of the apology, Pascal analyzed the reasons for man's difficulty in reaching truth. The contrast between the universe and man provided the contrast between infinity and nothingness (*l'infini – le néant*). Pascal points out the difficulty of instituting justice among men, the absurdity of war, of political regimes, the vanity of diversions (*divertissements*), the contradictions of philosophical systems, and finally the need for religion. The second part of the apology thus was to be the happiness of man in God.

The discouraging picture of man given by Pascal was not easily acceptable to the Church in the 17th century. Eighteenth-century thinkers, Voltaire in particular, attacked the Pascalian apology, but Chateaubriand and the romantics in the 19th century rehabilitated Pascal. The 20th century on the whole looks upon him as one of the great religious spirits of France, the leading converter, and one of the forerunners of existentialism. More than a polemicist, more than an apologist, Pascal today appears as a mystic whose fervor is evident in such fragments of his writings as *le mémorial* and *le mystère de Jésus*.

Le silence éternel de ces espaces infinis m'effraie. . . This is probably the first sentence one learns in Pascal, and it is the one remembered the longest. It is a good example of that type of *pensée* that resembles a cry. In this case, it is the cry of a scientist and the cry of a sick man. As a scientist, Pascal knew as much about the cosmos, *ces espaces infinis*, as anyone in his day. The emptiness, *ce gouffre*, that Pascal observed growing in every direction around the earth, was carried also in himself. He felt the presence of this void, always at his left. To protect himself from falling into this bottomless space, he used to place a chair on the left side of his bed whenever he hoped to sleep. The genius too has his neuroses, which today we accept more willingly because we have made some progress in understanding neuroses.

Pascal felt both terror and fascination for what he called infinity. By this word "infinity" he meant both the infinitesimal that man is and the infinite that God is. In his own way, Pascal warned us that in our voyages through space we would discover only ashes, and in our atomic research we would find mainly new resources for warfare.

Pascal is close to us today in his sensitivity to the paradoxes of human nature. He knew both the elevations of the spirit, the space flights, and the descents into the self, the experience of the *gouffre*. He spoke both of the loftiness of man the fallen king, *le roi déchu*, as well as the viscousness and the nausea of Sartrian man.

The intensity of his experience was such that it could not be articulated in any one coherent, falsely-coherent way. And that is why those who insist upon categorizing him are still asking: Was Pascal a saint or a fanatic? Was he a mystic or was he a realist?

Many of the thoughts of Pascal can be traced back to his three principal sources: the Bible, the essays of Montaigne, and the writings of the theologians associated with Port-Royal. He accepted the challenge to defend Christianity and at the same time he accepted the possibility of not winning. This dual acceptance was in keeping with his submission to the will of God. The obstacles that prevent the progress of religion have to be accepted by the believer, and even by the apologist, and borne patiently.

FOUR WRITERS FROM THE NOBLE CLASS

La Rochefoucauld (1613–1680)

After an early military career, le duc François de La Rochefoucauld joined the *frondeurs* in the civil war against the king and Mazarin. The active part of his life is narrated in his *Mémoires* (published in 1662), in which he gives a very full portrait of himself.

He frequented several salons, particularly that of Mme de Sablé. When he was fifty-two he met thirty-one-year-old Mme de Lafayette, and they remained lovers for the rest of his life, becoming the leaders of a small group of intellectuals to whom such writers as Corneille, Moliere, de Retz and Boileau often submitted literary works for approval.

There were five editions of *Les Maximes* of La Rochefoucauld in his own lifetime. The first publication was in 1664, and the full title was *Réflexions ou*

Sentences et Maximes morales. The game of writing and reading maxims was a worldly game of wit and incisive critical observations of manners. These aphorisms represent an often embittered pessimistic interpretation of human nature. La Rochefoucauld considered love of self, or egoism, the basis of the actions of men, even of those actions that appear disinterested. Such words as *amour-propre*, *égoïsme*, and *intérêt* seem to be synonymous. Even virtue dissolves in egoism, as he wrote in one of his most famous maxims: "Les vertus se perdent dans l'intérêt comme les fleuves se perdent dans la mer."

This thesis is supported by La Rochefoucauld's relentless analysis of all the noble sentiments of mankind: friendship, love, pity, generosity, forgiveness. The clear style in which they are written avoids all the ornaments of language, such as the antitheses and refined metaphors associated with the *ruelles* of the salons. His most cogent maxims were verdicts reduced to their essence, texts very much in harmony with the Jansenist spirit and with the general wave of pessimism of the century. La Rochefoucauld seemed to bar the way to any sincere repentance, to any hope for the moral betterment of man. Always courteous in his outward behavior of a 17th-century nobleman, he was inwardly as nihilistic as is Samuel Beckett in our day.

Cardinal de Retz (1614–1679)

Paul de Gondi, Cardinal de Retz, was more a political conspirator than a church prelate, more a Florentine than a Frenchman, who in the Fronde opposed Mazarin and probably hoped to become a second Richelieu. Without possessing any sense of a religious vocation, he was made a cardinal at the age of thirty-eight. Louis XIV never forgave him for his opposition to Mazarin. He frequented the salons of Mme de Sévigné and Mme de Lafayette, and finally befriended his enemy La Rochefoucauld, of whom he had painted a vindictive portrait in his *Mémoires*.

The chief subject of the *Mémoires* is the Fronde (1648–1652), the last phase of the long struggle for political power between the nobles (the great barons of the Middle Ages) and the king of France. Cardinal de Retz had read Plutarch, Tacitus, Machiavelli, and such sources are evident in his history of La Fronde, in which he shows himself to be a political theorist reminiscent of Machiavelli and a forerunner of Montesquieu. He himself is the center of the *Mémoires*—he is in the scenes and episodes he relates and his personal feelings are evident in the hostile portraits he gives of so many figures of the day.

Mme de Sévigné (1626–1696)

Marie de Rabutin-Chantal, better known as la marquise de Sévigné, was left a widow at twenty-six. She devoted her life to her two children, and especially to her daughter, who married le comte de Grignan in 1669. In 1671 Mme de Grignan followed her husband to Provence where he had been commissioned lieutenant-général, and this simple event helped make her mother, with Voltaire, the greatest letter-writer of France.

From Paris or from her estate Les Rochers, near Vitré in Brittany, she wrote letters to relatives and friends—to Mme de Lafayette (one of her favorite friends), to La Rochefoucauld, to Cardinal de Retz, and to Fouquet (especially when he was being persecuted and threatened by the king). But the majority of the fifteen hundred letters that have survived were addressed to her daughter in Provence. It would be difficult to imagine a colder, more indifferent correspondent than Mme de Grignan, but Mme de Sévigné's letters were really written to herself. A naturally joyous person, an understanding friend of many people, curious about every subject, and even at times speculative in a semi-philosophical way, she had one great passion—her daughter—and a great need to express the tenderness and solicitude she felt.

She wrote about political events (the court proceedings against the king's *surintendant* Fouquet), military events (the campaigns of Condé and Turenne and the death of Turenne), and French society *à la ville* (Paris) and *à la cour* (Versailles). She offered literary judgments on most of the writers of her time: on Mlle de Scudéry, Pascal, Corneille (for whom she had the highest regard), and Racine (on *Andromaque* and the première of *Esther*). She spoke of nature more frequently than anyone else (even La Fontaine) in the century. She was garrulous, but with such art and such keen power of observation and wit, such spontaneity of feeling, that her letters are the most entertaining introduction to the French culture of the 17th century.

Mme de Lafayette (1634–1693)

The art of Mme de Lafayette in her short novel *La Princesse de Clèves* (1678) represents the shift from preciosity (as in the long novel *L'Astrée*) to the aesthetics of classicism in its sobriety and in its emphasis on psychological analysis.

As a young woman, Mme de Lafayette frequented the Hôtel de Rambouillet and other salons. Her novel may have been somewhat influenced by La Rochefoucauld, with whom she lived. The background of *La Princesse de Clèves*, written over several years and talked about extensively prior to its publication, was the brilliant court of Henri II, between 1558 and 1559. But there are many reminiscences in the story of the even more spectacular court of Louis XIV.

The Princesse de Clèves esteems her husband, but falls in love with the handsome duc de Nemours. When he tries to seduce her she resists him, but confesses her love to her husband. The Prince de Clèves knows his wife is innocent but is tortured by jealousy. Nemours again approaches the princess after her husband's death, but she refuses him and retires to a convent.

There are obvious Cornelian traits in the novel: the conception of honor evidenced in the princess' resistance to the man she loves because of her husband, whom she does not love. The rich political-historical background of the Renaissance court is also in keeping with the Roman background of so many of Corneille's tragedies. But there are Racinian traits also in Mme de Lafayette's writing—action that is totally simple and based upon the tension of a fatal or a disastrous love. *La Princesse de Clèves* comes nearest in 17th century fiction to a Racine tragedy. The success of this novel in the age of Louis XIV as well as today is due in large part to the novelist's concentration on the sufferings of the heroine's heart and on her self-analysis.

MOLIÈRE (1622–1673)

Jean-Baptiste Poquelin was born and reared in the heart of Paris, on the rue Saint-Honoré. His father, a prosperous tapestry-maker and upholsterer (today he would be called an interior decorator), *tapissier ordinaire du roi*, provided his son with a Jesuit education at the collège de Clermont (today the lycée Louis-le-Grand). Jean-Baptiste studied law briefly, declined his father's desire to see him become a *tapissier*, and moved very early toward the world of the theatre. A family of actors, the Béjarts, intrigued him and initiated him to the arts of the theatre. He was drawn to Madeleine Béjart, the eldest daughter, four years older than he, and to the freedom of the actor's life that she represented.

With the Béjart family and in opposition to the bourgeois ideals of his father, Jean-Baptiste discovered an irresistible vocation in the art of acting, changed his name to Molière and founded with the Béjarts *L'Illustre Théâtre*. During the first months of 1644, the productions in Paris were failures and Molière was jailed in the Châtelet for debts. L'Illustre Théâtre, with Molière as actor and director, was unable to compete with L'Hôtel de Bourgogne and Le Théâtre du Marais, so the new company left Paris in 1645 and spent twelve years in the provinces: Toulouse, Albi, Carcassonne, and later in the vicinity of Lyon, where Molière met the Italian actors, the *Gelosi*, and observed carefully the improvisational theatrical skill of the *commedia dell'arte*. He profited from playing before a variety of publics—lords, bourgeois and peasants—and took good note of the language and customs of these social classes.

His first full-length comedy was probably *L'Etourdi*, performed in Lyon in 1653, and his second may have been *Le Dépit amoureux*, played in Béziers in 1656. Both plays have complicated plots and both are fairly close imitations of Italian imbroglios.

Molière's company, back in Paris in October 1658, played Corneille's *Nicomède* in the Louvre in the presence of the king. A year later, on November 18, 1659, in the theatre of the Petit Bourbon, Molière played *Cinna* of Corneille, which was followed by a new one-act prose play of his own, *Les Précieuses Ridicules*. Its success was immediate, and it is still played with seven or eight other plays of Molière in the permanent repertory of the Comédie Française. *Les Précieuses Ridicules* was the first *comédie de moeurs* in France, a farce which, rather than unravelling a complicated plot, studied the ludicrous aspect of exaggerated preciosity as it had developed in the provinces. It was not as much an attack on la marquise de Rambouillet as it was a vindication of simplicity of behavior and good common sense in society, and it defined what was to become one of Molière's principal themes.

The next success of Molière was *L'Ecole des Maris*, which was performed in the Palais-Royal in 1661. This three-act comedy in verse involves farcical elements and character studies on a sociological subject: the education of girls. In the following year Molière married Armande Béjart, sister or daughter of Madeleine (Armande is believed by some scholars to have been Molière's own daughter). He had known her from babyhood and had trained her as an actress. Armande's official début was as Agnès in *L'Ecole des Femmes*, first performed in 1662. This is the first complete and successful formulation of Molière's type of comedy, based on a close observation of reality, a clear psychology of character, and an attitude toward life which amounted almost to a philosophy of life. The middle-aged bourgeois Arnolphe tries to prepare his young *pupille*, Agnès, to be his wife. In this play, Molière underscored the danger of one person attempting to control and discipline the natural instincts of someone else.

The play was attacked by friends of the rival company of the Hôtel de Bourgogne, and the attacks were answered by Molière in two witty plays: *La Critique de l'Ecole des Femmes* and *L'Impromptu de Versailles*, both performed in 1663. In *L'Impromptu*, the actors appeared with their own names, and Molière used the occasion to expose his ideas on the art of comedy and the art of acting. He particularly denounced the artificiality of the Hôtel de Bourgogne's histrionic style.

Molière, now at the beginning of his greatest period, clashed with the Church. *Tartuffe ou L'Imposteur* was performed before Louis XIV in 1664 and then banned for approximately five years. The play was vigorously discussed by the theatre public and the clergy, drastically revised and reworked by Molière, and finally authorized for production in 1669. *Tartuffe*'s success is explained somewhat by the fact that it treated a serious problem of the day. Tartuffe is not only the hypocrite caricaturing religious practice but also the hypocrite using religion for political and material ends. He is an epicurean lusting after his benefactor's wife—a full-fledged scoundrel who attempts to control or demolish an entire household. Orgon's richly appointed home is the setting. And Orgon himself symbolizes the stupidity of the type of bourgeois eager to be hypnotized by a newcomer, by a new theory. He is the first of the fully drawn bourgeois figures in the comedies whom Molière is determined to ridicule.

On the dangerous subject of impiety, Molière wrote *Dom Juan ou Le Festin de Pierre*, a prose play in five acts which had fifteen performances in 1665 and then was withdrawn despite its commercial success. It was probably banned because of the *parti dévot*. The legend of Don Juan had passed from Spain to Italy, and from there to France. (The play's title is perplexing. Rather than *Don*, Molière used *Dom*, a spelling usually reserved for Benedictine and Carthusian monks. The word *pierre* refers to the statue of the *commandeur*.)

Dom Juan, *grand seigneur méchant homme*, is presented by Molière as a noble who is demonized. The play is not so much a series of duets between Dom Juan and the women he seduces as a duet between Dom Juan and his valet Sganarelle. Sganarelle is terrorized by his master. His servile nature illustrates the abjection of the servant class and helps to explain Figaro's revolt in the next century. Both *Tartuffe* and *Dom Juan* were accused of reflecting the spirit of *libertinage*.

Molière's third major play, *Le Misanthrope ou l'Atrabilaire amoureux*, a verse comedy in five acts, was first played in 1666 and was not very well received, although today many consider it Molière's greatest play. Alceste, the misanthrope, is Molière, who judges everyone and is always right—Moliere is thus able to ridicule himself. Célimène, a young widow of twenty, is intoxicated with her own beauty, wit and success. She illustrates the cruellest aspect of a society that demolishes the reputation of all those who are not present at a given social function. She represents Armande, who is deceiving Molière in real life. If Molière is Alceste in the play, he is also Philinte, Alceste's friend, who accepts the world as it is. At the première performance, Molière played Alceste and Armande played Célimène.

From then on, Molière suffered from continuing ill health and had continuing successes with each new play: *Le Médecin malgré lui* (1666), a farce on a charlatan doctor; *L'Avare* (1668), on Harpagon the miser; *Le Bourgeois Gentilhomme* (1670), a comedy-ballet with music by Lully; *Les Femmes Savantes* (1672), the most polished of the social comedies; and the last play, *Le Malade Imaginaire* (1673), on the subject of imaginary ill health, written at the moment when Molière's own sickness was at its worst. He was playing Argan, *le malade imaginaire*, on February 17, 1673, when he suffered an attack halfway through the play. He kept on, however, and finished the performance. He was carried home, rue de Richelieu. The actor Baron, whom Molière loved dearly, sought out Armande. The playwright died while friends were trying to find a priest. At first the funeral mass was denied, but the king intervened and Molière was given a rapid night funeral. He became, and still is, the best-loved genius of France.

RACINE (1639–1699)

Jean Racine was born in La Ferté-Milon, in Champagne, and raised in a Jansenist milieu by his grandmother. He studied first at Beauvais and then for three years, 1655–1658, was a pupil of the Jansenists at Port-Royal. To these fervently religious and scholarly teachers, Racine owed his knowledge of Greek literature and his love for Homer and Plato, Sophocles and Euripides.

In Paris at nineteen, he looked for a patron and received some financial reward for his first poems. In Uzès, in the south, he tried unsuccessfully for an ecclesiastical appointment. Back in Paris, he submitted odes to the king and was promised a *pension*. Encouraged by Molière to write on the subject of Oedipus, Racine turned out *La Thébaïde*, his first play to be performed (1664); it was unsuccessful. In his second tragedy, *Alexandre* (1665), Racine mingled the heroism of Alexander the Great with gallantry (probably that of Louis XIV, whom he was determined to please). A few months after *Alexandre*, first played by Molière's company and then by the Hôtel de Bourgogne, Racine broke off his relationship with Port-Royal. The religious men who had been Racine's family, so to speak, opposed his worldliness and his literary ambition. The Jansenist teacher Nicole seemed to be castigating Racine when he wrote that novelists and dramatists are public poisoners of souls: "Un faiseur de romans et un poète de théâtre est un empoisonneur public, non des corps, mais des âmes des fidèles."

Racine met a celebrated actress in Molière's company, Mlle du Parc, daughter of an acrobat (*saltimbanque*), seven years older than Racine, who became his mistress. He quite literally stole her from Molière and had her join the Hôtel de Bourgogne company. (At la du Parc's death, Racine was accused of poisoning her. The intervention of Mme de Montespan saved him from being arrested.)

For Mlle du Parc, Racine wrote his third tragedy, *Andromaque* (1667), his first success and one of the outstanding successes in the history of the French stage. It is a skillfully constructed tragedy on the conflict of opposing passions. Pyrrhus the king loves his hostage Andromaque, who loves her son Astyanax and the memory of her husband Hector. Oreste, ambassador of the Greeks, loves Hermione, who loves Pyrrhus. All four characters suffer from their passion. In this play, Racine developed his tragic style and the language of this style: the simplest and most commonplace words, which were given extraordinary pathos and dramatic value by using them at the right moment and adapting item to the immediate circumstances.

After writing a burlesque comedy, *Les Plaideurs*, Racine returned to tragedy with *Britannicus* in 1669: a play with which he hoped to quiet his critics, who preferred Corneille to him. *Britannicus* is taken from Roman history (Tacitus) and shows Nero at the very beginning of his life of crime and sadism. Nero was the emperor of poison (and all Paris had clearly in mind the death of Mlle du Parc). Racine called his Nero *un monstre naissant*, and that was exactly what Paris was calling Racine. In the play Nero is young and handsome, and commits his first crime by ordering the death of Britannicus. He is both male and female, almost hermaphroditic—a voyeur, hiding behind a curtain to watch the lovers Junie and Britannicus, the only pure, idealistic characters of the tragedy.

Bérénice (1670) is an elegy play about the love of Emperor Titus for Bérénice. Racine boasted of having written his play on three words of Suetonius: "*Invitus invitam dimissit*" [In spite of himself, he sent away the woman he had invited.]

With *Phèdre* (1677), his greatest tragedy, Racine turned again to Greek mythology. Guided by the text of Euripides (*Hippolytus*), he moved into the darker passions, into a family legend of bloodshed. Phèdre's father was Minos, king of Crete and judge of Hades, and her mother was Pasiphae, who had loved a bull and had borne a monster-son, the Minotaur. In Racine's play Phèdre, married to Thésée, slayer of the Minotaur (her half-brother), falls in love with her husband's son Hippolyte, born of Thésée and a Lesbian!

Although Racine remains close to his Greek models in writing *Phèdre*, and evokes a decidedly Greek atmosphere, the remorse felt by Phèdre, her public confession and her death, led many contemporaries of the playwright to see in it a Christian and even a Jansenist tragedy.

A cabale against *Phèdre* (his ninth tragedy) and problems of his personal life caused Racine to give up the theatre. He became reconciled with Port-Royal and religion, married, fathered seven children, and was appointed, with Boileau, historiographer of the king. Twelve years after *Phèdre*, with the behavior of a perfect courtier, he wrote two Biblical plays, *Esther* (1689) and *Athalie* (1690) for Mme de Maintenon's school for girls at Saint-Cyr. *Esther*, in three acts with choruses, is a work of piety. *Athalie* is a political play on the subject of a matriarch, an almost Cornelian queen.

The poetry of Racine is always in harmony with the situation of tragedy, character and emotion. In this sense it is functional verse, but it has also incantatory power. His conception of tragedy, the spectacle of fate that triumphs over human weakness, made the three unities simple and natural for him. Racine concentrated his art on the victim who is to be sacrificed, Britannicus (killed by Nero), Phèdre (killed by Venus). The crisis that opens each play is brief and intense. At the *dénouement*, the mechanism of fate functions and the irreparable is depicted.

Racine's Contemporaries

Other playwrights of Racine's day seem minor in comparison. Philippe Quinault (1635–1688) produced his most successful plays, sentimental tragicomedies, between the time of Corneille's masterpieces and the first successes of Racine. Between 1672 and his death he wrote several libretti for Lully's operas and ballets, such as *Alceste* and *Armide*. Jacques Pradon (1644–1698) is remembered today for his *Phèdre et Hippolyte*, written to compete with Racine's *Phèdre* in 1677. There were other playwrights, but it is obvious that the conventions of tragedy were best suited to the genius of Racine. During the first half of the 18th century, Corneille and Racine continued to be performed and also served as models for 18th century dramatists.

LA FONTAINE (1621–1695)

Like Racine, Jean de La Fontaine came from Champagne. He was born in Château-Thierry, where his father was a forestry official (*maître des eaux et forêts*). He was asocial, as were many great artists, submitting to various patrons when they attracted him by their wit and good taste.

In 1658 La Fontaine read his poem *Adonis* to the minister of finance for Louis XIV, Nicolas Fouquet, who recognized the gifts of the poet and granted him a *pension*. Fouquet, who had made his château de Vaux-le-Vicomte into a palace of arts and letters, was his first important patron. La Fontaine had just written his poem on the magnificence of the château, *Le Songe de Vaux*, when the young king, jealous perhaps of the lavishness with which he had been received at Vaux-le-Vicomte, accused Fouquet of theft and had him imprisoned. La Fontaine pleaded for clemency for his friend in his poem *Elégie aux nymphes de Vaux*.

Between 1665 and 1674, La Fontaine published his *Contes et Nouvelles en vers*, fairly scabrous stories drawn from many sources including Ariosto, Boccaccio and Marguerite de Navarre. *Les Fables* appeared between 1668 and 1694 (twelve books in all) and their success overshadowed all his other writings, including his *Amours de Psyché et de Cupidon* (1669), a long retelling in prose (with some verse) of the Greek legend.

At the age of fifty-one, in 1672, La Fontaine took up residence in the hôtel of Mme de la Sablière on the rue Neuve-des-Petits-Champs. She was thirty-three and separated from her financier husband. Cultivated to the point of reading Homer in the Greek text, she had become the center of an illustrious society of which Jean de La Fontaine was the most original member. There he saw Turenne, Mme de Lafayette, Mme de Sévigné, and writers also: Molière, who was the same age as La Fontaine, and two younger writers who were forging their way into Parisian society: Boileau and Racine.

Such a company as this encouraged La Fontaine to continue writing his *Contes* (although the king was vexed by their indecency) and his *Fables*. The verbal economy with which he wrote the fables, the vividness of the narration anecdote, the picturesqueness and sharp morality, made La Fontaine into the one fabulist who is still read in France. The *Fables* are miniature plays (La Fontaine tried persistently but unsuccessfully to write for the theatre), in which he invokes mountains and seas, forests, peasants, palaces, gardens, servants, winds and storms, the moon, the sun and the stars.

> Une ample comédie à cent actes divers
> Et dont la scène est l'univers.

Although he drew from all the earlier fabulists, his art is totally different from theirs. Portraying animals with very little attention to biological accuracy, he proved he was not a naturalist but a poet, and he made of a humble literary genre one of the most finished examples of French classical art. In his fables he passes judgment on all society: king, courtiers, priests, merchants and magistrates. Philosophically speaking, he took sides with Gassendi and the *libertins*.

Several times he presented himself as a candidate for the Académie Française, and was finally elected in 1683. In his reception speech (in verse), he called himself a

> Papillon du Parnasse . . .
> Je suis chose légère et vole à tout sujet . . .

At the end of his life, afflicted by the death of Mme de la Sablière and by his own illness, he returned to religious belief and piety and publicly retracted his *Contes*. His desire to expiate his earlier sins recalls the modern examples of Paul Verlaine and Max Jacob.

BOILEAU (1636–1711)

Nicolas Boileau was better known as Despréaux to his contemporaries. He was born in Paris, the fifteenth child of a lawyer's family, members of the solid French bourgeoisie who gave the 17th century such writers as Molière,

La Fontaine, La Bruyère and Racine. A small income allowed Boileau to make literature his profession.

Most of his twelve *Satires* were published between 1666 and 1668, and many circulated in manuscript prior to publication. In the first *satire* he attacked Fouquet in order to side with Colbert the prime minister, bent on weakening the power of all financiers. The second *satire* is an homage to Molière, written after *L'Ecole des Femmes* had been severely criticized. In this poem, Boileau, twenty-eight years old, spoke of Molière, aged forty-two, as a younger admirer of the dramatist:

Enseigne-moi, Molière, où tu trouves la rime.

Boileau used to read his *satires* in the cabarets, often in the company of his friends Racine and La Fontaine. So his *satires*, long before their appearance in print, had made him enemies who in turn wrote satires against him. He was patronized first by the king's favorite, Mme de Montespan and then by le grand Condé. Thanks to Colbert's protection and the king's, Boileau became the official poet and gradually assumed the position of literary critic of the age of Louis XIV. He translated Longinus' *Traité sur le sublime*, and wrote an *Art Poétique* (1674) which shows an appalling lack of knowledge of French litera-ture. In it he skipped over the Middle Ages, calling them *siècles grossiers*, and denounced Ronsard as one who spoke Greek and Latin in French. His famous exclamation, "Enfin Malherbe vint," seemed to indicate he believed French literature began with the grammarian poet at the beginning of the 17th century.

In writing his *Art Poétique*, Boileau continued the tradition of earlier poetics by Sébilet, du Bellay and de la Fresnaye. He drew abundantly on the contem-porary work by le père Rapin, *Réflexions sur la poétique d'Aristote*. Written in alexandrines, the four cantos of the *Art Poétique* emphasize 1) a love for reason-ableness and sobriety, and the need to rewrite endlessly, "Vingt fois sur le métier remettez votre ouvrage"; 2) definitions of secondary genres: elegy, ode, sonnet, epigram, satire; 3) the major genres: tragedy, epic, comedy; 4) maxims on the writer's vocation, the writer's morality, the role of the king.

Like Horace, Boileau cultivated the genre of the epistle (*épître*) which per-mitted him to write of the king, of moral themes, of literature (*épître VII* to Racine, on the cabale against *Phèdre*).

Named with Racine in 1677 as historiographer of the king, Boileau was thus rewarded for his constant attention to Louis XIV and his *arrivisme*. Prema-ture decrepitude kept him from appearing often at court. He became more religious under the influence of Mme de Maintenon and Bossuet. His final satire, *L'Equivoque*, was directed against the Jesuits and their practice of casuistry, but the poem was censured. Boileau died two months later.

BOSSUET (1627–1704)

Throughout the entire century religious oratory (*éloquence*) was a brilliant literary form. Bossuet's sermons and funeral orations surpassed all the others.

Two predecessors in particular had elevated the art of religious oratory and writing. Saint François de Sales (1567–1622) preached in Paris at the beginning of the century. He spoke directly from the heart and wrote with an almost mystical fervor: *Introduction à la vie dévote* (1608) and *Traité de l'amour de Dieu* (1616). Saint Vincent de Paul (1576–1660) was influenced by de Sales and lovingly emphasized the Gospels in his preaching. The style of "Monsieur Vincent," as he was called, greatly influenced young Bossuet.

Born in Dijon, capital of Burgundy, Jacques-Bénigne Bossuet came from a hard-working family. He had an early and very sincere vocation for the priesthood. Tonsured at nine, a pupil of the Jesuits in Dijon, he was a canon (*chanoine*) in Metz for seven years. There he gave his first sermons: *sur la loi de Dieu* (1653), *sur la Providence* (1656), and cultivated the genre of the panegyric (*panégyrique*): on Saint François d'Assise, Saint Bernard, Sainte Thérèse and Saint Paul. His language was rich in imagery and realistic detail.

In Paris, Bossuet was attached to Saint Thomas du Louvre where he often preached and delivered funeral orations (*oraisons funèbres*). He became the favorite prelate of Louis XIV and was often at court. In 1670, he delivered the funeral oration of Henriette d'Angleterre (after having been her spiritual director), and fifteen days later was appointed tutor (*précepteur*) of the Dauphin; soon after that he was elected to the Académie Française. Bossuet was part of the inner circle of Versailles, admired by Mme de Maintenon, La Rochefoucauld and Mme de Lafayette. He was spiritual director of Mme de Montespan, and induced her to break her liaison with the king.

Urged by the king, Bossuet defended gallicanism without breaking with Rome. At fifty-five he became bishop of Meaux (1681) and was from then until his death the most eminent prelate in the French Church. Strong in his body, a tireless worker, able to make his voice heard in the cathedrals, he did not scorn physical comfort and good food. He lived elegantly in his country house of Germigny where he received the Dauphin, Condé, Mme de Montespan. He grew proud with age and said once to Mme Guyon, "Je suis Père de l'Eglise."

His prolific work testifies to his genius and his abundant vitality. He attacked the Protestants on several occasions throughout his career, and as a forerunner of ecumenism labored for the uniting of the churches. He came to grips with quietism during the last years of the century, and defeated Fénelon in that important controversy. Joshua-like, Bossuet waged war on relaxed moralists, cartesians, jansenists, *ultramontains* (ultramontanists). For his pupil the Dauphin Bossuet wrote book after book, which, grouped together, would represent a full university course: *Histoire de France, Discours sur l'Histoire universelle, Traité de logique, De la connaissance de Dieu et de soi-même.*

Literary history has put aside all other parts of Bossuet's writings in order to make place for his sermons and funeral orations, in which he surpassed not only other preachers but also political orators of every century—Danton and Jaurès, for example. In delivering his sermons, Bossuet was the voice of God, rolling his Burgundian r's in a thunderous voice. Like Corneille and Racine, he had a theatrical sense. The *oraisons funèbres* were of course more spectacular and more dramatic than the sermons. And they attracted the most spectacular of audiences: the royal, the nobly born and the wealthy, in the atmosphere of a magnificent church and solemn liturgy. Bossuet always seized upon the contrast between the greatness of the deceased and the presence of death, the ending of life in the midst of triumphant life. In his sonorous cadences, Bossuet played on the immense antithesis between the living and the dead.

Henriette d'Angleterre, sister-in-law of Louis XIV, and a favorite figure at court, died at the age of twenty-six, and Bossuet, in the basilica of Saint-Denis, preached on vanity, ". . . et tout est vanité!" The young woman had possessed all the privileges of birth, yet had intelligence and modesty. And she had died, "Le matin, elle fleurissait, avec quelle grâce, vous le savez. Le soir nous la vîmes séchée."

Bossuet's Contemporary Churchmen

Four other bishops made distinct contributions to the art of the sermon and the funeral oration, although none of them reached the heights of Bossuet.

1. BOURDALOUE (1632–1700), bishop of Condom, a Jesuit, and more professorial than Bossuet, attracted in large numbers the ladies of the court who used to send their lackeys twenty-four hours in advance to hold their seats at church. Mme de Sévigné noted ecstatically, "Le Pere Bourdaloue prêche divinement aux Tuileries."

2. MASCARON (1634–1703), a *méridional*, bishop of Agen, gave Turenne's funeral oration.

3. FLÉCHIER (1632–1710), also a *méridional*, bishop of Nîmes, converted many Protestants. He was an habitué of the "Saturdays" of Mlle de Scudéry, and his style bore traces of preciosity.

4. MASSILLON (1663–1742), still another *méridional*, born in Hyères, bishop of Clermont-Ferrand. He delivered the funeral oration of Louis XIV in 1715, and preached the Lenten sermons of 1718 in the presence of Louis XV. These texts, *le petit carême*, were studied and appreciated by Voltaire.

FÉNELON (1651–1715)

François de Salignac de la Mothe-Fénelon came from an old aristocratic family of Périgord. As a young priest, he was sent on a mission to convert the Protestants of Saintonge. He was favored at court because he was at first favored by Bossuet, his elder by twenty-four years. In every way, Fénelon was the opposite of Bossuet. The contrast is as striking as that between the plays of Corneille and those of Racine.

Among Fénelon's earliest writings is a *Traité de l'éducation des filles* (1687), a work requested by the duke and duchess of Beauvilliers, who had eight daughters. Fénelon revealed himself a liberal-minded pedagogue who maintained that the nature of a young pupil should not be suppressed but encouraged. In 1689 Fénelon was named tutor of the duc de Bourgogne, heir to the throne, and became the only successful teacher of young princes in the 17th century. (Those entrusted to the care of Bossuet and La Bruyère made little response to their tutors.) With tact, patience, and a real aptitude for teaching, Fénelon converted an obdurate wild youngster into a student. He trained the sensitivity of the boy, stimulated his mind, and encouraged him to learn. He wrote fables to cure the young duke of moral defects and dialogues of the dead (*Les Dialogues des Morts*) to teach him history, mythology, literature and philosophy. He wrote an entire novel, *Télémaque*, to prepare him for the profession of a king.

In his *Télémaque* (1699), Fénelon added an episode to the *Odyssey*. He imagined Telemachus, son of Ulysses, went in search of his father accompanied by his guide Mentor. In this didactic work, primitive times appeared more utopian than Versailles. Fénelon preached certain ideas to the young prince that were dangerous for the age, a king is not above the law, a nation is not above humanity, war is a crime, social equality is an ideal that must be achieved.

Fénelon's success as pedagogue brought about many honors: the Académie Française and the archbishopric of Cambrai, one of the wealthiest dioceses of France. Nevertheless he was to know disaster and disgrace because of his friendship with Mme Guyon, a woman slightly older than he, and more determined and masculine in temperament than he was. She wrote mystical works, such as *Les Torrents Spirituels*, in which she analyzed the doctrine of quietism. The quietists, and especially Mme Guyon, were accused of teaching that the quiet contemplation of God was sufficient to efface all the disorders of sensuality. She flattered Fénelon with praise and adulation. She interested Mme de Maintenon. When her writings were examined by theologians, they found that in quietistic practices, the will of man and the dogmas and the hierarchy of the Church were dissolved.

At first Fénelon was not too much implicated. But soon Bossuet himself attacked Fénelon and had Mme Guyon cloistered. He publicly asked pardon of the king for having recommended Fénelon. Finally Fénelon was condemned by Rome, and made his submission. He never regained power at court. The duc de Bourgogne, who maintained a sense of gratitude toward Fénelon, died before reaching the throne. Mme Guyon retired to Touraine. The year before his death, Fénelon in his *Lettre à l'Académie* set forth his literary principles and his suggestions for future works of the Académie.

Outside of France, Fénelon has been studied for his religious thought, his skill as spiritual director, and his interpretations of doctrine. In New England alone there have been many editions in translation of his *Lettres Spirituelles*.

LA BRUYÈRE (1645-1696)

Jean de La Bruyère, a lonely meditative type of man from a middle-class family, might not have entered literary history if the Prince de Condé (le grand Condé) had not asked him to tutor his grandson, le duc de Bourbon. When his tutorship was over, La Bruyère stayed on at court or close to court, at Chantilly, where he continued to observe the world of courtiers. The notes he took on these observations, maxims, and portraits were called in the first edition of 1688 *Les Caractères ou les Moeurs de ce siècle*. Their success was immediate. Before his death, seven subsequent editions were published in which he outdistanced the work of the Greek philosopher Theophrastus who was his model.

This bachelor, one of the most perspicacious observers of his day, was religious by nature and by conviction, and had been recommended to Condé by Bossuet. In the château of Chantilly, where he taught his pupil, an ill-tempered dwarfish boy, La Bruyère was treated like a servant and made to feel his insignificance. When his pupil married, he was kept on as a retainer and named librarian of Chantilly. The dream of his life was to be elected to the Académie Française. After three defeats, he was finally elected. His *discours de réception* was something of a scandal because in it he dared prefer Racine to Corneille. In the same speech he praised both Bossuet and Fénelon, but later, when the quarrel over quietism broke, he took sides with Bossuet.

La Bruyère is the author of a single book, his *Caractères*. The body of the work is a series of portraits, grouped under such headings as *Des femmes, Du coeur, De la ville, De la cour, Des grands, De la chaire*, but there are also reflections reminiscent of Montaigne, and maxims reminiscent of La Rochefoucauld. He repeatedly states that he was born into a world already too old and that there was nothing left to say. His teaching had been a martyrdom and his *Caractères* makes him out to be a desperate man suffering from his lowly position, his unattractive appearance, his sense of being a victim. He wrote portraits of all types: the snob, the *parvenu*, the fop, the *nouveau riche*. At times he expressed indignation over social injustices. Like others of his day, he seemed to be trying to tell aging Louis XIV to institute social reforms. At other times, he uttered complaints of a more private nature—those of a man not loved.

La Bruyère was a transitional writer in the sense that his book is a document on French society during the last years of the reign of Louis XIV. He gave a clear picture of everyone except himself. He had the Parisian's satiric wit, the ambition of a man who wanted to rise above his social position, the pride of a writer who felt his worth was unappreciated, and the attitude of a sentimentalist who ranked the kindness of a man's heart above his intelligence.

In his social satire, La Bruyère is more indignant and bitter than the other leading satirists of that age: Molière, La Fontaine and Boileau. He stressed the fundamental perversity of human nature. He painted man in general, not only 17th century man, as a being who innately dislikes virtue and incapable of knowing happiness. Only the sage escapes condemnation because he, according to La Bruyère, does not try to govern others: "Il veut que la raison gouverne seule, et toujours." His philosophy of man is not original but it is persuasive perhaps because it is not controlled by any systemic view. La Bruyère rejuvenates, often with greater picturesqueness, the ideas of Montaigne, Pascal and La Rochefoucauld.

LA QUERELLE DES ANCIENS ET DES MODERNES

Throughout the 17th century, there was a growing opposition to the power that classical writers of antiquity exerted over literature. Descartes was among the first to question the need to learn Greek and Latin and to bow down before the ancient writers only because they were ancient. He claimed that modern man has a greater experience with everything than the ancient had. In Fontenelle's *Dialogues des Morts* (1683), when Montaigne and Socrates are conversing, the Greek philosopher tells the Périgourdin not to admire the Greeks excessively—"Les hommes sont toujours les mêmes." Saint-Evremond preached the idea that each age must cultivate the art that is appropriate to it.

The quarrel between the two opposing views exploded at a meeting of the Académie Française in 1687, when Charles Perrault (the future author of *Contes de ma mère l'Oye*) read his poem *Le Siècle de Louis le Grand*, in which he said that the age of Louis could be favorably compared with the age of Augustus. As he read this charter for the moderns, Boileau rose up from his seat and left the room in a fit of anger. As the quarrel developed, the second- and third-rate writers went over to the camp of the moderns under the leadership of Perrault, whereas the partisans of the ancients were the great writers of the age (according to the judgment of history): Boileau, as the leader, La Fontaine, Molière, Racine, La Bruyère.

In 1688, Fontenelle became an ardent defender of the moderns with his

Digression sur les anciens et les modernes, in which he claimed the moderns' superiority in science and at least their equality with the ancients in the arts. Fontenelle's subsequent election to the Académie in 1691 was a victory for his side. But in La Bruyère's *discours de réception* to the Académie in 1693, he quoted only those authors who were partisans of the ancients. This first phase of the quarrel was dominated by the antagonism between Perrault and Boileau. They were temporarily reconciled by le grand Arnauld in 1694.

Twenty years later, hostilities broke out again over a translation in prose of Homer's *Iliad* by Mme Dacier. Houdard de la Motte, a poet ignorant of Greek, made another translation in verse, based on Mme Dacier's prose version. The lady hellenist protested. La Motte, blind and infirm, answered in his *Réflexions sur la critique* (1715). Fénelon played the role this time of arbiter and reconciler.

The moderns came out victorious. The quarrel was somewhat revived in a penetrating treatise on aesthetics in the early 18th century by Abbé Du Bos, *Réflexions critiques sur la poésie et la peinture* (1719). In its deepest sense, the quarrel was waged between the consequences of Descartes' rationalism, according to which a man's mind maintains its individuality, and the principle of authority.

LES LIBERTINS

The growing power and influence of the *libertins* in the 17th century was not unrelated to the cause of the moderns. Free thinking (*libertinage* in the 17th century) naturally favored freedom in morality (*libertinage* in the 18th century). As a result of the wars of religion, centers or small societies of free-thinkers were formed at the beginning of the 17th century. The poets Maynard, Tristan l'Hermite, and Théophile de Viau were among the boldest representatives. A secret society was created that circulated anonymous tracts on problems of religion, the Bible, customs and dogma. The term "nature" was substituted for God, and the idea of a divine Providence gave way to belief in the operation of blind powerful forces in nature.

Richelieu persecuted the *libertins*, but tenaciously they kept creating new groups around such men as Gassendi and La Mothe Le Vayer. After the Fronde, or Mazarin's victory, the *libertin* groups became disorganized. Gassendi died in 1655. The secret Compagnie du Saint-Sacrement, the same organization that attacked Tartuffe, was used to track down and denounce the *libertins*. Pascal, first, and then Bossuet undertook the labor of converting and convincing the nonreligious.

But the *esprit libertin* persisted. Traces of it are in the satires of Boileau, in the comedies of Molière, and in the *contes* and *fables* of La Fontaine. Conversation in the salons as well as in the cabarets kept alive the *libertin* philosophy. It reappeared in vigorous form after the Revocation of the Edict of Nantes in 1685. From then on, there was little need for it to remain secret. Ninon de Lenclos' salon was only one of several worldly centers of *libertin* thought. It grew and spread in Holland and England, where the philosophy of Descartes was intensively studied. Locke and Spinoza criticized Christian metaphysics as well as the concept of an absolute monarchy. Three writers in particular illustrate the movement of *libertinage* at the beginning of the 18th century. They were the immediate forerunners of the philosophers: Saint-Evremond, Bayle and Fontenelle.

CHARLES DE SAINT-EVREMOND (1614–1703) was a Norman from the noble class who began as a musketeer of Louis XIII. He was impertinent with Mazarin when he served under him. At forty-seven he began a life of political exile which lasted forty-two years. To Holland he preferred London, where he formed a French group of *résistants* that has been compared to De Gaulle's exile and "Free French" in London. Three English kings provided him with a *pension*. He wrote about the philosophy of history in *Réflexions sur les divers génies du peuple romain*, a subject that was later more fully developed by Montesquieu. Saint-Evermond's temperament and way of life were perhaps greater contributions to French culture than his writings. His wisdom, his civic courage, his courtesy and dignity were his natural virtues. He combined the best traits of the *honnête homme* and the *libertin* of the 17th and 18th centuries. He disliked and attacked dogmatism and intolerance wherever he found them.

PIERRE BAYLE (1647–1706), born into a Calvinist home, was converted to Catholicism and then returned to Protestantism. He taught philosophy in Rotterdam and spent the last years of his life in Holland. In *Lettres sur la comète* (1682) he derided religious superstitions and the doctrine of Providence. His *Dictionnaire historique et critique* (1697) had a marked influence on his age. By pretending to correct errors in earlier dictionaries (especially the *Grand Dictionnaire historique* of Moreri, 1674) Bayle advanced his own theories on morality, theology and philosophy. Better than anyone else, he personified the *esprit libertin*.

He denounced dogmatic philosophy by claiming that there is not an idea that cannot be contradicted and proved false. His writings counted most heavily in the realm of religion, in which he fought doctrines concerning the supernatural and miracles, and every manifestation of sectarianism. Voltaire was greatly influenced by the writings of Pierre Bayle. The *Encyclopédie* was guided by the method and the spirit of his *Dictionnaire*. A fervent apostle of tolerance, he separated morality from religion in order to make it depend upon the social institution. His tone of irreverence was captured and deepened by Montesquieu and Voltaire.

BERNARD DE FONTENELLE (1657–1757), like his uncle Pierre Corneille, was born in Rouen and studied with the Jesuits. At first a *bel esprit*, a social wit, described by La Bruyère in his portrait of Cydias, he showed *libertin* tendencies in his *Dialogues des morts* (1683), in which Paracelsus and Molière, among other surprising couples, converse about literature and philosophy.

A popularizer of science, in *Entretiens sur la pluralité des mondes* (1686), he informed the general public of what had been accomplished by science in the 17th century. He attacked pagan oracles in *Histoire des oracles* (1687) but implied that the same attack could be levelled against Christian prophecies. A more universal writer than Bayle because he touched on politics and religion, literature and science, poetry and philosophy, Fontenelle had probably less influence than Bayle. He pontificated somewhat in the fashion that later characterized Voltaire.

At the age of one hundred, when Fontenelle was on his deathbed, his physician approached him and asked how he felt: "Comment vous sentez-vous, Monsieur Fontenelle?" The answer, "Je sens une certaine difficulté d'être," was used by Jean Cocteau in 1947 as the title of a book of essays, *La Difficulté d'être*.

EIGHTEENTH CENTURY

HISTORY		LITERATURE	
1715	death of Louis XIV		
1715–74	reign of Louis XV		
1715–23	regency of Philippe d'Orléans	1721	Montesquieu, *Lettres Persanes*
		1730	Marivaux, *Jeu de l'amour et du hasard*
		1731	Prévost, *Manon Lescaut*
		1734	Voltaire, *Lettres Philosophiques*
		1750	Rousseau, *Discours sur les arts*
1755	Lisbon earthquake	1751–80	*Encyclopédie*
		1755	Rousseau, *Discours sur l'inégalité*
		1759	Voltaire, *Candide*
		1762	Diderot, *Neveu de Rameau*
1774–91	reign of Louis XVI	1782	Rousseau, *Confessions*
		1784	Beaumarchais, *Mariage de Figaro*
		1787	B. de Saint-Pierre, *Paul et Virginie*
1789–99	French Revolution	1794	Chénier, *Iambes*
1789	Fall of Bastille		
1793	Louis XVI executed		
1794	Rule of Convention		
1795	Directory		
1799	first consul Bonaparte		

The 18th century is often called the age of enlightenment (*le siècle des lumières*) or *le siècle des philosophes* because of the significant contribution made by Montesquieu, Diderot and Voltaire. Traditionally a "philosopher" is concerned with great metaphysical questions concerning the origin of man, his being, and his destiny. But in the 18th century, the *philosophe* was more interested in social, political and moral problems than in metaphysics. He was concerned with those ideals that would assure a life of happiness for man on this earth. He was the man who admitted nothing unless it could be proved. This was his definition in the *Encyclopédie:* "Le philosophe n'admet rien sans preuve." He was the type of thinker resisting authority. Descartes had some of his traits; and the *libertins* of the 17th century were his immediate ancestors.

Travellers and missionaries in the 18th century brought back reports that people in primitive cultures reasoned as well as duchesses and fops in Paris. The theory of the "noble savage" (*le bon sauvage*) was cherished by the *philosophes.* They contrasted the purity of his life with the corruption of civilized man. England, too, was practically a new discovery for France in the 18th century. Both Montesquieu and Voltaire considered England a political paradise, with its tradition of individual freedom and religious tolerance. The satiric work of Defoe and Swift were much admired by the French.

Poetry lost out in the 18th century and prose took precedence as the better means of literary expression. In analyzing the effect of a work of art, Abbé Du Bos (*Réflexions critiques sur la poésie et la peinture,* 1719) calls it sentiment, the arousing of a physical emotion. The heart was considered a greater judge of the worth of art than the mind.

Politics, for the first time in French history, became the concern of everyone, not just of the professional. The many political errors perpetrated by Louis XIV, especially in his last years, encouraged ordinary citizens to discuss the errors and express their indignation, and finally led to their revolt. Le Club de l'Entresol, founded in 1695, was organized for the discussion of political issues, in the fashion of the English. Fénelon's *Télémaque* (1699) was the most literary of the many works at the turn of the century that proposed political reforms.

Under the domination of Mme de Maintenon, Louis XIV lost power and prestige in his advancing years. The once brilliant court of Versailles became an asylum. The art of conversation, in which political opinion could be expressed, moved from Versailles to the salons of Paris. Condé's granddaughter, la duchesse du Maine, created of her estate in Sceaux a miniature Versailles where conversation and literary games alternated with displays of fireworks and night festivities. La marquise de Lambert, in her salon in the rue de Richelieu, received on Tuesdays writers like Fontenelle, Montesquieu and Marivaux among others, and members of the aristocracy (*gens de qualité*) on Wednesdays. Mme de Tencin held a more mixed salon on the rue Saint-Honoré, where she received bankers, magistrats and clergy, as well as writers. Prévost, Helvétius and Lord Chesterfield from England, were among her favorites.

In addition to the salons, there were new public noisy meeting places called *cafés*, serving the new eastern drink of coffee that had reached Paris first in 1667. At the death of Louis XIV, a half century later, there were three hundred cafés in Paris, of which the most famous was le café Procope, founded in 1695 by the Sicilian Procopio, in what is today the rue de l'Ancienne Comédie. There, in a rowdy and much more animated atmosphere than the salon of the ladies, such figures as Fontenelle, Marmontel, Voltaire and Diderot congregated regularly. Such men often attracted a public that grouped around them in order to listen to the arguments and participate in political discussions and general verve.

SAINT-SIMON (1675–1755)

During the first half of the 18th century, the literary genres of fiction, tragedy and comedy continued, on the whole, the traditions established by classicism. The great exception was the *Mémoires* of Saint-Simon, a work quite independent of tradition and highly esteemed in the 20th century, especially by Marcel Proust.

Le duc de Saint-Simon's first ambition was military. At seventeen he was a captain in the king's army. He retired from the army in 1702, but remained attached to the court of Versailles, although Louis XIV detested him. He lived in the elaborately hierarchical world of the court through the last years of Louis XIV and through the years of the Regency (1715–1723). At first, Saint-Simon had placed his hopes on the duc de Bourgogne, the heir presumptive whom he believed would reign more wisely than Louis XIV. He was a friend of the regent Philippe d'Orléans, at whose death he withdrew from court to devote himself exclusively to the writing of his *Mémoires*.

From the age of nineteen, Saint-Simon had been writing his impressions of events and people. His *Mémoires* cover the years between 1691 and 1723, namely the last years of Louis XIV and the Regency. He drew largely on his own memories of the court, on gossip he culled from valets and grooms, and on stories he had from courtiers, priests, ladies, ministers, physicians and surgeons. He was fascinated by the intimate lives of the great, by their intrigues and adventures.

Saint-Simon's information is often inaccurate, and his style marred by defects of negligence, long wandering sentences, incoherences, latinisms and flat expressions. But these defects are easily forgotten because of the passion with which he writes. His portraits are memorable in their grotesqueness, and the big scenes (such as the death of the Grand Dauphin) are alive with color and movement. He had as much psychological insight into the life of his time as did La Bruyère and Mme de Sévigné.

The venom and the hatred of so much of the *Mémoires*, and the tumultuous style in which they were written remind readers today of Céline. At Saint-Simon's death, the work was seized by the government. Only official historiographers were allowed to consult it during the 18th century. Charles X permitted the first publication in 1829. There have been many editions since then, culminating in the Pléiade edition in 1949–1953.

VAUVENARGUES (1715-1747)

The thirty-two years of Vauvenargues' life coincided with the years in which Saint-Simon was writing his *Mémoires*. The works of the two men offer a study of contrasts: the ruthless vivid analysis of a world that Saint-Simon hated, and the noble abstract estimation of man's moral life as seen by Vauvenargues, who appears in every way a victim of fate.

Born in Aix-en-Provence, he suffered from ill health very early, but served as an officer in the War of the Austrian Succession. At twenty-eight, he resigned from the army (1744) with the same bitterness of disappointment in the military that Vigny expressed in the 19th century. A serious case of smallpox ruined his health, his appearance, and his hopes for a diplomatic career. Writing became, as it so often does, his consolation. Encouraged by Voltaire, to whom he had submitted a first manuscript in 1745, Vauvenargues settled down in a modest lodging in Paris and wrote. His writing was both his cure and his pleasure. Anonymously he published in 1746 his one book, *Introduction à la connaissance de l'esprit humain. Réflexions sur divers auteurs. Maximes.* This work has placed him among the leading secular moralists of France.

Literature was for him a religion, a remedy, almost an ascesis. This conviction allies Vauvenargues with two authors he greatly admired as a young man, Plutarch and Seneca, and with Montaigne in the French tradition. He was the principal secular saint in a century that tried its best to do without religion. His maxims and his *pensées* point to ways of reaching wisdom that are entirely human. He is opposed to Pascal, who tends to humiliate man, and to La Rochefoucauld, who is deeply pessimistic about man. The wise man, for Vauvenargues, sympathizes with human nature both good and bad: "Dans l'homme il y a autant de vérités que d'erreurs, de qualités que de défauts." Christian thinking in the 17th century, in Descartes and Racine, had denounced passion as the seat of all evil. Vauvenargues rehabilitated passion as the seat of all creativity: "Nous devons peut-être aux passions les plus grands avantages de l'esprit."

Voltaire was irreproachable in his relationship with Vauvenargues. The early death of a man so gifted, so noble in spirit, so unknown, saddened Voltaire, who measured his own fame and glory in the light of Vauvenargues' martyrdom.

MONTESQUIEU (1684–1755)

Charles-Louis de Secondat, baron de Montesquieu, was born in the château of La Brède, near Bordeaux, not far from Montaigne's country. Both writers, who were philosophic sages, had similar backgrounds in the legal profession, a lasting attachment to their province, and both led an aristocratic way of life.

The style of the Regency is in Montesquieu's first work, *Les Lettres Persanes* (1721), which combines the humorous and the serious. The Orient was very fashionable at that time; Galland's translation of *The Arabian Nights* (*Mille et une Nuits*) had appeared between 1704 and 1717. The use of the Orient was an easy device for Montesquieu. He imagined two Persians, Usbek and Rica, visiting Europe, France in particular. They write their impressions in letters to friends in Persia, who answer them. The work is vaguely an epistolary novel with a licentious harem intrigue and unlimited opportunity to describe and satirize Parisian society. There are portraits in the letters resembling those of La Bruyère, a *seigneur*, a farmer, a soldier and a poet. There are Parisian scenes: a café, a salon, strollers in the streets, the Académie Française, *ce corps à quarante têtes toutes remplies de figures, de métaphores et d'antithèses*. The social institutions are attacked: the king is called *ce grand magicien*, the pope *une vieille idole qu'on encense par habitude*, and monks are called derviches (*dervis*). The Utopian race of Troglodytes suffer misfortunes from the day they elect a king.

Les Lettres Persanes made Montesquieu famous. He wrote a somewhat pornographic novel, *Le Temple de Gnide* (1725), and travelled extensively on the continent and in England, where he was presented at court and where he studied the form of government. He was already thinking of what was to be his major work, *L'Esprit des Lois*.

After his travels, he settled down in his château of La Brède and spent three years writing *Considérations sur les causes de la grandeur des Romains et de leur décadence* (1734)—a long title and a long serious work, of which the key is the word *décadence*. It is a theory of history that sought to prove that moral and physical causes are at work in every form of government, uplifting it or destroying it.

Between 1734 and 1748, Montesquieu wrote *L'Esprit des Lois*, a massive work he had been preparing to write since the time he was a law student. After examining the constitutions of ancient and modern states, Montesquieu composed a study of political theory. He explains the variations in laws from country to country by the differences of climate and geography. Montesquieu's relativity of legal systems recalls Montaigne's relativity of moral customs. Three types of governement are analyzed: despotic (*le gouvernement despotique*), founded on fear; monarchic (*le gouvernement monarchique*), founded on honor; and republican (*le gouvernement républicain*), founded on virtue. He preferred monarchy, which he said could be kept from changing into tyranny by the establishment of a separation of powers. Laws should be made by a legislative body, and not by the sovereign (or the executive body). Their application should be carried out by a second body, the judiciary. Sources for such a system Montesquieu had found in the government of England and in the writings of Locke.

The writers of the American constitution incorporated many of Montesquieu's principles, and a few years later, the first revolutionary assembly, the Constituante (1789–91), was influenced first by *L'Esprit des Lois* which had proposed a program of reforms based upon a respect for individual rights and the dignity of man. He condemned *lettres de cachet*, slavery, torture, intolerance, poverty, war and capital punishment.

L'Esprit des Lois is a masterpiece of wisdom, but not a literary masterpiece, and today it is safe to guess that it is not read by many. Politically speaking, Montesquieu was as conservative as Montaigne. The Revolution would have shocked him, although it would not have surprised him. He found that constitutional monarchy best preserved the freedom of its citizens and the independence of the three powers: executive, legislative and judicial.

VOLTAIRE (François-Marie Arouet, 1694–1778)

There have been four or five examples of literary men enjoying enormous prestige in France and abroad during their lifetime: Ronsard in the 16th century, Chateaubriand during the First Empire and the Restoration, Victor Hugo during the few years that followed the Second Empire, and Jean-Paul Sartre in the middle of the 20th century. But no one dominated his age to the extraordinary degree that Voltaire dominated the 18th century. In himself he became a social force. When he returned to Paris after a long exile, at the age of eighty-four, he was given an hysterical welcome.

As a young man of twenty-four, he was hailed in his native Paris as the outstanding dramatist of the day. Unwilling to restrict his genius to one field, he took over all knowledge and wrote on every possible topic: God, physics, history. He corresponded with most of the famous people of his day, and many of these letters were concerned with social and religious abuses. In later middle age he created a model town in Ferney, near the Swiss border. His enormous activity continued until the day before he died. His complete work, on every subject and in every genre, is one of the longest in world literature.

Throughout his career Voltaire tried to imitate Racine in the writing of tragedies, and never succeeded. Between *Oedipe* (1718) and *Irène* (1778), he wrote twenty tragedies, of which the best are probably *Zaïre* (1732) and *Mérope* (1743). With most intellectuals of his day, Voltaire admired tragedy as the noblest literary form, but he was unable to see beyond a mechanical psychology in his characters, or give up using his plays for philosophical purposes.

His contemporaries lavished praise on his epic *La Henriade* and looked upon him as the official poet of France. Today he would be called a versifier and nothing more. Voltaire was always a defender of poetry, but many today agree with the 20th century critic Alain that there is not one line of poetry in all of his verse. It is hard to believe that his famous aphorism about the need to invent God if he did not exist is an alexandrine verse:

> Si Dieu n'existait pas, il faudrait l'inventer.

Far less original in his thinking than Diderot or Rousseau, Voltaire nevertheless made an important contribution to the writing of history. In calling the reign of Louis XIV *le grand siècle*, he emphasized the literary works written during the latter half of the 17th century, and avoided discussing the social and political problems. In his *Siècle de Louis XIV* and his *Histoire de Charles XII*, Voltaire added to military and political history notes on the arts and on civil institutions. His *Essai sur les moeurs* is a survey of world history which he finds to be the progress from superstition to rational enlightenment.

Voltaire was the outstanding disseminator of ideas in his century, although most of the ideas had already been expressed by others. He despised the supernatural mysteries of religion which he felt led to fanaticism. As a *philosophe*, he helped to make thinking about social problems and religious abuses fashionable. He loved humanity more than individuals (though Mme du Chatelet may have been an exception), and his human relationships were largely intellectual. His ideas are expressed in *Traité sur la tolérance* (1763) and *Dictionnaire philosophique* (1764). His *contes philosophiques* popularized those ideas: *Zadig* (1747), *Micromégas* (1752), and especially *Candide* (1759) belonging to the Ferney period, the best example of Voltaire's dry prose, which would have been flat had it not contained the ingredients of malice and wit.

Candide is a farcical tale of disasters. The first chapter parodies the temptation in Eden and the Fall of man. Cunégonde is Eve, or the Ideal, and Candide goes in search of her. But there is an impersonal evil in the universe represented in natural disasters: shipwrecks and earthquakes. Moral evil also exists in the form of injustice, cruelty and fanaticism. Voltaire is a deist in all his writings, but in *Candide* especially he depicts man as doomed to evil by God. As the allegorized human soul, Candide always expects good to be done to him rather than evil. Pangloss, the intellectual in the story (a caricature of Leibnitz) keeps proposing useless explanations of evil. The final sentence, "Il faut cultiver notre jardin," has many possible meanings: a pastoral conception of nature, an ironic statement of our limitations, a refuge from the disasters of the world, the praise of energetic work, or the archetypal pattern of the world as God's garden.

MARIVAUX and COMEDY IN HIS DAY

Three writers of comedy still dominate the repertory of the Comédie-Française: Molière, first and foremost, with his thirty comedies, and then, in fairly equal popularity, Marivaux and Musset.

Some of the actors at the turn of the century wrote comedies to fill out their company repertories. One of them, Florent Dancourt (1661–1725), wrote more than fifty comedies, many of them in one act. His best play concerns the corruption money brings to bourgeois and nobles: *Le chevalier à la mode* (1687).

Jean-François Regnard (1655–1709), from a rich bourgeois family in Paris, wrote plays especially for the Italian actors, such as *Arlequin homme à bonnes fortunes* (1690). Among his more ambitious plays for the Comédie-Française was *Le Joueur* (1696), on the subject of gambling.

La Comédie-Française was all-powerful, but constantly felt itself being threatened by the success of the Italian actors (*Les Italiens*), who at first were not allowed to play in French. But gradually they appropriated French, mimicked the comedies and tragedies of the Comédie-Française, and parodied even Mme de Maintenon. The king had their theater closed. (Watteau painted a picture showing their departure from Paris.) With the Regency, however, they returned, and this time played French comedies—later Marivaux wrote his best play for them.

Another group of actors, *les forains*, each one of whom was a combination of actor and acrobat, played at the great fairs. The public loved them and often took sides with them against the police, the Comédie-Française and the Italians. Lesage wrote for the *forains*.

Alain-René Lesage (1668–1747), who is better known for his novels, began writing for the theater when he left his native Brittany for Paris. In *Turcaret* (1709), he found an original subject in his study of a lackey, Turcaret, who acquires wealth through usury. He is as naive as Molière's Bourgeois Gentilhomme, fearful of the slightest physical danger, and morally corrupt.

The playwright Destouches (1680–1754) was more influenced by English comedies than by Molière in his successful play, *Le Glorieux* (1732), about a haughty individual, le comte de Tufière, who is deflated by love.

There were traces of the new genre, *la comédie larmoyante* (the "tearful comedy") in Voltaire's *Zaïre* and in Piron's *Le Fils Ingrat* (1728), but Nivelle de La Chaussée (1692–1754) made this type of play his speciality, and enjoyed a marked success with *Le préjugé à la mode* (1735). Women in particular approved of La Chaussée and wept at his plays far more than they laughed.

Pierre Carlet de Chamblain de MARIVAUX (1688–1763) created a new genre of comedy. Like Molière, he wrote more than thirty plays and seemed to prefer to have them played by the Italians.

Born in Paris of Norman parents, he was brought up in the provinces where he was a student in Riom and Limoges. He returned to Paris to study law but was more intrigued by the conversation in the salons of Mme de Lambert and Mme de Tencin. After trying his hand at adventure novels and a tragedy, *Annibal*, for the Comédie-Française (it was a miserable failure), he turned his attention to the Italians and the writing of comedies in prose. Marivaux wrote the type of 18th-century French prose in which there is more poetry than in 18th century French poetry.

Marivaux was able to free himself from Molière's tradition and create an original kind of play. He repeated himself from comedy to comedy, but used his own very personal style and his own world of characters. He avoided the tricks and practices of farce and gave to a traditionally burlesque character such as Arlequin more grace and ingenuousness, as in the play *Arlequin poli par l'amour*. He did not depict the manners of his day as Molière had done in *Les Précieuses Ridicules* and *Les Femmes Savantes*, but created a fantasy world that resembled a costumed scene painted by Watteau. Stock characters from the Italian repertory were used in his plays: two couples of lovers, two couples of servants, a jovial father, a tyrannical mother. He did not study an obsessive vice or a fatalistic passion, but evoked especially the varying sentimental moods of a character engaged in a crisis over love. Whereas Racine placed insurmountable obstacles in the way of love, Marivaux, whose genius was comedy, imagined transitory difficulties that tested a character without thwarting his happiness. For example, in his best-known play, *Le Jeu de l'Amour et du Hasard* (1730), the characters, by using disguises, create their own obstacles. Silvia and her servant Lisette change roles, and Dorante and his valet Arlequin also change roles.

The term *le marivaudage* is used to describe the very special art of Marivaux and the special psychology of the Marivaux character who hesitates before accepting happiness, who is tormented by scruples and worry, and whose egoism at first distrusts the sentiment of affection growing in him. Marivaux' writing is stylized without being *précieux;* the sentiments he analyzes are never trivial, although *marivaudage* sometimes refers to affected love-making. It was used in this pejorative sense by Marivaux' enemies, Voltaire, Diderot and the Encyclopedists.

Marivaux attempted to write two novels, *La vie de Marianne* and *Le paysan parvenu*, but never finished them. His plays, like the paintings of Watteau, are nostalgic, dreamlike situations in which the heart in its fluctuations is analyzed minutely. Marivaux was at his best when describing the unconscious beginnings of love in an adolescent character; he taught that love is born in the heart before the heart is conscious of it.

PRÉVOST and the NOVEL

Before the end of the 17th century, Antoine Furetière (1619–1688) published his *Roman bourgeois* (1666) as a parody of the heroic classical novel. It is a realistic type of novel depicting the Parisian bourgeoisie, and in this sense a forerunner of the 18th-century Parisian novel of Restif de la Bretonne, the 19th-century Balzac novel, and the 20th-century Jules Romains novel.

Lesage was the first novelist of importance in the 18th century. Like his predecessors in the 17th, he borrowed, or pretended to borrow from the Spanish. His method was picaresque, and his story the adventures of an unheroic hero, but his observations of society and the development of his characters were extremely sharp. In England, Defoe in his novel *Moll Flanders* was doing at the same time what Lesage was doing in *Le Diable Boiteux* (1709). The little devil Asmodée (Asmodius) flies over Madrid and, taking the roofs off the houses, shows the student Cléophas what is going on inside.

Lesage's best work, *Gil Blas* (1735), has all the traits of the Spanish pica-resque novel, although no exact sources have ever been found. The hero Gil Blas is the man-in-the-street who recovers from every adversity but remains incorrigible. He learns lesson after lesson that life gives him, but never relin-quishes his illusions. Greater novelists coming after Lesage fused better than he did the observations of society with the analysis of character.

In the history of the French novel, Antoine-François PRÉVOST (1687–1763) occupies a place similar to that of Richardson in the history of the English novel. He is known today for one short novel, of about the same length as *La Princesse de Clèves*, which is one part of a voluminous semi-autobiographical work *Mémoires d'un homme de qualité*. The full title of the novel, *L'Histoire du chevalier Des Grieux et de Manon Lescaut*, has been reduced today to *Manon Lescaut*. It is the story of a young priest whose life is changed by a girl. Manon is the central character. Two popular operas have been drawn from the novel by Massenet and Puccini, and also a film made by Clouzot in the early 1940s.

Educated by the Jesuits, Prévost became a Benedictine and very soon was a serious problem for the order. He preached at Saint-Germain-des-Prés among other places. He deserted the religious order for the army, and then deserted the army to go to England, where he was aided by the Archbishop of Canterbury, after a secret conversion to the Anglican Church. He probably wrote *Manon* in England in about 1730. It was first published in the seventh volume of *Mémoires d'un homme de qualité* in 1731.

Prévost spent some time in Holland, went back to England briefly, and then returned to France with a young girl he had met in Holland. He made a new submission to the Catholic Church, but was soon exiled briefly because of debts and other offenses. He translated three novels of Richardson—*Pamela* (1742), *Clarissa Harlowe* (1750), and *Grandison* (1755). At the end of his life, he under-took the writing of the history of the Condé family, and in order to be close to the archives he settled down in a village near Chantilly. One evening, returning home on foot from Senlis, the rather scandalous Abbé Prévost was struck down with an attack of apoplexy in front of a *calvaire*.

Manon is the story of Des Grieux' love for the girl Manon Lescaut as he tells it to a gentleman he meets in Calais two years after Manon's death in

Louisiana, where she had been sent with a group of prostitutes. He had met her first by chance in Amiens where he had just finished his studies for the priesthood. Des Grieux is undoubtedly the adventurous half of Abbé Prévost. Manon is a child-woman with an angelic face, a very sensual nature, both perfidious and affectionate, and able to awaken the sexual desires in most men she encounters. She is not the typical *femme fatale*, but more the teenager of today who takes one lover after another. Des Grieux states at the beginning of his confession, "Elle était bien plus expérimentée que moi." He is a cultivated young man from an excellent family who sincerely believes he has a priest's vocation, but who turns into a criminal and murderer because of his uncontrollable love for Manon. The subject matter of the novel is melodramatic, but Prévost does not write it as melodrama. Because the drama cannot be averted and because Des Grieux cannot act as he reasons, the subject of this work has often been classified as Racinian. Des Grieux justifies and excuses his passion as something human that he wishes. With this attitude toward his dilemma, he announces the romantic temperament almost one hundred years before it becomes exemplified in Rousseau's character Saint-Preux, and in Chateaubriand's René and Hugo's Hernani.

VOLTAIRE'S SPIRIT IN OTHERS: CHAMFORT and RIVAROL

Voltaire influenced almost every domain of thought and literature. Two moralists in particular illustrate his influence in both wit and in lucid intelligence: Chamfort and Rivarol.

From Auvergne, CHAMFORT (1740–1794) came to Paris at twenty as tutor and secretary for a wealthy bourgeois family. He was supported by the king, favored by women, and admired for his wit. He approved of the Revolution but became one of its victims. Chamfort wrote fables and poetry, but is remembered for his posthumously published *Maximes, Caractères et Anecdotes* (1803). He is more bitter, more caustic and less profound than La Rochefoucauld. Montaigne once wrote of learning how to die, and Chamfort answered, "Apprendre à mourir? On y réussit la première fois."

RIVAROL (1753–1801) inherited from Voltaire his impertinences and the nimbleness of his style. His skill as conversationalist was admired in an age of many remarkable conversationalists. In answer to a subject proposed by the Academy of Berlin, Rivarol wrote his *Discours sur l'universalité de la langue française* (1784), in which he analyzed the qualities of logic and clarity and harmony of the French language. The text is an echo of Du Bellay's *Défense et illustration de la langue française* of 1549, and measures the progress made by the French language during two hundred years.

FRENCH THOUGHT (*esprit philosophique*) IN THE SECOND HALF OF THE 18TH CENTURY

Salons

At the beginning of his reign, Louis XV was very much liked by the intellectuals, both men and women. But he eventually grew disillusioned and fell into a state of apathy, losing contact with the good minds of his kingdom. Intellectual life was concentrated in a series of brilliant salons in which the *philosophes* expounded their ideas. They attracted foreigners to such an extent that Paris became the capital of Europe. Intellectuals seemed to be bored elsewhere than in Paris. The new salons in the second half of the century encouraged the clearer and more courageous articulation of "philosophical" ideas—ideas that today would be called sociological or political ideas.

Mme Geoffrin (1699–1777) was a wealthy bourgeoise who, at the death of Mme de Tencin, inherited the habitués of the earlier salon. Her salon on the rue Saint-Honoré was known throughout Europe as being an intellectual center in which new ideas were welcomed and discussed. One of her favorites, Stanislas Pomiatowski, later became king of Poland. She received artists on Mondays (Boucher, Pigalle, Latour), on Wednesdays writers (Marivaux, Voltaire) and encyclopedists (Grimm, Helvétius, d'Alembert). She gave important financial help to the *Encyclopédie*.

La marquise du Deffand (1697–1780) presided over a salon which flourished from 1740 to 1780, first on the rue de Beaune and then on rue Saint-Dominique.

She received most of the encyclopedists as well as Fontenelle, Montesquieu and Marivaux. During the latter part of her life, she was passionately fond of Horace Walpole.

Her correspondence reveals very penetrating literary judgments as well as fearless estimates of her own psychological makeup, her loneliness and her boredom. She quite literally believed in nothing, but longed to believe and react vibrantly to all events and all sentiments. She became blind at the age of fifty-seven, and engaged as a reader a young orphan girl of twenty-two, Mlle de Lespinasse (1732–1776), who began secretly receiving some of the habitués of her mistress' salon. When this betrayal was discovered she was expelled, but she opened up her own salon almost next door.

Sensibilité

The strictness of intellectual inquiry was not always observed in the salons. Precisely, Julie de Lespinasse's salon represented a change of attitude. She favored the training and the exalting of sensibility. Her correspondence reveals a greater effusiveness of sentiment than the dry rationalism prevailing in other salons. This emphasis on sensibility had been observed first in the comedies of Marivaux and the novels of Prévost. Mlle de Lespinasse helped prepare the way for the greatest exponent of sensibility in the century, Jean-Jacques Rousseau. In one of her letters, she wrote, "Il n'y a qu'une seule chose qui résiste, c'est la passion et c'est celle de l'amour."

Illuminisme

Despite the rationalism of the *philosophes*, an "illuminist" movement grew in France which attracted some first-rate minds as well as some charlatans. The mission of the *illuministes* was to regenerate Christianity by developing the practice of communication between the human soul and the invisible world. The writings (in Latin) of the Swedish philosopher Swedenborg (1688–1772) were studied in various milieux throughout Europe. He taught that there is an exact parallelism (*correspondance*) between earth and heaven. In the 19th century, Swedenborg's work influenced the writing of Balzac, Baudelaire and Nerval, in particular.

Science and Buffon

Science became a fashionable pastime in the 18th century. Lords and ladies collected fossils, insects, and plants (*herbiers*). Experimental sciences were explored by Montesquieu, Diderot, Voltaire and Rousseau. Newton was revered as the founder of the experimental method. In a word, science, as we know it today, was being founded.

Georges-Louis Leclerc (1707–1788), from a Burgundian middle-class family, was made comte de Buffon by Louis XV in 1772. After his early training under the Jesuits in Dijon, Buffon studied medicine, developed a passion for botany, and travelled extensively in France and Europe with a young English nobleman, the duke of Kingston. In 1739 he was appointed *intendant du Jardin du Roi*. This work led to the writing of his monumental *Histoire naturelle de l'homme*, thirty-six volumes in all, which appeared at intervals between 1749 and 1788.

During his lifetime, Buffon was as famous in France as Voltaire and Rousseau. His books were in all the private libraries of the day. Although he is not read today as a scientist or a naturalist, he is still remembered as being the first scientist of modern times to deal with the problem of the origins of species, and who thus opened the way to the work of Lamarck, Darwin and Spencer. Thanks to Buffon, science became popular reading in the 18th century. His *Histoire Naturelle* was one of the best-sellers of his day, with Voltaire's *La Henriade*, Rousseau's *La Nouvelle Héloïse*, and *L'Encyclopédie*.

L'ENCYCLOPÉDIE

The origin of the *Encyclopédie* was a publisher's plan to exploit the increasing interest in science. Le Breton commissioned Diderot to translate and adapt Ephraim Chambers' *Cyclopaedia or Universal Dictionary of the arts and sciences*, which had been published in London in 1727. Diderot accepted, but soon decided to bring out instead an original work, conceived along lines that resembled Bayle's *Dictionnaire historique*. He secured the collaboration of d'Alembert, the outstanding mathematician of Europe, and enlisted the services of a large number of specialists. He announced the publication of the *Encyclopédie* in 1750.

When the first two volumes appeared in 1751, the *Encyclopédie* was temporarily banned, although it was never successfully suppressed. The work continued somewhat secretly, and by 1765 seventeen volumes, the main body of the work, had been published. Supplementary volumes, principally of plates, followed later and were sold legally.

Diderot, an indefatigable worker, always remained the prime mover of the gigantic enterprise. He wrote more than a thousand articles. Jean d'Alembert (1717–1783), Diderot's principal assistant, composed the *Discours préliminaire* of the *Encyclopédie*, in which he discussed the purpose and the method of the work. He wrote the article on *Genève* and many aricles on mathematics and physics. Several of the leading writers of the day collaborated—Voltaire, for example, was enthusiastic at first, but gradually withdrew his help when he saw himself in too large a company of writers.

Condillac (1715–1780), a friend of Rousseau and Diderot, contributed articles on philosophy and on his psychological theory of sensualism, in which he attempted to prove that the human personality is formed by physical sensations and not by innate qualities.

Helvétius (1715–1771) applied and developed the sensualist theories of Condillac and argued that personal profit is always the basis of an individual's actions. His book *De l'esprit* (1758) was condemned and increased the chances for censorship of the *Encyclopédie*.

Le baron d'Holbach (1723–1784) wrote articles on chemistry and mineralogy. A determined materialist, he explained everything in the world in terms of matter and movement.

For most of the encyclopedists, especially for those men just named, the main obstacle to happiness was religion. Priests, like tyrants, were thought to maintain man in ignorance and slavery. The soul was considered simply the center of sensations, and God was simply a word. In order to avoid censorship and imprisonment, the encyclopedists followed the principle of objectivity in the writing of the lead articles, but referred to other articles, usually more obscure and briefer, in which their special philosophic interpretations were revealed. For example, Diderot's article *Christianisme* would shock no one, but in the articles referred to in *Christianisme* his ideas are reversed. Under the article *Cordeliers*, the Franciscans are praised, but under *Capuchons* they are severely criticized.

DIDEROT (1713–1784)

In the history of literature and thought, Denis Diderot has continued to grow in importance. Today he is read and studied as one of the most original minds of the 18th century. Like Stendhal, Diderot became known long after his death.

Like so many other writers of his century, Diderot was educated by the Jesuits in his native city of Langres. After a few years of study in Paris, he became an independent hack-writer. In his *Lettre sur les Aveugles* (1749), he tried to prove that a blind person could not believe in God. For proposing such a theory, he was imprisoned three months in the donjon de Vincennes. The huge labor of the *Encyclopédie* did not interrupt his own writing, and it put him in contact with other writers and with the influential salons.

In reacting against classical tragedy, which had been languishing for some time, Diderot proposed a new type of play, *le drame bourgeois*, in prose—an intermediate type between tragedy and comedy. His theory is well illustrated in two of his plays, *Le Fils Naturel* (1757) and *Le père de famille* (1758), which seem static and unplayable today. He advocated realistic themes and characters, with emphasis on pathos and morality. In his stimulating essay *Le paradoxe sur le comédien* (1773), Diderot developed his thesis that the great actor must intellectually control the role he is playing and not let himself go to it emotionally. In this sense, he must learn to be hypocritical and insensitive and aware every moment that he is acting. "Method" acting taught by the Actors' Workshop in New York in the 20th century has some relationship to Diderot's theories in *Paradoxe*.

In his practice of art critic, Diderot saw painting as the art that arouses emotions and reveals truth. His preference was for scenes of mute pathos—seascapes of Vernet, for example, the sentimental family scenes of Greuze, the realism of Latour, the simplicity of Chardin. With the exception of three years, Diderot wrote the criticisms of the *salon* exhibitions between 1759 and 1781.

Diderot's philosophy is clearly outlined in his fiction, in his licentious *Bijoux indiscrets*, in *La Religieuse* (1760), in which he condemned the rule of celibacy of religious orders, in *Jacques le fataliste* (1773) in which he preached that man is predestined by the physical world he lives in, and finally in his masterpiece, *Le Neveu de Rameau* (written between 1762 and 1773, and first published in 1821). This novel is a dialogue between the narrator and the old Bohemian music teacher of the title. The two voices have been variously interpreted. For Karl Marx, they represented the honest consciousness (static values) and the disinterested consciousness (flux and confusion). At one time Diderot idolized

Rameau (as opposed to Lully), but his taste changed in time and he turned against Rameau for newer composers. His hero, le neveu de Rameau, is presented as a tramp, a pimp, a gourmandizer, a frequenter of cafés, a friend of the prostitutes of the Palais-Royal, and a lover of ideas, of love, and of music. Diderot incarnates the frenzied actions of the picaresque hero, but especially in his passion for music.

It is not difficult to see Diderot himself in Rameau's nephew, a kind of bistro prophet and gesticulating conversationalist. In his real life, Diderot was uninhibited and exuberant. Catherine II of Russia was one of his sponsors, and during his six-month stay at St. Petersburg, she had a table placed between them to keep Diderot from constantly slapping her on the thigh.

ROUSSEAU (1712–1778)

Born in Geneva, Rousseau lost his mother at his birth and was brought up by an emotional and somewhat eccentric father who left his son Jean-Jacques at the age of ten. The boy was then cared for by a pastor and others. At sixteen he left Geneva and asked for help from a Catholic priest in a village outside of Geneva, who turned him over to Mme de Warens of Annecy. She undertook the conversion of Jean-Jacques and became attached to the boy emotionally and sexually. For some years Rousseau was intermittently dependent upon Mme de Warens, whom he called *maman*.

Rousseau was first a composer of music, and then, during two summers he studied philosophy and literature in Les Charmettes, a country house in Chambéry lent to him by Mme de Warens. When he moved to Paris in the 1740s he was determined to be a dramatist and composer. He began a life-long liaison with an inn servant, Thérèse Levasseur, who bore him five children placed by Rousseau in an orphange (*enfants trouvés*).

One summer day in 1749, Rousseau walked the eight kilometers to Vincennes to visit Diderot in prison; on his way he read of a competition offered by the Académie de Dijon for an essay to be written on the subject of whether the study of arts and sciences contributed to an improvement of morals. "Si le rétablissement des sciences et des arts a contribué à épurer les moeurs." Rousseau later claimed that the central idea of his philosophy came to him as an illumination on that walk to Vincennes. He was probably encouraged by Diderot to write this first important text, usually called *Discours sur les sciences et les arts* (1750), in which he answered the question of the competition topic in the negative and developed his theory of the natural goodness of man. Rousseau won the prize in the competition and suddenly became famous.

It was a paradoxical success because Rousseau went against the spirit of his age in opposing the doctrines of materialistic progress and the perfectibility of human nature. He composed at that time an opéra-bouffe, *Le devin du village*, performed before the king and the court at Fontainebleau in 1752, and a work very much in keeping with the simple country life he was determined to lead.

A new subject was proposed by the Académie de Dijon in 1754, one that involved two questions: "Quelle est l'origine de l'inégalité parmi les hommes, et si elle est autorisée par la loi naturelle?" In this second essay, usually called *Discours sur l'origine de l'inégalité* (1755), Rousseau developed the conclusion of his first essay by claiming that the source of inequality is the social institution itself—society, he felt, was responsible for its own corruption.

This time Rousseau was not awarded the prize, but the *discours* was read more avidly and more widely than the first. Rousseau named the principle of property and ownership of land as the primal cause of social injustice and inequality. The exposition of this sociological theory was autobiographical to some extent, because Rousseau was already considering himself an outcast, persecuted and solitary, but pure and good. He was already playing the role of anachoret by selling all he owned and living in the "desert," where he earned his sustenance by copying music. Voltaire and other *philosophes* were outraged by Rousseau's thesis on society as the source of evil.

In 1756, Jean-Jacques, Thérèse, Thérèse's mother, and a favorite cat moved to L'Ermitage, a small house in the forest of Montmorency given them by a new patroness, Mme d'Epinay. For almost five very productive years, Rousseau occupied L'Ermitage and then a house in the village of Montmorency, where he wrote four important books.

Lettre à d'Alembert sur les spectacles (1758)

By this time Rousseau had renounced Catholicism and returned to his early Calvinist faith. He had read in *L'Encyclopédie* d'Alembert's article on *Genève*, in which certain Genevan ministers were praised for their liberalism and for wishing to institute a theater in the city. Rousseau attacked d'Alembert and raised the problem of the relationship between the theater and morality. The attack was fundamentally waged against Voltaire, who had urged d'Alembert to exalt the theater. Rousseau in his *Lettre* took sides with moralists, Nicole and Bossuet, among others, who had opposed the theatre for two hundred years. He pointed out in his text that the sincere hero Alceste in Molière's *Le Misanthrope* is made fun of, whereas Philinte the compromiser is praised. (Jean-Jacques was probably thinking of himself as Alceste, and the typical *philosophe* as Philinte.) With such a publication as the *Lettre à d'Alembert*, Rousseau appeared in open war with the *philosophes* and the *Encyclopédie*.

La Nouvelle Héloïse (1761)

After attacking the theme of love in the theatre, Rousseau wrote a love story in which he lived the kind of love he longed to know and felt he had not known with Mme de Warens or Thérèse. He was forty-four years old, in ill health, hated by his enemies, famous, and worshipped by a large public of women. This novel, begun in L'Ermitage and completed in the house in Montmorency, is first a love story about a young, handsome and pure tutor, Saint-Preux, and his pupil Julie, a composite heroine of the women Rousseau had loved, including Mme d'Houdetot, a friend of his benefactress Mme d'Epinay. The book is also a thesis novel (*un roman à thèse*) in which the simplicity of pastoral life is the ideal setting for happiness and nature provides a source of purification and serenity. The 12th-century story of Abélard and Héloïse, the seduction of a young girl by her philosophy tutor, is recast in the story of Julie and Saint-Preux.

Whereas Voltaire stimulated the minds of men of his century, Rousseau, especially in *La Nouvelle Héloïse*, so successful a novel that it went through seventy editions in forty years, appealed to women, for whom he became a kind of spiritual director.

Le Contrat Social (1762)

This third book was a part of a long work on political science that Rousseau planned to write. It still remains today a key text on the principles of democracy in which the people are sovereign, making laws by a general vote. The state was conceived of as being the protector of individual liberties, and the government must respect the will of the people. This work, in which Rousseau shows himself to be a proletarian Montesquieu, was not studied until after the Revolution. For many readers today, Rousseau is known essentially as the author of *Le Contrat Social*.

Emile (1762)

This treatise on pedagogy continues the tradition of several major French writers—Rabelais, Montaigne, Bossuet and Fénelon—who tried to enact reforms in the education of children: Rousseau was influenced by Montaigne and Locke's work of 1693, translated into French in 1695 as *L'Education des enfants*. In Rousseau's system, everything should be done to preserve the natural freedom of the child: the baby should be free in its bodily movements, the boy in his games, and the adolescent in the choice of his religious faith. Emile must learn the power of the natural laws. He should not be given prefabricated ideas from books. "Je hais les livres; ils n'apprennent qu'à parler de ce qu'on ne sait pas." The fables of La Fontaine could make a child envious of the lion and the wolf, so *Robinson Crusoe*, the story of natural man, was thought to be preferable reading.

In the fourth chapter, *Profession de foi du vicaire savoyard*, the vicar explains to Emile, aged fifteen, that he has a soul, that there is a God and a religion. God is revealed in the harmony and beauty of nature, and a man's conscience tells him what is right and what is wrong. These are doctrines of Rousseau, the deist, who will not accept religious dogmas or the belief that there has been a revealed religion. Too religious to satisfy the atheists of the age and not religious enough to please Protestants and Catholics, *Emile* was condemned by the Parlement de Paris, and Rousseau entered upon the most painful part of his existence, in which he suffered from an ever-increasing paranoia. Repulsed in Paris and in Geneva, he took refuge in England on the invitation of David Hume, but soon began imagining that Hume was in league with his persecutors. He returned to France, lived briefly in Paris in almost total solitude between 1770 and 1778, and then settled in Ermenonville, near Senlis, where he died two months later.

During Rosseau's last years, his writing became frankly autobiographical. Before settling in Paris, he wrote his *Confessions* between 1765 and 1770, in which, like Saint Augustine, he tells of the good and the bad of his life. The elegant opening sentence, "Je veux montrer à mes semblables un homme dans toute la vérité de sa nature," is the claim to total sincerity. The work, a model for countless subsequent autobiographies, was published after Rousseau's death.

During the last Paris years he wrote three curious dialogues: one was *Rousseau, juge de Jean-Jacques*, an appeal to his readers to understand the two characters he is: Rousseau the man, and Jean-Jacques the writer. His last work, left unfinished, *Rêveries d'un promeneur solitaire* (1776–1778), was an idealization of himself, a series of meditations on his life and his sensibility, and especially on the ecstasy he felt in nature. In the tenth *Promenade*, he recalled his first meeting with Mme de Warens and celebrated in the final pages the fiftieth anniversary of the happiness he knew at Les Charmettes.

Rousseau died two months after his enemy Voltaire, and was buried at night by torchlight in a lake on the île des peupliers. Having been born with a malformation of the bladder which caused urine retention, he had had to care for this painful and humiliating malady from his twenty-fourth year on—this physiological predicament explains to some degree his seeming madness, his uneasiness in society, his desire for solitude and his paranoia. It is impossible to measure the influence of Rousseau on modern civilization. His deep feeling for the country and country life, his exaltation of the ego (*le moi*), his theories on progressive education and the natural goodness of man, and his lack of class consciousness, are just a few of his themes that have become part of our modern heritage.

NOVEL, THEATER, POETRY
AT THE END OF THE 18TH CENTURY

The Novel

BERNARDIN DE SAINT-PIERRE (1737–1814) became a friend of Rousseau in 1772. He had already at that time travelled to the île de France, called today île Maurice. Temperamentally he was as unstable as Rousseau but far more difficult and vindictive. His *Etudes de la Nature* is a long work of nature descriptions and a back-to-nature philosophy derived from Rousseau. One part of this work is the novel *Paul et Virginie* (1787), set in the île Maurice and devoted in part to a description of exotic landscapes. It is an innocent love story which ends with the death of Virginie in a shipwreck. Today the writing of this novel seems mannered and over-refined. (Chateaubriand soon after did better in his similar story of *Atala*.) With its theme of purity in love, it is the antithesis of *Manon Lescaut*. Some of the scenes give the romantic sense of the infinite. *Paul et Virginie* is one of the first books of exoticism in French literature, a form destined to have success in the writings of Chateaubriand, Lamartine and Pierre Loti.

Nicolas Restif de la Bretonne (1734–1806) was the son of a Burgundian farmer, and wrote exhaustively, in a verbose careless style, about Paris. *Le Paysan perverti* (1776) illustrates the demoralizing effect of the city on a country fellow; *Les Contemporaines* (1780–1785) describes the countless trades of Parisian women; *Monsieur Nicolas* (1796–1797) is an autobiography. Restif was a voyeur in the *bas-fonds*, a visionary who showed the symptoms of a psychopath, a fetichist and a paranoid.

Pierre Choderlos de Laclos (1741–1803), from Amiens, had a military career culminating in his becoming a general in Napoleon's army. He wrote only one novel, *Les Liaisons Dangereuses* (1782), by far the best novel in the libertine tradition of the 18th century.

Like *La Nouvelle Héloïse* of Rousseau and *Clarissa Harlowe* of Richardson (very much admired by Laclos), *Les Liaisons dangereuses* is an epistolary novel in which the sophisticated libertines, Valmont and Mme de Merteuil, undertake the seduction of two innocent people, Cécile de Voltanges and the chevalier de Danceny.

The couple Valmont and la marquise de Merteuil are monstrous in the coldness with which they analyze their sentiments and the sentiments of the people they seduce. Their pleasure is intense only when they win over virginity or God or a pure love promised to someone else. At the end, their evil is punished; Valmont dies in a duel and la Merteuil is disfigured by smallpox.

The character of the marquise de Merteuil is complicated—she is concerned quite directly and unashamedly with the satisfaction of elementary desires. Sade might well see in her the beginnings of what he would call the natural woman. The "little house" in which she receives her suitors retains a good deal of 18th-century gallantry, but it also has elements about it reminiscent of the deserted castle of Sade, in which crimes and debauchery are perpetrated. Mme de Merteuil is an aristocrat and a thinker; she is also something of a demiurge in that she distributes roles and causes actions and crimes to be carried out. Her letters to Valmont create an exceptional complicity between the two characters. She is stronger and bolder than the man, more intelligent and more implacable.

Valmont, her partner and rival in this philosophy of sexual pleasure which excludes sentiment and emotion, often fails to understand her completely. He is more devious and patient than she is, but they are equal in the degree to which they have liberated their sensuality from all constraint. In the sensual satisfactions Valmont seeks, he is more complicated than the marquise, more given to tastes that later develop in the heroes of Sade and the gothic tale. He too has something of the demiurge in him, and many traits of the dandy and the dilettante who will appear in the following century and be exalted by Charles Baudelaire. The vicomte de Valmont, as the libertine of Laclos, treats the women he loves as victims. He constantly uses the image of warfare: "Conquérir est mon destin." His basic impulse is the most primitive of all.

Mme de Tourvel, called *la Présidente*, is the marquise's opposite; she lives in devotion to man, and even sacrifices her own salvation to the happiness of Valmont. She and the ingénue of the story, Cécile, are both tragic examples of the dangers of such "acquaintances." The naïveté of Cécile reminds one of the heroines of Molière and Marivaux. Mme de Tourvel might well have been in the previous century a penitent of François de Sales. In the long series of temptations offered by Valmont to Cécile and la Présidente, one has the impression of watching a condemned society, a drama whose end is announced at its very beginning. The Paris houses and the provincial châteaux are like places of exile where the inhabitants vegetate in their solitude and boredom. The action of what Baudelaire later calls "satanism" is more visible in the two victimized women than in the convinced libertines.

Mme de Tourvel is the only character belonging to the bourgeoisie (as Baudelaire pointed out in his notes on Laclos) and she alone attains to something like nobility of character. She plays an important part in the military metaphor pervading the book because she is the woman destined to be defeated. Her boudoir is a battlefield, and her *gloire* means sexual success. On one level, Valmont's seduction of la Présidente is an attack on the conventional morality of the century, but behind the problem of social laws and tradition there is a more profound study of male strategy and male domination. It is the problem of *gloire* or of whatever word happens to be substituted for male conquest.

The form of *Les Liaisons Dangereuses*, completely composed of letters, permits the characters to carry on a constant introspection. It also permits them to construct their own personalities, to invent and falsify their actions. A dialogue carried on by letters is far more thoughtful and planned and significant than any ordinary spontaneous dialogue; for example, the adroitness and implacable skill of Valmont's writing contrasts with the despair of some of Mme de Tourvel's letters. The letters of this novel, by comparison with the letters of Rousseau's and Richardson's novels, are closer to action than to narrative. They are instruments to cause suffering or to act as defense—often masks put on to conceal some vice or to compromise their correspondent. The constant answering back and forth gives the entire work an antiphonal quality both lyric and ceremonious, like the parts of a Greek ode. The total effect, particularly with the gruesome endings of the characters, is that of a tragedy. The two novels— *Les Liaisons Dangereuses* and *Manon Lescaut*—are more basically tragic than the literal tragedies of the 18th century.

The language of the book represents an extraordinary degree of clarity and precision. The exaggerated traits of preciosity and bombast allowed by the 17th century have practically disappeared. There are almost no remainders of poetic ornamentation, of pietistic verbiage, or of picturesqueness for its own sake. The speech is direct and the answer is direct. The words mean only what they say. The restricted vocabulary reminds one of Racine. The elegance of the style comes from its sobriety.

The strong current of sentimentality in 18th-century writing is nowhere present in *Les Liaisons Dangereuses*. Before 1782, and after it in the early romantic period, much of French and European literature was well watered with tears. In *La Nouvelle Héloïse* and in *Werther*, all the virtues had languished and wept. Laclos was contemporary with Bernardin de Saint-Pierre and Chénier, a curious moment indeed for the flourishing of his dry prosaic genius. His novel came one hundred years after the tragedies of Racine, but in many ways, in the ruthlessness, cruelty and penetration of the psychological analysis, Racine is the ancestor of Laclos. In both Racine and Laclos there is a strong alliance of politeness and intransigency. The protagonists know what their desires are and what their fate is, and they speak directly of these matters with their *confidents*.

Les Liaisons Dangereuses has been looked upon as a compromising book for humanity. Libertinism, when it no longer concerns a single man, as with Don Juan, but is studied in a man and a woman who are equal in intelligence and brilliance, becomes a subject of deep scandal and deep shame. It is possible that the sophistication of this *libertinage* is as extreme as can be found in any book of any nation. The pure scandal of the book might have turned it into a study merely of eroticism, but it is much more than that, largely because of the wit of its sophistication, of the almost terrifying equality of the sexes in their pursuit of sexual conquest, and in the comparative silence of Laclos regarding the ancient legend of woman's resistance to man.

The position of the marquis de SADE (1740–1814) is much more than that of a libertine writer. He is unique in being the only writer whose name is used to designate a perversion. In its most specific sense, sadism refers to the sexual pleasure derived from torturing or murdering the partner. De Sade's writings are used today in the study of modern sexual psychology. He was looked upon as an important writer by Baudelaire, Swinburne and Nietzsche in the 19th century, and was rediscovered by Apollinaire and the surrealists in the 20th century.

De Sade spent twenty-seven years of his life in prison, principally in the Bastille, and the end of his life in the insane asylum at Charenton, where he died. *Justine* (1791) is a novel about an innocent girl who undergoes all forms of defilement and torture; *Juliette* is a novel about the thoroughly depraved sister of Justine; *La Philosophie dans le boudoir* (1795) is the initiation of a young girl to all forms of sexual experience; *120 journées de Sodome* is an elaborate repertory of sexual perversions. The narrative of these four principal novels of Sade is interspersed with philosophical interpretations, Sade being both philosopher and novelist. At intervals pauses in the orgy scenes permit the characters to explain at great length the principles of their immorality.

It would seem that the long periods of imprisonment made Sade into a writer by allowing him to explore his obsessions, characterize them, and interpret them. The elaborate system of perversions described and analyzed by Sade outlined a cathartic-psychoanalytical process that has been developed in the 20th century. Aristotle taught that the spectator is purified of his passions by watching the performance of a tragedy. Sade taught that a man is exalted in his passions by watching or participating in an orgiastic sexual scene. Scenes reminiscent of those in Sade's novels are being introduced in new films of 1970 and could be justified in moral-psychoanalytical terms by Sade himself!

The novels of the marquis de Sade represent a declaration of the rights of eroticism. His philosophy was based on what he believed was man's absolute solitude and absolute egoism. The motivations of man's actions were presented as being purely selfish. He developed endlessly his theoretical ideas in a language that was always very clear and very firm. Throughout his philosophy where evil takes precedence over the good he refused the "social contract" by which the weak are protected. His idea of *libertinage* was the organization of small groups or clubs of very privileged people—nobles, kings, and popes—*petites sociétés* founded for the sole purpose of allowing these people to indulge their passions. Herein lies the principal thesis of Sade: that no evil can befall the man who accepts evil as the one reality.

In *Marat-Sade*, by the German playwright Peter Weiss, performed in Paris in 1966, Sade is seen in Charenton where Weiss imagined he had written, in 1808, a drama on the death of Marat, performed by the inmates of the asylum. In this play (and film) Sade stands for haughty pessimistic individualism, and Marat seems to represent a type of political theorist, possibly Karl Marx.

The Theater of Beaumarchais

Pierre-Augustin Caron (1732–1799) was the son of a watchmaker who lived in the rue Saint-Denis in Paris. His life was more dramatic, more varied, more spectacular than his plays. He learned early the trade of watchmaker. At twenty-four he married a rich widow, age thirty-five, who died ten months later. From her he inherited not a fortune, but the name Beaumarchais. (Some property of hers, near Arpajon, was called *Bois-Marché* and pronounced by the peasants *Bômarchais*.)

Beaumarchais became harp teacher of the four daughters of Louis XV, engaged in various business deals, including gunrunning for the Americans in the War of Independence, and married a second time at the age of thirty-six. His second wife was also a rich widow who died soon after the marriage. (Like Racine, Beaumarchais was suspected of committing murder by poison.)

Le Barbier de Séville, the first of the two plays for which Beaumarchais is remembered today, went through various versions before reaching its definitive form in 1775, when it was played with great success. Borrowing from Molière's *L'Ecole des Femmes* and from other playwrights, Beaumarchais produced a work that seemed new, refreshing and lively. Figaro, who carries the action of the play, is a descendent of the valet of the Italian comedy and of Molière's Scapin. Does the name come from *Fils Caron, Fi-Caron, Figaro*? The opera that Rossini made from *Le Barbier de Séville* in 1826 was already in the verbal music of the French text. The play is a comedy of intrigue (*imbroglio*) in which Count Almaviva, aided by his barber-servant Figaro, wins Rosine and thereby thwarts her guardian Bartholo.

Three years later, in 1778, Beaumarchais finished *Le Mariage de Figaro*. The play was banned for six years. Its first performance in 1784 was memorable. The playwright used the characters from *Le Barbier* and added the *soubrette* Suzanne and the page Chérubin. The main plot of this second comedy is Figaro's determination to marry Suzanne despite Almaviva's desire to make her his mistress.

The first performance at the Comédie-Française has been looked upon as one of the first skirmishes of the Revolution. The impertinent actions and speeches of Figaro influenced public opinion. He preaches the doctrine of equality in his fiery monologue of act V, when he asks what the count did to deserve his good fortune and the privileges he enjoys: "Vous vous êtes donné la peine de naître, et rien de plus." The virulence of the satire in *Le Mariage de Figaro* makes the play a document on public opinion in France on the eve of the Revolution. In the more purely literary tradition, Beaumarchais' art was obvious in the skill with which he complicated (*nouer*) and uncomplicated (*dénouer*) a plot in the Italian style. The picture he gave of social customs and his characterizations place him as a disciple of Moliere. His two best comedies are so stamped by his personality that they have not been used as models in subsequent French comedy.

Although Beaumarchais had been called the champion of freedom at the time of *Le Mariage*, the revolutionists were hard on him and considered him an opportunist.

Poetry: André Chénier

Throughout the century the art of poetry was dominated by the theories of Boileau. It remained primarily an intellectual exercise, and the deeper emotions of the age were expressed in prose.

Epics had been written in the 17th century with religious or national subjects: Saint-Amant's *Moïse sauvé* (1653), Chapelain's *Pucelle d'Orléans* (1656), Desmarets de Saint-Sorlin's *Clovis* (1657). The 18th century chose as its epic Voltaire's *La Henriade* (1724–28), the story of Henri IV.

Voltaire was not only the official poet of the century but also the best defender of poetry. There were many versifiers—Jean-Baptiste Rousseau (1671–1741), for example, a cobbler's son who was called *le grand Rousseau* in order to humiliate Jean-Jacques. His *Odes et Cantates* (1723) was first published in London. Jean-Baptiste-Louis Gresset (1709–1777) wrote a lighter kind of poetry, somewhat in the tradition of Marot. *Vert-Vert* is a poem about a parrot brought up by nuns, Les Visitandines of Nevers, which, in moving from one convent to another, picks up the language of sailors.

Le Franc de Pompignan (1709–1784) in his *Odes chrétiennes et philosophiques* (1771) and Ponce-Denis Lebrun (1729–1807), author of *Elégies* and *Epîtres*, were considered disciples of Jean-Baptiste Rousseau.

Les Saisons (1769), a pastoral poem by Saint-Lambert (1716–1803), was undoubtedly inspired by *The Seasons* of the English poet Thomson. Jacques

Delille (1738–1813), a mediocre poet, became famous for his translations of Virgil (*Géorgiques*), Milton (*Paradis perdu*), and Pope (*Essai sur l'homme*). Parny (1753–1814) should be mentioned because Lamartine at the beginning of his career considered himself a disciple of Parny. His poems do have some fluidity and delicacy.

But there was only one real poet in the century, ANDRÉ CHÉNIER (1762–1794). He was born in Galata, on the outskirts of Constantinople. His mother was a highly cultured Greek woman who gave her son an understanding of Greek civilization deeper than any French poet had had since the time of Racine. His early poems, *Bucoliques*, testify to his extensive knowledge of Greek and his skill in restoring the Greek gods in poetry (as in *La mort d'Hercule*), and scenes of Greek life, such as the marriage scene in *La Jeune Tarentine*.

At the outbreak of the Revolution, Chénier was in London, where he held a position in the French embassy. He returned to Paris in a state of enthusiasm for the Revolution, which he celebrated in the only two poems of his work that were published before his death. But he soon began protesting against the Jacobins and the excesses of the revolutionists. He collaborated in an attempt to spare France from the shame of a regicide.

After the execution of Louis XVI, horrified by so much bloodshed, Chénier went into hiding in Versailles for a few months. On his return to Paris he was arrested in Passy in March, 1794. After four months of imprisonment in Saint-Lazare, he was condemned by the Revolutionary Tribunal (who confused him with his brother Sauveur) as "an enemy of the people." In the tumbril that took Chénier and the poet Roucher to the guillotine, the two men recited the opening scene of Racine's *Andromaque* and thus restored for their death the atmosphere of ancient Greece. After assassinating Lavoisier, the greatest chemist of the century, the Revolution killed the greatest poet, at the age of thirty-two. It was two days before the fall of Robespierre, bringing the change of events that could have saved the life of Chénier.

The first edition of Chénier's work appeared twenty-five years after his death, in 1819. The most complete edition was published between 1907 and 1919 under the editorship of Paul Dimoff. For the romantics, André Chénier was the luminous poet emerging out of the night of the Revolution. He was revered by Lamartine, by Hugo (who called him the romantic among the classicists, and who entitled one of his poems in *La Légende des siècles*, *André Chénier*), and by Sainte-Beuve (who named him the forerunner of romanticism.)

He tried to create a new kind of epic in his poems *Hermès* and *Amérique*, in which he denounces ignorance and fanaticism as the monsters of modern times and celebrates as the new heroes such figures as Galileo, Newton and Buffon. His extensive literary knowledge reminds one of the Pléiade poets and their eagerness to learn from poets of antiquity. Chénier knew the Italian poets and the Bible, the *Arabian Nights*, and the English poets: Shakespeare, Young, Thomson and Ossian. Ronsard, La Fontaine, and Chénier are the three French poets who were inspired and guided by their study of antiquity and yet who never imitated the ancient poets in any servile manner.

The romantics recognized Chénier as a brother because he claimed that the heart is the source of poetry:

> L'art ne fait que des vers, le coeur seul est poète.

Two of his most famous poems show two captive girls: *La Jeune Tarentine*, a girl who drowns on the eve of her wedding, a prisoner of the sea; and *La Jeune Captive*, a young duchess imprisoned by the revolutionists. In the pity he shows for these two women, cut off so young and in such tragic ways, Chénier seemed to be prophesying and lamenting his own death.

His strongest, most virile poem is his last, *Les Iambes*, written in prison just before his execution on bits of thin paper he secreted in the laundry sack that was sent to his father from Saint-Lazare. It is poetry of despair written by a young man whose life is condemned and who is powerless to avert the tragedy. The *iamb* was the Greek meter used in satire, but there is no connection between the Greek metrics and Chénier, who in *Les Iambes* alternates the alexandrine with the octosyllabic line:

> Au pied de l'échafaud j'essaie encor ma lyre.
> Peut-être est-ce bientôt mon tour.

The violence of this prison poem is equal to the violence in poems of Villon's *Le Testament* and Agrippa d'Aubigné's *Tragiques* and Hugo's *Châtiments*.

NINETEENTH CENTURY

HISTORY		LITERATURE	
1801	Le Concordat	1801	Chateaubriand, *Atala*
		1802	Chateaubriand, *Génie du Christianisme*
1804	coronation of Napoleon	1810	Staël, *De l'Allemagne*
1815	Waterloo	1816	Constant, *Adolphe*
1815–24	reign of Louis XVIII	1820	Lamartine, *Méditations poétiques*
1824–30	reign of Charles X	1827	Hugo, *Préface de Cromwell*
		1829–48	Balzac, *Comédie Humaine*
1830	Revolution of July	1830	Battle of *Hernani*
1830–48	reign of Louis-Philippe	1831	Hugo, *Notre-Dame de Paris* Stendhal, *Le Rouge et le Noir*
		1835	Musset, *Lorenzaccio*
		1839	Stendhal, *La Chartreuse de Parme*
1848	Revolution of Feb.	1848–50	Chateaubriand, *Mémoires d'Outre-Tombe*
1848–51	Second Republic		
1851	Coup d'état du 2 déc.	1852	L. de Lisle, *Poèmes Antiques* Gautier, *Emaux et camées*
1852–70	Second Empire; Napoleon III	1853	Nerval, *Chimères, Aurélia*
		1856	Hugo, *Contemplations*
		1857	Flaubert, *Madame Bovary* Baudelaire, *Les Fleurs du Mal*
		1862	Hugo, *Les Misérables*
		1869	Verlaine, *Fêtes Galantes* Lautréamont, *Maldoror*

HISTORY		LITERATURE	
1870–71	Franco-Prussian War	1871–93	Zola, *Les Rougon-Macquart*
1871–1940	Third Republic	1873	Rimbaud, *Une saison en enfer*
1871	La Commune	1876	Mallarmé, *Après-midi d'un faune*
		1884	Huysmans, *A rebours*
		1885	Laforgue, *Complaintes*

EMPIRE AND RESTORATION

EVOLUTION OF IDEAS
AT THE TURN OF THE CENTURY:
idéologues, Maine de Biran, Joseph de Maistre,
Saint-Simon, Fourier, Senancour, Constant

At the end of the 18th century, a new group of *philosophes,* known as
idéologues, succeeded the real *philosophes.* These men gave to the main theses
of the encyclopedists extreme interpretations. Their goal was to found the
science of ideas. As disciples of Locke and Condillac, they believed in the power
of reason and in the doctrine of progress. They wrote a form of psycho-phy-
siology which inspired Stendhal and Taine and other positivists later in the
century. Psychology and morality must be joined with science, according to the
idéologues: Condorcet (1743–1794), the mathematician who edited the *Pensées*
of Pascal and wrote a *Vie de Voltaire;* Destut de Tracy (1754–1836), the most
doctrinaire of the group, with his *Eléments d'idéologie;* Cabanis (1757–1808),
a physician and the most intransigent of the *idéologues* in his *Traité du physique
et du moral de l'homme.*

Napoleon disliked such theories and made life difficult for the *idéologues.*
But the principal opposition came from such metaphysical-minded writers as
Maine de Biran (1766–1824) and Joseph de Maistre (1754–1821). According
to Maine de Biran (*Considérations sur les rapports du physique et du moral des hommes*), the nature of man is formed not by his thinking (as Descartes would claim)
and not by his sensations (as the *idéologues* would claim), but by the effort of
his will. Maine de Biran drew semi-religious conclusions from his analysis of
man's effort.

With such a writer as Joseph de Maistre we encounter an interpretation of
the Revolution as a curse of humanity. He was born in Chambéry, in Savoie,
and when the revolutionary troups invaded Savoie in 1797, he took refuge in
Lausanne. The king of Sardinia then sent him to Saint Petersburg where he stayed for fourteen years as *ministre plénipotentiaire.* His masterpiece, *Les Soirées
de Saint-Pétersbourg* (1821), is a series of eleven conversations (*entretiens*) of a
noble French émigré, a Russian senator, and himself. As in his earlier work,
Considérations sur la France (1796), he denounces the Revolution as a sacrilege

that had attempted to put man in the place of God, that had executed Louis XVI who was both king and pontif. De Maistre wrote like a prophet, with the violence of d'Aubigné and Bossuet, and tried to restore, after what he considered the sins of the 18th century, the sanctity of the throne and the altar. The subtitle to *Les Soirées* is indicative of his thesis: *Entretiens sur le gouvernement temporel de la Providence*. He accepted and incorporated in his writings illuminist and theosophist theories when they did not contradict doctrines of the Roman Church.

Joseph's younger brother Xavier de Maistre (1763–1852) was less polemical. He served for years in the Russian army and wrote his semi-amused, semi-malicious reflections in the form of an unpretentious novel, *Voyage autour de ma chambre* (1794).

Whereas the duc de Saint-Simon, author of the *Mémoires*, described the collapse of French society under Louis XIV, his great-nephew le comte de Saint-Simon (1710–1825), without being a socialist in any strict sense, helped to prepare the advent of socialism in France. He served first as an officer in the American War of Independence, and when he returned to France he amassed a fortune, lost it, and died in abject poverty. He wrote innumerable tracts on social and economic problems. At one time he had as secretary a young *normalien*, Augustin Thierry, the future historian, and at another moment his secretary was Auguste Comte, the future social philosopher and positivist.

Saint-Simon launched a new religion based on the principle of a society that must "produce," using the term *producteurs*. The wealth of a country, he thought, comes from those who produce: scholars, writers, industrialists and inventors. In the new society a man would be rewarded in terms of the work he does and his capacity for work. Saint-Simon attacked *les oisifs* and praised *les producteurs*. *Le catéchisme des industriels* (1823) was written just before his death.

The son of a cloth manufacturer (*drapier*) from Besançon, Charles Fourier invented an elaborate system to solve all social problems. The new society was to be based on *la phalange*, the "phalanx" or social unit. In a *phalanstère* (from *phalange* and *monastère*), a group of men and women would work willingly and enthusiastically for a greater productivity than if they were coerced to work. Work would be divided, labor alternated with leisure, and women would be emancipated. *Le fouriérisme* played a role in the revolution of 1848. It spread as a social doctrine in England and especially in the United States. Zola's last three novels, *Fécondité*, *Travail* and *Vérité*, drew upon Fourier's theories.

Some years before the major novelists began publishing in the 19th century, about 1830, two brief "confessional" books continued the French tradition of the analytical novel: *Obermann* (1804) of Senancour (1770–1846), and *Adolphe* of Benjamin Constant (1767–1830), written in 1807 and published in 1816.

The sadness, the sentimental disappointments, and the solitude of Senancour's life are reflected in *Obermann*, composed of eighty-nine letters. This is the intimate journal of a man attracted by spiritual problems, by those doctrines that offer an experience of transcendence over life. The novel contains dissertations on Pythagoras and the symbolism of numbers, on Swedenborg, and on illuminist doctrines. In the midst of mankind, Obermann feels alone and dreams of an unrealizable happiness. He is one of the first romantic heroes doomed to unhappiness because of his temperament as well as the circumstances in his life.

Constant, born in Lausanne of a French family that had expatriated itself after the revocation of the edict of Nantes, became a French citizen in 1794. A much-travelled European, his tumultuous liaison with Mme de Staël lasted sixteen years. Constant was with her in Coppet (Switzerland) between 1805 and 1807, when he wrote *Adolphe* as a way of ending his love affair and escaping from an over-demanding difficult mistress.

Adolphe, a model for the short psychological novel, gives a fairly accurate portrait of Constant himself, as the hero who is brilliant but unstable, more interested in self-observation than any kind of action. Ellénore has traits of Mme de Staël and other women Constant had known. The details of the analysis are unmercifully precise. Adolphe grows tired of Ellénore, but pities her. After her death, his life seems empty to him. The book is more analytical than *La Princesse de Clèves* and less cynical than *Les Liaisons dangereuses*. The lover is much younger than the mistress (although Constant and Staël were almost the same age.) Adolphe is both a coldly determined seducer and an impassioned lover. The analysis of the basic contradiction is remarkably sustained. "Il n'y a point d'unité complète dans l'homme, et presque jamais personne n'est tout à fait sincère ni tout à fait de mauvaise foi"—this psychological ambiguity of Adolphe separates him from the classical hero. Constant studies in his novel the psychology of the subconscious—the automaton type of gesture, speech and attitude that love, or the semblance of love, is able to bring about.

Napoleon too was a writer during the early years of the century. His proclamations were succinct and imperious, effective when read to the troups or when posted on public buildings. He read widely, and even during military campaigns insisted on having the new publications sent to him from Paris. Napoleon understood the power that writers can have, a power that Caesar and Louis XIV knew, as did De Gaulle in our time. His two rivals for fame were the writers Mme de Staël and Chateaubriand.

Legally, Mme de Staël was not French. Her German grandfather had been naturalized a Swiss. Germaine Necker was born in Paris because her father, Jacques Necker, was a Genevan diplomat at that time in the French capital. The girl grew up in Geneva, one of the truly cosmopolitan centers of Europe. Her mother held a typical 18th-century salon in Paris where the young girl listened avidly to the conversation. Of all the literatures of Europe, she probably knew French the least well. Fiercely independent in spirit, somewhat mannish in appearance, Germaine Necker did not attract the type of man who might have dominated her.

Le Baron de Staël, a Swede, married her for her dowry. (She was one of the wealthiest heiresses of Europe.) Unhappy in her marriage, she turned passionately to literature and politics. Her first salon, in the rue du Bac (Staël had been appointed the Swedish ambassador in Paris), favored the Revolution. From time to time she withdrew to her château de Coppet on Lake Geneva. She had several lovers, of whom Benjamin Constant was only one. She believed in the rights of passionate love, and expressed herself on the subject as flamboyantly as had Louise Labé in the 16th century, Mlle de Scudéry in the 17th, or Mlle de Lespinasse in the 18th century. At one point she longed to appropriate the young military genius Bonaparte, but their relationship disintegrated quickly; their last meeting was in the winter of 1800-1801, when she felt insulted by the Corsican. Both figures seemed almost ridiculous: Napoleon in his eagerness to escape from her, and Mme de Staël in her defiance of the emerging tyrant. He exiled her in 1803, depriving her of Paris and the conversations that only Paris provided.

Mme de Staël had published in 1800 an ambitious book, strongly influenced by Rousseau, who had abolished for himself the concepts of literary models, literary recipes and literary rules. The title seemed Rousseauistic: *De la littérature considérée dans ses rapports avec les institutions sociales*. In this work, Mme de Staël studied the many relationships existing between literature and all aspects of civilization: religion, government and customs. She tried to prove that literature and social institutions are allied and change and develop together— Latin literature, for example, she thought superior to Greek because it came after Greek.

In *De L'Allemagne* (1810), she distinguished between literatures of the north, permeated with the fog of England and Germany and illustrated in Ossian, and literatures of the south, sunlit and characterized by the formal perfection of the Greeks and Latins and illustrated in Homer. Literatures of the north were "romantic," according to Mme de Staël, and those of the south "classical."

Since in France classical literature was transplanted from antiquity, it was not indigenous and not popular. She predicted the development of romantic literature in France because it *was* indigenous and could be perfected. Largely under her influence, critics began to examine works of art not so much in themselves but as products of a culture.

Between these books of theory, Mme de Staël wrote two novels: *Delphine* (1802), an epistolary novel, and *Corinne* (1807) the story of a superior woman, a poet in Italy who is not able to find happiness in love. *Corinne* announces the drama of woman's liberation which Simone de Beauvoir analyzed in the 20th century.

Napoleon continued his persecution of Mme de Staël, and she, at the end, had her revenge by joining the coalition against him. After the emperor's defeat, it became a commonplace to say that there were three great powers in Europe: England, Russia and Mme de Staël.

CHATEAUBRIAND (1768–1848)

A Breton, born in Saint-Malo of an aristocratic family, François-René de Chateaubriand described in detail his childhood in *Mémoires d'outre-tombe:* his daydreams, the austere sadness of the château de Combourg where he lived for two years, his elderly unsympathetic father who had made a fortune in slave trade, his cold, superstitious mother, and his sister Lucille, whom he loved. In this autobiography, which he began writing when he was forty, in 1809, he created the type of predestined hero, the male counterpart of *la femme fatale.* More then any single writer, Chateaubriand inaugurated and defined the great romantic spell in French literature.

Napoleon, the *parvenu* who became emperor, needed poets to immortalize him and develop his legend, but Chateaubriand was a legitimate noble who needed only himself, and he deliberately described himself in pose after pose that created the type of romantic hero: the lonely Breton boy who fell in love with the sea and the wind and the birds nesting in the turrets of his feudal castle; the handsome French officer in the New World, in Baltimore and Philadelphia; the civilized European in the virgin forests of America; and later, the writer who was world-famous, representing his country and defending the traditional religion of his country. He always remained an aloof feudal figure. Saint-Malo was his birthplace and Chateaubriand saw to it that a rock in the harbor became his tomb. He slightly altered most of the facts of his life in order to make his life legendary and "romantic." In describing his sister Lucille as Amélie in *René*, he exaggerated her incestuous feelings for her brother. He spent five months in America in 1791, and invented a large part of the information in his *Voyage en Amérique* (1827). In order to describe the parts of the country he did not visit, he simply pillaged travel books of the day.

On his return to France in 1792, he married a rich heiress in Saint-Malo whom he soon deserted for twelve years. He fought in the émigré army (*l'armée des Princes*), was wounded, and settled in England for seven years. His first book, *Essai sur les révolutions* (1797), published in London, was a potpourri of Montesquieu, Voltaire and Rousseau, in which he tried to prove that the French Revolution was nothing new in the history of mankind. At the same time he was working on a huge prose epic, *Les Natchez*, the story of an Indian tribe in America, which he hoped would exalt natural man, the noble savage (*le bon sauvage.*)

He was still in London in 1799 when two letters reached him telling him of the death of his mother and his sister Julie. His answer was the phrase: "J'ai pleuré et j'ai cru," announcing his return to Catholicism, and the undertaking of his work, *Le Génie du Christianisme*. But he had already made plans for the writing of this apology. He knew that such a work was needed—that since the Revolution many Frenchmen wanted to return to their religious faith. Bonaparte also realized this. Chateaubriand returned to France in May, 1800, and Bonaparte, who was the same age as Chateaubriand, returned at the same time from the Egyptian campaign.

In 1801, Chateaubriand published *Atala*, a short love story, as exotic in its new world setting as *Paul et Virginie* had been fourteen years earlier. Atala is a Christian girl who loves the Indian Chactas but cannot marry him because of a vow made to her dying mother. The story had all the necessary ingredients to assure its success at that particular moment: the picture of a primitive world, the religious theme, a tragic and very sensual love story.

Atala was the publicity announcement of *Le Génie du Christianisme* (the word *génie* here means "spirit" and not "genius.") Its publication on April 15, 1802, was synchronized with the Concordat made legal by the First Consul Bonaparte, April 14. The 18th of April was Easter Sunday, when a *Te Deum* opened the doors of Notre Dame.

From that moment on, Chateaubriand's pose was that of defender of the faith, of the apologist for Christianity who opposed Voltaire's war cry: "Ecrasons l'infâme." As apologetics, the book argues for the truth of Christianity by demonstrating its achievements in art, learning and social action. It is also a landmark in the history of literary criticism, rehabilitating the Middle Ages as a glorious past in French national life. In the wake of Rousseau and Bernardin de Saint-Pierre, it called attention to the color and movements of exterior nature. Chateaubriand claimed that he had replaced the sterile criticism of faults by the fertile criticism of beauty.

Bonaparte gave Chateaubriand a diplomatic post in Rome, but the writer soon broke with the First Consul. In 1805, he published separately *René*, an extract from *Le Génie*. In this brief story, Chateaubriand analyzes what he called the malady of the day, *le mal du siècle*, a form of melancholy unknown to the ancients and not sufficiently observed by the moderns. An entire generation recognized itself in René, as an entire generation recognized itself in Eliot's *Prufrock* in the 20th century. René is the romantic hero *par excellence:* aristocratic, narcissistic, proud, sterile, bored, suffering from the incestuous love of his sister. René is the hero who remains adolescent in feelings and outlook, *l'enfant du siècle* of Musset, Hernani and Ruy Blas of Hugo, and later, in the 20th century, Lafcadio of Gide, Paul of Cocteau, and even James Dean in America.

Less successfully than in his portrayal of the new hero, Chateaubriand evoked early Christian times in *Les Martyrs* (1809) and wrote a biography of a 17th-century Trappist monk, *La Vie de Rancé* (1844). Today his greatest literary achievement seems to be *Les Mémoires d'outre-tombe*. During his last years, some of the more purely autobiographical parts of *Les Mémoires* were published as *feuilletons* in newspapers. The first posthumous editions were incomplete. Not until 1948 was an authoritative critical edition brought out by Levaillant. The larger part of the work is devoted to Chateaubriand's role in politics. The earlier part presents a stylized picture of Chateaubriand, in an elaborate prose, a religious style of a Massillon secularized by a Rousseau and made colorful by a Bernardin de Saint-Pierre. We see French society under the *Ancien Régime*, the Revolution of 1789, the Empire, the Restoration, the Revolution of 1830. Some of the memorable portraits in the work are those of the writer's great friend Mme Récamier, of Talleyrand and Danton, of Louis XVIII and Louis-Philippe, and of the man Chateaubriand both admired and hated: Napoléon premier.

Romanticism was, first, in France, a new spirit attempting to define itself in periodicals (*La Muse Française*), in newspapers (*Le Globe*), and in manifestoes (*la préface de Cromwell*), in literary circles: le salon de l'Arsenal and le cénacle de la rue Notre Dame des Champs. It ended by becoming a successful struggle for a renewal of literature and art. The flamboyant triumph of Hugo's *Hernani* in 1830 marked the success of the new school.

Charles Nodier (1783–1844), poet, novelist, and short-story writer, was appointed librarian of the Arsenal in 1824. For six years, on Sunday evenings, he was a gracious host of gatherings that danced, recited poetry and talked. There some of the balding classicists mingled with the youthful long-haired romantics: Lamartine, Hugo, Vigny, Musset, Mérimée, Dumas, Nerval, Gautier, Balzac, the painter Delacroix, and the sculptor David d'Angers.

In 1827, Hugo published an important doctrinal preface to his drama *Cromwell*, which consecrated him leader of the new school. With Sainte-Beuve, Hugo founded a *cénacle* whose meetings were held in the poet's apartment, rue Notre Dame des Champs. (*Cénacle* is from *cena*, "supper." *La cène* is the French for "last supper." *Cénacle* came to mean a club gathering of writers, artists and philosophers.) In his preface to *Hernani*, Hugo defined romanticism (*le romantisme*) as *le libéralisme en littérature*. "La liberté littéraire est fille de la liberté politique. Ce principe est celui du siècle."

The movement of romanticism was extremely complex, but fundamentally it represented the determination of the artist (see, for example, Delacroix), of the composer (Berlioz) and of the writer (Hugo) to express this individualism. If classicism was the search for universal, abstract truth, romanticism was the description of the particular experience of a single individual. Rather than following "reason" (*la raison*) as Boileau had advised, the typical romantic preferred to analyze the mysterious aspects of his sensibility, of his emotions, his aspirations, and even his madness. The rules of classical art had to be put aside so that the freshness of emotions and personal experiences and dreams might be transcribed. Hugo opposed some of the rules of versification, as well as the classical distinction between comedy and tragedy, and the three unities.

The romantic revolt was also against some aspects of religion and the social order. The new type of somber predestined hero was in revolt against society and even against God. *Le beau ténébreux* appealed to the younger generation under the Restoration. He was characterized by a vague ill-defined melancholy that made him unsuitable for bourgeois society. Baudelaire and Flaubert both gave extreme expressions to this hero's break with society.

More frenzied, more *maudit* than *le beau ténébreux*, was the hero of the horror stories, the *romans noirs*, that attracted Balzac, Nodier, and Hugo. The real initiators of the demonized romantic hero were Lewis and Byron in England, Maturin in Ireland, and Sade in France. The *macabre* was an important development of romanticism. It has been assigned its rightful place by the Italian scholar Mario Praz in his book *The Romantic Agony*.

Under the influence of the German writer Hoffmann, a literature of fantasy enjoyed a considerable vogue in France. This theme of the fantastic is not to be confused with *le merveilleux* of the Middle Ages or with the fairy story or mythological tale. It is a tendency toward the cultivation of the morbid, the phenomena of nightmares and hallucinations. The short story, such as Poe later used in America, was the principal form used for the fantasy experiences, as seen in the writings of Nodier, Balzac, Nerval, Gautier, Mérimée and Pétrus Borel (1809–1859), who called himself *le lycanthrope*, the "werewolf"; or the prose poems of Aloysius Bertrand (1807–1841) in his collection *Gaspard de la nuit, fantaisie à la manière de Rembrandt et de Callot* (this title is perhaps an imitation of Hoffmann's *Fantasie Stücke in Callots Manier*); and the prose poems of Baudelaire (*Spleen de Paris*).

The influence of Walter Scott's historical novels, in which a picturesque resurrection of the past is emphasized, is clearly visible in Vigny's *Cinq Mars*, in Balzac's *Les Chouans*, in Mérimée's *La Chronique du règne de Charles IX*, and in Hugo's *Notre-Dame-de-Paris*. It is also apparent in the dramas of Hugo and of Alexandre Dumas (*Henri III et sa cour*), and in poems of Hugo (*Les Orientales*), Théophile Gautier, Leconte de Lisle, and other parnassians.

The romantics followed, therefore, an aesthetics, and a social philosophy which became more clearly defined after the Revolution of 1830. Man must be liberated as well as art. Many of the romantics dreamed of and wrote about a future for mankind where justice and brotherhood would reign: Lamartine, Hugo, George Sand, Lamennais, Michelet. They expressed an idealism in writing about society, and at times a mystical idealism that was religious. The illuminist doctrines of Swedenborg and the search for God and the Eternal Woman are in Balzac (*Seraphita*) and the sonnets of Nerval (*Artémis.*)

Rousseau used the term *romantique* in speaking of the lac de Bienne. (The "lake" is a romantic theme for both Rousseau and Lamartine.) The word reached its fuller meaning when it was opposed to *classique*. Perhaps the best definition of *le romantisme* is that developed by Stendhal when he calls it the right of a generation to express its own sensitivity in new art forms. *Le classicisme* would then be the imposing of the aesthetic rules of earlier generations on the present generation. Romanticism refers therefore to what is dynamic and spontaneous and individualistic. Classicism is the defender of the past, of inherited positions and principles. Romanticism is a youthful force that upsets and welcomes other literatures from other countries.

Before Rousseau there was no direct communication between the reader and the personality of the writer. But since Rousseau the writer takes his reader into confidence about himself, his personal life, his neuroses and idyosyncrasies, his moral and immoral sensitivity. A bond of familiarity is established between the writer and his reader. Romanticism was the first literary movement that defined the gap between the generations of the young and the old, that defined the right of the young to express their most intimate feelings and oppose the older generations. Classical literature had no trace of this opposition between young and old.

LAMARTINE (1790–1869)

The 19th century was an age of great poetry in France, Alphonse de Lamartine was the earliest in date of the major poets. His *Méditations Poétiques* (1820) was a new kind of poetry, the first volume of romantic verse. Forty to fifty years later, the poetry of Baudelaire and Rimbaud was destined to have a far greater influence on the 20th century than the poetry of the romantics, with the possible exception of Hugo's.

Lamartine was a Burgundian, born in Mâcon and raised in the village of Milly, fifteen kilometers from Mâcon. The family, somewhat impoverished by the Revolution, lived on the produce of their simple country estate: wheatfields and vineyards. As a child, Alphonse led the life of a peasant. He was educated in a pension in Lyon. At eighteen, he returned to Milly where he lived until 1820. He hunted, rode horseback, oversaw the vineyards, and avidly read Rousseau, Ossian, Mme de Staël, Chateaubriand, and Goethe's *Werther* (which inspired thoughts of suicide in him, as the book did with countless other young men.)

Lamartine was one of the many writers of the age—Byron, Shelley, Goethe, Mme de Staël, Chateaubriand, Stendhal—whose travels to Italy inspired them to write of it as a romantic dreamworld. Of all these writers, Lamartine was the least interested in the landscapes and ruins of Italy, and the most interested in the Italian gambling houses. *Graziella*, a short novel written in Ischia in 1844, is a much altered account of his love (in 1811) for a Neapolitan girl who probably worked in a tobacco factory (similar to the situation in Mérimée's *Carmen* of 1845).

After the Italian episode, and after the return to power of Louis XVIII, on Napoleon's abdication (1814), Lamartine resumed a life of boredom, a type of life that Chateaubriand and Vigny also described. Threatened with tuberculosis in 1816, he was sent to Aix-les-Bains, on the Lac du Bourget in Savoie. There he was treated and cured, and there he met Mme Julie Charles, a young tuberculosis patient with whom he fell deeply in love. (M. Charles, seventy years old, was permanent secretary of the Académie des Sciences in Paris). Julie died the following year. Largely because of this experience of love, death and religious faith, Lamartine became a poet.

After the prose writers Rousseau, Mme de Staël and Chateaubriand, Lamartine recast his personal experience in poetry and sought, successfully, to turn it into a universal experience. The first edition of *Les Méditations Poétiques* contained twenty-six poems. *Le Lac* and *L'Immortalité* were written before Julie's death, and *L'Isolement* is on the poet's grief after her death. There is a sense of appeasement in *Le Soir*, *Le Souvenir*, *Le Vallon*, *L'Automne*. And still other poems *La Foi*, *Dieu*, *La Prière*, *L'Homme*; speak of a renewed religious fervor. These poems are among the original messages of French romanticism. *Le Lac* is a plea for memory: "O temps, suspends ton vol!" The large number of French readers of this light volume believed that an authentic poet had been born.

Lamartine continued to write about Julie's death (he calls her Elvire in the poems), and three years later he published *Nouvelles Méditations*. With his collection of poems of 1830, *Harmonies poétiques et religieuses*, he took on the definite position of a religious poet. He spoke of God as present in nature, present in the voices of plants and trees (*Hymne du Matin* and *Novissima Verba*).

He felt impelled and inspired to compose a vast epic poem of which he ᴠ ⸱ ᴄᴛe only two unrelated parts, *Jocelyn* (1836), in the form of a diary of a country priest, the inspiration of a humble man for God's love; and *La Chute d'un ange* (1838), his only publication that was a failure in his time. In approximately 11,000 lines, the poem narrates the love of the angel Cédar for Daïdha, a descendent of Cain. Cédar, because of his guilty passion, is doomed to become a man, lose the woman he loves, and die at the stake. He recovers his angelic form after nine incarnations. There are memorable passages: the description of the earth before the flood, the chorus of the cedars of Lebanon (*le choeur des cèdres du Liban*).

Despite his hostile feelings toward Lamartine, Leconte de Lisle, in the next generation, was the first to praise *La Chute d'un ange*, and today critics admire it, not as remarkable poetry in a technical sense, but as a myth in which Lamartine developed his idea of man. It is seen today as the poem announced in *Le Génie du Christianisme*, an attack on the encyclopedic spirit and that form of sensuality characteristic of the 18th century.

Lamartine is important for having taught France that poetry is a part of human nature. Subsequent poets, between Baudelaire and Valéry, later taught France that poetry is an art. The best poetry written during the Second Empire was to a large extent a reaction against Lamartinian poetry. Immediately after 1820, Lamartine was applauded unanimously, and soon after 1850 he was no longer in fashion.

ALFRED DE VIGNY (1797-1863)

Vigny was born in Loches, in Touraine, at a time when it was dangerous to be born a noble. The revolutionists were hard on his family. His father had been an officer in the king's army. Alfred studied mostly at home, was gifted in languages, and prepared for Polytechnique. After Waterloo, he began a dreary inactive existence in barracks, in Courbevoie, Vincennes, Rouen.

Vigny married an English girl, who soon became an invalid, half mad, unwilling to learn French and unwilling to read the poems of her husband. At the age of thirty, Vigny resigned from the army. Already at that age he appeared as a man aloof from everyone, a solitary figure who scorned society and human relationships.

As a poet—his first collection, *Poèmes*, appeared in 1822—he showed none of the facility or fluidity of Lamartine, none of the delicacy of romantic verse. The Bible had taught him the greatness of myths, from Chénier he learned of the voluptuousness of Greek marble, and from Byron, the insolence and the independence of the dandy.

Eloa, a long poem of 1824, inaugurated the use of the Bible in romantic poetry. Eloa is a feminine angel born from a tear of Christ. She hears about the story of Lucifer, the fallen archangel, and tries to find him in the depths of the earth. *Moïse* was written just before *Eloa*, and included in the collection of 1826,

Poèmes antiques et modernes. Moïse is the solitary romantic speaking with God at the top of Sinai, as Byron's *Manfred* (1817) speaks with God at the top of the Jungfrau. He is the genius misunderstood by men and feared by women..The poem is a picture of geography and history as well as an analysis of one of the poses of the romantic hero, *le génie incompris.*

The prose work *Stello* (1832) and the play *Chatterton* (1835) both develop the theme of the poet persecuted by society. Especially in *Chatterton* (based on the life of the English poet), written for and played by Vigny's mistress Marie Dorval, Vigny shows the modern genius transformed into a pariah, and his solitude and unadaptablity to society. The play's hero refuses any compromise. The only solution is suicide.

Servitude et Grandeur Militaires (1835) is made up of three stories which depict the soldier as another pariah rejected by society. Vigny did not exalt the soldier and militarism as Joseph de Maistre had done, but saw the ordinary soldier (*le troupier*) and even officers as slaves. But in the soldier's law of obedience and sacrifice, Vigny found an example of man safeguarding his honor.

After a seven-year liaison, Vigny broke with the actress Marie Dorval and composed in his poem *La Colère de Samson* a vituperation against woman in general, in which the goodness of man (*la bonté d'Homme*), Samson, is contrasted with the cunning of woman (*la ruse de Femme*), Dalilah.

> Et plus ou moins, la Femme est toujours Dalila.

Feeling himself betrayed by his mistress, by God, by society, by the literary world in Paris, by politics, Vigny shut himself up in his estate of Maine-Giraud in the department of La Charente. His pessimism was somewhat offset by the lesson in stoicism which the writing of his poem *La mort du loup* gave him in 1843. The wolf, tracked by dogs and hunters, and dying in silence, is another symbol of the desperate romantic hero, another candidate for suicide as Chatterton had been.

In his life of a feudal lord (Sainte-Beuve called Vigny's castle *une tour d'ivoire,* by which he implied that the poet was escaping from society and betraying his duty to the world), he continued until his death to write philosophical poems, of which the most celebrated are *Le Mont des Oliviers, La Maison du Berger,* and *La Bouteille à la mer.* These poems appeared in the posthumous volume, *Les Destinées* in 1864. He also wrote his *Mémoires* and discussed the subjects of his poems in his *Journal d'un poète.*

The writings of Alfred de Vigny are very much the image of his temperament and the translation of his personal experience and philosophy. He felt humiliated as a noble no longer powerful, as an officer without wars, as a poet misunderstood by his generation, and as a lover who was deceived. He was tormented by problems of politics, religion, and metaphysics. Unable to express himself easily in the kind of effusive lyric poetry that Lamartine wrote, he chose concrete symbols suitable for the themes and ideas of his writing: Moses as the terrifying unloved genius (*Moïse*); the bottle containing important discoveries and thrown into the sea by a captain, illustrating the obstacles to man's progress and the positive message that knowledge and experience must be passed on to future generations (*La Bouteille à la Mer*).

VICTOR HUGO (1802–1885)

The name of Victor Hugo is as well known in France and abroad as Jeanne d'Arc, Louis XIV and Napoleon. In a purely literary sense, he was the leader of the romantics, successful in every genre: novels, plays, poetry. He believed his mission was sacred. In exile for twenty years (1850–1870) on the islands of Jersey and Guernsey, he wrote with the conviction of a chastiser (*Les Châtiments*) and the exaltation of a visionary (*Les Contemplations*).

He was born in Besançon, in La Franche-Comté (*Ce siècle avait deux ans*) because his father, a colonel, was stationed there. The boy accompanied his father, who soon became a general of the Empire, abroad, notably to Italy and Spain. He was a student in Paris where he discovered very early a literary vocation. At fourteen he wrote in one of his notebooks, "Je veux être Chateaubriand ou rien." Hugo considered himself a royalist when he published his first book, *Odes et Poésies diverses*, in 1822, and was given a pension by Louis XVIII. The collection was augmented in 1824 and 1826, and given its definitive form in 1828: *Odes et Ballades*. These were poems of commonplace themes and conventional language.

His drama on *Cromwell* was unplayable, but his *préface de Cromwell* (1827) made Hugo famous. An English company had been playing Shakespeare in the Odéon in 1827. Prior to that time, Stendhal had discussed the controversy over the theater that romantics and classicists had been carrying on. In his *préface*, Hugo distinguished three ages of poetry: primitive times, represented by the lyric, in the use of odes; antiquity, represented by the epic, Homer's; and the modern age by drama, because Christianity had revealed to man his dual nature of spirit and body, and the ceaseless struggle between the two. Shakespeare best illustrated this modern genre for Hugo, but it is obvious that he considered himself the French Shakespeare.

The first performances of *Hernani* in 1830 were important in the annals of the French theatre. They consecrated the triumph of the young long-haired romantics (*Les Jeune-France*) led by Théophile Gautier, who in his *Histoire du romantisme* described the performances as the alignment of two armies, and even two civilizations. Gautier's costume, worn only on opening night, has passed into French mythology: green trousers with a black velvet band on the side, and a rose-colored vest. All the celebrities of the day were present—Berlioz, Balzac, Sainte-Beuve, Mérimée, Delacroix, Benjamin Constant, and, ancestor of them all, François-René de Chateaubriand.

Notre-Dame-de-Paris (1831) was Hugo's re-creation of a monument and his first prose masterpiece. His sources were several technical books and his own imagination. He resurrected medieval Paris, with its narrow streets, its smells and its darkness, the court of miracles, the slums where thieves congregated (*le quartier des truands*). The deformed bell-ringer of Notre-Dame, Quasimodo, resembled a gargoyle. Unable to analyze complicated characters, Hugo created either monsters or the pure gypsy girl Esmeralda. The compelling atmosphere of the novel is a literary achievement.

The poems Hugo wrote for four collections published between 1831 and 1840 were primarily on emotional experiences. *Les Feuilles d'automne* (1831) has pages on the poet's suffering for the disinherited of the earth: *pour les pauvres*. *Les Chants du crépuscule* (1835) contains some of his first poems about his love for Juliette Drouet. *Les Voix Intérieures* (1837) evokes his childhood and memories of his brother; *A Eugène, vicomte H. Les Rayons et les Ombres* (1840) is an enlarging of earlier themes: the innocence of childhood, the mysteriousness of nature (*Oceano Nox*), and his passion for Juliette (*Tristesse d'Olympio*). Hugo is Olympio evoking the past as he walks in the valley of La Bièvre.

His play *Les Burgraves*, more static than dramatic, was a failure in 1843, and he published nothing for the next nine years. After the Revolution of 1848, he had at first some faith in Louis-Napoleon, nephew of Napoleon I, but as a result of the Coup d'état of December 2, 1851, when Louis-Napoleon became Napoleon III, Hugo went into exile—first to Brussels, where he was penniless, and then to the island of Jersey, an English island in the Channel where French is spoken. Between 1852 and 1853 he wrote *Les Châtiments*, 7000 lines of angry accusation against Napoleon III. This collection surpasses the other French works written in the satiric mode: the *Discours* of Ronsard, the *Tragiques* of d'Aubigné, and the *Iambes* of Chénier. *L'Expiation* is a short epic poem in *Les Châtiments* in which Hugo verbally punishes Napoleon I for the 18 Brumaire when Bonaparte made himself First Consul, Napoleon III for his insignificance and pettiness, and himself for ever having given his support to the nephew of the great Napoleon.

When he was expelled from Jersey in 1855, he went to the neighboring island of Guernsey and bought Hauteville House with the royalties he received from *Les Contemplations* (1856). At the top of the house he had a glass cage built, a look-out, where he worked for fifteen years. He rose at dawn, drank a cup of cold coffee, ate two raw eggs, and wrote, standing, in full view of the sky and the sea.

Les Contemplations, in two volumes, of more than 11,000 lines, were poems on all of Hugo's interests: spiritualism and tipping tables, saint-simonism, efforts to describe the experiences of his youth, and his loves and sorrows. The collection is the history of his heart. *La Fête de Thérèse* is a poem reminiscent of a Watteau painting, with the poet setting out for the island of love. *Pauca meae* is a group of poems on his daughter Léopoldine. *A Villequier* is about a visit Hugo made to the grave of Léopoldine, who had died in a drowning accident. It is perhaps the greatest poem in French on paternal love. *Les Mages* is a poem on eighty colossal figures who, according to Hugo, had served humanity best: poets and philosophers, writers and theologians (no statesmen and no generals); and including men like Michelangelo, Aeschylus, Shakespeare, Phidias, Socrates, Beethoven, Saint Paul.

On the advice of his publisher Hetzel, Hugo prepared next *La Légende des Siècles* (1859), short epic poems based on the Bible, mythology and world history. He considered *La Légende* the first part of a triptych, to be completed by *La Fin de Satan* and *Dieu*. *La Légende des siècles* is the story of the ascension of humanity during which there are constant struggles between the forces of good and evil. The poet called upon history, religion, science and fables to describe the successive phases of man's ascent, beginning with the story of Eve, mother of men, and ending with the Revolution, mother of the people.

Les Misérables, in ten volumes, was published in 1862 in Belgium, and represents a rest for Hugo from the gigantic effort of *La Légende des Siècles*. The title of the long novel designates the victims of the social order. Somewhat inspired by Eugène Sue's very successful *Mystères de Paris*, also in ten volumes (1842–43), Hugo had had the idea of *Les Misérables* in his mind for some time. The theme of pity for those oppressed by society is also found in *Les Contemplations*. Hugo's imagination favored the use of antithesis: good and evil, light and darkness, God and Satan. In *Les Misérables*, it is Jean Valjean the convict (*le forçat*) and Javert the detective (*le policier*). Jean Valjean is redeemed and in-spired by the charity of Mgr. Myriel, bishop of Digne. The novel includes many genres: it is a work of edification, of adoration, and of personal confession. It is the masterpiece of popular fiction, and its success encouraged Hugo to write other novels: *Les Travailleurs de la Mer* (1866), *L'Homme qui rit* (1869), *Quatre-vingt-treize* (1874).

The Prussian invasion of France in 1870 brought about the fall of Napoleon III. As soon as the Republic was proclaimed, Victor Hugo returned to Paris, where he was elected *député* to the Assemblée Nationale. He was dissatisfied with both the Communards and the Versaillais in 1871, and returned to Hauteville House in 1872 for eleven months. Although elected a senator in 1876, he partici-pated very little in public life. His eightieth birthday in 1881 was celebrated by all of Paris. In 1883, he completed *La Légende des Siècles* with a final volume. At his death, his casket was exposed under the Arc de Triomphe, and it was es-timated that 200,000 persons visited it in homage to the writer. His body was then taken to the Panthéon. It was the most spectacular funeral in the history of France.

The two unfinished parts of Hugo's epic were published posthumously: *La Fin de Satan* (1886) and *Dieu* (1891). They represent his most sustained ap-proach to the mystical experience and attempt, in very remarkable passages, to show the merging of evil with the good. The verbal richness and the vision of these last works make it impossible to deny the greatness of Hugo. Most of the major French poets who followed him were in his debt, particularly Baude-laire, Leconte de Lisle, Rimbaud, Mallarmé, Claudel. When André Gide was asked to name the greatest French writer, his answer, "Victor Hugo, hélas!" confirmed the greatness of the man and at the same time recalled the defects of his greatness.

ALFRED DE MUSSET (1810–1857)

The youngest of the four principal romantic poets, Musset was born in Paris, and exemplified the sophisticated critical mind of the young Parisian, as Villon, Moliere and Voltaire had before him. He was a brilliant pupil at the lycée Henri IV, and, like Voltaire, won most of the prizes at the end of each school year.

Between the ages of seventeen and twenty, Musset appeared often at L'Arsenal, where he played the role of dandy, of young prince bored with life, or of young *gavroche* scorning his elders. His first volume, published when he was twenty, *Contes d'Espagne et d'Italie*, was an indirect jibe at Hugo's *Les Orientales*. Unlike Hugo, Musset had never been to Italy and Spain, but he wanted to prove that his imagination of a Parisian could be equally exotic. He was insolent, *l'enfant terrible*, in his mocking of Chateaubriand and Lamartine and Hugo. He drank heavily and at an early age suffered from dipsomania. And yet Musset remained, despite those excesses and despite his posturing of *enfant terrible*, a curious combination of idealist and sceptic.

In 1830, his play *La Nuit Vénitienne* was performed at the Odéon, and hissed. Musset sulked over his failure, and decided to write his future plays only for himself (*le spectacle dans un fauteuil*) and for readers sitting under the light of a lamp.

At twenty-three, Musset was initiated to love in a semi-tragic way that involved considerable suffering. George Sand, six years older than the poet, had divorced le baron Dudevant and had come to Paris with her two children in order to live by her writing. She had just broken off her relationship with Jules Sandeau (whose name had given her part of her pseudonym) and had been placed beside Musset at a dinner of *La Revue des Deux Mondes*. Musset's effusive praise of her novel *Indiana* was the literary beginning of their love affair. Even at the outset, with two such striking personalities, there were scenes of near-madness on the part of Musset, which were narrated in Sand's novel *Elle et lui*, written twenty-six years later. She was the dominant member of the couple, famous for her novels *Indiana* and *Lélia*, a forerunner of the women's liberation movement, a woman who smoked cigars and supported herself by her writing.

Their voyage to Venice was a disaster. At first George Sand fell ill with fever and was abandoned by Musset. Then he fell ill with what the Venetian doctor Pagello diagnosed as *une typhoïde nerveuse*! Mme Sand and Pagello became lovers. On his return to Paris, Musset found that everyone was interested in the Venice episode. He asked and received his mistress's permission to write about their love affair. In 1834, he published in *La Revue des Deux Mondes* two plays (*proverbes*, as he called them): *Fantasio* and *On ne badine pas avec l'amour*, and completed his long drama of *Lorenzaccio*. He also began writing his *Confession d'un enfant du siècle*, in which he tried to equate the couple Sand-Musset with famous legendary lovers: Romeo and Juliet, Abélard and Héloïse.

To exhibit her Venetian lover, Sand brought Pagello back with her to

Paris, but he was ill at ease in Parisian society and soon returned to his patients. After breaking off all relationship with George Sand in 1835, Musset finished *La Confession d'un enfant du siècle* and wrote *La Nuit de Mai* and *La Nuit de Décembre*. The suffering poet Musset in the four *Nuit* poems is not as convincing as the ironic, capricious elegant dandy author of the plays.

In 1837, a French actress saw in Saint Petersburg a Russian performance of Musset's *Un Caprice*. Ten years later she played *Un Caprice* at La Comédie-Française. It was a success and from then on most of the comedies were performed, and some have become part of the permanent repertory: *Il faut qu'une porte soit ouverte ou fermée, Le Chandelier, Il ne faut jurer de rien*. Today Musset seems the best dramatist of the romantic movement. The short plays have remained the most popular, but his long historical drama, *Lorenzaccio*, has been revived in recent years. The setting is 16th-century Italy—Lorenzaccio, somewhat reminiscent of Hamlet, assassinates the tyrant Alessandro dei Medici although he knows that his act is futile, since another tyrant will succeed Alessandro. The theater-going public in Paris at the time found Lorenzaccio's act in keeping with existentialist teaching.

STENDHAL (1783–1842)

Henri Beyle spent his first sixteen years with his fairly well-to-do bourgeois family in Grenoble. Even before byronism struck France, he was a youthful Byronic hero whose nature was developed by his longing for happiness. He never ceased being the adolescent, the romantic, in the French sense of *romanesque*, who lived on the stimulation of his senses and the mysterious power of his fantasies.

He went to Paris in 1799 to study at the Ecole Polytechnique, but joined the reserve army in 1800 and reached Milan the day after the victory of Marengo. Milan was a place of enchantment for him. After eighteen months of military service, he resigned from the army and returned to Paris where he was less successful than he had been in Milanese society. Literature was his constant preoccupation. He longed especially to become a dramatist.

He returned to the army in 1806. During the next few years he saw, not the battles of Napoleon, but the aftermath of the battles, the scenes of horror on the battlefields. From 1814 on, Milan became more than ever his favorite city. His first book, *Vies de Haydn, de Mozart et de Métastase*, did not solve the question of what kind of writing he should do. For the publication of *Rome, Naples et Florence*, in 1817, he used the pseudonym of M. de Stendhal, borrowed from the name of a German city, and subsequently life took on for him a new glamor that he was to lose and recover in successive moments of depression and exaltation.

Stendhal returned to Paris in 1821 and published there during the next nine years six books: *De l'Amour, Racine et Shakespeare, Vie de Rossini, Armance* (his first novel), *Promenades dans Rome*, and *Le Rouge et le Noir*. In 1830 he became a consul in the service of Louis-Philippe and was appointed first to Trieste and then to Cività Vecchia, close to Rome. He was bored by everything in Civita Vecchia—by the pettiness connected with his profession and by the dullness of the city. It was there he probably wrote most of *La Chartreuse de Parme* and *Les Chroniques italiennes*.

Just before his death he had the joy of reading Balzac's glowing article on *La Chartreuse*. This praise was the first indication of what "the happy few" were to propagate in the years to come when Henri Beyle had definitively grown into Stendhal.

The writings of Stendhal are an extraordinarily accurate reflection of his personality and his thoughts, combining countless paradoxical conflicts and desires. But these very contradictions made of Stendhal the writer a representative man in the sense that Emerson made of such a figure as Montaigne. Stendhal the sceptic in everything that related to philosophical or theological absolutism and Stendhal the lover of that willed forcefulness in man he called "energy," the deployment of *espagnolisme*, are behind those moments in his work that call forth in the reader a feeling of sympathy for the writer's understanding of foibles and dreams and fantasies, and a feeling of respect for man who—despite foibles, dreams and fantasies—is able to achieve lasting monuments of art.

Alone in Paris, on the rue Neuve-des-Petits Champs (today called the rue des Capucines), almost at the door of the ministry of foreign affairs and close to the Place Vendôme, apoplexy struck Stendhal down on a March day in 1842, and a few hours later he died in his hotel room. Stendhal never had a permanent address, nor a permanent profession. He had no home, no children, and, one can almost say, no mistresses. Those love affairs that had some duration in his life were unhappy.

Each book of Stendhal is the account of a young man's charm that attracts the people around him or instills envy in those who are attracted in a hostile way. When the sensations of Julien (*Le Rouge et le Noir*), of Fabrice (*La Chartreuse de Parme*), of Octave (*Armance*) were described in the present, during the course of the novel's action, the novelist was dramatizing his memories. The novels were an autobiography in retrospect. Stendhal relived in them his own emotional life, and only partly disguised the gestures and costumes. They are what he became in his imagination, in his fantasy-making world. A scandal related in a newspaper or an historical chronicle, found almost by chance, provided a sufficient background for *Le Rouge et le Noir* and for *La Chartreuse de Parme*. Such settings and such starting-points in reality were all Stendhal needed to convert autobiography into fictional biography.

He himself was so struck by what his books represented, by his strange compulsion to write them, by the needs of his nature they satisfied, by the pleasure and the therapeutic cure they provided, that he had to invent a word with which to name this mystery. He used not his pseudonym but his family name, by which he was known as a youth: *le beylisme*. This was the name given by Stendhal to his method, which designated two things at once: a sense of style and composition, and the search for happiness that was indispensable for that method of writing. These two words "search" and "happiness" recapitulate Stendhal's life and art. Later, Marcel Proust used the same word, *la recherche*, in the title of his novel, and referred to Stendhal's phrase in which beauty is defined as *la promesse du bonheur*.

Stendhal's literary autobiography is to be found in two books: *Souvenirs d'égotisme* of 1832, and *Vie de Henry Brulard*. *Souvenirs* is a scrupulous self-analysis. The cult of the self, as found in such a romantic work as Musset's *Confession d'un enfant du siècle*, was not what Stendhal meant by *égotisme*. He exhibited an interest in himself because of a greater interest in the very process of analysis itself. Stendhal was not self-admiring, as was Rousseau in his *Confessions*; neither was he presenting himself as an exceptional human being whose sensitivity sets him apart from mankind, in the way developed by Chateaubriand in *Mémoires d'Outre-tombe*.

In these two books, as well as in his letters, Stendhal appeared the moralist in the manner of a Montaigne and a Gide—a man inhabiting a moral world, who is determined to analyze his conduct in that world in terms of the prevalent moral conventions and in terms of the hypocrisy by which moral conventions are sustained. Henri Beyle was the lonely hero of these two books, and he himself was actually far more lonely than his lonely heroes Julien Sorel, Octave and Fabrice del Dongo.

HONORÉ DE BALZAC (1799-1850)

The name of Balzac evokes the thought of something gigantic and power-ful. This writer was able, in the space of twenty years (1828–1848), to create a literary work of unusual proportions to which he gave the name *La Comédie Humaine*. He completed ninety-one novels and novellas before his death.

His physical size and the variations of his temperament announced the vast-ness in scope and detail of his work that he called *la cathédrale balzacienne*. Al-though often a heavy eater and drinker, he was able to follow for long periods a Spartan regimen of existence, when he consumed a minimal amount of food and wrote for fifteen hours out of a twenty-four hour period. He combined in his nature a deep interest both in mystical studies and "illuminism," and the scientific beliefs of the 18th-century encyclopedists.

Born in Tours and educated at the Collège de Vendôme, Balzac was always attached to la Touraine. In 1814 his family moved to Paris. There Honoré continued his studies and served for a time as an apprentice in a notary's office. At twenty, he secluded himself for two years in an effort to test his writer's vocation. The results were failures. He undertook then the writing of a series of novels, principally "Gothic tales," which he signed with various pseudonyms. In 1829, he published his first successful novel, *Les Chouans*, the first of his books to be ultimately included in *La Comédie Humaine*.

This marked the beginning of a more worldly life for Balzac. He was received in the most select salons of Paris, carried on a series of amorous affairs, fell in love with Eveline Hanska, a Polish countess. In an effort to diminish the debts he had incurred during his early years of poverty, he promised book after book to his publishers and thereby committed himself to a harsh schedule of labor. Dressed in a monk's habit, he wrote assiduously at a small table in a heavi-ly curtained room lit by candles day and night. He left Paris only for brief trips, often for the purpose of meeting Mme Hanska. He married her in March 1850 and died five months later, exhausted from the heavy program of work he had followed for so many years.

The title *La Comédie Humaine* was first announced in 1841, and the first edition in seventeen volumes appeared in 1842. The preface of 1842 contains the clue to Balzac's vast literary enterprise. There he protrayed society as a nature within the natural world—a nature showing all the varieties of zoological species plus something else. Society was not for Balzac the duality of the sexes, but rather the triple reality of men, women and things (*hommes*, *femmes*, *choses*). By "things," he meant furniture, houses, cities—all those things created by man that help form his temperament.

More even than Dante, Shakespeare and Moliere, Balzac was the creator of the largest number of characters in literature; *La Comédie Humaine* has approximately two thousand characters.

The words "creator" and "creation" were sacred for Balzac. The mystical experience of paternity explained the novelist. Of all the novels in *La Comédie Humaine*, *Le Père Goriot* (1835) is the most explicit on this subject of fatherhood. It contains several of the key characters: Vautrin the criminal, Eugène de Rastignac the *arriviste*, Bianchon the medical student, and the Nucingen family. The two daughters of Goriot turn against their father, and for this reason Balzac calls Goriot *le Christ de la paternité*. But Balzac himself is the father-creator of Père Goriot. At one point in the novel, Goriot claims that his condition and the suffering of fatherhood permit him to understand God: "Quand j'ai été père, j'ai compris Dieu."

Balzac used the term *spécialité* not in the usually accepted modern sense but as a means of explaining the gift and the function of the novelist—the man trained to see through things and human beings to the ideas they represent. This principle of *spécialité* is reminiscent of the Platonic use of ideas. Goriot is not only the father of two daughters who reject him and cause him great anguish, he is also the mystical incarnation of paternity. In his death agony, Goriot calls out that if children do not love their father, all of the social structure will collapse.

La pension Vauquer in *Le Père Goriot* is the microcosm of humanity. There, Eugène de Rastignac, a young man, meets Goriot, the example of paternity, and Vautrin, who is the satanic parody of the father. Underneath the levels of society described in the novels of Balzac lies the world of evil, comparable to hell in the theological sense, and to the lower depths of society and the prisons of mankind. The convict prison, *le bagne*, has its hero in Vautrin. When Vautrin is seized by the police, the expression on his face is described as that of the fallen archangel.

Balzac defined his vocation as that of writing the drama of three to four thousand characters presented by a given society. His ambition exceeded his realization, but the margin between the project and the work was not very wide. His methods of observation and documentation have been the subject of controversy. Some scholars look upon him as the research man, the detective-discoverer of documents, the reader of files and notebooks, and others see him as the diviner and the prophet, the intuitive visionary who had little need of factual documentation. Between the theory that everything was observed and the theory that every fact was reached intuitively, there are various theories that compromise these extremes. In an early letter to Mme Hanska, Balzac wrote that "la mémoire n'enregistre bien que ce qui est douleur."

It is known that Balzac often went to the sites of his novels for documentation. He would look at the houses and streets and monuments. He went to Aix-les-Bains, for example, for certain scenes in *La Peau de Chagrin;* to Angoulême for *Les Illusions perdues;* to Saumur for *Eugénie Grandet.* For the reconstruction of his famous character Vautrin, whose real name was Vidocq, a former convict who had spectacularly become head of the secret police force, Balzac had recourse to the published *Mémoires* of the man, and sought him out for interviews and conversations. For the writing of *La Recherche de l'Absolu*, he studied chemistry. For *Seraphita* he became acquainted with the texts and mystical theories of Swedenborg.

The two statues of Balzac in Paris indicate two contradictory interpretations of the man. On the right bank, at the corner of the rue Balzac and the avenue de Friedland, stands the motionless figure sculptured by Alexandre Falguière. It is Balzac, the right-bank conformist. On the left bank, at the intersection of the boulevard Raspail and the boulevard Montparnasse, stands the very different statue by Rodin. It is a gigantic form, depicting an attitude of scorn— is it the form of a wrestler or an ancient menhir? This 'left-bank Balzac' is the man of mystery, bent upon ferreting out the secrets of all those he observes.

The Balzac creation has such magnetism that it draws the unsuspecting reader into its center. This power has to do with the attraction of Balzac's vitality, with the feverish intensity he had for life. When the thought came to him for the first time, in the summer of 1833, that he could fuse all the parts of his work into one system, he became as exalted as a Pascal or a Descartes or a Rousseau when each saw the vision of his life work. He never compared himself to other writers of his century, but rather to Napoleon, who had dreamed of uniting all of Europe.

After he had used the device of letting characters reappear in novels, and after he had divided his novels into seven groups, he began to fit his early books into the general plan. Some of his critics have called this system an after-thought, based upon a false sense of unity. Marcel Proust, the most Balzacian of novelists, argued that precisely because the system of unity was originally a subconscious thought, it has all the more validity.

Fifty years ago, the general critical view on Balzac was different from that held today. The leading factor in this change of appraisal was the publication and success of *A la recherche du temps perdu* of Proust, which brought about a revised judgment of the novel as a literary genre. The critic Albert Thibaudet, in 1936, judged Balzac in the light of Proust.

L'ART POUR L'ART:
The Development of an Aesthetics

Romanticism has always been looked upon as a literary revolution, and it was the first in the history of French literature that cannot be separated from a comparable revolution in painting. The *salon* of 1827, the painting exhibit held the same year the *préface de Cromwell* was read and published by Hugo, showed Delacroix' *Le Christ au jardin des Oliviers*, and the work of a twenty-one year old artist, Louis Boulanger, a painting called *Mazeppa* that was enthusiastically received by the painters. Boulanger became momentarily Hugo's favorite painter.

This union of poetry and art was further consecrated by another *cénacle*, quite different from Hugo's, which is sometimes considered the birthplace of the movement called *l'art pour l'art*. It was a studio workshop, an *atelier* in which painters worked, on the rue du Doyenné, today replaced by the place du Carrousel, in front of the Louvre. The two leaders and principal spokesmen of the group were Théophile Gautier and Gérard de Nerval.

The word *rapin*, first designating a fine-arts student and then, by extension, a bohemian artist, is most apt in describing the type of artist frequenting the group on the rue du Doyenné. The *rapins* were eccentrics, hostile to all the bourgeois standards, truculent in their behavior, often very gifted, and usually representing failures in their vocation.

At the beginning of his career, Gautier hesitated between poetry and painting. When he finally chose poetry, he brought to it the style, ideas and habits of the painting studio. In his book *Les Jeunes-France*, he gave an animated picture of the young left-wing romantics.

The questions relating to "art for art's sake" have been raised in every age, but the phrase, in its most precise meaning, applies to this French movement, originating with Gautier, Nerval and Pétrus Borel, in their avowed aversion for the bourgeois spirit and saint-simonism or humanitarianism. Most scholars agree that the first reference to *l'art pour l'art* is in a work by the philosopher Victor Cousin, of 1818, *Questions esthétiques et religieuses*, in which he says that art is not enrolled in the service of religion and morals or in the service of what is pleasing and useful. Art exists for its own sake: "Il faut de la religion pour la religion, de la morale pour la morale, et de l'art pour l'art."

With the founding of the Second Empire, in 1852, the opposition between those writers concerned with the defense of a national morality and the cause of progress and those writers representing the tradition of art for art's sake became clear. In his preface to *Poèmes Antiques* (1852), Leconte de Lisle quarrels with everyone on every subject, and sees the political future sullied for a long time with bourgeois meanness, industrialism and utilitarianism. As the politics of the Second Empire (1852–1870) continued, the younger writers and artists looked for a new faith not in participation in active life but in rejuvenated forms of art.

The "bourgeois" art of the day had no originality and no style, according to the strong attacks made against it by Baudelaire, Flaubert, Gautier, Leconte de Lisle, Théodore de Banville. The younger Hugo of 1830 was still revered, and Vigny was respected for having said that a book must be composed, cut and sculptured as if it were a statue of Paros marble. Gautier represented the continuation of that tradition. Baudelaire regretted having come too late, after the glorious days of romanticism, after *le coucher du soleil romantique*. At the end of his career Gautier, in his *Histoire du romantisme*, spoke of the early period as a golden age. The beginnings of the new movement, between 1851 and 1853, resembled the beginnings of romanticism. The new bohemianism was celebrated and idealized. Henri Murger is perhaps the best historian of this renaissance, in *Scènes de la vie de Bohème*, of 1851, a novel made famous years later by Puccini in his opera *La Bohème*.

In reality, there was no "school" uniting such different temperaments as Flaubert and Renan, the Goncourts and Leconte de Lisle. But there were common aspirations and a belief in the principle of the independence of art. The historian of parnassian art, Catulle Mendès, went to great pains to point out that Le Parnasse never represented a school. It was a theory—a doctrine—similar to art for art's sake, a form of faith coming directly from romanticism. Théophile Gautier was the central figure, who had proclaimed as early as 1836 the doctrine of art for art's sake in his preface to *Mlle de Maupin*.

Flaubert admired Gautier, and at least during the early part of his career, considered himself Gautier's disciple. They were joined in their dislike for their contemporary world. In his home in Neuilly, Gautier often received at his Thursday dinners Flaubert, Banville, Jules and Edmond Goncourt, and Baudelaire. Baudelaire, who had probably met Gautier for the first time in 1849 at the hôtel Pimodan, where both of them lived briefly, dedicated *Les Fleurs du Mal* to Gautier: "Au poète impeccable, au parfait magicien ès lettres françaises, au très cher et au très vénéré maître et ami." Gautier, in his turn, wrote the laudatory introduction to the complete works of Baudelaire.

The new poets were published in three anthologies by the publisher Lemerre in 1866, 1869, and 1877, under the title *Le Parnasse Contemporain.* The word *parnassien* can be applied to theories of *l'art pour l'art.* There was very little development or change in these theories after 1870. Gautier died in 1872. Flaubert seemed to look upon the new democracy, the Third Republic, as the end of art. He was convinced that a reign of utilitarianism was going to triumph: "Nous allons devenir un grand pays plat et industriel comme la Belgique." (Correspondance, IV, 55)

For almost fifty years the principles of art for art's sake were current in France. Belief in the artist's freedom was clearly stated in Hugo's preface to *Cromwell,* but the specific doctrines themselves were analyzed and clarified best in such works as Flaubert's letters, the Goncourts' journal, the prefaces of Leconte de Lisle, the critical writing of Baudelaire. The best examples of art based upon these theories are in the novels of Flaubert and the poetry of Banville, Leconte de Lisle and Baudelaire.

Flaubert was the least charitable of these writers. He examined the bourgeoisie as if it were a world reserved for his research, and he collected a long series of extracts from conversations he had overheard, out of which he made a *Dictionnaire des idées reçues.* He and Baudelaire referred endlessly to examples of bourgeois stupidity—*la bêtise,* as they called it.

These French writers and artists often analyzed the difficulties in creating a work that would match their ideals. Their pages on the slow painful process of artistic creation are among their most valuable contributions. The achievement of anything like perfection demands time and labor and constant revision. The emotions of the artist in the process of creating his art are brilliantly studied in Delacroix' *Journal,* in Flaubert's correspondence, in the Goncourt journals. Whereas romanticism emphasized the sentiments and the sorrows of the individual, the parnassian creed emphasized the passion for beauty felt by the artist, which separates a man from everything that is vulgar and banal.

The principal theories on morality and art, as developed by Flaubert, Baudelaire and the Goncourts, are still the bases for the aesthetics of modern art. These writers would say that truth is not immoral, and art is not immoral. Obscenity is immoral only when it is untruthful. Intellectual honesty is a leading characteristic of the true artist, and such honesty is in itself a moral principle. Such men, for whom art is everything (Flaubert, Baudelaire, Mallarmé, Joyce, Henry James) were morally unified in their temperaments and in the scrupulosity with which they carried out their work as artists.

Art contains in itself its own principle of morality. With this thought in mind, the exponents of *l'art pour l'art* advanced the theory that there is more moral dignity in a work of art when it is devoid of a specific moralizing intention. A vigorous bold depiction of vice and passion can have a moral effect on the public. The morality of a great artist is in the forcefulness and the truthfulness of his treatment of whatever subject he chooses. In other words, the morality is in the form of the art and not in its subject matter.

THÉOPHILE GAUTIER (1811–1872)

Born in Tarbes, in the Pyrenees, Gautier was a Parisian by adoption. He studied at the lycée Charlemagne with Gérard de Nerval. At eighteen he worked in a painter's studio, but ultimately chose the career of writer. He played an important part in the *claque* for Hugo at the première of *Hernani* in 1830.

After his first collection, *Poésies*, of 1830, he published a long poem in 1832 about a young painter who damns himself for a sorceress (*Albertus*). *Les Jeunes-France* (1833) is a series of humorous sketches on the young bohemians of the day. In the preface to his first novel, *Mlle de Maupin*, Gautier celebrated the cult of pure beauty and denounced any utilitarian use of art. His long poem *La Comédie de la Mort* (1838) is the expression of metaphysical anguish over man's fate. *España* (1845) is a collection of poems on his travels through Spain in 1840, in which he created an art criticism in verse in his poems on Zurbaran and Ribera.

Emaux et Camées (1852) with the additional poem *L'Art*, in the edition of 1857, best illustrates Gautier's belief in the parnassian ideal of art for art's sake, according to which beauty is the triumph over matter. Baudelaire not only hailed Gautier as his master, but borrowed many lines from his work, although in almost every case, he altered somewhat the original phrasing of the lines.

GÉRARD DE NERVAL (1808–1855)

Gérard Labrunie, who later adopted the pseudonym Nerval, spent his first years in Le Valois, the region north of Paris, where he was enchanted by legends of the Ile-de-France. He was a schoolmate and friend of Gautier, frequented the cénacle on the rue de la Doyenné, and played the role of dandy. He became imbued with Germanic culture and translated in 1828 the first part of Goethe's *Faust*.

For Nerval, the dream world was the world of the subconscious controlled by its own laws. His works, and especially the sonnets called *Les Chimères*, are more than a distillation of experiences. They create a new compact life in which the settings are more real than the landscapes of the Valois, and the characters are more living than Adrienne, who kissed his forehead in the children's *ronde* in the park of the château when he was a boy, and more real than Jenny Colon, the actress and singer in Paris with whom he fell in love in 1836.

Nerval's wisdom was obscure because it was composed of magnetism, esoterism and occultism, but his madness (he had two serious mental crises in 1841 and 1853) was lucid because it constructed the world of dreams. As a traveller, Nerval pursued the symbolism of numbers and the memories of magic and of cabala, but as a poet he constructed the existence of a man who loves and suffers.

The figures of the women who inhabit his work resemble a phantom from a dream. Adrienne, Jenny Colon, a Neapolitan girl (*la brodeuse*), the English girl Octavie are all synthesized into Aurélia, the only woman Gérard could love since, never having seen her in life, he was able to make her divine. Nerval encouraged his madness because it abolished time and plunged him into a distant past where all was illuminated with joy.

The spiritual experience of love is tenacious, according to Nerval. It binds us to time gone by, to a past that becomes present and future. Love is metempsychosis. It is the same experience we relive ceaselessly.

La treizième revient . . . c'est encor la première.

The sumptuous resonances of this sonnet of *Artémis*, while falsifying the truth, reduce the fragments of real experience into a single experience as simple as it is profound, as permanent as it is inaccessible.

The principle of metempsychosis (revealed in the first line of *Artémis*, in the meaning of the words *treizième* and *première*) abolishes any tragic notion of love.

Et c'est toujours la seule—ou c'est le seul moment.

"The one moment" referred to was that love always sought by Nerval because it had once existed and because it continued to exist in his dreams.

Romanticism of all the centuries and not solely of the 19th is the dream of life, the harsh disproportion existing between imagined life and daily life. Rousseau, on certain pages of his *Rêveries*, bequeathed to the sensitive hearts of the 19th and 20th centuries ways and exercises by which to attain the ecstasy of dreams, but the Rousseauistic romantics in their dream of life have today been replaced by Gérard de Nerval's life of dreams. The climate desired by Jean-Jacques was the dream of nature, but the climate desired by Nerval was the nature of dreams. He says this in the opening sentence of his short novel, *Aurélia*: "Le rêve est une seconde vie."

CHARLES BAUDELAIRE (1821–1867)

After a century, Baudelaire appears today a classical writer—classical not simply in the sense that he is established and recognized and studied, but classical especially in his lucidity and power of analysis. In *Bénédiction* he speaks of the poet's *esprit lucide*. *Les Fleurs du Mal* (1857) occupies such a central position in the history of modern poetry because it satisfies this need of analysis and exploration of man's consciousness which the Frenchman has always demanded of his writers and even of his poets.

Baudelaire is classical also in the importance he places on the sense of order and architecture of a poem. One of the principal passions of the poet, according to Baudelaire, is the passion for order, for symmetry and structure. The writing of a poem is the discipline of form imposed upon emotion and experience and ideas. Baudelaire professed an exalted belief in the willpower of the artist. He practiced his willpower, not in his personal life, but in the writing of his poems. "Il n'y a pas de hasard dans l'oeuvre d'art," he wrote in 1846.

The influence of this basic classicism of Baudelaire did not diminish during the symbolist period and during the past seventy years. Modern poetry presupposes a system of metaphysics. It affirms, first with Baudelaire and later with the philosophy of Bergson, that the poet should place himself in the very center of what is real and merge his consciousness and his sensibility with the universe. Whereas the parnassian poet, in his descriptions of the phenomena of the world, stayed within the domain of the relative, the symbolist poet, taking Baudelaire as guide, tries to penetrate beyond the physical phenomena and reach what he calls the heart of reality.

All three terms—classicism, romanticism, and symbolism—have been applied to Baudelaire's art. The classical trait of this poet is represented in his longing for perfection, his lifelong striving to discover the ideal form of art and beauty. Romanticism is, at its beginnings and in the personal drama of Baudelaire, a longing for the infinite. Symbolism was already for Baudelaire what it was to be for subsequent poets, a longing to reach the essence of poetry, to reach the subconscious and thus to enter into communication with supreme Reality.

"Baudelairism" has become a frequently used term in modern criticism. It involves many matters: attitudes of the dandy, an attraction to the unhealthy and the morbid, habits of provocation and scorn. Baudelaire was essentially a man who felt the contradictions of his nature more acutely than most, who waged a spiritual struggle between the opposing forces of his greatness and his weakness, and who engaged his entire being in the adventure of poetry.

At the poet's death in 1867, his obituaries stressed sensational details in his life—his eccentricities, his diabolism, his dandyism. It is true that he lived the role of dandy in the Hôtel Lauzun on the Ile-saint-Louis, that he often shocked the French bourgeoisie with his cynicism, that he cultivated an attitude toward satanism and the Gothic tale or *roman noir*. But today, thanks to the accessibility of all his writings, we know that far more important than his exterior appearance and behavior was the "inner dandyism" of his spirit. Baudelaire is the first modern poet because of his awareness of disorder in the world and in himself. Satanism is at the center of his work, not by histrionic black-magic values, but by the poet's horror of man's fate and his obsession over guilt. The pathology of Baudelaire's sado-masochism has been elaborately studied in recent years.

When Baudelaire was writing his earliest poems, in about 1845, his principal references and directions came from romanticism. He felt a close affinity with the enthusiasms of Gautier and Banville, with the esoteric interests of Nerval, with the macabre audacities of Pétrus Borel. These men, more than the leaders of the romantic movement—Hugo, Lamartine, Vigny—helped him define modern poetry by its secrecy, its spirituality, its aspiration toward the infinite. He was among the first to define romanticism as a way of feeling (*une manière de sentir*). The examples of Delacroix, Poe and Wagner, as well as the more philosophical Swedenborg and Joseph de Maistre, confirmed the intuition of Baudelaire concerning the modern form of melancholy and nostalgia. In his search for beauty through the *forêts de symboles*, where every element is hieroglyph, he practiced the art of symbolism instinctively long before it reached its consecration in theory and manifesto.

For many Americans, Baudelaire is still the French poet who was influenced by Poe and who exaggerated the importance of Poe. He recognized himself in the American poet. He translated Poe because of their common traits: hysteria, which often replaced the free functioning of the will; a lack of harmony between the nervous tensions and the intellect; a scorn for the concept of progress and for the materialism of their century; a love for the secrecy and the suggestiveness of dreams. The psychological analyses of Laclos, the prose style of Chateaubriand, the philosophy of Joseph de Maistre probably exerted a far deeper influence on Baudelaire than any aspect of Poe's writing. But the American poet had for the Frenchman the power of a myth, and the particular significance that Baudelaire found in Poe was to play an important role in the development of Mallarmé's genius and Valéry's.

At the time of *Les Fleurs du Mal*, philosophers had been humbled in the presence of the positivistic scientists. Baudelaire's revelation of poetry revindicated belief in the spiritual destiny of man. His example and his art convinced his readers that man has the right to ask of poetry the solution to the problems of human destiny. The parnassians created a purely descriptive art of exterior concrete objects. Baudelaire's revelation was to provide a metaphysical conception of the same universe. His famous sonnet on synesthesia and symbolism, *Correspondances*, reassigned to the poet his ancient role of *vates*, of soothsayer, who by his intuition of the concrete, of immediately perceived things, is led to the *idea* of those things, to the intricate system of "correspondences." The sonnet was to become the principal key to symbolism as defined by subsequent poets. Already, for Baudelaire, nature was a word, an allegory. To the poet is revealed *une ténébreuse et profonde unité* which is the unison of the sensible and spiritual universes. The experience of the poet is the participation of all things invading him, with their harmonies and analogies. They bear the sign of the First Word, of their original unity.

Today *Les Fleurs du Mal* is the most frequently edited book in world literature. It is undoubtedly the book translated into the largest number of languages during the past fifty years. The introductory poem, *Au lecteur*, which is a study of modern man's spiritual malady, an analysis of his famous *ennui*, ends with the challenging apostrophe, "Hypocrite lecteur, mon semblable, mon frère!" It is a line that Eliot takes over whole into *The Waste Land*.

In *L'Albatros*, one of his easiest and most frequently anthologized poems,

Baudelaire projects the story of his deepest drama. The poet is caught by the world as the albatross is caught on the deck of a ship. His large wings, the source of his strength and beauty in the air, make it impossible for him to rise when he is placed on the deck. Baudelaire turns the drama into an almost comic picture of frustration. This personal tragedy of the poet far outdistances the lesser conflicts in Baudelaire's life: his endless arguments with his mother; the long, more than twenty-five years' liaison with Jeanne Duval; his constant quarrels with creditors and notaries; his struggles with a hostile press.

The elements of pathos in the poems are so universal and so humble that we can easily fraternize with this poet as we read of the indefinable sadness of a large city, the dreams and idealizations of a drunkard, the heart of an old servant woman. Whatever can be called metaphysical suffering in Baudelaire is so joined with daily anguish of the most commonplace kind that one illuminates the other and provides an experience of warmth and love.

Baudelaire has been psychoanalyzed, first by a doctor, René Laforgue, and recently by Jean-Paul Sartre. But before those writers, he psychoanalyzed himself, and derived a principle which psychoanalysis has extolled: the principle of compensation: "Tout mystique a un vice caché."

His childhood love, his pure love for his mother, *le vert paradis des amours enfantines*, never left his thoughts for long. This carefully protected memory of early happiness led him to write that poetry is childhood willfully recovered (*l'enfance retrouvée à volonté*). Baudelaire defines genius as *l'enfance nettement formulée*.

School after school of poets have chosen objects that seemed at the time distinctive and privileged. Voiture and other *précieux* poets favored chains and fires of love, the blushing dagger, compendious oceans (to designate tears). Hugo and the romantics chose twilight, stars, meadows. The emblems of Mallarmé and the symbolists were vases, swans, jewels. Baudelaire described a world as unpoetic, in the traditional sense, as possible: skeletons, cemeteries, barracks, hovels, prostitutes, gamblers, clowns. His art involved the creation of their beauty. These words were related to his personal experience, which was undeniably an experience in pessimism. Baudelaire had a distinct distaste for the advocates of optimism, for those who denied the existence of evil or who justified it, or for those who dissimulated it under concepts of evolution and racial perfectibility. In distinguishing himself from those advocates, Baudelaire became the poet and the thinker of our age, of what we like to call modernity.

PÉTRUS BOREL (1809–1859)

Pétrus Borel is known today to students of French literature largely through Baudelaire's short article on him, printed in the collection of prose pieces, *L'Art Romantique*. When Baudelaire wrote this article in 1859, Borel's name was used by journalists to express their scorn and distaste for the macabre type of romantic poetry and for the type of flamboyant genius characterized by excesses of bohemianism and excessive affectation. Baudelaire, who revered Borel and felt strong sympathy for him, explained the aptness of the name *lycanthrope*, associated with Borel. This "wolfman" or "werewolf" behaved as a man demonized and living in the dark forests of melancholy. He exemplified a favorite word of Baudelaire, *le guignon*, which signifies evil fate pursuing a man and from which he is unable to recover. *Le Guignon* is a goddess possessing, more than any pope or lama, the privilege of infallibility. Baudelaire explains by *le guignon* the irreconcilables in the life of Borel, the genius of the poet in the preface poem of *Madame Putiphar*, and the epic skill of the writer in several scenes of the novel, and the endless difficulties and hardships he encountered throughout his life.

No theory is proposed by Baudelaire to explain the number of *guignons* in the career of Pétrus Borel. He merely hinted at the symptoms of morbidity in the man's nature which maintained and even nurtured flagrant contradictions. Signs of psychic disturbance were evident even in Borel's handwriting, in his spelling, in the agony which the writing of the simplest letter caused him. The romantic movement would not have been complete without the lycanthropy of Pétrus Borel. Baudelaire distinguished between the early phase of romanticism when the imagination of the poets was concerned with the past, with nostalgia and regret, and the second phase, more active and violent and earthy. Borel was one of the most picturesque and vehement characters of this second phase. He incarnated the spirit of the *Bousingos* in his attire and in his hatred of the king and the bourgeoisie. During the years 1830–1835, when he was famous and influential, he expressed his disapproval of the emphasis on excessive color and form in literature and art, and he sympathized with the dandy's creed, with the Byronic pessimism and dilettantism of an entire generation which, paradoxically, was both turbulent and bored.

Champavert (1833) is made up of five tales and two autobiographical sketches, the second of which is *Champavert le lycanthrope*, the writer's own account of his life. The tales are not immoral, as was alleged at the time, but they are tales of horror, with elements of sadism, that would illustrate André Breton's category of *humour noir*. *Madame Putiphar* was written in Le Baizil, a small village in Champagne, where Borel lived in a wooden shack, in extreme poverty and solitude. The book describes almost every kind of horror and cruelty. When it appeared, in 1839, it passed almost unnoticed. One critic, Janin, compared Borel to the marquis de Sade, an unjustified comparison, but one which pleased Borel.

Le petit cénacle emerged in 1827, a group of ten or twelve poets and artists headed by Pétrus Borel, who undertook a fight against classicism in French art and letters. Théophile Gautier and Gérard de Nerval are today the best-known figures of le petit cénacle, but at the time Borel himself best represented the new spirit of literature. He amazed and amused the group with his stories and his paradoxes, in much the same way that Baudelaire was to shock his contemporaries a few years later. Victor Hugo turned to Borel to help him form a claque for the première of Hernani. For that momentous occasion, Borel organized a group of one hundred students from the Latin Quarter and taught them the passages of the text where they should express themselves vocally.

Borel's rise to fame and the decline of his reputation transpired within just a few years, but they were colorful violent years in French history, the July Revolution of 1830, the cholera of 1832 which exterminated 20,000 Parisians, the carnival of 1832, when all of Paris was turned into a bacchanalia. Borel was also an important leader of les Jeunes-France, made up of members of le petit cénacle, who used the new name to indicate that they were the youngest and most adventurous opponents of Louis-Philippe. They finally adopted the name of Bousingos (from bousin, meaning "a noise"). Borel's supremacy was being questioned by 1835. At that time, Gautier broke away from the Bousingos and founded his own circle in the Impasse du Doyenné, near the Palais Royal. The new group, referred to as La Bohême du Doyenné, included Delacroix, Corot, Chassériau. A house-warming party at Gautier's in November 1835 marked the end of Borel's influence.

LECONTE DE LISLE and the PARNASSIANS

Leconte de Lisle (1818–1899) was born on the island of La Réunion (in the Indian Ocean), and came to France in 1837 to complete his education. He was converted to the new socialism in France in about 1845, but with the advent of the Second Empire in 1851 he gave up all political activity. To earn his living, he became a translator of classical Greek works, notably *The Iliad* and *The Odyssey*. At Hugo's death in 1885, Leconte de Lisle was elected to his chair in the Académie Française.

The first edition of *Poèmes Antiques* (1852), with thirty-one poems, was augmented in the definitive edition of 1874, with twenty-five additional poems. They are poems essentially of two inspirations: Hindu and Greek. *Bhagavat* is the meditation of three Brahmins, embittered by life and desirous of merging their being with the absolute. The philosophy and art of ancient Greece were exalted by Leconte de Lisle at the expense of Christianity.

Poèmes Barbares (1862–78) continued to show the poet's disgust for modern times. He invoked the Bible in *Caïn*, and nordic myths in such a poem as *Le Coeur d'Hialmar*. His fundamental pessimism and his hostility to Christianity continued to be expressed in *Poèmes Tragiques* (1884) and *Derniers Poèmes*, posthumously published by Heredia in 1895.

In his loathing for the ugliness and vulgarity of modern life, Leconte de Lisle deliberately cultivated historical and exotic picturesqueness. His poetry is the worship of beauty, of which the greatest example for him was Greek art. Like Gautier, he emphasized the difficulty of writing poetry, the need for strict versification, and the control of language.

His influence was felt on all the poets associated with the parnassian ideals as well as on *Le Parnasse Contemporain*, the publication promoting the work of the new poets.

Leconte de Lisle's principal disciple was José-Maria de Heredia (1842–1905), a Cuban by birth, who composed one hundred eighteen sonnets, published in 1893, under the title *Les Trophées*. These are meticulously composed poems celebrating Greece and Sicily, Rome and the barbarians, the Middle Ages and the Renaissance, the Orient and the Tropics. For each sonnet, Heredia chose a striking detail or event able to evoke a moment of civilization.

Théodore de Banville (1828–1891) was one of the most gifted parnassians. His *Odes funambulesques* (1857) are graceful, comic and technically successful. Sully Prudhomme (1839–1907) was more a personal poet than a strict parnassian. François Coppée (1842–1908), in his *Intimités* (1860), cultivated a familiar everyday realism. He tried to become the people's poet in *Les Humbles* (1872).

GEORGE SAND (1804–1876)

Aurore Dupin grew up in Nohant, in the province of Le Berry. At a very early age she married le Baron Dudevant. She left him after eight years of marriage and settled down in Paris where she earned her living by writing. She took the pen-name of George Sand, based on the name of her lover Jules Sandeau. Her first novels (*Indiana*, 1831, *Lélia*, 1833) exploited her own sexual and emotional experiences. In them she vindicated, as a feminist, woman's equality of freedom to have emotional experiences. George Sand's distinguished list of lovers included Musset and Chopin.

Her second group of novels reflected her conversion to socialism. In these works, such as *Mauprat* (1837), she defended the cause of the humble on the earth, preached the joining of social classes and the solidarity of mankind, and predicted the advent of peace in the world.

During the last phase of her career, from approximately 1845 on, she lived in her country house in Nohant, where she was known as *la bonne dame de Nohant*, surrounded by grandchildren and tenants, and where she wrote a series of pastoral novels that seem today the least outdated of her works: *La Mare au diable* (1846), *La petite Fadette* (1849), *François le Champi* (1850).

George Sand had the temperament of a novelist, but suffered from too great a facility in writing. She won over her readers by the exaltation of her themes: love, belief in progress and in the natural goodness of man.

With the heroes of her novels, so many of whom are consumptive, and with her lovers, Sand played the role of mother or even praying mantis (her critics accused her of being *une mante religieuse*). After her break with Musset, she wrote to him about her infatuation for Pagello, the physician who had cared for Musset in Venice: "Je l'aimais comme une mère, et tu étais notre enfant à tous deux."

Mme Sand found happiness in her long association with Le Berry, and in the sympathy she felt for the peasants she knew there (*les paysans berrichons*). Ever since the *fabliaux* of the Middle Ages, the French peasant had been either ostracized from literature or converted into an idealized shepherd in works of a pastoral nature. George Sand rehabilitated the peasant, with his *patois*, with his habits of a farmer, and his sentimental adventures.

Inspired by the Revolution of 1848, the novelist embraced the cause of the people. Her life in Nohant resembled Voltaire's life in Ferney. At Musset's death in 1857, she published *Elle et Lui*, a work lacking in any sense of delicacy, in which she claimed she had become Musset's mistress through charity. Paul de Musset, Alfred's brother, replied with the book *Lui et Elle*. And Louise Colet added her word on the famous affair with *Lui*.

Sand was revered by the peasants during the last years of her life in Nohant and by Flaubert, seventeen years younger, for whom she became a remarkable friend, addressing him in letters as *mon bénédictin, mon troubadour*. Greatly disturbed by the war of 1870, she continued writing and publishing, but received no attention from the critics. She was buried in Nohant, which she had made famous in her books, as other regionalist writers were to do: Flaubert for la Normandie, Mauriac for Le Bordelais, Jean Giono for la Provence.

GUSTAVE FLAUBERT (1821–1880)

Literature was for Flaubert the province of the bachelor, or of that type of married man who, like Montaigne, isolated himself from the world, as in a tower, and in reality led the life of a bachelor. Flaubert chose the vocation of a writer as another man would choose a religious vocation and the celibate life of a monastery. After the deaths of his father and sister, 1845–46, Flaubert cloistered himself in the large estate in Croisset, near Rouen, on the bank of the Seine. There he was to live with his mother and his niece. He seemed predestined to such an existence by his failure as a law student in Paris, between 1840 and 1843, and by a serious nervous malady in 1843 which affected his entire life and made of him a man perpetually apprehensive of further attacks.

He was as securely chained to his writing table as Balzac had been, a prey to that creative energy he cultivated in himself and to that particular form of anxiety that creative work generates in the artist. He was as self-critical, as worried over the number of syllables in a word, as Malherbe, another Norman writer, had been before him.

Between 1846 and 1855, when he was finishing the composition of *Madame Bovary*, he carried on a strange love affair with Louise Colet, an exasperating *bas-bleu* of the period who was well-known in literary circles for her poetry— far better-known than Gustave Flaubert, who had published nothing. She was eleven years older than Flaubert, a self-centered demanding woman whose claim to glory is having served as inspiration of some of Flaubert's greatest letters, written about his temperament as an artist, his method of writing, and the daily suffering caused by such a method. When Flaubert met Mme Colet in the studio of the sculptor Pradier, he believed he had found the woman of his dreams. It was an unusual love affair for anyone except Flaubert, because it lasted nine years and was carried on largely through correspondence. Louise Colet's rival was Emma Bovary. The mistress was jealous of her lover's heroine, who occupied fifty-five months of Flaubert's life.

La Tentation de Saint Antoine was the work he would have liked to have made his masterpiece. Three times he attempted to write it—in 1849, 1856 and 1872. His first inspiration for the work was a painting of Breughel he had seen in Genoa, at the age of twenty-four. It was a typically nightmarish Breughel, representing a mass of monsters, in which fish are devouring drowning figures. When Flaubert completed the first version of La Tentation, he read it to his two closest friends, Louis Bouilhet and Maxime du Camp, and both, with unusual frankness, declared it a failure. In order to recover from the disappointment, Flaubert, in the company of Du Camp, left for what was the most extensive voyage of his life, to Alexandria, Cairo, Jerusalem, Tripoli, Rhodes, Smyrna, Constantinople, Athens, Naples, Rome, Florence, Venice. By June 1851, he was back in Croisset after an absence of twenty months.

On September 19, he began work on a vastly different kind of novel, one that had been suggested by Bouilhet and Du Camp. When they had pointed out the weakness of La Tentation de Saint Antoine, they had urged him to avoid lyricism at all costs. His predilection for the composing of lyric passages in his early writings had kept him in a state of literary puberty. He was now, in 1851, to choose a subject that would do violence to his nature. Eugene Delamare, the model for Charles Bovary, had been a pupil of Flaubert's father on the medical faculty in Rouen. Delamare's wife, Adele-Delphine, had turned against the realities of life and indulged in moods of extreme romantic fantasy and feeling. She had died at the age of twenty-seven, possibly by her own hand. Flaubert's counselor-friends urged him to take such a banal subject as the story of the Delamares, such a typical *fait divers*, in order to bring him down to earth. The Norman celibate, in his retreat at Croisset, accepted his penance.

Thus Flaubert began writing his novel, presumably about the exaggerations and the tragedy of a romantic temperament, but which was in reality for him the expression of his loathing of the bourgeois temperament. *Madame Bovary* has a dual subject matter. It is the story of a romantic heroine who commits the error of considering her dreams reality, and at the same time it is a story of the bourgeois world responsible for her suicide. The bourgeois type of individual, according to Flaubert, thinks in terms of clichés, of what he calls *idées reçues*. Flaubert collected these clichés and assembled them in a *Dictionnaire d'idées reçues.* Then he transformed them into a novel, published eight months after his death, *Bouvard et Pécuchet.*

In order to write *Madame Bovary*, Flaubert entered upon a regimen of hard labor. He worked on an average of twelve hours a day. For four years and seven months he wrote assiduously, especially during the long hours of night, when his lighted lamp literally served as a beacon for boats on the Seine. He created a Norman village, Yonville, for the main action of his novel. There he placed the church, the vicarage, the pharmacy, the market place and the hotel Le Lion d'Or. The source of the name Bovary is not known with certainty, but the word *boeuf* is in it, and the heaviness and stupidity of an ox.

It is certain now that Delphine Delamare was not the sole model for Emma. Like Proust and countless other novelists, Flaubert composed a character from several models. Mme Pradier, wife of the sculptor, is in Emma. A famous Mme Lafarge, accused of poisoning her husband with arsenic and acquitted by Louis-Napoléon Bonaparte in 1853, is also in Emma, as is Louise Colet, who insisted on seeing Flaubert for a few days in Paris or Mantes every three months or so during their liaison.

But the most famous model for Emma was Gustave Flaubert himself. "Madame Bovary, c'est moi!" was a revealing statement he once made. Flaubert's own romantic dreams are in Emma. Her defeat in life—a defeat that forced him to find consolation in writing—was his also.

What emerges clearly from the vast amount of documentation now available, even from the novel Flaubert wrote at the age of sixteen, *Passion et Vertu,* is the fact that he did not need the prodding of Bouilhet and Du Camp to write *Madame Bovary*. The rain and the fog of Normandy were merely the setting for the dissatisfied soul of a woman (and of a man). "Ma pauvre Bovary," he wrote, "souffre et pleure en ce moment dans vingt villages de France." The critic-philosopher Jules de Gaultier coined the word *bovarysme*, and used it to designate the sickness of a person who believes himself destined to a life far superior to the life he leads. Such a term defines Emma Bovary, and it can be extended to Flaubert himself, and to France as a country, especially France of the Second Empire, to an entire section of the bourgeoisie that had grown jealous of the very aristocracy it had ruined.

PROSPER MÉRIMÉE (1803–1870)

After writing a series of short plays (*pochades*) and an historical novel (*Chronique du règne de Charles IX*, 1829), Mérimée found in the short story or *nouvelle* the literary form that best suited his talents.

One of his farces, *Le Carrosse du Saint-Sacrement*, has become a minor classic, thanks to the film of Jean Renoir, Copeau's production at the Vieux-Colombier, and its inclusion in the Comédie-Française repertory.

Mateo Falcone, first published in 1829, is Mérimée at his best and most typical: a ten-page *nouvelle* of a tragic Corsican story in which a young boy is slain by his mother because he betrayed a bandit to the police by means of a simple gesture.

In his official career of inspector of historical monuments, Mérimée discovered material or suggestions for his stories. *La Vénus d'Ille* (1838), for example, is the story of a young man who places his ring on the finger of a bronze statue of Venus while playing a game; the finger tightens over the ring as if the statue considers herself married to the man.

Colomba (1840) is almost the length of a novel. It is a tragic Corsican story of vendetta. *Carmen* (1845) also is almost a novel, of Spanish origin, and has become famous because of Bizet's opera (1875), a recent ballet of Roland Petit, and the American film *Carmen Jones*.

Mérimée was a friend of Stendhal and, like Stendhal, looked for an integrity of feeling in civilizations other than that of Paris. He was one of the first Frenchmen to take interest in Russian literature, and translated Gogol and Turgenev.

CHARLES-AUGUSTIN SAINTE-BEUVE (1804–1869)

The goal of Saint-Beuve's gigantic work, contained in approximately seventy volumes, was to infuse new life into criticism, to enlarge its scope and transform it. In his short critical papers, collected under the title *Causeries du lundi*, and in his long solid works, such as *Port-Royal*, he produced criticism which was a review of French literature in all its forms and which was guided by a desire to understand rather than to judge. He attempted to give as full a portrait as possible of the writer under consideration, and there raised points about him that had hardly been thought of in previous systems of criticism— points including physical and anatomical characteristics of the writer, his educa- tion, his psychological traits, and his temperament as explained by provincial or Parisian mores.

By the middle of the century, Sainte-Beuve was the master critic in France. His weekly article, appearing every Monday, was an important force in shaping literary opinion. He clung doggedly to his own method, although he foresaw the emergence of the new type of criticism that developed in the last part of the century—sometimes called impressionist criticism because of the use of individual criteria in making judgments and impressions.

The criticism of Sainte-Beuve may have little value today if judged by the criteria of the new critics in America and the new French criticism of Blanchot, Bachelard, Picon, Starobinski and Jean-Pierre Richard. Historically, however, his position and his method remain important. Because of his work, as it appeared during his lifetime, the public turned more and more to the literary critic for help in reading and in seeing relationships between life and literature.

Under the pretext of historical accuracy, Sainte-Beuve often investigated biographical data of a very intimate nature. The agility of his mind and his intelligence illuminated whatever problems he considered. He was interested primarily in the writer as an individual, and he looked upon a book as the expression of a temperament. His judgment of a book was his judgment of the author as a man.

Sainte-Beuve was best when, with the curiosity of a psychologist, he analyzed the background of a writer, or the defects of character and the noble aspects of a writer's nature. In each essay he offered an impressive documentation in biography and character study and tried to establish general laws to explain various types of minds. He applied this method to major writers (Montaigne and Voltaire) as well as to minor writers (Mme Geoffrin and Grimm), and it applied better to explanations of moderately gifted writers than to analyses of geniuses. The creative work of the genius interested him less than the characters, emotions and personal dramas of the genius himself. He constantly tried to discover the characteristics of a man's mind; "la forme de l'esprit" was one of his favorite phrases. But he was hostile to any absolute theory. He experimented cautiously with the data and the facts he had at hand.

The critical method of Sainte-Beuve, fundamentally a moralistic method, resembles no method employed today by the leading French critics. The pene- tration into the literary work itself by such critics as Sartre (in his long book on

Genet), by Georges Poulet (in his recent *Métamorphoses du cercle*) by Jean-Pierre Richard (in his dissertation *L'Univers imaginaire de Mallarmé*) represents another mode of criticism. Each of these critics is distinct in himself, and not one occupies the place once occupied by Sainte-Beuve, but together they have created a new intellectual climate, and their work is sufficiently prolific and stimulating to be called the "new French criticism."

POSITIVISM: HISTORY and CRITICISM

Three men in particular, accepting at least in part the principles of positivism, became the intellectual leaders of a new generation in France, enamoured of science and objective truth: Renan, Taine and Fustel de Coulanges.

Ernest Renan (1823–1892) was born in Tréguier, in Brittany. He studied for the priesthood in three different seminaries: Saint-Nicolas du Chardonnet, Issy and Saint-Sulpice. Eventually losing his faith in the truth of religion, Renan gave up all thoughts of becoming a priest and threw himself into the study of science and philology. *L'Avenir de la Science* was written in 1848, but not published until 1890. In 1861 he visited Palestine and two years later published his *Vie de Jésus*. This biography divests the figure of Christ of any divine character and presents the founder of Christianity as a gentle persuasive apostle. The pastoral quality of the book caused Oscar Wilde to call it the Fifth Gospel. The seven volumes of Renan's principal work, *Histoire des origines du christianisme*, ends with a study of Marcus Aurelius, *Marc-Aurèle et la fin du monde antique* (1881).

At the end of his life, when he was professor and administrator at the Collège de France, Renan turned toward his past and wrote about his early life in Brittany and his seminary years in *Souvenirs d'enfance et de jeunesse* (1883). This volume contains his famous *Prière sur l'acropole*, a text reflecting his religious doubts and the drama of a man in search of truth.

The hope of making literary criticism into a science is more apparent in the work of Hippolyte Taine (1828–1893) than in Sainte-Beuve. His theories of criticism systematized and developed the earlier theories of Mme de Staël and Chateaubriand. As he conceived it, as all the parts of an organism maintain necessary connections, so all the parts of a work, a man, a period, or a people form one system. Every system has an essential or dominant characteristic. Taine proposed to study all the variations of given literary data as influenced by what he called race, environment and period (*race, milieu, moment*). He looked upon literature and art as the expression of society, as documents awaiting the scholar, philosopher and historian.

Taine developed a method of criticism that was intended to apply the rigor of the natural sciences to the human sciences. It is an elaborate system of causes and laws based upon the belief that art is the result of such knowable factors as race, environment and historical moment. This theory owes its existence, in part, to writings of Montesquieu, Stendhal and Michelet. Taine stated the terms of his formula in the preface to his *Histoire de la littérature anglaise* (1863) after developing a detailed example in his book *La Fontaine et ses fables* (1860), a revision of his earlier *Essai sur les fables de La Fontaine* (1853). A genius is for Taine a product that can be explained by a process resembling a chemical analysis. La Fontaine, for example, is a *Gaulois* (race), a *Champenois* (from the province of la Champagne, the *milieu*), and a courtier of Louis XIV (*moment*). His *faculté maîtresse* (leading gift) is his poetic imagination.

Fustel de Coulanges (1830–1889) ended his career as a professor of medieval history at the Sorbonne, after teaching at the Faculté de Strasbourg and serving as director of the Ecole Normale Supérieure. He looked upon history not as an art but as a pure science demanding solid documentation. He was therefore anti-Michelet. *La Cité Antique* (1864) is his best book. It is a study of ancient societies and their worship of the dead. He explored the evolution from family religion to municipal religions and institutions until the advent of Christianity, which he saw as founding a universal religion and thus bringing to a close the ancient world. Many of the proofs used by Fustel de Coulanges to support the thesis of *La Cité Antique* no longer seem authentic.

SOCIAL THINKERS:
COMTE, LAMENNAIS, LACORDAIRE

For several years Auguste Comte (1798–1837) served as secretary of Saint-Simon, and called himself a disciple of the socialist writer. Then he gave in his home, and published later in six volumes his *Cours de philosophie positive* (1839–42). He was the founder of *le positivisme*.

According to Comte, philosophy has passed through three stages: *l'état théologique, l'état métaphysique* and *l'état positif,* which began with the 19th century. Religious and metaphysical thinking were outdated. Henceforth man's thinking must be based on the positivistic study of facts which will lead him to the discovery of the laws of phenomena.

Comte's system first attracted scientists: Claude Bernard and Pasteur, for example, and then ultimately, writers, such as Zola, were won over to his doctrine of positivism. In the university world, Comte was never given the recognition he deserved, probably because of an attempted suicide in 1827, when he jumped into the Seine at a moment of mental derangement. He was a staunch representative of the cult of science, the generosity of socialism, the denial of religions, the veneration of the Revolution of 1789, and the desire to bring about the founding of a new and perfect political order. He was the founder of a new science which he called *sociologie*.

Félicité-Robert de Lamennais (1782–1854) was born in Saint-Malo, in Brittany, fourteen years after the birth of Chateaubriand in the same harbor city. He was converted to Catholicism at twenty-two, and ordained a priest at thirty-four. In his *Essai sur l'indifférence en matière de religion* (1817), he denounced the apathy of his contemporaries and the rationalistic scepticism of the 18th century.

After the Revolution of 1830, Lamennais felt himself a liberal and, asking for support from the generation of young romantics, and young Catholic writers such as Lacordaire and Maurice de Guérin, he founded a newspaper, *L'Avenir*, in October 1830. The newspaper argued for the separation of Church and State, and for the liberation of the proletariat from the exploitation of the bourgeoisie. Two years later the papal encyclical *Mirari vos* condemned the principles promulgated by *L'Avenir*.

Lamennais made his submission to Rome, but in 1834, in publishing *Paroles d'un croyant*, a book written in Biblical-like verses, he restated his faith in a Christian socialism. In another encyclical, *Singulari vos*, Pope Gregory XVI condemned him as a heretic. Almost all Lamennais preached and predicted has come about today: the separation of Church and State, the reunion of Christianity and the proletariat, the reform of the liturgy, and the adaptation of the Church to the modern world.

Lacordaire (1802–1861), a Burgundian, was first a lawyer and then, greatly influenced by Chateaubriand's *Génie du Christianisme*, studied at the seminary of Saint-Sulpice and was ordained a priest in 1827. With Lamennais, he fought for a liberalizing of Catholicism. He entered the Dominican Order in 1839, and helped bring about a restoration of that order. His sermons and *conférences* at Notre-Dame became famous. The young romantics looked up to him as a Bossuet because of the fire of his eloquence, and as a Chateaubriand in the pulpit because of the imagery of his style.

HISTORIANS:
THIERRY, TOCQUEVILLE, MICHELET

Both the *philosophes* of the 18th century and the romantics emphasized the importance of history. It became, especially in the writings of Michelet, a literary genre.

Augustin Thierry (1795–1856) was born in Blois. At fifteen, at the collège de Blois, he read *Les Martyrs* of Chateaubriand and there discovered his vocation of historian. On graduating from the Ecole Normale, he taught at the Collège de Compiègne, became Saint-Simon's secretary, then a journalist, and finally an historian with his *Histoire de la conquête de l'Angleterre par les Normands* (1825).

By 1837, Thierry was almost totally blind, and yet was able to continue his research with the help of his wife and disciples. In 1840, he published his most popular work, *Récits des temps mérovingiens*. History, for Thierry, became an art as well as a science. He was the type of scholar who in his research, carried on at the Bibliothèque Nationale, Sainte-Geneviève, the Arsenal and the Institut, sacrificed his life to his work.

Jules Michelet (1798–1874), one of the great prose writers of France, came from a very humble family in Paris. After receiving his *agrégation* degree, he became an admirable teacher of history, first in the Collège Sainte-Barbe, then at the Ecole Normale Supérieure, and finally at the Collège de France, where he was appointed professeur d'histoire et de morale, in 1838. "L'enseignement c'est une amitié," he once wrote.

In developing his theory and practice of history, Michelet was influenced by the Italian philosopher Vico, who helped him see history as a series of vast syntheses, an endless drama with episodes. For eleven years (1833–1844), he worked on the huge project of an *Histoire de France*. The first six volumes carried the history to the death of Louis XI.

Important political preoccupations interrupted the work, however. Michelet was moved to help the proletariat (*le peuple*) by demonstrating liberal democratic ideas. He became belligerently anticlerical in his conviction that the Church was the enemy of progress and social emancipation. At that moment in his career, Michelet, having interrupted work on his *Histoire de France*, wrote *Histoire de la Révolution*, based upon new documentation.

After the *coup d'état* of 1851, he lost his chair at the Collège de France. He resumed work on his *Histoire de France* and published volumes seven to seventeen between 1855 and 1867. These volumes carried French history from the Renaissance to the Revolution.

Michelet called history *une résurrection de la vie intégrale*. By the words "integral life" he seemed to mean documentation and scholarship. By the "resurrection" of distant historical periods, he seemed to mean the work of the artist. In writing history, Michelet emphasized not only the constant use of original sources, but also geography, geology, climate, the specific culture of provinces, and the customs of each region. History is a synthesis of all these elements. From all of this material the historian should, he thought, try to derive the fundamental law of the evolution of humanity. Michelet called France the daughter of her freedom: "la fille de sa liberté."

Michelet's powerful imagination (often compared to Hugo's) encouraged him to transform historical scenes into things grandiose and almost supernatural. He transformed into symbols the great figures of history: Charlemagne and Jeanne d'Arc, for example. Charles Péguy, in the next century, recalled Michelet in his effort to create an *idea* of France, and in the *idea* of Jeanne d'Arc.

FROM *L'ART POUR L'ART* TO
LE SYMBOLISME AND *LA DÉCADENCE*

When Sainte-Beuve used the phrase "ivory tower" to designate Alfred de Vigny's retreat from the world and from the activities of Paris, he could not have realized how the phrase would be used subsequently by those exponents of *l'art pour l'art* to describe precisely the site of the artist's isolation—not for the purpose of exile, not to manifest his scorn for the world of everyday actuality, but for the purpose of understanding his world more deeply and discovering the means of expressing his thought in a richer and more original manner. The ivory tower (*la tour d'ivoire*) will be used this way, with this precise meaning, by Flaubert and Henry James, by Pound and James Joyce, by Proust in his cork-lined room, and by Yeats.

The word associated with Baudelaire in the new aesthetic credo was *bizarre*, "strange and unusual." In announcing in his *salon* of 1855, that "le beau est toujours bizarre," he indicated that the artist's attraction to the strange is an element of his personality and separates him from most men who submit easily to the conventional and the traditional, who prefer not to be startled by originality. Those impulses that often manifest themselves in the subconscious—fantasies, hallucinations and sentiments of fear—and which in most men are not allowed to develop, represent the sources of experiences in man's moral and physical life. The artist, for Baudelaire, feels a desire to know and explore such fantasies that border on dreams and nightmares. Thanks to them, a man is able to escape from the humdrum routine of existence.

The word *maudit*, used by Verlaine in three essays in 1883 to designate the new type of poet, was more aggressive than the word *bizarre*. The three poets he discussed were Corbière, Rimbaud and Mallarmé—"Satanic" poets whom normally constituted citizens would repulse through fear that their work contained the germs of dissolution.

More vigorously than the essays of Verlaine, the novel of J. K. Huysmans, *A rebours* (1884), developed the theme of decadence in art. The book's protagonist, des Esseintes, represents all the positions of Huysmans: a philosophical pessimism about the world strongly reminiscent of Schopenhauer's thought, and a horror for what he considered the stupidity of most people in the world and the malice of fate. Des Esseintes is as refined as the comte de Montesquiou (who participated later in the makeup of Charlus in Proust's novel). The tapestries of his house are chosen as carefully as are the bindings of his books. The sensations of smell are as acute for him as they were for Baudelaire; indeed all forms of sensuality are celebrated as if they were part of a mystical cult. Perfumes have an effect on his spiritual life. He creates symphonies of smells as if he were illustrating Baudelaire's sonnet *Correspondances* and the doctrine of synesthesia. He is as refined in his analysis of sensations as he is unusual in his taste for so-called decadent literature. In modern literature, his predilections start with Baudelaire and continue with Poe, Ernest Hello, Barbey d'Aurevilly, Verlaine, Corbière, Mallarmé. Neurosis and decadence (*névrose, décadence*) are terms freely expressed throughout the novel, in des Esseintes' passion for Gustave Moreau's and Odilon Redon's paintings.

A rebours created a sensation. It revealed to a fairly wide public the work of the *poètes maudits* as continuing the work of the parnassians and illustrating the renewed belief in *l'art pour l'art*. Such works and such theories formed the basis for attitudes that were struck in the nineties in France and in England, and often referred to as aesthetic and decadent attitudes. But it is impossible to confine such terms to one or two decades. The history of taste and morals and aesthetics is difficult to describe chronologically. The English terms "gay nineties" and "mauve decade," and the French term *fin de siècle* are applicable to at least fifty years and even more of literary and art history.

In 1883, in *Le Chat Noir*, a poem of Verlaine, *Langueur*, was published, which called attention to the word "decadence." The opening line is the poet's self-portrait as he calls himself the empire at the end of the age of decadence:

Je suis l'Empire à la fin de la décadence.

In England, where the term was associated with certain aspects of French civilization, writers were, on the whole, worried about the term being attached to them. To offset the evil implied in the word decadence and a purely aesthetic view of life, comic elements were added. The tone of dead seriousness in *A rebours* is quite altered in Oscar Wilde's *Picture of Dorian Gray*. English levity offset French grimness. Swinburne, as well as Wilde, was able to parody himself. The high camp of Wilde and Max Beerbohm probably testifies to an English reticence and puritanism in the face of French extravagance and "immorality." However the thesis that Wilde develops so brilliantly in his essay *The Critic as artist* (*Intentions*) is one of the significant conclusions to be drawn from the entire movement of *l'art pour l'art*.

Undoubtedly inspired by Gustave Moreau's painting, Wilde's play *Salomé* (written in French), in which the heroine is turned into a sadist, was one of the more serious English contributions. But even here, the seriousness of the text was parodied by Aubrey Beardsley's illustrations. Arthur Symons, in his analysis of what he called "the decadent movement in literature," did not minimize the French sources and examples. Despite his defense of France, he called decadence a "beautiful disease," and tried to show how it developed into the more respectable movements of symbolism and impressionism. Yeats never approved of the term "decadence," and suggested that a more appropriate name to use was "symbolism." This may have influenced Symons in naming his book-length study of 1899 *The Symbolist Movement in Literature*. The words "decadent" and "aesthetic" were thereby given in England a healthier terminology. Corruption was given a new chance and a new garb.

At the time, in the Second Empire, when art for art's sake came into its own, Gautier, perhaps because of his limitations or perhaps because he never felt with the intensity of a Baudelaire, reached a degree of impassiveness in his behavior and outlook and gave in his writing the clearest example of a belief in laborious difficult technique. In his poem *L'Art*, printed in the second edition of *Emaux et Camées* in 1857, he defined the precept that only those forms of art that are technically difficult and demanding of an artist's patience have any chance for survival. The harder the material is to work in, the more beautiful the work will be. Gautier lists as examples poetry, first, and then marble, onyx, and enamel:

> Oui, l'oeuvre sort plus belle
> D'une forme au travail
>   Rebelle
> Vers, marbre, onyx, émail.

If these requirements of robustness and strength are met, the piece of sculpture and the poem whose versification is complex will endure longer than the city.

> Tout passe.—L'art robuste
> Seul a l'éternité:
>   Le buste
> Survit à la cité.

Ezra Pound, in *Mauberly*, of 1920, recapitulated this theory of Gautier, and imitated the versification of the French poem. The art of Flaubert is compared to Penelope's tapestry, patiently and everlastingly begun over again each day, in the artist's hope to reach perfection:

> His true Penelope
> Was Flaubert
> And his tool
> The engraver's
>
> Firmness
> Not the full smile,
> His art, but an art
> In profile.

In a much earlier poem of Gautier, *L'Hippopotame*, the new attitude of the parnassian poet was described by comparison of his indifference to the hostile world of the bourgeoisie and the traditional critics with the thick hide of the hippopotamus. The poet's convictions, his aloofness and aloneness, were evoked in the hippo's stolid heaviness as he wanders through the jungles of Java:

> L'hippopotame au large ventre
> Habite aux jungles de Java . . .
> Je suis common l'hippopotame:
> De ma conviction couvert . . .

T. S. Eliot wrote the same kind of poem, in terms of form and tone, in *The Hippopotamus*, but gave a different meaning to the metaphor by comparing the hippopotamus to the Church of Rome:

> The 'potamus can never reach
> The mango on the mango-tree;
> But fruits of pomegranate and peach
> Refresh the Church from over sea.

The cult of formal beauty and the application of elaborate technique were always present in art for art's sake. And in France, the passion behind this cult was, to some extent, hatred of successful mediocrity. The ascetic dignity and conscientiousness which Leconte de Lisle in *Poèmes Antiques*, and Hérédia in his *Trophées*, gave to pure craftsmanship were admired by the English—by Swinburne, for example—but the art was never directly copied by them. The French prose writers had perhaps more tangible influence. Walter Pater's essay on *Style* recapitulates theories of Flaubert.

It will forever be impossible to estimate how much Baudelaire's so-called "morbidity" and taste for extracting beauty out of unusual experiences developed because of his hatred for the world in which he lived. At one time, and not very long ago, Baudelaire was looked upon, both in England and France, as an isolated psychopathic case. Today, largely because of Eliot's three essays on him, he is studied in England and America as the modern poet—the modern Dante, in fact—who has given to the doctrine of morality in art its profoundest meaning. The wide range of themes in contemporary poetry, extending from the classical theme of Corso's poem *Uccello*, to poems classified as "pop" art, is owed in some degree to Baudelaire's example.

The word "symbolism" has come to have as many meanings as "romanticism." Ibsen's plays and Wagner's operas have been called "symbolist." For some, decadence became a means to religious conversion—in the cases, for example, of Barbey d'Aurevilly and Verlaine. Rimbaud's *Une saison en enfer* and *Les Illuminations* played a part in Paul Claudel's conversion. The decadent symbolist Huysmans of *A rebours* became a Catholic in *Là-Bas*.

At the very end of the century, several events seemed to make clear that art for art's sake and its survival in decadence were over. The triumph of Edmond Rostand's play *Cyrano de Bergerac* in 1897 indicated that the public wanted heroics and sentiment, action and wit. The Dreyfus Case encouraged many writers to turn into fighters. Nationalism, an outgrowth of imperialism, was pioneered by Maurice Barrès, whose cult for human energy was an attack on art for art's sake. In England, Rudyard Kipling put his art in the service of energy and imperialism. The odor of decadence seemed to diminish before the socialism of Jean Jaurès and Zola and Anatole France. And yet some disciples of art for art's sake were to survive the turn of the century movements and continue their work far into the century, although never occupying a central position in their day: Pierre Louÿs in France, for example, and George Moore in England.

The twenties were characterized by the appearance of many signs of art for art's sake: a philosophical pessimism, an arch-sophistication, a renewed interest in literary techniques, the emergence of somewhat defiant forms of immorality. Abbé Bremond's discussion with Paul Valéry over the theory of *poésie pure* was a worthy topic for art for art's sake. In describing European art in 1925, José Ortega y Gasset called it "new," and yet the traits he analyzed are those we associate with the pure art created in an ivory tower.

Such a doctrine as art for art's sake can be born and develop only in a blatantly materialistic age. The prosperity of Louis Napoleon's era when Gautier, Baudelaire and Flaubert wrote their best works was not unlike the Victorian atmosphere of austerity in which Oscar Wilde and Walter Pater flourished. The letters exchanged between Gide and Valéry during the last

decade of the 19th and the first of the 20th century refer frequently to the useless-
ness of art and the characteristic of poetry as not serving any definable function.
The type of man unable to understand and feel art is Flaubert's pharmacist
Monsieur Homais, in *Madame Bovary*. He was the type easy to scandalize.
Epater le bourgeois had once served almost as a battle cry. In America he was to
become Sinclair Lewis' Babbitt. Such literary creations as Homais and Babbitt
inevitably beget art for art's sake.

Since the time Jean-Jacques Rousseau revealed so much of himself in his
Confessions to a public eager to know the personal details of his life, the artist's
life and personality have been a part of literary study. There have been two
moments in the history of literary criticism when marked opposition to biography was felt: in the 1930s in America, in the "new criticism," the back-to-
the-text movement; and in the 1950s and 1960s in France, with the new
"structuralist" critics. From Rousseau's day on, despite the fact that most artists
have led quite conventional and moral lives, the general public has grown to
believe that they are temperamental and irresponsible, if not immoral.

The great importance given to aesthetic theories in Baudelaire's generation,
theories either identical with those of art for art's sake or closely related to them,
tended to conceal or disguise the moral and philosophical problems felt by that
generation. An attitude toward life which in the age of romanticism was called
le mal du siècle is in evidence at the end of the century, when it is called *le mal de
fin de siècle*. Paul Bourget's *Essais* and *Nouveaux essais de psychologie contemporaine*
(1883 and 1885) still offer today a penetrating analysis of a drama taking place
in the moral conscience and intellect of a generation. The suffering studied by
Bourget was more than the familiar phase of melancholy that most young
people go through when their world seems limited and their aspirations limitless. It was something more than introversion. The poetry of Jules Laforgue
reveals many aspects of a dissatisfaction and even resentment that had to do
with the prodigious development of the large cities, with the monotony of
provincial life, with the routine existence of employees and civil servants
(*fonctionnaires*), with *la vie quotidienne* in general, coming after two generations
of romanticism in the arts in which individualism had been exalted.

Baudelaire occupied a central position in the Bourget essays as the artist
who had the courage to call himself a decadent and adopt an attitude of sympathy with artificiality and strangeness. The mysterious word "decadence" would
seem to mean the will of the artist to understand the basic drives of his nature,
to explain what Baudelaire called the inner abyss or cemetery of the self, and
to use the creations of art as a remedy for ennui or spleen or what might be
called by the more simple term "pessimism."

The artists in France in 1885 were far more cut off psychically and soci-
ologically from society than their elders in 1820. Their suffering was more
neurotic and morbid. Their inability to adapt to society was more radical.
The themes of their poetry were more personal, more introverted, more symp-
tomatic of serious psychological upheavals. A fatigue with life is at the basis of
such a poem as Baudelaire's *Chant d'automne*. A disenchantment with everything
that life had promised him pervades the verse of Jules Laforgue. The need to
escape from the mortal boredom of provincial life is studied in Flaubert as well
as in the poetry of the decadents. The desperate need to live in a distant legendary land is sung by Verlaine in *Fêtes Galantes*, by Baudelaire in *L'Invitation au
voyage*, and by almost all of the lesser poets during the last part of the century.
But finally, dreams themselves become impossible, and all hope disappears.
Albert Samain, in *Au jardin de l'infante*, says that the sense of the void, of nothingness, has forged a new soul for him:

> Et le néant m'a fait une âme comme lui.

Around 1890, the proliferation in Paris of literary magazines was proof
that *le symbolisme* had grown into something comparable to a movement. *La
Vogue, La Plume, L'Ermitage, Le Mercure de France* provided the new writers
with the means of publishing and propagating those trends of the new literature
that still preserved from the earlier parnassian days an emphasis on art forms,
especially those forms that would bring out the musical qualities of language.
Less importance was granted to the shape and color of objects, those plastic
qualities celebrated by the parnassians, and there were new traces of moral and
psychological preoccupations, of metaphysical problems, and of a style of
writing more impressionistic than parnassian.

At the Saturday-night gatherings in the Latin Quarter, under the auspices
of *La Plume*, the Bohemian extravagances and enthusiasms for art recalled the
rue du Doyenné meetings, where Gautier and Nerval once discussed their
theories. Yet, on the whole, the *fin de siècle* gatherings were less bohemian than
those of the *rapins* of 1835. Pierre Louÿs warned his new friends André Gide
and Paul Valéry that Hérédia was a *mondain* and that Mallarmé was so serious
and correct in his behavior that they would have to give up wearing their
wide-brimmed hats and long neckties. Mallarmé's *mardis* had almost an official
air about them in 1890. Mallarmé had won out, at least in a social sense, over
Verlaine. The salon had replaced the café.

While Gide was still attending the *mardis* of Mallarmé, he wrote and published a manifesto on art which, although it is called in its subtitle *théorie du
symbole*, was also a recapitulation of parnassian theories on the role of the artist

and on his quest. The full title was *Traité du Narcisse*. Narcissus is the man seeking to find his own image, and who sees at the same time the image of everything else in the world. Narcissus is presented by Gide as the myth of man's return to the beginning of time, when all forms were paradisaical and crystalline. Poetry is the nostalgia for Paradise that has been lost. Adam had seen this wonder before he had seen himself. When, according to Gide's interpretation of the myth, he saw himself, he then distinguished himself from everything else, and fell from grace.

By defining the poet as the man able to look, able to see paradise behind appearances, Gide indicated affiliations with one part of the parnassian creed. Every phenomenon is the symbol of a truth. The poet's duty is to manifest it. As the poet contemplates the symbols of the world, he penetrates at the same time their deepest meanings. This is why Gide calls the work of art a crystal, a partial paradise where the idea unfolds as a flower does, in its original purity. As an admirer of Mallarmé, Gide, in *Traité du Narcisse*, wrote a profession of faith in platonic idealism.

The symbol in Mallarmé's art, which can be as visible and precise as in parnassian art—a swan, a vase, a faun—is that creation of the poet capable of suggesting. *Suggérer* is a key verb in Mallarmé's aesthetics. It means first to awaken, to indicate without specifically naming or defining, to propose a meaning without dogmatically imposing it. *Suggérer* can also mean to incite and prolong an emotion on the part of the reader. During the decade of the 90s, Mallarmé and his disciples unquestionably enlarged the meaning of the symbol to include certain aspects of myth and allegory. Whereas an allegory is primarily didactic, a myth is addressed as much to the emotions of the reader as to his intelligence. It tends more to move a reader than to convince him. Allegory is therefore moralistic and myth is religious by nature. The object in parnassian art and the symbol in symbolist art are primarily aesthetic, intended to give to the reader a sense of the beautiful. But the literary symbol, as it has been used since Baudelaire's time, in its aesthetic power, has a closer relationship with the religious spirit of man than with any reasonable or practical or didactic use.

Symbolism has been a major preoccupation of literature since Baudelaire published his sonnet *Correspondances*, which can be seen as a succinct manifesto. It has provided an aesthetic basis for works that have elements both of myth and allegory. They are literary works, among the most impressive and notable since 1850, which have reacted strongly against a realistic art of precision in order to reflect preoccupations that are religious and philosophical: the poetry of Rimbaud, Mallarmé, Yeats and Eliot; the novels of Proust and Joyce.

It would be difficult to exaggerate the prevalence of pessimism throughout

Europe between 1880 and 1900—the doubts and reservations expressed about science, the influence of Schopenhauer's philosophy, the negativism of Ibsen and Nietzsche. The aesthetic beliefs, often designated as "decadent" came in part from the spread of intellectual and moral pessimism, from an exalting of Baudelaire's theme concerning the decadence of aging civilizations. Each country offered its own brand of decadent pessimism: Verlaine and his group of *décadents* in Paris, Stefan George in Germany, with his *Blätter für die Kunst*, and Oscar Wilde in England, with the turbulent group of writers associated with *The Yellow Book* and *The Savoy*.

From today's perspective, it is fairly clear that decadence was one aspect of the development of symbolism. Stefan George's activities were efforts, without any subversive characteristics, to rally young German writers around a set of beliefs that were almost identical with art for art's sake. English decadence was more complex to follow and understand, and in fact was so complex that the word decadence seems inappropriate. It was used, of course, because of the scorn on the part of some writers for conventional morality and for certain morbid elements of art that were esteemed. The English origins of this cult for beauty may be found in the poetry of Keats in the early part of the century and later redefined and reformulated by Rossetti, Morris and Swinburne. John Ruskin's teachings on esthetics had a more direct influence, whereas the writings of Walter Pater rallied very little marked support. French influence was felt to some extent in the work of Swinburne and Pater, but especially in the writings of George Moore. In the 90s, when the figure of Wilde dominated all others, the movement of decadence was openly a revolt against tradition.

The cult of art for art's sake continued well into the 20th century. The assumption of this cult, as illustrated by Joyce and Proust, is that art by itself is capable of conferring value and meaning upon life, and even ultimate value. Such writers as Yeats, Eliot and Pound, who were in closest sympathy with the theories of art for art's sake and whose work reflects strong influences of those French writers associated with the movement, continued to show a similar attitude toward the world, at least toward the world of politics. They tended to look upon democracy as a standardizing process. Yeats felt almost a resentment of the prestige of science. To indict these men as "fascists" is erroneous, but they have often given evidence of a preference for an earlier social order. The cultural atmosphere of the early 20th century was characterized by yearnings for the religious, the mystical, the occult, by the development of a new romanticism that merged with belief in the sovereignty of the word in literature.

LAUTRÉAMONT (1846–1870)

In 1970, the hundredth anniversary of Lautréamont's death, two new biographies were published (ironically, perhaps, because there are very few known facts about his life) and also the Pléiade edition of the *Oeuvres complètes* by P. O. Walzer. The introduction and notes of this edition take into account all of the writings about Lautréamont and all of the many hypotheses concerning the interpretation of his work and his character.

Isidore Ducasse was born of French parents in Montevideo, Uruguay. He was sent to France for his schooling, first to the lycée of Tarbes, and then the lycée of Pau. He was in Paris in the fall of 1867. In 1869, he gave to a publisher the complete manuscript of the six *Chants de Maldoror* under the pseudonym "Comte de Lautréamont." The edition was printed but not sold. The young writer died in November 1870, in his room at 7, faubourg Montmartre, at the age of twenty-four. The first edition of *Maldoror* that had been printed in 1869 was put on sale in 1874, without any success. Fifty years later, the surrealists, especially André Breton, who published the *poésies* of Lautréamont in his magazine *Littérature*, made him into a god. He represented for the surrealists an absolute revolt against society, the only writer who did not leave behind him any equivocal trace of his life on earth. All trace of his bodily remains and his manuscripts was lost. The mysteriousness of Isidore Ducasse's life is quite in keeping with the sinister mysteries of the writings of le comte de Lautréamont.

During the past thirty years, several critics have called attention to the importance of *Les Chants de Maldoror*—Bachelard, first, in 1939, Marcel Jean and Arped Mezei, in 1947, Maurice Blanchot in 1945 (*Lautréamont et Sade*) and Marcelin Pleynet in 1967. In depicting the monsters of Maldoror who threaten the establishment (the family and society), Lautréamont was unquestionably influenced by the gothic tales (*le roman noir*) of such writers as Sade, Eugène Sue, Anne Radcliffe, Lewis, Hoffmann, Pétrus Borel. The rational and the irrational were not separate worlds for Lautréamont. He established communication between them.

Lautréamont had the conviction that the artist must be different from other men, must live in some other way than in accordance with the fixed standards of the bourgeoisie. His writings represent an attack on the traditional poses of romanticism, on the languorous and sentimental attitudes of the poets, on the moonlit scenes of peacefulness and meditations. He followed and exalted the more vigorous romanticism of a Berlioz in his resounding periods and inflated style, and of a Delacroix, in the rich colors of his scenes. He was the youthful writer who, with Rimbaud, felt he had been cheated and tricked by destiny. He refused, during the brief span of his career, to compromise with society or with any of the forces that habitually promise success to the aspiring artist. In this regard, Rimbaud and Lautréamont closely resembled one another.

Les Chants de Maldoror was written during a brief period of time and was the product of an intense intellectual fervor in a personality that would traditionally be classified as highly abnormal. In his systematic visions, in his tone of scorn and sarcasm for what is human, Lautréamont revived and prolonged the romanticism of despair and revolt. *Maldoror* is the work of an unhappy and even desperate adolescent. In the beauty of his writing, he derived some degree of satisfaction by demolishing the world, by upsetting its moral values. In his experience of solitude, Lautréamont saw only himself and his Creator. All the scenes he depicted have to do with the epic struggle, the oldest struggle of mankind, between man himself and God.

Maldoror is both man and animal, resembling the minotaur or a beast of the Apocalypse. On horseback he rides over the surface of the earth, and takes on innumerable metamorphoses: eagle, octopus, cricket, black swan. Everything is presented as enigmatic in the long series of episodes that compose *Les Chants*: dreams, myths, symbols, realistic effects. The son's hostility toward his father (or man's efforts to liberate himself from his Creator) is the most apparent theme of the work. There are examples of the traumatic experience of a child being brutally separated from his parents: in the second canto, the child running after the omnibus; in the fourth canto, the child taking refuge in the ocean and being transformed into an amphibian; and the episode of Mervyn in the sixth canto, which is the story of a spiritual seduction and a physical assassination.

To know oneself is dangerous, and this danger is emphasized throughout the cantos. Lautréamont seems to be saying that the individual first recognizes himself as such in his relationship with his father, both his human father and his supernatural Creator. But as soon as this recognition takes place, a combat follows, a combat for survival that will challenge all the power of a man. Mervyn's story is both his renunciation of his father and his search for a father.

The strong symbols of "minotaur" and "labyrinth" are in Lautréamont's text. In his subconsciousness man creates his own labyrinth, and then in his conscious life he tries to explore it. Each man plays the two roles of Minotaur, of monster for whom the labyrinth is designed, and of Theseus, who heroically tries to find the monster and slay him. *Les Chants de Maldoror* is the meeting between Theseus-Lautréamont and the Minotaur-Maldoror. The cantos are the labyrinth, the literary expression of man seen in his labyrinthine ways.

The writer is always to some degree the recreator of a myth. In the figure of Maldoror, whose name could mean the dawn, the light of evil (*mal-d'aurore*), one can see the re-creation of the Christian myth of Lucifer, the fallen archangel whose name means light (*lux, lucis,* and *ferre*—to bring). In the name Ducasse chose for himself, Lautréamont, some critics believe they can see *L'autre Amon,* or *Amon-Râ,* the Egyptian sun-god, the other sun. The defiance of Maldoror is of such proportions, the violence of his actions and his thoughts is so extreme, that he becomes the personification of evil, an epic figure (of a modern *chanson de geste*) in the very greatness of that which he opposes.

Lautréamont established a relationship with forms of anxiety that reappear virulent and provocative in the 20th century. These anxieties, in a histrionic and highly stylized manifestation, are the subject matter of *Les Chants de Maldoror.* The macabre is deliberately cultivated in the themes of lycanthropy, vampirism, murder, bestiality. We are at the beginning of time, because each human being, in his subconscious, relives the history of man. The fears of primitive man are orchestrated by Lautréamont in his stanzas. All the instinctive impulses of sexuality and egoism are celebrated as if they were necessary rites of purification. Monsters of the sea, animals of prey, insects and vermin are everywhere on these pages. Pictorially they appear as they would in the imagination of a child, but they symbolize the basic drives of man in his destructiveness.

The literary creation of Maldoror and the writer Lautréamont were also the young man Isidore Ducasse, living alone in his room on the fifth floor of a Paris hotel. At the same time, Rimbaud, the author of *Le Bateau Ivre,* was a young boy living in his room on the top floor of a hotel in the rue Monsieur le Prince—Ducasse had been a student imprisoned in the collège de Tarbes in the Pyrenees, and Rimbaud a student prisoner in Charleville, in the northern Ardennes.

ARTHUR RIMBAUD (1854–1891)

Rimbaud began writing at an early age in Charleville. In 1869 a Latin poem won a first prize in the Concours Académique. His first known French poem, *Les Etrennes des Orphelins* was composed in the same year.

During 1870, he wrote twenty-two poems. The young teacher Georges Izambard became Rimbaud's mentor and friend during his last year at the

Collège de Charleville. On the 29th of August, Rimbaud made his first escape to Paris, by train, and was put into Mazas prison at the end of the trip, because he had not purchased a full ticket. Later, on foot, he set out for Belgium, an experience that inspired such poems as *Ma Bohème, Le Buffet* and *Au Cabaret Vert*.

There was another trip to Paris, in February 1871, and a return on foot to Charleville. His two letters of May to Izambard and Paul Demeny are in reality treatises on Rimbaud's conception of poetry. The boy's disposition was strongly anti-religious at this time, testified to in such a poem as *Les Premières Communions*. At the end of September, Rimbaud, armed with new poems, including *Le Bateau Ivre*, went to Paris, where he had been invited by Verlaine, after a first exchange of letters.

The next year and a half were dominated by Verlaine in an enthusiastic, troubled, and at times tragic relationship. Rimbaud undoubtedly began writing some of the *Illuminations* in London in 1872, and was engaged in writing *Une Saison en Enfer* in April 1873, at his mother's farm in Roche. The definitive break between the two poets occurred in Brussels in July 1873 as the result of a violent quarrel. Verlaine fired a revolver, wounding Rimbaud in the left wrist, and was arrested and condemned by the Belgian police court to two years in prison. His arm in a sling, Rimbaud returned to Roche, where he completed *Une Saison en Enfer*. He was nineteen, and his literary work was over, save for some *Illuminations* which he may have written during the next two years.

After extensive travelling in Europe, Rimbaud went to Aden in 1880 to work for an export company. In 1887 he sold guns to King Menelik in Choa, and between 1888 and 1891 he worked for a coffee exporter in Harar. A tumor in his right knee caused him to return to Marseille in May 1891. His leg was amputated. After a brief return to Charleville to be with his mother and sister, he was again hospitalized in Marseille and died there at the age of thirty-seven.

Most of Rimbaud's work was written between the ages of sixteen and nineteen. After the Brussels drama, he published *Une Saison en Enfer*, but as soon as the work was printed and a few copies distributed, he lost all interest in it. *Les Illuminations* was published by Verlaine for the first time in 1886; the first edition of the poems came out in 1891.

Today most of the poems in verse present few difficulties to a reader trained in the reading of modern poetry, but *Une Saison en Enfer* is still a troublesome text. The psychic experience related in it is as much that of our age as it is of one adolescent poet. The prose poems of *Les Illuminations* are still more difficult to fathom.

Etiemble's thesis of gigantic proportions, *Le Mythe de Rimbaud*, appearing in 1952–54, denounced the critical method of turning Rimbaud into a mythical figure—angel or demon, Catholic or surrealist, *voyant* or *voyou*. A new type of study has begun in which the focus is on the problems of poetic expression.

Our age is one of revolt, and Rimbaud has given, in his literary work and in the example of his life, one of the most vibrant expressions of this revolt. There was nothing unusual about his life, save that the major events, transpiring while he was a practicing poet, were swift: the interruption of formal study, hatred for his provincial life, his friendship with Verlaine, the discovery that very few people in Paris were interested in him or in his talent, the break with Verlaine, the writing of *Une Saison en Enfer*, and soon after that, the irrevocable giving up of literature.

The strange masterpieces of Rimbaud, and of other artists and writers who followed him—Apollinaire, Joyce, Picasso, Chagall and Satie—show a proclivity toward enigma and infantile imagination. All of Rimbaud's poems are on childhood, but especially the one called *Mémoire*. The river crossing the prairie reflects all the memories of the boy Rimbaud: the nude women bathing in it, the young girls playing, the mother dressed in black standing erect and watching over the children, the yellow and blue flowers growing out of the water—and finally the boat immobilized by a chain.

Rimbaud, at sixteen or seventeen, when he composed *Mémoire*, speaks of a child but evokes the most austere dramas of man and woman. The character of woman is analyzed by the symbol of the river, as Anna Livia Plurabelle is analyzed in Joyce's *Finnegans Wake*. In *Le Bateau Ivre*, the poet, after all his hyperbolic adventures, has to return to the parapets of Europe, and in *Mémoire* he cannot cut the cables of his boat.

And yet Arthur Rimbaud is still associated with the theme of flight and poetry of exploration. The youthful poet who in his *Bateau Ivre* names so many places and visions—fish traps, glaciers, singing fish, cataracts, gulfs, Floridas—is a kind of primitive mystic, as Claudel described him, because the universe he sees is not seen by other men. The art of poetry is the opposite of the art of science. Science consists of the discoveries of men which are known and which are sure of succeeding, but poetry is that voyage into the unknown where no discovery is assured, where nothing is certain of success. The metamorphoses of the horizons we follow in *Le Bateau Ivre*—the liberation of the boat, its going down the river, its marine adventures, its return to the parapets of Europe—are the metamorphoses of Rimbaud's character by which he forces his imagination to plunge into the unknown.

In his practice of poetry, which is neither exclusively sentiment nor music, Rimbaud laid the basis for a new opening out onto a supernatural and surreal world, an art that later will be associated with Claudel and Char. In the mind's search for that absolute, which began in modern poetry with Baudelaire and Nerval and continued in diverse ways with Rimbaud, Mallarmé, Claudel and Apollinaire, poetry changed from an art of lyricism to one of inquiry and exasperation, to a search for values and metaphysical assurances. The basis is the charter as set forth in *Correspondances*—the visible world is the image of a secret universe. The alchemy Rimbaud alludes to is one term for an age-long quest for certainty, the survival of a tradition that parallels the history of mankind. Man has to learn how to work back from the visible to the invisible.

STÉPHANE MALLARMÉ (1842–1898)

Mallarmé enunciated in many ways and on many occasions the belief that poetry is something akin to magic. After passing through the two phases of individualistic and social poetry with the early romantics and Victor Hugo, this became, especially with Mallarmé, a metaphysical exercise. He married the arts without hesitation. His defense of the new painting in his day was undertaken with as much fervor as was his defence of the new poetry.

Recent critics and biographers of Mallarmé have tried to discover the philosophical books and authors that might have served as the foundation of his aesthetics. But Mallarmé was probably not an assiduous reader of the German metaphysicians, even of Fichte and Hegel, with whom his name has been associated. He doubtless read very little technical philosophy, and had no characteristics of the erudite which Flaubert, for example, possessed. He was of course aware of the philosophical concepts in his day, but his mind deepened by means of perceptions rather than dialectics. Pascal would have called Mallarmé *un esprit de finesse*. The series of seemingly unrelated or discontinuous images which many of his poems demonstrate place them beside the work of post-impressionists, cubists and surrealists.

The comparatively few poems he published, his avoidance of clichés and of verbal facility, his unwillingness to hasten the writing of any line or of any stanza, were elements of his excessive scrupulosity. Unlike those writers for whom writing was a constant career—Voltaire or Victor Hugo—Mallarmé was one of those poets like Baudelaire and Valéry whose far rarer productions were the result of certain privileged moments in a lifetime. As with the painters who were his friends—Manet, Degas, Berthe Morisot—and with the great painters who followed him, Mallarmé had only a few subjects in his poems. Like a portrait painter, he waited for commissions. His poems were of circumstances.

In the early years, what seemed to him poetic sterility, or lack of material, was the cause of a great personal anxiety. It became one of the personal principles of his aesthetics. Poems like *Le pitre châtié*, *L'Azur*, *Les Fenêtres*, all testify to the merging of a personal anguish with an aesthetic belief. The poet's struggle with the white page is comparable to the painter's struggle with the white canvas. The infrequent sonnets of Mallarmé and the still-lifes of Braque, for example, represent a difficult attitude toward nature and the familiar objects of a room. The newer artist, both poet and painter, is more isolated from the world in his almost obsessive treatment of a few familiar objects and figures and scenes. The often recurring treatment of the same objects in the sonnets of Mallarmé and the paintings of Picasso lent itself to the art of deforming the presences and the objects.

Symbolism and impressionism both were reactions against the data, the given subject material, the rigor in order and composition of an Ingres or a Leconte de Lisle. The so-called cult of obscurity, as opposed to an oratorical or expository art, is certainly to some degree the art of doubt and nuance, an art based on a predilection for ellipsis. Mallarmé, in the very title of his collected essays, *Divagations*, warns that he will turn the reader's mind from the usual ways and channels. He was fully aware that his poetry was an arduous exercise for the mind and a delicate testing of the sensibility.

Mallarmé's habit of living in his apartment more than in the world parallels his withdrawal from popular literature and his creation of a highly esoteric poetry. The fans, vases, books and bibelots of his parlor helped to constitute the scene of a refuge not unlike *la chambre bleue* of Mme de Rambouillet, in which manners and the art of poetry were preserved from the coarseness of the court of Henri IV. Beyond any doubt, Stéphane Mallarmé believed that the highest or the purest expressions of art were accessible to very few.

Words have familiar meanings, and this fact represented for Mallarmé the constant trap or obstacle to the creation of his kind of poem. Likewise, the objects painted by Braque and Matisse were to suggest rather than signify. Mallarmé turned more and more to the negative word, the word of absence, as in his toast sonnet,

Rien, cette écume, vierge vers (Salut)

and the use of a series of seemingly disjointed or discontinuous images, as in the sonnet on Baudelaire's tomb. The successive images, flaming and fulgurant, in *La chevelure vol d'une flamme*, present a solemn exercise of relationships that have to be seized by the reader. Such demands on the reader are not unlike the demands on the spectator implied in such a painting as *Les demoiselles d'Avignon* of Picasso.

The difficult and often painful existence of the poet and the artist such as we associate with a Baudelaire, a Mallarmé, a Cézanne, or a Van Gogh, with its failures, exile, sadness seems a necessary part of the scheme whereby he will see the purer, more spiritual vision of things and their relationships. Proust has spoken in detail about the disparity between the artist's life and his work. Alfred de Vigny's ivory tower is the symbol of the poet's isolation and dignity. Mallarmé's salon and Verlaine's café were in one sense their ivory tower.

In the history of French poetry, Mallarmé represents today a turning point and a point of achievement. His art and his theory are of such a nature that his moment has the significance of the *trobar clus* of the troubadours in the 12th century, of the Platonist poets of the Renaissance, of romanticism and the parnassian ideal which immediately preceded him in the 19th century. By his concentration on language, by his skill with ellipsis and synecdoche, he purified language. Only the most efficacious words remained in the finished line to designate the object and the way in which it was seen. This purification of language was such that the object revealed was elevated to a metaphysical value—the swan, the punished clown, the helmet of the girl empress (*Victorieusement fui le suicide beau*) reach meanings far beyond the usual.

A poem is a privileged moment when words are revealed in a new context, in an unusual lighting, an unusual drama: the sunflooded noon of the faun in the forest, or the cold midnight of Hérodiade in her tower. But whatever the object—a lascivious faun, an hieratic princess, a garden of irises, an empty bibelot—the theme of the poem is always the same: the poetic act.

In his letter to Verlaine in 1885, the important text called *Autobiographie*, Mallarmé names the book, the ideal book he hopes to write: *Le Livre, explication orphique de la Terre*. Metaphors are in reality metamorphoses and transmutations, and thus the poet, creator of metaphors, is a kind of alchemist and magician. The attempt to recreate the world by means of the poetic word is a quasi-divine ambition.

Mallarmé is fully conscious of the immemorial prestige of words: the meanings they have today in their human context, and the more esoteric meanings that still cling to them from their uses in a remote past. The moral theme, so strong in *Les Fleurs du Mal*, diminishes in Mallarmé's poems. The theory of verbal incantations, defined by Baudelaire, is more fully applied by Mallarmé, until the power of the words, with their associations and their relatedness, replace the moral allusions. This would be a major distinction between Baudelaire's *Le Voyage*, in which the various kinds of voyage are moral quests, and Mallarmé's *Prose pour des Esseintes*, in which the island voyage is the poet's quest for beauty. The reality of Paris in such a poem as *Le Cygne* is the basis of Baudelaire's art, whereas the real world is nullified in *Toast Funèbre* as Mallarmé celebrates the poetic universe created by the poet.

To the experience of sterility, evident in such a poem as *L'Azur*, succeeded the experience of purity. *Hérodiade* is perhaps the work that best designates this very marked change in Mallarmé's poetic process. What had once been for the romantics and even for Verlaine poetry of the ephemeral became, for Mallarmé, an experience cast in the form of a drama—a drama of the mind in its search for the absolute.

The poems of Mallarmé and his teaching about poetry mark a change in the history of an art. Poetry before him, on the whole, translated sentiments and ideas, and usually without ambiguity. Poetry after him is more difficult because it conforms to other powers of language, because it is the expression of mysterious aspects of existence. The charm and the processes of Mallarmé are visible in such different and original poets as Apollinaire, Valéry, Claudel, Eluard. He created an art form that is antioratorical and antisocial. By writing a poetry in which the concrete is always vanishing, he created a counter-creation. The flower he holds up in his verse is not a flower—it is the one absent from all bouquets, *l'absente de tous bouquets*.

PAUL VERLAINE (1844–1896)

Of the three major poets who wrote in the second half of the 19th century, Verlaine is the least difficult, and his work has in recent years been more neglected than Mallarmé's and Rimbaud's. His first collection, *Poèmes saturniens* (1866), contains many poems written in the parnassian manner. *Fêtes Galantes* (1869) evokes the delicacy and licentiousness of Watteau's paintings. *Romances sans paroles* (1874) has some of his first allusive poems. His *Art Poétique*, written in prison in 1873, became a manifesto for the symbolists. It insists upon music, imprecision and shading. Verlaine advocated lightness of tone and no rhetoric, no "literature."

Et tout le reste est littérature.

Verlaine is usually described as weak and unstable. This judgment can be justified, but he had also a tenacity of spirit and determination of will that at times made him appear almost a fanatic. He was fervently *communard* at the time of the Commune in 1871. After his conversion, he denounced in vigorous terms aspects of the modern spirit he believed erroneous.

According to his own confession, his life was dominated by a number of indiscreet and wrongful acts—chiefly stemming from his turbulent relationship with Rimbaud, which culminated in disgrace and imprisonment for Verlaine.

For many years after his release from prison, he tried to restore his marriage and recover a social status. Neither his wife nor society was willing to help him. The poverty and dereliction of the last years of his life, when he fell victim to drink and debauchery, were not planned by him. They were imposed upon him by forces beyond his control.

If the human experience and suffering of Paul Verlaine seem beyond our comprehension because they are so personal, we are better able to follow his poetic transcription of them. His poem on the adventure with Rimbaud, *Crimen amoris*, makes it resemble a marriage of heaven and hell. It is a theological explanation by a poet who for the first time perhaps understands the meaning of remorse and integrates it within his nature.

During his last years, he was looked upon by many as the greatest living poet. In France he is still one of the few poets who have reached the general public. His influence on the development of French poetry has been slight, despite the fact that he exploited brilliantly the resources of the French language. Today he is associated with impressionism. When a critical judgment is now made on Verlaine, it usually asserts his incapacity to move beyond a transitory and subjective impression of his themes.

JULES LAFORGUE (1860–1887)

Laforgue called himself "un bon Breton né sous les tropiques." Born in Montevideo, at the age of six he was brought to Tarbes in southern France, where, with his brother Emile, he attended the lycée de Tarbes for several years of intense solitude. The family moved to Paris in 1875, and Jules finished his lycée years at Fontanes (called today Condorcet). He took courses at the Ecole des Beaux Arts, listened to Taine lecture, and frequented museums and libraries, especially the Bibliothèque Nationale. Some of his early poems date from 1879.

He was quite alone in Paris in 1880–81 when Charles Ephrussi, an art historian of exceptionally fine taste, engaged in writing a book on Dürer, hired him as secretary. Laforgue's life in Paris was typical of the talented young provincial, in love with literature, ambitious to become a writer, and leading a miserable and solitary existence.

A change came at the end of 1881. Ephrussi secured for Laforgue the post of French reader to Empress Augusta of Germany. For five years he lived in Berlin in a magnificent apartment in the royal palace, *unter den Linden*. He had a personal servant and usually ate with the ladies-in-waiting of the court. He resembled a clergyman in his impeccable black suit. Whenever the Empress travelled, Laforgue followed the court—to Baden, Hombourg, Coblentz. He made a few friends in Berlin where he studied German art and attended concerts, operas and the circus.

After the five years in Germany, he married in England a young English girl, and then settled in Paris. Poverty and ill health again beset his last few years. He died at the age of twenty-seven, unable to secure enough funds to leave Paris for a warmer climate.

Laforgue felt all the principal literary influences of his day: Vigny, Hugo, Gautier, Balzac, but was most deeply affected by Baudelaire, Corbière, Rimbaud and Mallarmé. He felt a close affinity with the type of sad Pierrot, a familiar symbol of the young Parisian intellectual of 1880. The prophetic tendency in him was curiously fused with the clown. He was exactly the type of hero, of artist-intellectual whose psychology and drama he wanted to describe in his writing: the genius-failure.

Gradually Laforgue's work has been assuming a place of importance in the history of symbolism. The first really constituted group of symbolist poets was active during 1880–1885, years when Laforgue was absent for the most part from Paris and was writing his major poems. The word "decadent" has been associated with this particular group of poets (Moréas, Morice, Tailhade, Fénéon, Kahn). The decadent reacted against the platitudes of his day and opposed to them the unusual, the precious, the refined. Des Esseintes, hero of Huysmans' novel, *A rebours*, was the leading type of decadent. Verlaine subscribed to the new emphasis. Gustave Kahn, who had maintained correspondence with Laforgue in Germany, asked for contributions to *La Vogue*, a magazine he began publishing in April 1886.

To students of Laforgue today, the characters in his prose book, *Moralités légendaires* (1887)—Pan, Lohengrin, Hamlet, Salomé—appear as thinly disguised self-portraits of Laforgue rather than as symbols of universal import. "Decadence," if it has any meaning at all, applies better to Laforgue than the term symbolism. Baudelaire had taught Laforgue's generation significant lessons on self-analysis and on the morbid pleasure to be derived from such analysis. Bourget, in his *Essais de psychologie contemporaine*, pointed out that the word "decadent" became the battle-cry of the new school. He called it a *pessimisme parisien* that spread outside of France.

Laforgue's first poems, published after his death as *Le Sanglot de la Terre* (1901), are the easiest to read and the most recognizable to readers of Baudelaire in their litanies of "spleen" and in the various exorcisms he practices to recover from the spleen. There are many pictures of Paris, more localized and less universal than Baudelaire's, and cosmological visions in which the earth is seen as some abysmal mediocrity, a dying star in the vertigoes of universes.

The central image of *Le Sanglot de la Terre* is one of the heart—the heart of a solitary man, amassing so much remorse and adoration that it burns and bleeds like a rose window in a cathedral (see *Rosace en vitrail*). The poet comes to read into this symbol of the hypertrophied heart the illusion of life. Laforgue is really considering the heart of the earth and his poem is the passion of the earth, but his intelligence keeps a careful watch over his heart. No matter how cosmic his vision becomes, he always ends by parodying his own anguish. He is the type of passionate intellectual, "Hamlet without a sword," as Camille Mauclair called him, who refuses to take himself seriously and whose most heartfelt cries are always silenced by the clown's grimace. Not even the pessimistic philosophy of Schopenhauer, whose works Laforgue read in Paris, and that of Hartmann, whom he read later in Germany, prevented his writing verse which is essentially a parody of sensibility.

The second group of poems Laforgue wrote, and the first to be published, *Les Complaintes* (1885), represented a new aesthetics and a new philosophy. His new language he called more "clownish." His boldness in vocabulary and style gave the collection a complex, bizarre effect, a kind of poetic laboratory of hundreds of unexpected combinations. Some of the "complaints" are semi-philosophical, like the opening one, a propitiation addressed to the unconscious, in which the poet prays to be released from thought in a parody of the Lord's prayer:

> Non, rien; délivrez-nous de la Pensée
> Lèpre originelle, ivresse insensée.

The complaint of daily living is the most poignant of all:

Ah! que la vie est quotidienne!

Hurdy-gurdies, pianos, billboards, photographs, October days, and Sundays are themes of the incurable complaint. As far back as the poet can go in his memory, he has been something of a clown, something of a genius *manqué*.

Comme on fut piètre et sans génie...

("Almost at times the fool!" Eliot will say through his Prufrock.)

The character Pierrot gradually came to life in the poetry of Laforgue, and with the group of poems, called *Imitation de Notre Dame la Lune*, Pierrot assumed first place, combining the irony and the metaphysics of the earlier poetry. He and the moon carry on a dialogue, under the protection of Gustave Kahn and the priestess Salammbô, to whom the work is dedicated. Through the sensibility of these lunar inhabitants, called Pierrots, Laforgue was describing his own sensibility. Like them, he wanted to become legendary before the beginning of the false ages.

Derniers Vers, a series of twelve poems, are meditations on love. Their setting is always the same: the slums and the suburbs of cities. Their 816 lines appear almost as a single continuous poem. There was nothing in the later Laforgue of the grand style of romantic poetry. He was concerned with depicting the shifts and variations of feelings in scenes of the modern city. Both the system of multiple allusions and the general atmosphere of spiritual sterility relate the work to *The Waste Land*. The dominant mood Laforgue expressed was one of emotional starvation and emotional inhibition. It was already the negative wit, the brevity of Prufrock.

The parody of his own sensibility became, in Laforgue's *Moralités légendaires*, the parody of some of the great myths of humanity. He recapitulated the stories of the masters: Shakespeare's Hamlet, Wagner's Lohengrin, Mallarmé's faun, Flaubert's Salomé, and altered them in order to infuse new meanings into them. No such thing as a pure hero existed for Laforgue. He saw the so-called heroes as ordinary creatures, and gave them psychological characteristics of his Pierrots—nervousness, anxiety, an ephemeral existence. By parody and by anachronism, he created new characters out of the old. Each "morality" defined a concentrated action, a single crisis, which gave it a highly dramatic tone.

The most deeply hidden theme in his work, and probably the most important for an understanding of Laforgue as man and poet, is that of woman and love. He never concealed the anguish he felt over his celibacy. He was a recluse and always depressed by his solitude. He feared not love, but the deceit of love.

He worried for fear that love was always a deceit of nature and denounced what he believed to be the false myth of woman—very much the same myth Mme Simone de Beauvoir denounces in *Le Deuxième Sexe*, in which she quotes Laforgue. He spoke against the deification of woman, against the mystery with which she has been surrounded. Either he vituperated against what he believed her falseness or regretted plaintively the disappearance of man's comradeship with women, or a simple natural relationship between the sexes.

With Rimbaud, who was the most influential poet in France to emerge after World War I, a different metaphysics of poetry came into prominence. On the whole, the surrealists disapproved of Laforgue. "Lisez Rimbaud. Ne lisez pas Laforgue," was their admonition. Jean Cocteau tells the story of Picasso, Max Jacob and Apollinaire once shouting in the streets of Montmartre: "Vive Rimbaud! A bas Laforgue!"

TRISTAN CORBIÈRE (1845–1875)

The first edition of Corbière's one book, *Les Amours Jaunes*, appeared in 1873, which was also the year of Rimbaud's *Une saison en enfer* and Verlaine's *Romances sans paroles*. Corbière died two years later, at the age of thirty. Not until 1883, in Verlaine's series of essays on *Les Poètes Maudits*, was Corbière presented to the Paris public as a poet of importance. This first label of *poète maudit* has remained associated with his name. He refused to write poetry in accordance with traditional forms. He even refused to be a traditional bohemian. "An ocean bohemian," Jules Laforgue once called him, since most of his life was spent in Brittany, in the towns of Morlaix and Roscoff, and since the themes of his personal suffering are mingled with the dominant theme of the sea.

In many ways Corbière was the spiritual descendent of Villon, and especially in his self-disparagement. He looked upon himself as a failure both as man and poet, and he looked upon his life as a marriage with disaster. His early suffering seemed to come from the nostalgia of a youth who longed to be a sailor and whose ill health prevented him.

His first poems, grouped under the title *Gens de mer* and placed at the end of his volume, celebrate the harmony existing between sailors and the natural forces that they learn to control. Corbière's life of solitude and poor health forced him into the role of eccentric, which he took pleasure in exaggerating. The rheumatism from which he suffered strangely altered his appearance when he was still very young—his body grew excessively thin, his complexion turned yellow, and his nose and ears appeared large in proportion to his face. His self-portrait is the sketch of a monster.

He used to eat in the one restaurant at Roscoff, a pension called Le Gad, where in summer he fell in with a convivial group of painters from Paris. This contact, which was continued during several summers, influenced the cynicism and moral laxity of *Les Amours Jaunes*, the licence in verbal expression, the puns, the care for picturesqueness, the need to shock. Bohemianism was his climate, both in Roscoff and in Paris, where he went on a few occasions to follow the girl with whom he had fallen in love. Marcelle was the mistress of a rich man who had visited Roscoff. Corbière met the couple in the pension Le Gad and was introduced as the "character" of the place. It was the spring of 1871, a few months after the end of the Franco-Prussian War. The strange idyll between Corbière and the beautiful Italian girl was in keeping with the poet's life and character. The misogynist turned lover but never believed for long that any woman was capable of loving him.

The admirable poem, *Le poète contumace*, was inspired by Marcelle's departure from Roscoff in October 1871. It is in the form of a love letter or a long complaint in which Tristan Corbière assimilates himself with the medieval Tristan of the legend whose name he had chosen and whose story he had just reenacted. The two Tristans were sailors, Bretons, and victims of fate and passion.

Corbière followed Marcelle to Paris in 1872, where his behavior was even more eccentric than in Roscoff. He seemed to take a perverse delight in exaggerating his ugliness and the traits of cruelty and stubbornness in his character. Tristan Tzara, in the preface to his edition of *Les Amours Jaunes*, develops the theory that Corbière was acting the extreme pose of dandy and remembering the lycanthropy of Pétrus Borel in his efforts to startle the bourgeois by playing wolf and vampire. Not until the surrealists, fifty years later, recognized Corbière as one of their most authentic ancestors, was any serious attention paid to his work.

There are strong reminiscences of Baudelaire in *Les amours jaunes*, and Baudelairian traits in Corbière's impenetrability and will to hide the deepest secrets of his heart. There are concetti and antitheses almost in Gongora's style, and rhythmical innovations and patterns which Verlaine later developed. An art of living preceded this new art of poetry which is articulated in such a line as:

L'Art ne me connaît pas, je ne connais pas l'Art.

This would seem to mean that only when the strict conception of a poem as a work of art is abandoned will the poet really become the poet. Rhetorical devices and verbal clichés that form a serious defect in *Les Fleurs du Mal* are absent from *Les amours jaunes*. Yet Corbière's control of his art is less strong than Baudelaire's and Rimbaud's, and his revolt against order and convention is less metaphysical than Rimbaud's. His defiance, his insolence, and even his obscenity are traits of one of the *poètes maudits*, one of the lost children in revolt who differed from the other major poets of the 19th century in France only in the degree of intensity and hopelessness that characterized their human drama. The despair which is the basis of Tristan Corbière's poetry comes from his feeling of having made some fatal alliance with a cause or a malediction he is unable to define clearly.

The society of their period was only slightly perturbed by the waywardness and idiosyncrasies of the *poètes maudits*, because their lives were far less revolutionary than their writings. They rejected a certain orderliness in man's human destiny that had held sway for centuries, and they felt that in order to reach the new salvation, they had to risk damnation. Corbière has often been compared to Villon, and there are many linguistic and thematic traits in the two works to justify this comparison. But in a deeper, more metaphysical sense, they are almost antithetical. The wretchedness of man's fate and of his daily occupations is clearly in evidence in Villon and Corbière, but such disaster in Villon is never considered without its relationship to the poet's religious faith and hope.

The poet's defiance of God, the Luciferian attitude of Baudelaire and Rimbaud, had no place in Corbière's writing. The creature's torment is all the greater because of the absence of God. His self-debasement seems total as he passes from one phase to another—his failure in being a sailor or an adventurer or a lover. The first writers to comment on Corbière's art, men like Bloy and Laforgue, Rémy de Gourmont and Huysmans, all spoke of his failure as a poet. But today his verses seem as solid and permanent and deliberately articulated as those of the best technicians. A Corbière poem limps and breaks off and recovers when the poet wishes it to express the corresponding sentiment. His range in feeling and style permitted Corbière to move from a disarming tenderness to a coarse joke. He felt closest to those Bretons pursued by bad luck, the invalids and the criminals he saw in the *Pardon de Sainte-Anne*, and who seemed to him an extension of himself. He was refused by the sea as he was refused by love, and most of his poems speak of his enthusiasm and his disillusionment with respect to these two experiences.

LITERARY CRITICISM AFTER SAINTE-BEUVE

During the last twenty years of the century, three academic critics exerted considerable influence. Ferdinand Brunetière, who taught for several years at the Ecole Normale Supérieure, stressed the moral and social values of works of literature and studied the evolution of literary genres. Jules Lemaître was perhaps the most brilliant of the subjective impressionistic critics. Emile Faguet, who lectured at the Sorbonne, was particularly concerned with elaborating and explaining the ideas of the authors he chose to study.

Paul Bourget's *Essais de psychologie contemporaine* (1883) are still read today. They continued the form of criticism associated in particular with Brunetière in representing primarily a sociological analysis. Bourget spoke very little about the personality of the authors he studied (as Sainte-Beuve would have done) in order to stress the social value of the work. Literary works were for him the transmission of a psychological heritage. Rather than a critic, he was the historian of French moral life during the second half of the 19th century. He denounced a pessimistic turn of mind in his contemporaries which he studied as being the result of dilettantism, of cosmopolitanism, of the impotency of modern love. He concentrated his efforts on analyzing the moral crisis of his age. Literary analysis in Bourget led to social and political analysis. The ten writers he discusses in the *Essais*, including Baudelaire, Flaubert, Stendhal, Amiel and the Goncourts, were chosen not for the literary value of their writing but for the influence they exerted on their readers. He approved of Taine's formula: "La littérature est une psychologie vivante."

At the turn of the century, approximately from the year of Bourget's *Essais* to the First World War, the term "impressionism" occurred frequently in critical circles and quarrels. The word is difficult to define. The dogmatic and scientific type of critic, in the wake of Taine, hoped to reach objective judgments concerning a work of art, but *les impressionnistes* preferred to analyze their own feelings about a work of art. Their criticism was the result of an encounter between a text and themselves as readers. The most resolute of these critics would confess that criticism was a way of speaking about themselves. The goal of this kind of criticism would be the opposite of Sainte-Beuve's, which was aimed at analyzing and explaining the subjectivity of whatever writer he was studying.

There is probably no such thing as a pure impressionist critic. No matter how subjective his writing, he does have recourse to rules and doctrines and criteria in formulating his critical judgments. Jules Lemaître (with his five volumes of articles, *Les Contemporains*, 1885–1918), and Anatole France (with his four volumes of articles, *La vie littéraire*, 1888–1894) are examples of critics who believed any objective critical judgment was fundamentally impossible. The merit of a work being criticized, they believed, is judged by the pleasure it gives. Lemaître revealed his personal taste in extolling those classical works that represent traditional values. He depreciated the symbolists and the so-called decadents who threatened the sense of proportion French classicism meant for him. Anatole France did not condemn the symbolists, but he refrained from speaking of them.

Remy de Gourmont's criticism appeared somewhat later than France's, his *Promenades littéraires* being published between 1904 and 1927. His form of impressionistic criticism was different from that of Anatole France and Lemaître. He remained close to his period, close to symbolism, to the moment when *A rebours* of Huysmans represented a cult. He defined his own writing as a process of "dissociation," a form of analysis of the ideas in a work of literature in which he demonstrated principally a negative tendency, a destructiveness. There was no such thing as absolute beauty for de Gourmont; every author, he felt, has his own personality and his own personal conception of beauty which it is the critic's duty to explicate. He followed this principle in his articles on the leading symbolist poets, published in his two volume *Livres des masques* (1896–1898).

His numerous essays, collected in several volumes, form a very perceptive record of the thought, the literature, the sentiments, and the customs of the fifteen-year period between 1895 and 1910. The kind of essay written by Remy de Gourmont modified to some extent literary criticism at the beginning of the century. In the history of criticism he appears as an adversary of Brunetière's dogmatism. He accepted neither the rigors of any dogmatic view nor the uncertainties, the wavering qualities of impressionism. There was no one code for the critic to follow, but his taste should be sufficient for the development of his writing. He saw the critic's mission as that of helping his generation to overcome prejudice and to recognize the beauty being created by the writer. The critic should call attention to the new beauties of art, and avoid at all cost the danger of scholarship and pedantry, the temptation to turn his criticism into a treatise on morality, philosophy, or justice.

The scholars and the literary historians have been the principal scorners of impressionistic criticism. Their study of a book involves the collecting of documents and information that will serve as an elucidation of the book. They emphasize biographical and historical data in order to propose a maximum of objectivity. With Gustave Lanson (1857–1934) the form of literary history and scholarly research became clearly defined and coordinated. He was largely responsible for replacing a rhetorical somewhat bombastic academic criticism with a "scientific" criticism based upon a minute study of facts, but which always stressed as the goal of literary criticism the forming of the reader's taste and understanding.

Whereas Emile Faguet's articles analyzed the ideas of a writer and his style (a form of criticism that has continued to our day and is often visible in the brief articles of the French literary weeklies), Lanson, obviously influenced by Taine and Brunetière, went much farther in attempting to analyze the conditions that surrounded the work of art and the precise place occupied by the work in literary history.

To a large extent, the method of research for the preparing of a monograph, promulgated and advocated by Lanson at the Sorbonne and the Ecole normale supérieure, remains in Europe and America the principal method for training young scholars of literature. The hunt for "sources" is an important element of Lanson scholarship. These sources may be found in earlier books of the author or in his biography. Lanson tended to believe that every part of a work had sources that could be tracked down; ideas, phrases, themes. A discovery of the sources of a work, he said, helped establish how an author worked and the degree of originality he possessed. The end of the typical monograph would be devoted to a study of the influences of the work, its posthumous fame, its success in influencing other writers, and the place it occupies in the history of literature.

THE GONCOURT BROTHERS:
Edmond (1822–1896), Jules (1830–1870)

At first the Goncourts wrote books on the society and the art of the 18th century, and then they turned to the writing of novels about contemporary life: *Renée Mauperin* (1864) and *Germinie Lacerteux* (1865), one of the first proletarian novels in France. After his brother's death, Edmond continued to write novels and also continued the *Journal* which the two brothers had begun in 1851. This work is a storehouse of anecdotes and observations on writers and artists in Paris, and on Paris society.

The Goncourts attempted to relate the present as historians relate the past, by collecting documents and taking notes on conversations overheard and scenes observed. Emile Zola was deeply affected by the pathetic story of *Germinie Lacerteux*, and was probably encouraged by it to move in the direction of *le naturalisme*.

Edmond's will founded the Académie Goncourt, whose ten members award the still-prestigious *prix Goncourt* in literature every year.

GUY DE MAUPASSANT (1850–1893)

A Norman, Maupassant studied at the Catholic *collège* in Yvetot and at the lycée de Rouen. In Paris, he was a *fonctionnaire* in two ministries, and began writing under the direction of his literary godfather Flaubert. He belonged to the younger group of writers, including Alphonse Daudet and Huysmans, who were following the examples of Flaubert, Zola and Edmond de Goncourt. Maupassant entered literature *comme un météore* and soon separated from the group of *naturalistes*. Between 1880 and 1891 he wrote three hundred short stories and six novels, of which *Une Vie* (1883) and *Bel Ami* (1885) have been the most successful. At the end of his life he lost his sanity and died in the clinic of Dr. Blanche, in which Gérard de Nerval had been a patient thirty years earlier.

Maupassant was the naturalist version of the *libertin*. He was best in his depiction of a peasant's ruse, of the covetousness of narrow-minded provincials, of the simplicity of prostitutes. His vision of the world was totally pessimistic.

With regularity he negated all expressions of hope in mankind. He felt close to Schopenhauer's philosophy. He became and has remained the French master of the realistic short story.

THE THEATER AFTER HUGO

Even during the romantic period there was a reaction to the *drames* of Hugo. The very prolific Eugène SCRIBE (1791–1861) wrote more than three hundred and fifty plays that represented a tendency toward realism and the *comédie de moeurs*. Emile Augier, in such a comedy as *Le gendre de M. Poirier* (1854), adapted the theme of Molière's *Le Bourgeois Gentilhomme* to modern life. He depicted in most of his plays the wealthy bourgeois, plays in which the plot centers about the subject of money.

Throughout the Second Empire and into the first years of the Third Republic, one playwright in particular enjoyed considerable success. Alexandre DUMAS fils (1824–1895), the natural son of the famous novelist, created in 1852 *La Dame aux Camélias*, which is still performed today. It was written on the theme of the courtesan regenerated by a sincere love. (Verdi's *La Traviata* is an adaptation of *La Dame aux Camélias*.) In such plays as *Le Demi-Monde* (1851) and *Le Fils Naturel* (1858), examples of thesis plays (*pièces à thèse*), Dumas confronted serious social problems and attacked prejudices.

After 1850, the tradition of naturalism was best represented by the plays of Henry BECQUE (1837–1899). Two of his plays were kept for many years in the repertory of the Comédie-Française: *Les Corbeaux* (1882) and *La Parisienne* (1885). Becque avoided using the usual tricks and devices of the theater, with the result that his writing gives the impression of verisimilitude. The plays are bitter in tone; the genre is often called *comédie rosse*.

More important than Becque in the history of the theater was the influence of André ANTOINE (1858–1943), the director and founder (in 1887) of Le Théatre Libre, who produced plays in it for nine consecutive seasons. This was long enough to establish his revolution and make of it the standard type of realistic production which is the basis of the modern French theater.

Antoine performed in France the theatrical renovation that Wagner carried out in Germany. He demolished the conventions that had dominated the French stage since the time of Louis XIV, such as the declaiming of the alexandrine line, stylized artificial acting, and the ornate spectacular productions that the Sun King had once favored in the festivities of Versailles. Dominating the French stage for approximately twenty-five years, Antoine instituted greater naturalism in speech and acting and an extreme realism in his care for details and use of real objects on the stage. He was imitated in Berlin, in London, and especially in Russia, where Constantin Stanislavsky (1867–1935) founded the Moscow Art Theater in 1897.

FICTION AT THE END OF THE CENTURY

Eugène FROMENTIN (1820–76) was a traveller, painter, art critic and novelist. In *Dominique* (1863), the young man Dominique de Bray is in love with his childhood friend Madeleine. Madeleine, who is married, discovers Dominique's love and falls in love with him. He leaves her and isolates himself in a small village. There is no revolt, no outpouring of feelings that a more typically romantic writer would have given. Dominique quite simply gives himself over to the failure of his love and of his life. This autobiographical novel, like *Adolphe* of Constant, is based upon a secret and a confession. André Gide was later influenced by *Dominique* in writing *La Porte Etroite*.

After the book's success, Fromentin turned again to his interest in painting, and travelled to Egypt, Italy, Belgium and Holland. The last two countries inspired one of the finest books of art criticism in French: *Les Maîtres d'autrefois*, articles first published in *La Revue des Deux Mondes* and then collected in book form in 1876.

Barbey d'AUREVILLY (1808–1889), originally Jules Barbey, who appropriated his uncle's name of d'Aurevilly, was a Norman who studied law in Caen and then settled in Paris where he led an aloof and impoverished existence. An early essay on *le dandysme*, in 1845, called attention to his name. He had met Beau Brummell in Caen where the English dandy was British consul. Barbey became known as an ultra-Catholic, an ultra-Royalist, and a provocative literary critic. After writing several novels (such as *Le prêtre marié*, 1865), he published a collection of six stories, *Les Diaboliques* (1874), on which his fame rests today. They are melodramatic stories, *nouvelles*, of diabolic possession, infanticide, adultery, and flamboyant lust.

VILLIERS DE L'ISLE-ADAM (1838–1889) was born in Saint-Brieuc, in Brittany, and often claimed that he came from one of the oldest families of France. By many in his day he was looked upon as a mad genealogist. His literary vocation was undertaken in part to restore fame to his family. He published poetry, a philosophical tale (*Isis*, 1862) and two dramas. His best book is thought to be *Contes cruels* (1883), satiric stories of contemporary life. He attacked such matters as the pretentions of science, the stupidity of the masses, the tyranny of money, the triumph of mediocrity in the modern world.

Villiers claimed fidelity to orthodox Catholicism and occult doctrines. In his long play *Axel*, published the year after his death, the hero and heroine willfully sacrifice wealth, power, and love so that in their death they may take refuge in eternity. *Axel* is important in the development of symbolist drama. Villiers de l'Isle-Adam was very much admired by Mallarmé, Huysmans and Edouard Dujardin.

Léon BLOY (1846–1917), during his career of journalist and novelist, expressed a great loathing of his time. As an ardent Catholic he denounced all the signs of impiety in his century. He wrote one of the most violent denunciations against the materialistic traits of *la belle époque*. His eight-volume *Journal* (1898–1920) and his two novels, *Le Désespéré* (1886) and *La Femme pauvre* (1897), were attacks against the bourgeois values of the last years of the century. Living like the beggars he praised, he set out to humiliate the rich by the example of his life and by his incontinent writings. Appropriating some of the Catholic lessons of Barbey d'Aurevilly, and with the fervor of an Ezechiel, he vituperated against his age. He triumphed after his death in the influence he exerted on the 20th-century revival of Catholic literature.

Paul BOURGET (1852–1935), a prolific and popular writer in his day, is remembered for his critical writings more than for his psychological novels, such as *Le Disciple* (1889). This novel, which is concerned with a teacher's responsibility in his disciple's crime, is a denunciation of Taine's psychological determinism and the moral system of Stendhal. The generation of 1900 admired Bourget, but today the theses of his novels appear too obvious or even false.

At first, during the so-called period of naturalism, Joris-Karl HUYSMANS (1848–1907) wrote proletarian novels, but his best known work, *A rebours* (1884), reflects impressionist painting, symbolist poetry, and the darker side of Baudelaire's art. Des Esseintes is the symbolist hero who lives among beautiful things and tests sensations that come to him from "decadent" literature and art.

Là-bas (1891) develops themes of diabolism and black magic. *La Cathédrale* (1898) and *L'Oblat* (1903) testify to Huysmans' interest in Christian mysticism and medieval art.

ÉMILE ZOLA (1840–1902)

The leading exponent of the "naturalist" novel in France, Zola was the son of an Italian engineer, Francesco Zola and a French woman from Dourdan, in northern France.

When Zola was still a child, the family moved from Paris to Aix-en-Provence, where his father began the ambitious engineering feat of building a canal to supply the city with water. Francesco Zola died soon after beginning this work, and the family suffered greatly from poverty. Emile, however, was happy in Aix because of his many young companions, of whom Paul Cézanne was one.

In 1858, Zola was studying in Paris at the lycée Saint-Louis. Failing to pass the examinations for the baccalaureat degree, he began work first as a clerk on the Paris docks, and later at the Hachette publishing house. By this time, 1861, he was reading widely in Dante, Shakespeare, Montaigne, Stendhal, Balzac and Flaubert, and had met, thanks to Cézanne, some of the young painters of the day who gathered regularly at the Café Guerbois.

After leaving Hachette's in 1866, he supported himself for several years by journalism. He was an art critic, in his fervent defense of Manet and the impressionists, and he was also a drama critic. His first fiction had been published in 1864 (*Contes à Ninon*). He looked upon the novel as the genre the most suited to his century and the true descendent of the ancient epics. In 1870 he published the first of the series of twenty novels, to be called *Les Rougon-Macquart: histoire naturelle et sociale d'une famille sous le Second Empire*. Zola's composition of this long series of studies, both social and physiological, was based on observation in accordance with the realist theory of Flaubert, and on scientific laws of heredity.

World success came to Zola with the publication of *L'Assommoir* in 1877, the story of Gervaise, a young laundress married to a drunkard, and forced eventually to become a prostitute in the slums of Paris. Zola continued writing the volumes of *Les Rougon-Macquart* under the influence of the biologist Claude Bernard and the literary critic Hippolyte Taine. The psychological traits of his characters were subordinated to the physiological. He thought environment (*milieu*) of prime importance in the formation of a personality. *Le Roman Expérimental* of 1886 is a series of articles and manifestoes in which Zola elaborated his aesthetic and scientific theories.

His history of a family was studied during generations. In each of the books, Zola analyzed one aspect in particular of society: in *La Curée* (1872) it is the world of high finance; *Le Ventre de Paris* (1873) describes Les Halles, the Paris market, which no longer exists today; *Germinal* (1885) is the world of miners; *L'Oeuvre* (1886), the world of artists; *La Terre* (1887), the life of peasants; *La Bête Humaine* (1890), the railroad; and *La Débâcle* (1892), concerns war.

Zola dreamed of doing for the Second Empire (1851–1870) what Balzac had done in *La Comédie Humaine* for the Restoration a generation or two earlier. Like Balzac, he created a huge cyclical work involving the reappearance of characters, but unlike Balzac, he knew from the beginning the general plan of his work.

Since approximately the middle of the 20th century, Zola's work has gradually assumed the position of importance he deserves as one of the major novelists of the 19th century. At first, his work was denounced as obscene. In England, where his name was once anathema, his translator was put into prison. He is still remembered for his ardent defense of Dreyfus, and one critic at least has called *J'accuse*, the document he published in *L'Aurore* on January 1898, his last great novel.

Zola has had a strong influence on the writers, both in and out of France, who have been directly or loosely associated with naturalism: Jules Romains and the movement of unanimism; the *roman-fleuve* of Roger Martin du Gard; Tchekhov and Gorki in Russia; Silone in Italy; and in America Dreiser, Steinbeck, and Dos Passos. These writers, and many others, have been guided by Zola's basic principle of a novelist that art, like science, will find its truth by modelling itself on nature.

Although most serious critics of Zola's work emphasize the social impact of his proletarian fiction (see Henriette Psichari, *Anatomie d'un chef-d'oeuvre*: *Germinal*, 1964), a few recent critics, such as Angus Wilson, are studying the novelist's obsessions and the major traits of his personality. Zola's mother fixation and his haunting fear of sexual sterility are not unrelated to moral preoccupations clearly visible in his fiction. These new probings into Zola's character and into the nature of his writing have helped to demonstrate how far his work is from pornography.

Not only in his vituperation against the bourgeoisie, but especially in the mythic patterns of his best novels, notably *Germinal*, Zola is now seen to represent a break with the past, a break with the decadence and the pessimism of his age, and to play a major role in cultural rejuvenation. The greatness of Zola no longer seems to be in the scientific statements on naturalism that can be read in *Le roman expérimental*, but in certain affinities he has with D. H. Lawrence's mystique of eroticism and with Nietzsche's belief in the cyclical return of history.

New readings of *Germinal* have stressed the prophetic and apocalyptic scope of the work, and have justified both Gide's selection of it as one of the ten greatest French novels, and the high consideration that Henry James and Havelock Ellis had for it. Thus interpreted, the strike in the coal mines of *Germinal* was Zola's picture of class warfare and the means by which he prophesied the future. Both Christian and pagan myths of the underworld were used by Zola in depicting and interpreting the "hell" of the mines. The catastrophes that Zola described with such vehemence do not represent the end of the world, the passing of the Christian humanistic world, as much as they represent the beginning of a new era, of a new society, of a new kind of paradise.

TWENTIETH CENTURY

HISTORY		LITERATURE	
		1900	Péguy founds *Cahiers de la quinzaine*
		1909	*La Nouvelle Revue Française* founded
		1912	Claudel, *L'Annonce faite à Marie*
		1913	Apollinaire, *Alcools*
1914–18	World War I	1913–28	Proust, *A la recherche du temps perdu*
		1922	Valéry, *Charmes*
		1924	Breton, *Manifeste du surréalisme*
		1925	Gide, *Les Faux-Monnayeurs* Mauriac, *Désert de l'amour*
		1933	Malraux, *La Condition Humaine*
		1936	Bernanos, *Journal d'un curé de campagne*
1939–45	World War II	1938	Sartre, *La Nausée*
1940	Invasion of France	1942	Camus, *L'Etranger*
1946	Fourth Republic		
		1953	Beckett, *En attendant Godot*
		1957	Robbe-Grillet, *La Jalousie*
1958	Fifth Republic: De Gaulle president		Saint-John Perse, *Amers*
		1963	Barthes, *Sur Racine* Lévi-Strauss, *Tristes Tropiques*
		1966	Le Clézio, *Le Déluge* Genet, *Les Paravents*
1970	death of De Gaulle		(in Paris)

French Poetry: 1900–1950

In the mid-20th century, French poetry was still fully engaged in one of the richest periods of its long history. Its roots were essentially in symbolism and in the achievements of poetry between *Les Fleurs du Mal* of Baudelaire (1857) and the death of Mallarmé (1898). Especially in France the creative spirit has always been fully conscious of its heritage of belonging to the past, of its destiny to continue and perfect a tradition.

The years 1900–1950 were dominated by four major writers who were all born around 1870 and who have reached now the status of classical writers. Two of these were prose writers: Proust and Gide; and two were poets: Valéry and Claudel. Their common background was symbolism—they were all initiated into literature by the stimulation, the achievements, and the manifestoes of symbolism, and each reacted to symbolism in his own way and according to his own purposes. They were the most illustrious members of the oldest generation still writing in 1950. They all felt the combined influence of Mallarmé and Rimbaud, which proved to be more permanent and more vital than any others in the 20th century.

The word "purity," a concept with which modern poetry is permeated, is associated primarily with Mallarmé and the doctrine he expounded on Tuesday evenings for so many years (1880–1898) in his apartment on the rue de Rome. There his most brilliant disciple, Paul Valéry, listened in his early twenties to the master's conversations on poetry. The leading symbols of Mallarmé's poetry—his virgin princess Hérodiade; his faun, more interested in his own ecstasy than in the nymphs; his swan caught in the ice of the lake—all reappear changed but fully recognizable in the leading symbols of Valéry's poetry: Narcissus and the contemplation of self pushed to its mortal extreme; his Jeune Parque and his marine cemetery.

La Jeune Parque, which may well be Valéry's greatest poem, composed during the war years (1914–1917), reflects in no way the event of the war. This poem, with the major poems of Mallarmé, Rimbaud's *Les Illuminations*, and the early prose pieces of Gide, treated so pervasively the theme of solitude and detachment that it created a new mythology of poetic purity and human absence. It is poetry anxious to live alone for itself and by itself. It is poetry of exile, written outside the social sphere. It bears no relationship to the society of the world that might be comparable to the bond between the tragedies of Racine and the monarchy of Louis XIV.

After writing his poetry of exile, Rimbaud lived in exile in the deserts, cities, and mountainous regions of Abyssinia. The same need for voyage and solitude was felt by Paul Claudel, who always claimed Rimbaud as his master in poetry, as the writer who revealed to him the presence of the supernatural in the world. Rimbaud's greatest ambition was to move beyond literature and poetry, and this was realized to some degree by Claudel, whose vocation as poet was always subordinated to his role of apologist of Catholicism. The entire universe was the site of the Christian drama for Claudel. The form of the *verset* is reminiscent of the rhythms in *Les Illuminations*. He continued Rimbaud's dionysian turbulence, whereas Valéry, in his more chastened, more classical style, represented, with Mallarmé, the apollonian tradition.

The second generation of poets were born at the end of the century. On the whole, they participated in the experience of World War I much more directly than the generation of Valéry and Claudel. This group of writers, particularly in the years after the war, demonstrated a changed attitude toward the role and the activity of the writer. The poet was for them a far less exalted being than he had been for Mallarmé and Rimbaud. The excessive intellectualism and aestheticism of the late symbolist period were drastically modified and diminshed.

The experience of the war and the rise of the cinema were only two of the many new forces that were shaping the younger poets at that time. Surrealism was the most significant literary movement in France between symbolism and existentialism. Its leading spirit and theorist was André Breton, who even after World War II and until his death in 1966 made attempts to revive surrealism as an organized movement. But most of the poets who at one time or another adhered to the tenets of surrealism are today writing poetry that is no longer strictly surrealist.

Breton and Benjamin Péret remained closest to the beliefs and practices of orthodox surrealism. Péret took part in the Civil War in Spain, and lived after that in Mexico. He was perhaps the best satirist of the group, the closest spiritual descendant of Alfred Jarry, whose *Ubu Roi* (1896) was a major text for the surrealists. Several of the surrealist poets have died: Crevel, whose suicide was interpreted as an act of heroism; Desnos, a victim of a German concentration camp; Artaud, who spent the last nine years of his life in an insane asylum; and Paul Eluard, who appears today as the best of the Resistance poets.

The miracle of Eluard's work is in the extremes it contains and the ease with which it moves from one extreme to the other—from the poet's solitude, from his deep and secret intimacy, to his sense of communion with everyone, to his civic hope. He is the poet of love in one of its highest forms—love that will not allow a man to remain within himself.

Several important poets who wrote during the decade of surrealism and since that time had no formal connection with any literary school. Pierre-Jean Jouve in recent years has grown into a poet of influence. His universe of catastrophe is described in poetry of a lofty Christian inspiration. Since 1940, Saint-John Perse lived in the United States, where he wrote *Exil*, one of the profoundest statements on the war. Jean Cocteau wrote poetry intermittently throughout his career. He remained one of the most gifted poets of his generation, even if the signal success in his other genres—theater, cinema and novels—detracted somewhat from his position of poet.

Henri Michaux enlarged the domain of poetry. The character he created, Plume, is the type of innocent who never escapes the violence and the cruelty of the world. He is innocent but tormented by a sense of guilt. A comparison of Plume with the characters of Kafka has often been pointed out, but there is a greater struggle in the Kafka characters than in Plume, who accepts whatever happens to him as part of his fate.

Prévert was probably the most widely read French poet around 1950. But more important than his poetry was his writing for the cinema: *Les Visiteurs du soir* and *Les enfants du paradis* were two of his outstanding successes. René Char first allied himself with surrealism and always retained in his subsequent poetry the boldness and profusion of imagery one associates with surrealism. He was maquis captain in Provence at the end of the war and has written movingly in his poetry of his war experience.

The third generation of poets writing in France at the turn of the mid-century was more dramatically allied with action, with the war and the Resistance, than the poets of the other two generations. Sartre defined the new literature as being "engaged," and this term applies to the poetry of this generation, so directly concerned with actual circumstances and events. The greatness of Jouve (who chronologically belongs to the previous generation) brilliantly illustrates this use of immediate events in poetry. Pierre Emmanuel has written generously of his admiration for Jouve and of the influence that Jouve's poetry has had on his own. One of Emmanuel's achievements is the vigor he has given to poetry of a well-defined subject matter. His mingling, for example, of the Orpheus theme with the redemptive power of Christ is in one of his early works, in which the mystery of man is not separated from the mystery of the exterior world.

The ambition of this youngest generation has been, in general, to recall the poet to reality after the long experimentation of poetry with language, with the symbol, and with the hieratic role of the poet. The new writer has felt a greater desire for immediate communication with the reader. On the whole, he is less subjective than the earlier poets. He appropriates the common basis of world events and world problems for his verse.

Existentialism, as a literary movement, did not develop any poets, with the exception of Francis Ponge, on whose work Sartre himself wrote a long essay. Ponge's first important publication was in 1942, *Le Parti-Pris des choses*, a work of great rigor and objectivity, and one completely lacking in any subjective lyricism. Although Raymond Queneau has written principally and prolifically in the domain of the novel, he is also a poet. His central preoccupation with language, with what he considers a needed revolution in language places him centrally among the poets. His influence is wide, exceeded only by the more massive influence of Sartre. By advocating the reintegration of the vitality of spoken language, each book of his is a "stylistic exercise." In the freedom of composition he practices, his work is often reminiscent of surrealism, with which he was at first associated.

CHARLES PÉGUY (1873-1914)

The vast amount of critical writing in France and outside of France during the past thirty years which has been concerned with assessing and explaining modern French poetry has given no place of importance to Charles Péguy. The work of Valéry, for example, born two years before Péguy, has elicited a large number of critical and exegetical studies, and his place is firmly established in the tradition of modern French poetry founded by Baudelaire. Péguy's poetry has nothing to do with that central tradition. It cannot be approached in the same way because it presents no linguistic and no metaphorical difficulties, and any other approach to a serious study of Péguy as poet has been impeded or discouraged by the tenacious and picturesque legends of his life.

In his case, hagiography very early replaced criticism. This was true even during the last years of Péguy's life, between the founding of his publishing business, *Les Cahiers de la Quinzaine*, in 1900, and his death on the first day of the battle of the Marne. It was largely true for the years between the two World Wars. He was remembered particularly as the patron-poet of peasants and as the pilgrim of La Beauce. Numerous biographies have repeated the same anecdotes: the childhood in Orléans, the lycée years in Paris, the shop of the *Cahiers*. Not until the recent study of *Eve* by Albert Béguin in 1948 and his earlier work, *La Prière de Péguy* (1942), was there a real critical effort to understand and explain the poet.

A few fragments of his poetry have become popular: *La présentation de la Beauce à Notre-Dame de Chartres*, and the passage beginning "Heureux ceux qui sont morts," but such popularity has not assured Péguy's place among the élite of the French poets. His ultimate reputation as a poet will doubtless rest on *Eve* and his three *Mystères: La Charité de Jeanne d'Arc, Porche du mystère de la deuxième vertu*, and *Mystère des Saints Innocents*. Although it was generally acknowledged that Péguy had fashioned an alexandrine that was peculiarly and recognizably his own (there are ten thousand alexandrines in his work), he was accused of having exaggerated its monotony.

In September 1908, Péguy confided to his friend Joseph Lotte that he was becoming a Catholic again. A year previously he had said the same thing to

Jacques Maritain, but had pleaded for secrecy. On one level, *Eve* is Péguy's literary expression of his return to the Church. It is a vision of human history as well as a poetics. It is the poem of Christianity with a circular composition moving from the Incarnation to the Redemption. All other themes center around these two, which appear as a long dialogue carried on between the flesh (Incarnation) and the soul (Redemption), between the Fall, associated with Eve, and the Redemption, associated with Christ.

What some readers of Péguy call repetition is actually a deepening of understanding, a widening of theme and perception. After finishing the "cahier" *L'Argent*, he wrote *L'Argent suite*. Whatever theme Péguy chose to write on, he amplified to such a degree that all themes were finally incorporated in it. Only the mere beginnings of his justification as poet have been written. If there is to be a future exegete to continue the analysis of Béguin's study of *Eve*, he will have to be a combination of aesthetician, fully aware of the ambitions and achievements of modern poetry, and theologian, able to discover how poetry was the instrument given to Péguy to reach the love of God.

Charles Péguy founded his *Cahiers de la Quinzaine* in order to convert the public to his principles, and he grouped around him men such as Romain Rolland, André Suarès, Daniel Halévy, and others who were guided and inspired by his thought. They were moved by Péguy's heroism, by his violent criticism of critics and professors. In his praise of Hugo and Corneille and writers of antiquity (see *Les Suppliants Parallèles*), he defined himself and the fervent generosity of his ideas.

He associated the perils that beset the modern world with the practice of and the belief in rationalism. The philosophy of Henri Bergson was for Péguy the antidote. Bergson claimed that passion is not obscure and that reason is not clear. In attacking what he called the "scientific method" of literary criticism, Péguy derided the habit of the critic (as he saw it in Taine's study of *La Fontaine et ses fables*) of never staying close to the text itself, of always moving outside the text to some vaguely defined beginnings. He attacked the so-called scientists of literature for never discovering within the text its meaning (see *Victor-Marie, comte Hugo*, 1910).

Not one of the *Cahiers* could be looked upon purely as literary criticism, and yet Péguy's work and the books he sponsored contributed important elements of criticism. He was probably the only *normalien*, the only student of the Ecole normale supérieure of the rue d'Ulm, to show unequivocally the spirit of the school, the only one to show open hostility to the traditional form of humanism represented by the school. He contributed more than anyone else in making Gustave Lanson a scapegoat by ridiculing the methods of erudite scholarship. The publication of the *Cahiers* and the discussions carried on by the writers of Péguy's group revived some of the oldest debates in French literature: the antithesis between Corneille and Racine, the opposing philosophies of Voltaire and Rousseau, the concept of France as reflected in the writings of Michelet and Hugo.

PAUL VALÉRY (1871-1945)

The summer of 1970 marked two Valéry anniversaries, celebrated in literary periodicals: the 25th anniversary of his death and the 50th anniversary of the first publication of *Le Cimetière Marin* in *La Nouvelle Revue Française*, of June 1920.

This poem, not his greatest perhaps, but the one that has received the greatest attention, restored the forgotten resources of the decasyllabic line of French poetry. In the twenty-four stanzas of six lines each, *Le Cimetière Marin* demonstrated a diversity of tones in the rhythm of this line, first used in *La Chanson de Roland*, eight hundred years earlier. The long poem is a monologue in which the poet's voice speaks of the most basic and constant themes of his emotional and intellectual life associated with the sea and the sunlight as it strikes certain parts of the land bordering on the Mediterranean. These themes, pursued by Valéry in his adolescence and thereafter, lead quite naturally to the subject of death and the thinking powers of man.

Paul Valéry was born in Sète, the town of the poem's cemetery, where he is buried today, and he lived in Sète through his childhood and into his adolescence. He completed his lycée years and studied law in Montpellier. Thanks to Pierre Louÿs and Gide, in Paris he met Mallarmé, who became his acknowledged master and friend. Two essays appeared in 1895 and 1896: *Introduction à la méthode de Léonard de Vinci* and *Une soirée avec M. Teste*. These were attempts to understand and describe the functioning of his mind. Da Vinci was the universal man for Valéry, and M. Teste, an imaginary character, the intellectual ascetic who removes himself from the pointless activities of the world in order to reach a lucidity of thought and reflection.

After twenty years of solitude and study (1897-1917), Valéry broke his silence in 1917 with a five-hundred line poem, *La Jeune Parque*. His early poems were collected in 1920 in *Album de vers anciens*, and in 1922 his major collection, *Charmes*, appeared; this contains *Le Cimetière Marin*, *Fragments du Narcisse*, *Ebauche d'un serpent*, *Palme*, and other poems. *Charmes* (meaning "incantations" or "poems") placed Valéry in company with the purest of the French poets—with Mallarmé, in particular, and with Chénier, La Fontaine and Racine.

After *Charmes*, Valéry returned to prose in two Platonic dialogues: *L'Ame et la danse* (1923), a meditation on the movement of a dancer that transforms her from an ordinary woman into a supernatural being; and *Eupalinos* (1923), a discussion on the genius of the architect and, more generally, any artist who is able to create out of his chosen materials a masterpiece.

In a series of five volumes of collected essays, *Variété* (1924–44), Valéry discussed various problems of his age and analyzed various literary problems, especially those related to poets with whom he felt close affinity; such as Mallarmé, Verlaine, Baudelaire, Poe, La Fontaine.

For Valéry, the poet is the artist who does not stifle any of his inner voices or any of the hidden desires of his nature. His particular vocation forces him to translate and interpret those voices and desires. To do this, he must remain lucid and fully rational. He is not a man inspired by the Muse, but must cultivate a universal intelligence and thus not close himself off from any reality. *La Jeune Parque*, for example, describes the successive stages of consciousness in a young girl as she moves from sleep to a full awakening. *La Pythie* is the oracle (Pythoness), convulsed before she can deliver herself of the divine message (or the poem). In composing sonnets (*L'Abeille*, *Les Grenades*) or odes (*Aurore*) or the long poems of *Le Cimetière Marin* and *La Jeune Parque*, Valéry accepted all the discipline of the classical style, all the demanding rules of vocabulary, rhythm, and rhyme. He used metaphors, alliteration, and harmonious effects to sustain the mystery and the enchantment of the poem.

Charmes is the last landmark of French symbolism. From the time of its publication until his death, Valéry was an almost official representative of his country's culture. He was elected to the Académie Française in 1927, and between 1938 and his death he held the chair of poetry and poetics at the Collège de France. In today's language Valéry's mind and attitude would be called that of a *contestataire*. He decried any doctrine that named literature something sacred and, like his master Mallarmé, pointed out the discrepancy between the thought of a man and the words in which he tries to express the thought. The composition of a poem interrupts and distorts the purity of the inner dialogue the poet carries on with himself.

Valéry ushered in a moment in French literature in which the poem was preferred to the poet, the study of poetics were preferred to the study of the poem, and a literary work was studied in its relationship to the general power of language. He treated poetry as something comparable to architecture and music. All three of these arts were for Valéry the offspring of the science of numbers. Almost in spite of himself, his work was expressed in words, in poetry, and in accord with that "inspiration" (a word he disliked) which the contemplation of the sea offered him.

No thinker has considered this age with greater perspicacity and penetration than has Valéry, and no thinker has demolished it more totally. His fame has been built upon fragments—upon poems, aphorisms, dialogues, brief essays. He was the supreme example of a writer indifferent to his public, detached from any need to please his public. The actual "subjects" of his pages are varied: the beauty of a shell, the prose of Bossuet, the method of Stendhal, the degree of conscience and consciousness with which he considers each subject. He tells us that *le moi pur* is unique and monotonous. Yet it is the deepest note of existence that dominates all the "varieties" of existence. To hear this note clearly was the goal and the ecstasy of Valéry's intellectual search. And this search was also closely related to Bergson's search for the freedom of the ego which he thought could be reached by deep reflection within the most personal states of our being.

With each essay, with each fragment of prose writing and each poem, Valéry extended the hegemony of his thought over most of the intellectual problems facing man today. But the subtlety and suppleness of his writing were such that he never reached, nor wished to reach, the creation of a philosophical system.

It has often been claimed that all of French literature, more than other national literatures, is of a social origin. It seems to come into its own under the stimulation of debate, in an atmosphere of worldliness and *mondanité*. Paul Valéry was for many years, and particularly during the decade of the thirties, looked upon as an esoteric poet, as a difficult thinker who never left the realm of abstractions, and hence as a writer who stood apart from the central tradition of French letters. But he was in reality a fervent observer of humanity and a man who always strove to express himself in the most meaningful and the most "social" way. The conquest of *le moi pur* led Valéry through a labyrinth of human experience and human sentiment, from the seeming indifference of M. Teste to the tenderness of the character Lust in the posthumously published volume, *Mon Faust*. Our entire historical period is in his work—the gravest problems that worry us and the oldest myths that enchant us.

Despite the high praise of Charles Du Bos, who called him the greatest genius in the west, and despite the judgment of Jacques Madaule, who compared him with Dante, Paul Claudel's place in literature and in Catholic thought is still vigorously disputed. At the time of his death, in his middle eighties, Claudel appeared as belligerent as ever, having maintained to the end not only his full powers as a writer but also his violent temper and his animosities. His detractors are still legion and his admirers come from many varying quarters, differing widely in their religious, political, and aesthetic beliefs.

He was born in Villeneuve-sur-Fère, a small village in the Tardenois, a locality which lies between the provinces of Ile-de-France and Champagne. For many years Claudel maintained contact with that village by spending vacations there. He always remembered how difficult it was to walk against the wind, and how the church steeple, bent by it, resembled the mast of a schooner.

He received his schooling in Paris at the lycée Louis-le-Grand, which for the young Claudel was a prison whose stifling atmosphere he described in *Ma Conversion*. At the graduation ceremonies of 1883, Ernest Renan made the now famous principal address, in which he told the students assembled before him that the day would come when one of them might denounce him as a poisoner and a corruptor. This prediction was truer than he realized, because Claudel never ceased denouncing him.

During his last year at the lycée, he read Baudelaire and Verlaine, but the first great revelation to Claudel of both a literary and spiritual order was to be Rimbaud. He has described in a passage justly celebrated and justly disputed the profound effect which the reading of *Les Illuminations* had on him. He first came upon some of the prose poems in the July issue of *La Vogue* of 1886. To him it meant release from what he called the hideous world of Taine, Renan, and other Molochs of the 19th century—"J'avais la révélation du surnaturel," he wrote to Jacques Rivière.

Rimbaud was the vehicle of Claudel's return to his faith. Certain sentences of *Une Saison en enfer*, such as "Nous ne sommes pas au monde," never ceased to impress him by clarifying the real significance of his own revolt. For, not unlike Rimbaud himself, Claudel was a revolutionary, a Dionysian ecstatic. Such prose poems as Rimbaud's *Après le déluge* and *Enfances* affected the rigid philosophical system that Claudel believed his. They taught him something concerning the mysterious character of poetic inspiration preceding personal experiences that were to come later, and that were secretly related to it.

Claudel recorded that in the same year, 1886, on Christmas day in Notre-Dame, during the singing of vespers, he experienced a spiritual awakening, a revelation of faith that was never to be impaired or endangered thereafter.

This mystical experience was followed by four years of bewilderment and struggle to harmonize the new force in him with his former self. He began to study the Bible, the history of the Church and its liturgy, and discovered that what he had once valued as poetry was indissolubly associated with religion. He attended Mallarmé's Tuesday evening gatherings and learned from the master of symbolism to look at the universe as if it were a text to be deciphered.

At the age of twenty-five, Claudel left for Boston to serve there as vice-consul for France. This marked the beginning of a long diplomatic career that took him to many parts of the world. When he went to China in 1895, he entered upon a period of solitude, silence and meditation; his *Vers d'exil* echo something of the spiritual experience of his five years there. *Connaissance de l'est* is a poetic form of journal accompanying the poems. One of the prose poems in this journal speaks of his return to Paris and his realization that he is unknown in his own country. This book constituted his farewell to his family, his past, and his country—he was free and disengaged, ready for the unknown.

Unlike Mallarmé in his career of teacher, Claudel, who had a highly developed sense of obligation, derived pleasure and satisfaction from his diplomatic and administrative duties. Everything in China interested him: the optimism and good humor of the people, their simplicity and sense of comradeship, their politeness, their art and their theater. His studies in China centered on the Bible and St. Thomas Aquinas. To Rimbaud's doctrine on the power of poetic language and to Mallarmé's doctrine on the symbolism of the universe Claudel added the gigantic synthesis of Aquinas and the religious interpretation of metaphorical language.

In September 1900, Claudel entered the Abbey of Ligugé in order to test his religious vocation. If he discovered in himself the vocation of a religious, he was ready to give up art and literature. He became an oblate of the Benedictine Order, but was discouraged by his superiors from continuing with a religious vocation.

As ambassador, Claudel represented France in Tokyo, Washington and Brussels. His diplomatic career, which included posts in Prague, Frankfurt, Hamburg and Rio-de-Janeiro, kept him away from France and literary groups. His travels helped make him one of the most cosmopolitan of French writers. The scope of his interests and studies was unusual for a French poet: Chinese theater, Italian and Dutch painting, Japanese poetry, Spanish culture and English Catholic literature, some of which he translated. The latter years of his life were spent in Brangues, in Savoie.

As a writer, Claudel never made concessions to his public. The Catholic world in France and outside of France has been slow to accept him. When he presented his candidacy for the Académie Française, just before the war, he failed to win the election. Not until after the war, in 1947, was he invited to become a member of the group.

Taken as a whole, Paul Claudel's work is praise to God and praise to His creation. It does not reflect the exaltation of a mystic but is rather the expression of the natural joy of a man who has found an order in the universe and believes in a certain relationship between this world and the next. In whatever he wrote —poems, letters, plays, essays, Biblical exegesis—he steadfastly explored the central drama of the human soul engaged in its adventure with eternity.

The Claudel plays are unlike anything in the tradition of the French theater. They follow none of the conventions of Racine's classical tragedy, of Hugo's romantic drama, of Augier's realism, or of Villier's symbolism. The first impression they give is one of unreasonableness, of chaos, and even of irreverence. They were composed in isolation, far from Paris, and in a seeming opposition to the taste of the day. Claudel created a dramatic form that is unique in French and that bears a somewhat vague resemblance to the dramas of Shakespeare and Lope de Vega rather than to the tragedies and comedies of his own country, which adhered closely to the Aristotelian precepts and the classical models. Claudel's dramas are not a combination of the comic and the tragic; they are works of one piece and one texture—simultaneously dramatic speech and poetry.

For Claudel the universe was *one* at every moment of every man's existence. Every story he undertook to tell, he found to be an anecdote or an element of the same drama of man which is continuously unfolding in the world. He wrote of the exaltation he derived from contemplating the millions of things that exist at the same time: "Que j'aime ce million de choses qui existent ensemble!"

The first version of his first play *Tête d'Or*, was written in 1889. Claudel called this play the introduction to his work. In its theme and even partially in its style it is, of all the works of Claudel, the closest to Rimbaud. It is the drama of a man, an adventurer, who attempts to assert himself by the sole means of his own strength and intelligence. The play raises many of the persistent problems of man's fate—without, however, the problem of woman's love, which is to be central in the later plays.

In all the many versions Claudel wrote of his best-known play, *L'Annonce faite à Marie* (first called *La Jeune Fille Violaine*), he stressed the mystical paradox of human relationships. The bonds uniting the young girl Violaine and Pierre de Craon, the builder of cathedrals, are as mysterious and as strong as those uniting Prouhèze and Rodrigue in *Le Soulier de Satin*. Pierre loves Violaine, and yet she represents for him everything he is called upon to give up: woman, happiness, the world itself. His love scene (the prologue) is actually his scene of farewell to the world.

The première of *Partage de Midi* took place on December 16, 1948, in Paris, exactly forty-two years after the play was written. The drama concerns only four characters. Each scene resembles a musical composition of two or three voices which reproduce a great variety of moods and tempi. The principal theme is adultery, and the secondary theme is the struggle in a man between a religious vocation and sexual love. Mesa, the leading male character, is the one Ysé desires most and who is for her the most inaccessible. The action of the play takes place between the moment of noon (*partage de midi*) when each character (Ysé, her husband, and her two lovers) makes a decision separating himself from his previous life, and the moment of midnight (*partage de minuit*) when the tragedy occurs, and death—a death of violence and sacrifice—joins Ysé and Mesa.

Claudel spent the years between 1919 and 1924 composing *Le Soulier de Satin*. He was living in Japan most of that time. The first performance took place twenty years later during the German Occupation of Paris, on November 27, 1943, at the Comédie-Française. For this performance Claudel rewrote the play, producing a considerably shortened version. It was staged by Jean-Louis Barrault, and the music was composed by Arthur Honegger.

Themes concerning the fatality of passion, dealt with in such works as *Tristan*, *Phèdre* and *Manon*, are reiterated in *Partage de Midi* and *Le Soulier de Satin*: here Claudel explored the meaning of passion, the reason for human love, the reason for its particular force, its destructiveness, the Christian attitude toward it, its spiritual meaning.

The conquest of the world and the tragedy of passionate love, two themes that are related, comprise the subject matter of *Le Soulier*. Adventurers, merchants and kings, in their will to possess the earth and unite the parts of the earth, provide the background for the human tragedy of Rodrigue and Prouhèze. Just a few episodes serve to prevent the total tragedy and announce the salvation: the slipper left with the statue of the Virgin, the angel watching over Prouhèze, Saint James and the other saints, the young daughter of Prouhèze. All the elements of tumult and upheaval in the long play find their place and their reason when Rodrigue releases Prouhèze (at the end of the Third Day) and by this renunciation welcomes the peace of God and the silence which had been announced by the Jesuit priest in the prologue.

ANDRÉ GIDE (1869–1951)

By the end of his life, Gide had received the official sign of consecration, the recognition of his century, that he was one of its major writers. The Nobel prize, awarded to him in 1948, indicated that his work had attained a degree of accepted universality. The miracle was that Gide had become a "classical" writer by the time of his death while remaining a "dangerous" writer. This man who, more than any other artist, invented for his age the term "restlessness" (*inquiétude*), ended his life in a seeming calm and resignation. A tone of affirmation, a marked denial of God, and a belief in the void of death provided a different portrait of Gide that has been added to the long series of self-portraits his books had already fashioned.

The vast work of Gide is, in a sense, a written confession, initiated by a need to communicate what he felt to be true about himself. He claimed that the central drama of his existence was his love for his wife, a drama which was revealed a few months after his death in his own words in *Et nunc manet in te*. The picture of Gide that this book gives was already seen, to some degree, in *L'Immoraliste* (1902), in the character Michel, who causes the death of his wife Marceline but who also exalts her. The same man is also in Jérôme, of *La Porte Etroite* (1909), who exalts Alissa and who at the same time experiences the futility of such an exaltation.

Madeleine Rondeaux was born in 1867 and was therefore two years older than her cousin André Gide. They were married after Gide's first visit to Algeria. In his *Journal*, Gide refers to her as Emmanuèle or as Em. Not until the posthumous work does he call her by her real name. The title is a hemistich from a line attributed to Virgil concerning the lost Eurydice: "et nunc manet in te [and now she remains in you]". Long in advance of this volume, Gide's conjugal idealism was fully expressed in his first book, *Les Cahiers d'André Walter* (1891).

Gide knew that he possessed nothing of the anguish of a Pascal. That trait he left to Mauriac, and accepted for himself the characteristics of a Montaigne—of a wavering and diverse mind, as Montaigne had described himself: *esprit ondoyant et divers*. He remained at all times the writer who profited from every kind of experience, important or trivial.

Marc Allégret's film *Avec André Gide* opens with a few solemn pictures of the funeral at Cuverville and Gide's own reading of the opening pages of his autobiography *Si le grain ne meurt* (1926). There are pictures showing the two contrasting family origins of Gide: Normandy and Languedoc, the north and the south, the Catholic and the Protestant background. The landscape pictures of Algeria and Tunisia provide a documentation for many of his works, from the earliest, such as *Les Nourritures Terrestres* (1897) to his *Journal* in 1941–42.

Among the most curious episodes are the trip to the Congo, the walk with Valéry, the home of his daughter Catherine in Brignoles, the speech made in Moscow in the presence of Stalin, the visit with Roger Martin du Gard in Bellème.

A genius is a man who considers passionately what other men do not see. In the tradition of French letters, Montaigne was preeminently this type of genius, seizing every occasion of pleasure, every experience, every meeting, for the subject matter of his writing. "Jusques aux moindres occasions de plaisir que je puis rencontrer, je les empoigne," wrote Montaigne. The art of both the 16th-century essayist and the 20th-century moralist is based upon an indefatigable curiosity and a relentless critical spirit. Gide's enthusiasm for whatever came within his vision was usually followed by an admirable detachment from it. Once the conquest was made, he refused to be subjugated by it, to be dominated by his conquest. The image of the minotaur's labyrinth, elaborated in his last important book, *Thésée* (1946), represents any body of doctrine that might constrict or imprison the thinking powers of man. The problem for Theseus, as it was for Gide himself, was that of surpassing his adventures. The one moral error to be avoided at all cost was immobility, fixation. The meaning of Gide's celebrated word *disponibilité* seems to be the power of remaining dissatisfied, capable of change and growth.

From his avid curiosity about everything, whether it was the coloration of a leaf or the first book of a new author, his ideas were engendered. In the manifold forms of attentiveness with which his life seems to have been spent, there were no traces of misanthropy, of pessimism, of class prejudice, or of fatuous satisfaction with self. From a nature that was dominated by curiosity, that accepted all contradictions—a will to freedom as well as a sense of destiny, good as well as evil—Gide's mind grew into one of the most critical of our age, a mind of infinite subtlety and unexpected boldness.

Gide began writing in about 1890, at a moment of great peacefulness in Europe, and continued to write during the next sixty years. He remained a constant and fervent witness to every ominous development in Europe and the world, from the period in which a religion of science and a rational vision of the universe dominated Europe to the present period of deep unrest.

There is little doubt that Gide hoped to compose a new gospel. With his favorite themes of adolescence, revolt, escape, the gratuitous act, he was able to upset the convictions of his readers, particularly the youthful readers, and yet he never created in them the feelings of terror or dismay that a writer like Lautréamont was able to arouse. Gide tried to write in all the genres because he was unwilling to restrict himself to any one form and because each book, once it was well under way, became irksome to him; he would finish it off quickly in order to move on to a newer work. He had planned, for example, several further chapters for *Les Faux-Monnayeurs* (1925), but when he wrote the sentence, "Je suis bien curieux de connaître Caloub," it appeared to him such an admirable final sentence that he felt freed from continuing farther.

Whenever Christianity appeared to him in the form of a system, of a body of principles, he refused to accept it. His was an attitude of detachment and adventure, which permitted him the practice of what has been so often called his sincerity. Problems of ethics worried Gide far more than religion. He was more concerned with justice than salvation. His knowledge of the Bible and his love for the Gospels always gave hope to his Catholic friends (Claudel, Jammes, Du Bos, Ghéon, Copeau) that he would finally submit.

Gide's morality was based upon the belief that each man is elected to play a role unlike every other role. Any deviation from that role, in order to pattern oneself on the predestined role, represented for Gide a betrayal of oneself. This peculiar separateness of man is a Gidian theme to which Jean-Paul Sartre, some years later, gave his own coloring and importance.

Sentence after sentence in the first books, *Voyage d'Urien* (1893), *Retour de l'enfant prodigue* (1907), and the early entries in the *Journal*, repeat the same belief that each man's way is unique. No one book, no one house, no one country can represent the universe. The Gidian hero refuses to shut himself off from any part of the world before he has tested it, and he reserves the right to judge it lucidly. Somewhere between dogmatism and total freedom Gide fixed his ethical behavior.

What appears as conformity to the world's law was seriously castigated in *Les Nourritures Terrestres* and in *L'Immoraliste*. And yet in the two books that followed, *Paludes* (1895) and *Saül* (1904), Gide criticized the other excess of giving oneself over to one's instinct. He never underestimated the perils of freedom. After the first movement of liberation from all societal constraints, as described in *Les Nourritures Terrestres* and *L'Immoraliste*, Gide the moralist advocated a close examination of the new freedom won. He presented in his play *Saül* a tragedy resulting from the misuse of freedom. The very difficulty involved in living with this new freedom provided the moral problem of most of his subsequent books, such as *Les Caves du Vatican* (1914), *Les Faux-Monnayeurs*, *Thésée*.

Rather than offering to the public what was peculiarly charactersitic and personal, as the typical romantic artist tends to do, Gide advocated a revindication of self in order to stress not its peculiarity but its universality. There are traits of Gide in many of his characters—in Michel (*L'Immoraliste*), in Jérôme

(*La Porte Etroite*), and in Edouard (*Les Faux-Monnayeurs*)—but each one represents a part of Gide's nature that he had renounced. From the role of immoralist, of the young man defiant of the fixed moral standards of his day, Gide passed to the role of self-examiner and self-inquisitor, a role lasting until the end of his life, when he reached the final state of moralist.

For the expression of human freedom, for its power and its peril, Gide created massive classical formulas that have returned, only slightly modified, in the writings of Sartre and Camus and René Char. His principal theme was the relationship between man and God, and fortunately his family fortune and background permitted him the leisure and luxury of pursuing such a theme. His long life was one of self-examination, of courage in liberating himself, of testing himself in such experiences as his African visit, communism, Catholicism. His attentiveness and the freedom of his spirit kept him from accepting any one doctrine. Gide developed one need—that of doubting everything—and one obligation—that of never doubting himself.

MARCEL PROUST (1871–1922)

In *Du côté de chez Swann*, the first of the seven parts of Proust's novel, *A la recherche du temps perdu*, we see a young boy, Marcel, who is to grow up into manhood as he looks for certain kinds of experience which represent happiness for him. But at the same time, and even in the earliest part of the novel, this youthful hero (who is also the narrator) is trying to find the subject for a book. He would like to be a writer. This subject matter is not discovered until the end of the novel when his search for happiness becomes identical with the creation of the very book we have finished reading. The narrative of a boy's life in his search for happiness is progressive and is presented as a series of disappointments, as an almost despairing experience of disillusion.

Gaëtan Picon, one of the recent critics to reevaluate Proust, looks upon his novel as the first work in French literature in which the voice of Balzac and the voice of Baudelaire are fused and heard simultaneously. We hear the voice of the historian, of the memorialist who depicts an entire age, as Balzac had once depicted the Restoration, and also the voice of the poet, of the man who feels the apprehensions and the anxieties of our modern world, as Baudelaire had felt them in the middle of the 19th century.

By comparison with the traditional 19th-century novel, *A la recherche du temps perdu* seems a new form in which the psychological analysis is far more developed, but is not conclusive, not dogmatic. Proust is a secretive writer. Despite the elaborate analysis of scenes and characters, we never learn his complete thought about the significance of a scene, nor does he ever reveal his complete understanding of a personality. The novel is secret and esoteric, and the countless critics of Proust tend to be exegetes in their efforts to explain the allegory, to pierce the secret of Proust and of his work.

Proust believed that the self a man exhibits in his daily habits, in his social life, in his vices, is artificial and even false. His real self is inner and concealed. More than in his biographies, he is visible in his own novel. His real self is described in the three major cycles of the novel, all of which engage in different ways the personality of the protagonist Marcel: first in the cycle of Swann, where we see the boy as an admirer of Swann the esthete, the connoisseur of art, and the father of Gilberte. Marcel the social being is portrayed in what might be called the cycle of the Guermantes, especially in his relationship with the duchesse Oriane and the baron de Charlus. The third cycle, that of Albertine, is Marcel in love, going through all the tortured phases of love, associated with Proust.

Proust watches himself in all of his characters. He is predominantly in Marcel, but very recognizable traits of Proust are in Swann, in Charlus, in Bergotte. He is in some of the female characters—in tante Léonie's hypochondria, and in Oriane's skill at imitating people. Three characters are saved ultimately by their devotion to creative work. They are the three artists: the writer Bergotte, the composer Vinteuil, and the painter Elstir—representing three aspects of the same type of man Proust undoubtedly wished to be or to emulate himself.

The hierarchy of society and the various circles of the Guermantes' world represent temptations of social power for Marcel—tests of endurance and skill, related to all the pleasures of worldliness. One after the other, Marcel savors each, is disillusioned, and passes on to the next. Before he enters it, each salon seems foreign and terrifying to him, but when he comes to know it, he sees its moral defects and its trivialities. In his quest for love, Marcel also passes through a series of tests and disillusionments. His love as a boy for the young girl Gilberte, his love as an adolescent for the older woman Oriane, duchesse de Guermantes, and finally his long painful suffering and jealousy over Albertine, represent initiatory degrees of love and passion.

These tests, these initiations to the world and to love, are the great scenes in Proust's novel, and they continue until the moment, at the end of the novel, when Marcel discovers the key to the one blessing in which he can believe. The title of the last volume, *Le Temps Retrouvé*, is in reality the recapturing of the lost vocation of writing, the vocation we learned of in *Combray* (the first chapter of *Du côté de chez Swann*), when Marcel's father discouraged his son from thinking of such a vocation, when Norpois, his father's dinner guest, encouraged him, and when Bergotte, encountered a bit later at Mme Swann's luncheon, incited him to reconsider his vocation.

Proust's original plan was to publish his novel in two volumes, the first to be called *Du côté de chez Swann*, and the second *Le côté de Guermantes*. These terms are carefully explained in the first volume as designating the two walks the family could take in Combray on leaving tante Léonie's house in order to reach the countryside beyond the town. Swann's way, or Méséglise, leads through a field landscape past M. Swann's property. Guermantes' way leads through a river landscape in the direction of the Guermantes' country house. The two "ways" designate two social worlds that seem far apart at the beginning of the novel. Swann belongs to the rich bourgeoisie, which was the social class of Marcel's own family. The Guermantes are members of the aristocracy, one of the oldest families of French nobility. To young Marcel, the Guermantes at first appear inaccessible, living in a world by themselves, in a kind of fortress. When Marcel grows up, this inaccessibility of the Guermantes dissolves, and he enters the world of the aristocracy with total ease.

The many moral defects which are forced upon the attention of Marcel as he encounters one after the other of the Guermantes help to prepare the general picture of social transformation that Proust is concerned with presenting in his long epic story of time. Even during the twenty years of the novel's action, the Guermantes family is changed by marriages and deaths and adoptions. The most ironic and spectacular social change in the novel is that brought about by Mme Verdurin's entrance into the Guermantes world. This almost comic figure at the beginning of the novel, in *Du côté de chez Swann*, an over-ambitious despotic lady of the bourgeoisie, eventually becomes the loftiest figure of the noble family, la princesse de Guermantes, in *Le Temps Retrouvé*. She is a metamorphosis, explicable by the passing of time and by a large number of moral deficiencies in the makeup of man: greed, infidelity, egoism, sloth; by all the pettinesses of gossip and envy; by the mirage of grandeur. She is as relentless in vying with the Guermantes and ultimately conquering them as Marcel is eager to know and understand them.

The vast social changes studied by Proust are recapitulated in the novel's two major love stories and in the several secondary love stories. The episode of Swann in love is placed near the beginning of the work, and the longer episode of Marcel in love is placed near the end. The torment of the heart in love, more swift and intense than a social change, does not parallel the upheavals of history whereby entire social classes emerge with lessened or increased power.

In the first episode there is greater emphasis on the slow and almost naïve way by which love for Odette grows in the heart of Swann. At one point, he suddenly realizes it is there in him, as if it were a malady that has taken over all the organisms of his body. He has to submit to its torment. When it is over, he marries Odette. In Marcel's love for Albertine, the emphasis is on the prolonged phase following the acknowledgment of love. Marcel studies the spasms of jealousy as his experience spreads out toward its dissolution and ending. The image of a malady, of a contagion, applies equally well to Marcel's love. The organism of the lover is devoured by the suffering of love.

Out of a life of oscillation and dreams, the mind of the artist creates order and richness of detail. In his creation of the two girls Marcel falls in love with—Gilberte and Albertine (whose names are so similar that they might be the same heroine)—Proust went far beyond his own experience. Everything is recognizable in his universe, but also everything is new. The temperament of Proust is everywhere visible in his book: in the man's intensity of feeling, his subjectivism, his own personal adventure on this earth. But Proust the writer was the technician who adapted all of that to the laws and the architecture of the work. His depiction of society and his analysis of the heart were revealed to him not as the man living in society and suffering from his sentiments, but as the writer who, alone in his room, filled the large *cahiers* with the writing that constituted his search for the absolute beyond time.

Proust's mother, Jeanne Weil, came from a Jewish family of Metz, in Lorraine. Throughout his life, Proust remained in close contact with his mother's family and often visited the graves of his Jewish ancestors in the cemetery on the rue du Repos in Paris.

His father, Dr. Adrien Proust, came from a Catholic family long established in Illiers, a town near Chartres, in the region of La Beauce. Proust's grandfather was a maker of wax candles and tapers in Illiers. His daughter married Jules Amiot, an important business man in Illiers. She was Proust's *tante Amiot*, who became *tante Léonie* in the novel. Her house on the rue du Saint-Esprit, with its front door opening onto the street, and the back door onto a small garden, is today a museum where one can visit the kitchen of Françoise and the dining room, mount the famous stairway at the top of which the young boy waited for his mother, enter the bedroom of Marcel and that of tante Léonie, and walk in the garden where the family, in the novel, used to listen for the ringing of the bell announcing Swann's arrival.

Proust placed credence in the belief that the family determines a writer's vocation, and that immediate influences count as well as distant atavistic influences of ancestry. A man writes from the accumulation of memories that reach far back in time, far beyond his own life. And when he writes, he is not free in facing the work to be written. An artist expresses not only himself but hundreds of ancestors, the dead who find their spokesman in him.

The genius of Proust's art is nostalgia for childhood, for the happiness of certain moments when, for example, he played with children in the Champs Elysées, particularly with Marie Bénardaky, some of whose traits are unquestionably in Gilberte. Like most artists, Proust remained a prisoner of his childhood. His lucidity is that of a child sorrowfully conscious of the world.

It was Proust's privilege to know Paris society at all levels of its prestige and power. He was attracted to this experience not by *snobisme* but as the observer of a world he was to transmute. He inspired affection and loyalty in a large number of friends. Hyperbolic in his expression, obsequious in his manner, he seemed worldly to a perilous degree and avid to know every stratum of society, every social type. And yet Marcel Proust was a solitary figure, anguished over his health and the gradually increasing threat of death, tormented by his ambition to be a writer.

In 1906, after his parents' death, Proust moved to an apartment at 102, boulevard Hausmann, where he lived until June 1919. There he created the room which is the real unity of place for *A la recherche du temps perdu*. He had the walls lined with cork, the door covered with heavy tapestry, and the windows closed so that no noise or odors from the street below would reach him. This cork-lined room where he wrote and slept is as famous now in the history of French literature as residences of other exiles in solitude: Montaigne's tower room where the *Essais* were written, Hugo's island posts on Jersey and Guernsey, and Flaubert's retreat at Le Croisset, on the Seine.

GUILLAUME APOLLINAIRE (1880–1918)

This very pure French poet had a Polish mother of Slavic ancestry and an Italian father. After a Mediterranean childhood (he was born in Rome), where he studied in Monaco and Nice, he came to Paris. Following a brief Rhineland voyage of great importance to his personal life and his poetry, he gradually assumed in Paris the role of impresario of the arts, especially of poetry and painting. But Guillaume Apollinaire (he had been baptised in Rome as Wilhelm Apollinaris de Kostrowitski) was far more cosmopolitan than most of the Paris poets. He espoused and then helped to direct the intellectual and artistic bohemianism of Montmartre and Montparnasse.

Apollinaire dominated and illustrated the new art of his age—the first fifteen years of the 20th century—not by inventing the new art forms, but by adopting them instantly, by using them in his own work and by interpreting them to others. During the First World War and the years that immediately followed it, it was Baudelaire who influenced two generations of writers: Proust, Valéry, and the Catholic writers Claudel, Bernanos, Mauriac and Maritain. Not until World War II and the years following it did Apollinaire reach a comparable position in his effect upon writers and the life of literature.

He came midway between the two generations of the symbolists and the surrealists, but he does not appear overshadowed by either one. The case of Rimbaud had somewhat fixed the portrait of the youthful poet as a vindictive, sullen, and even persecuted adolescent, hostile to family and state and religion. The case of Apollinaire changed this portrait to that of a young man without family and country, and without a sentiment of vindictiveness. His attitude was one of gratitude to France for receiving him (an attitude similar to that of many artists Picasso, Picabia, Chagall, Giacometti), of constant gratitude to his family of friends.

L'Esprit Nouveau, a lecture given by Apollinaire shortly before his death and published a month afterward in *Le Mercure de France*, is the synthesis of his major theories on poetry and the modern spirit in art. A sense of exuberance or exaltation must preside over the new spirit, as well as a desire to explore everything, to explore regions of the world and regions of the mind, to bring to every experience that critical sense and that common sense which the Frenchman believes he inherits at birth. The artist must never neglect the new popular forms of art—the cinema, for example, for which Apollinaire was a prophet.

The passage on the closed night world of dreams in *L'Esprit Nouveau* was to be a valuable guide for the surrealists. The life of dreams exemplifies man's perpetual renewal of himself, the endless creation of himself, so comparable to poetry, a force that is always being reborn and by which man lives.

The year 1913–14 was remarkable in the annals of French literature and art, the *annus mirabilis*. Apollinaire published *Alcools* and his book on the new painters, *Les Peintres Cubistes*; Proust, *Du côté de chez Swann*; Alain-Fournier, *Le grand Meaulnes*; Gide, *Les Caves du Vatican*; Jacques Copeau opened his theater of Le Vieux Colombier; Stravinsky directed the first performance of *Le Sacre du Printemps*. Cubism, as a new school in painting, had been founded in 1908, with the first cubist paintings of Braque and Picasso. By 1913, it was a fully established school. The paintings Apollinaire contemplated during the period he was composing his poems of *Alcools* reflected the universe of phantoms juxtaposed with the real universe of humanity.

In the epigraph preceding *La Chanson du Mal-Aimé*, Apollinaire tells us that this love poem, *cette romance*, was written in 1903, when he knew his love affair with Annie Playden was over, when he was still suffering from her rejection, and before he realized that his love, like the phoenix of mythology, would rise up again. It is primarily a poem on the violence of that special kind of suffering that comes from unreciprocated love. Every encounter, every memory that the lover experiences brings back his love and the knowledge that his life is, at least momentarily, emptied of every reason for living.

The first poem of the volume *Alcools*, called *Zone*, was actually the last poem to be composed. One evening in the summer of 1913, Apollinaire was in a small bar on the boulevard de Clichy, between the Place Blanche and the Place Pigalle. His companions, among others, were Marcoussis, Juan Gris and Raoul Dufy. Apollinaire was depressed because Marie Laurencin had deserted him. The conversation caused him to consider the whole experience of his life, the development and evolution of his character. He went home alone, and in the space of one night composed the poem *Zone*. It is an expansive freely written piece, part spiritual autobiography, part condensed history of Apollinaire's age. At the beginning of the poem stands the Eiffel Tower in the image of a shepherdess watching over her flock of bridges:

Bergère, ô Tour Eiffel le troupeau des ponts bêle ce matin.

Initially in the poem this line illustrates an aspect of surrealist art in its unexpected and slightly humorous analogy. Throughout the poem Apollinaire accentuates an urban magic, the new poetic force visible in bridges and machines, in automobiles and airplanes. During the café conversation, which perhaps initiated the poem, Juan Gris had pointed to some *affiches*, exclaiming; "Voilà notre poésie!" Some of the lurid and multicolored modern advertising is carried over into Apollinaire's verse. Catalogues, billboards and newspapers have their own dynamic rhythms, which are those of the modern city.

Apollinaire's *Zone* originated in a Paris *bureau de tabac* (*devant le zinc d'un bar crapuleux*) on the boulevard de Clichy in 1913, and W. H. Auden's poem of 1947, *The Age of Anxiety*, originated in a New York bar on Third Avenue. The two titles *Zone* and *Age* are not dissimilar, and the prewar *inquiétude* of Apollinaire, or his lassitude of the first line ("A la fin tu es las de ce monde ancien") bears a relationship to Auden's war-engendered existentialist *anxiety*.

Modern poetry owes almost everything to Baudelaire. Mallarmé, in a sense, became not only the philosopher of Baudelaire's theory that poetry is a method of knowledge but also the most extraordinary abstractionist of modern poetry. Lautréamont and Rimbaud were the dazzled initiates, the victims of the strange illumination. Apollinaire, however, without possessing the poetic genius of Mallarmé or Rimbaud, was very necessary in the unfolding of the poetic theory. He was able to bring poetry back from its Mallarmean hermeticism and Rimbaldian violence to tenderness and nostalgia, to the gentleness of the clown.

With Apollinaire's period the clown became the most sensitive of the modern heroes, the living receptacle for all dramas. The surrealist hero is visibly the clown, whether he be Chaplin or Donald Duck, the sad *saltimbanques* of Picasso and Apollinaire or the *voyou* who has temporarily forgotten the meaning of his heart. There is a significant *rapprochement*, quite easy to make, among the adjectives "clowning" and "surrealist" and the 1970 word "camp"—as in "camp" art and "camp" sensibility. One could read *La Chanson* of Apollinaire as if Petrouchka were the *mal-aimé*.

This is the psychological diagnosis of the poet in Apollinaire's poem *La Jolie Rousse*, the final poem of his volume *Calligrammes*, published in 1918. He is judging the order of Adventure. While in the 19th century the romantic hero judged the order of his heart, in the 20th the surrealist hero judges the order of his adventure. The word itself, when considered in its strict etymological meaning (*advenire*), explains an aspect of surrealism. It is experience without design, a hazardous enterprise of uncertain issue, the peril of jeopardizing oneself. But this order is limitless—it is the future, the adventure of the spirit that lies ahead of us. Adventure is the drama of the conscious and the subconscious, of the vast and strange domains we know and don't know. The most courageous type of hero to embark on such an adventure is the clown-*voyou* and the "easy rider." The final stanza of *La Jolie Rousse* is Apollinaire's cry of a clown. It begins:

Mais riez riez de moi
Hommes de partout surtout gens d'ici

This is Pagliaccio's invitation to laughter, the clown's dismay in the ring that incites laughter in the public. Then comes the confession:

Car il y a tant de choses que je n'ose vous dire

which is the silence of the songs, the literal silence of the performing clown, the hermeticism of Mallarmé and the surrealists, the enigmatic silence of the "midnight cowboy."

NINE NOVELISTS

Anatole France (Jacques Anatole Thibault, 1844-1924)

One of the most famous French writers in the first two decades of the century, Anatole France was awarded the Nobel Prize for literature in 1921. His influence and his fame have declined in recent years. Initiated to literature by his father, a bookseller on the Quai Malaquais in Paris, he wrote some of his early books on his memoirs of childhood, notably *Le Crime de Sylvestre Bonnard* (1881) and *Le Livre de mon ami* (1885).

France emulated to some degree the learned dilettantism of Ernest Renan, whom he greatly admired. His sceptical attitude toward highly respected values and doctrines gave to much of his writing a tone of mockery and wit. He fused with great skill and elegance themes of sympathy and irony. Before the Dreyfus affair, at the turn of the century, Anatole France seemed to be an amateur of philosophical ideas, but after the Affair, in which he espoused the cause of Dreyfus, he became a more polemical writer who denounced the forces of power and lent support to the meek in heart (see *Crainquebille* of 1901.)

When Anatole France was a prominent literary personality in Europe he was looked upon as a stylist of classical clarity and perfection. Today his style seems artificial, a combination of rhetorical effects learned from Chateaubriand and Flaubert and Renan. But the finesse of his writing is still apparent, as is the charm he exerts over the intelligence and the sentiments of his readers. His most lasting work may well be the four volumes of *Histoire Contemporaine*, in which his hero, Professor Bergeret, is the wise observer of small-town intrigues.

France always used his knowledge of the world and his erudition as weapons against dogmatic ideas, religious and secular alike.

Maurice Barrès (1862–1923)

Under the general title of *Le culte du moi*, Barrès grouped three of his early novels: *Sous l'oeil des barbares* (1888), *Un homme libre* (1889) and *Le Jardin de Bérénice* (1891). These were the writings of an aesthete in revolt against naturalism and eager to analyze the refinements of his personal experience. His second trilogy, *Le roman de l'énergie nationale*, was more concerned with political problems of the day. He belonged for a time to *L'Action Française* and the royalist movement. *Les Déracinés* (1897), first of the trilogy, develops the thesis story that a group of young men from La Lorraine (the native province of Barrès) failed in Paris because they were "uprooted." Barrès advocated fidelity to all the basic traditions—religious, national, provincial and family. And yet as a stylist he broke with the tradition of novel writing that had flourished between the time of Balzac and Zola.

Romain Rolland (1866–1944)

During the First World War, Rolland lived in Switzerland, and explained in his book *Au-dessus de la mêlée* (1915) a belief in internationalism, which he hoped would solve the problems of the world. Prior to the war, he had published biographies (*Beethoven*, 1903; *Michel-Ange*, 1905; *Tolstoï*, 1911), studies of the greatness of humanity and the highest form of fraternity. At the end of his life, he returned to the study of Beethoven, and wrote a six-volume work, *Beethoven: les grandes époques créatrices* (1927–1943). In the year of his death he published a study of Péguy, who had been his friend during the first decade of the century. Péguy, in his *Cahiers de la Quinzaine*, began the publication of Rolland's ten-volume *roman-fleuve*, *Jean Christophe* (1904–12). The hero is a musician, born in Germany. The novel is in the form of a fictionalized biography.

Colette (1873–1954)

Colette was famous for her analyses of young girls, of aging courtesans, of animals (*La Chatte*, 1933), gardens and orchards. In her novel *Chéri* (1920), on the theme of a mature woman in love with a young man, she proved herself a perceptive artist in her analysis of instincts and sensations. *Le blé en herbe* (1923) reveals an exceptional knowledge of adolescence. *Gigi* (1945) is a document on French gallantry at the turn of the century. Colette told of her childhood in Burgundy in *Sido* (1929), her first experiences in Paris, her marriage with Willy and its breakdown. Hers was the universe of the senses whose perceptions she expressed with great skill.

Valéry Larbaud (1881–1957)

Larbaud was a globe-trotter revealing influences of Baudelaire, Barrès and Gide, and an ingenious translator of Joyce, Whitman, Samuel Butler and Borgès. He was the first of several French cosmopolitans in the 20th century, including Blaise Cendrars and Paul Morand. The very wealthy Valéry Larbaud gave the portrait of a very wealthy poet, *A. O. Barnabooth* (1908), a traveller, a cosmopolitan of culture and taste who sings of luxury trains and luxury boats.

Roger Martin du Gard (1881–1958)

Between 1922 and 1940, Martin du Gard composed his long *roman-fleuve, Les Thibault,* in nine volumes. It is the story of two families, and particularly of two sons in the families, one a doctor and the other a revolutionary intellectual, who lived during the same historical period that Proust chose for his novel. Martin du Gard's work is an excellent example of the traditional 19th-century novel, well-organized and clearly written. He was awarded the Nobel Prize in 1937. At his death he left a *Journal* which, unlike the *Journal* of his close friend André Gide, who influenced his thought and writing, will not be published for some time.

Georges Duhamel (1884–1966)

In addition to shorter works, Duhamel wrote a *roman-fleuve* in ten volumes, *La Chronique des Pasquier* (1933–45), which is the story of his own family, a long novel showing the strength and the weakness of the bourgeoisie when it was the chief power in France, between the end of the century and the 1920s. Today

Duhamel appears as a disillusioned humanist. In 1906, with Jules Romains and others, he founded the "Abbaye" group at Créteil, and appropriated in his writing many of the principles of unanimism.

Jules Romains (1885–   )

After writing first for the stage (*Knock*, in 1923, was his major success), Jules Romains turned to the novel. His *roman-fleuve*, *Les Hommes de bonne volonté*, was published in twenty-seven volumes between 1932 and 1947. The work deals with the period in Europe between October 6, 1908 and October 7, 1933. The conception of the work draws upon the doctrine of unanimism. Many influences are merged in this doctrine, including the theories of symbolism and the writing of Whitman and Durkheim. Unanimism was a kind of social mysticism, and Romains' novel attempted to describe the collective soul of a society. The realistic Jerphanion and the dreamer Jallez are the two principal characters in *Les Hommes de bonne volonté*, the two opposite halves, possibly, of Jules Romains.

Henri Alain-Fournier (1886–1914)

The only novel of Alain-Fournier, *Le Grand Meaulnes*, has gone through many editions in French, has been translated into several languages, and has become a minor classic. It by no means ranks with the great French novels, but it does hold an honorable second place in company with *Dominique* by Fromentin and *Adolphe* by Constant. It has been compared with Nerval's *Sylvie* and with medieval tales of chivalry. It has been attacked as a good example of escapist literature, but on the whole it has been praised for the analysis it makes of late adolescence, and of the mingling of dream and reality, of love and adventure. Critical praise has centered especially on the first part of the novel, which forms a complete whole and deals with a dreamlike picture of an inaccessible girl.

The characters of *Le Grand Meaulnes* lead an enchanted existence. They look ahead to some ineffable dream. Alain-Fournier tried to join the dream experience of his adolescent heroes with the world of reality around them. The cult of memory dominates all the characters. They are obsessed by a lack of faith in happinesss. The secret of this mysterious story may never be fully revealed. Meaulnes' sin is perhaps his refusal of happiness. His despair grows poignant when his early happiness and his early delight with nature disappear. He eventually learns to refuse happiness and even to cultivate a certain degree of cruelty.

JEAN COCTEAU (1889–1963)

Cocteau was first introduced to the literary and artistic world of Paris by his family, through whom in his adolescence he met Rostand, Proust, Catulle Mendès, Anna de Noailles. Precociously he published his first volume of verse at the age of seventeen. A small public flattered him and applauded the facile brilliance of the poems. In his first meetings with the Ballets Russes and Serge de Diaghilev, he was not totally successful in captivating the attention of the impresario—Diaghilev's famous command, addressed to young Cocteau, "Etonne-moi," was a salutary interruption in the series of youthful triumphs.

The years immediately preceding the First World War marked the end of the school of impressionism in painting and the first works of the *fauves*, of cubism, and of the early interest in negro art. The paintings of Manet, with their scenes of picnics, straw hats and shaded gardens, gave way to the strong studies of Picasso, Braque and Rousseau, exhibited in the Salon des Indépendants. Cocteau closed himself off from those first rich contacts and began the writing of his first novel, *Le Potomak*, which he completed in 1913 at the home of Stravinsky, in Leysin.

Between 1917 and 1919, with three very different works, Jean Cocteau became a public figure. *Parade* of 1917, a ballet performed in Rome, was his first experiment with the theater. *Le Coq et l'Arlequin* (1919), a manifesto against the disciples of Debussy and Wagner, revealed his interest in aesthetics and his perceptive powers of a critic. *Le Cap de bonne espérance* (1919), a volume of war poems in which he celebrated the acrobatics of his aviator friend Garros, placed him in the ranks of the best young poets. Poetry was the mark of all three works, and the principle which was thereafter to direct the varied activities of Cocteau.

Raymond Radiguet, a boy of fifteen, called on Cocteau one day in 1918 with an introduction from Max Jacob, and was subsequently adopted by

Cocteau, Picasso, and their friends as the youthful prodigy who opposed dadaism. Although he died of typhoid in 1923 at the age of twenty, during the few years of their friendship Radiguet taught Cocteau a lesson on independence and on traits of style, conciseness and soberness that belong to the tradition of French classicism.

The two principal schools of French style have often been ascribed to the Latin rhetorical style, as illustrated in the sermons of Bossuet and the rich periodic prose of Chateaubriand, and to the Greek tradition, in which the sentence is brief and concise, as in Voltaire and Stendhal. In his Académie speech of welcome, André Maurois placed Cocteau in this second lineage. The Cocteau sentence is swift and seemingly lucid, but the content is mysterious and enigmatical. Cocteau's style became a manner of expressing complicated matters with discerning simplicity.

After *Parade*, Cocteau produced the pantomime-farce of *Le Boeuf sur le toit* of 1920, for which Darius Milhaud wrote the music. *Les Mariés de la Tour Eiffel*, first performed in 1921, was a parody of bourgeois attitudes at the turn of the century. The poems of *Vocabulaire* (1922) contained the key words of Cocteau's poetic experience, symbols and characters projected out of his imagination that were to form in time his mythology—episodes, myths, and characters charged with the duty of narrating the poet's drama. Kidnapers, sailors, angels and cyclists appear and disappear as if searching for their poet.

The companion volume of *Plain-Chant* (1923) is a more personal poem on the suffering of love which is constantly forcing the poet toward the void or into sleep. This poem reflects the moral crisis which followed Radiguet's death and out of which Cocteau sought refuge in the use of opium.

In *L'Ange Heurtebise* (1925) the poet engaged in violent combat with the angel, but Cocteau used the poem as an exorcism—for at the same time, he was beginning a cure for his opium addiction. The play *Orphée*, performed in Paris in 1926 by Georges and Ludmilla Pitoëff, was the first work of Cocteau to reach a fairly wide public. Reinhardt produced the play in Berlin, and Rilke began a translation of the text into German just before he died. In *Orphée*, the poet appears to be the combined characters of Orpheus and Angel Heurtebise. The action of the play is both familiar and esoteric; in it Orpheus is both poet and hierophant, both husband and priest.

Les Enfants Terribles was written in the three weeks Cocteau spent in the clinic at Saint-Cloud, and published in 1929. During the past thirty years this book has become a classic, both as a novel belonging to the central tradition of the short French novel and as a document of historical-psychological significance in the study it offers of the type of adolescent referred to in the title. The intertwined destinies of brother and sister, Paul and Elisabeth, with the dark forbidding figure of Dargelos behind them, provides an unusual picture of adolescence in its actions and speech and games.

The theme of Cocteau's first film, *Le Sang d'un poète* (1932), was an idea close to the romantics a century earlier, in which the poet writes with his own blood. He had always looked upon the "poetic" as antipoetic and had avoided using the fantastic (*le merveilleux*) in the traditional sense, but had found it, as in *Sang d'un poète*, in the ordinary objects of everyday life. All the episodes of the film—the scene in the artist's studio, the hotel scene, the snowball scene—compose the life and trials of the poet. Much later, in the film *Orphée*, of 1950, Cocteau developed this lesson of the poet and borrowed from *Le Sang d'un poète* and from his play *Orphée*. These films are two esoteric poems for the screen. The first one set a style that has been widely imitated, and the second represented the achievement of that style.

In *La Machine Infernale* (1934), a play on the Oedipus theme, Cocteau focuses on the machinations and ingeniousness of the gods in destroying man. He is closer in this play to the Greek prototype of tragedy than to Corneille and Racine. From his earliest *Parade* and *Mariés*, through his adaptations of Sophocles, to the major dramatic works of *Orphée*, *La Machine Infernale*, *Les Parents Terribles* (1938) and *Bacchus* (1951), Cocteau presented experimentations on the stage with the enthusiasm of a dramatist enamoured of the theater and of the idea of a spectacle.

Not least among his many roles is that of impresario and interpreter. Such moderns as Satie, Braque, Picasso and Stravinsky owe some of their glory to Cocteau. The group of *Les Six*—Honegger, Poulenc, Milhaud, Taillefer, Auric and Durey—owes him its name and the early support it received in Paris. He passed quite easily from an histrionic and tumultuous fame in the 20s to a more judicious central position in the 30s. Between the death of Apollinaire in 1918 and his own death in 1963, Cocteau occupied an active position in all the domains of French art.

RAYMOND RADIGUET (1903–1923)

Before writing his two novels, Radiguet practiced with poems (*Les Joues en feu*, 1920) composed in accordance with a type of preciosity that bears some analogy to the early poems of Cocteau and the paintings of Marie Laurencin. They are written with few words and ingeniously combine a formal elegance with licentiousness.

Raymond Radiguet was born in Saint-Maur, just outside Paris. As a young boy he came into Paris frequently. He wrote his poems on small bits of paper which he kept crumpled in his pockets. He had to iron them out with the palm of his hand, and then, because of his myopia, raise them to his eyes in order to read them. Although he claimed to be eighteen, he was only fifteen when he first appeared before Cocteau, announced by a servant's words: "Il y a dans l'antichambre un enfant avec une canne."

Radiguet's first novel, *Le Diable au corps*, was published in 1923, and his second, *Le bal du comte d'Orgel*, in 1924, after his death. The principles of his art were as austere and controlled as his personal behavior was erratic and unpredicatable. These novels depict a new *mal du siècle* that had appeared during the years following the war. *Le Diable au corps* involves a sense of limitless freedom felt by the young, and *Le Bal* analyzes the sense of bewilderment resulting from that very freedom.

Le bal du comte d'Orgel bears close affinity with the 17th-century *Princesse de Clèves* of Mme de Lafayette. Both novels are stories of a wholly admirable woman who loves two men in different ways but incompatibly. In Radiguet's novel, the passionate love Mahaut feels for her husband le comte d'Orgel diminishes until it becomes a conventional attachment. The third character, François de Séryeuse, is a friend of the count. The love he feels for Mahaut and her love for him exist at the beginning of the book and do not change.

Radiguet's sentences have a colorless purity that creates an effect totally different from that of the far more romantic and diffuse novel of Alain-Fournier, *Le Grand Meaulnes*. This novel, popular in the 20s and 30s, seems to be losing out today in favor of *Le bal du comte d'Orgel* and *Les Enfants Terribles* of Cocteau. The purely descriptive passages of Radiguet and Cocteau are more swift and condensed than even those in Stendhal's writing.

The theme of love in Radiguet is comparable to the high moral conception of love in the works of Racine and Mme de Lafayette. And it also bears analogies with the theme of love as dealt with by Cocteau, for whom love is never a moral problem but rather a willingness and a curiosity for exploration. Radiguet's treatment of passion in *Le bal* resembles a strange fascination for the perilous, for the dangerous properties of an object such as the snowball in which the pupil Dargelos had perhaps concealed a stone (*Les Enfants Terribles*). In their will to avoid the monotony of the novel and the inherent heaviness of its form, both Cocteau and Radiguet created semi-mythological characters who do not have the same need of speech and action as ordinary creatures. It is enough to see them briefly, in a brilliant setting.

In *Le bal du comte d'Orgel*, Radiguet refuses the type of poetic beauty that comes from the description of atmosphere and from the analysis of imprecise states of feeling, and he announces that another kind of poetry is to be found in the notation of what is precise and direct. The art of Stendhal, whose novels have been exceptionally enjoyed in the 20th century, also has this poetic element, which is a concentration or a denuding, a swift precise expression of critical judgment. Stendhal sees more than he feels, but remains in the tradition of the French moralists—of Mme de Lafayette, of Choderlos de Laclos, and in the category of French artists in which we would place Raymond Radiguet, who gave primacy to the senses and to the reason of man.

MAX JACOB (1876–1944)

After a childhood in Quimper (Brittany), Max Jacob came to Paris in 1896. Poverty plagued him all his life, particularly in the early years in Paris between 1896 and 1911. In *La Défense de Tartufe* (1919), Jacob tells of the event that changed or reorientated his life: the apparition of Christ in his room at 7, rue Ravignan, in Montmartre, on September 22, 1909. Between 1909 and 1924, Max lived as both penitent and sinner, and the extremes were so obvious that his close friends refused to take seriously his desire to become a baptized Christian.

A second apparition occurred in a movie house on December 17, 1914— as a result he renewed his request to become a Catholic, and was baptized on February 18, 1915. Picasso was his godfather. Between that year and the end of the decade, he wrote an extensive number of prose poems and lead a life of piety characterized by drastic penance because of his sexual sins.

By 1920, just prior to his first visit to Saint-Benoît-sur-Loire, where he was to find some degree of peace for a few years, Max Jacob had become a well-known figure in the avant-garde circles. He belonged to the somewhat older group that included Apollinaire and Reverdy. The younger poets who embraced the freshness and originality of Apollinaire and Jacob were Breton, Soupault, Eluard and Aragon, all destined to play major roles in the surrealist movement, and Cocteau and Radiguet, who remained independent of any school. The most revered figures in French literature in about 1920, whose work seemed the most certain of survival, were Gide, Claudel, Valéry, Léon-Paul Fargue and Proust. In music, Cocteau was promoting the work of Erik Satie and patronizing the group of new composers he called *Les Six*. In painting, the school of cubism had taken over first place with the work of such painters as Picasso, Braque, Roger de la Fresnaye, Juan Gris and André Lhôte.

For all the arts, the period was exuberant and fertile. Max Jacob had not only announced the period, but he incarnated its characteristics—its love of parody and humor, its nonconformity, its manner of considering philosophical and aesthetic problems.

He returned to Paris in 1928, but resumed his life in Saint-Benoît in 1936, where he lived until he was arrested by the Gestapo in February 1944. He died in the concentration camp at Drancy in March of that year.

Max Jacob's religious spirit penetrated everything, even his most burlesque writings. He needed to confess his acts and thoughts. André Blanchet, in his critical edition of *La défense de Tartufe*, justified his belief that Jacob remained always close to Jewish tradition in his life of a Christian. He studied Judaic theosophy, both orthodox and nonorthodox. The apparition of Christ on the wall of his room in 1909 never ceased to count in his life, however, and never lost its mysteriousness of an enigmatical sign. Both as a poet and as a believer, Max waited for signs.

Some of Jacob's earliest friends, and notably Picasso, who called him the only poet of the period ("Tu es le seul poète de l'époque"), looked upon his work as a major expression of modern poetry and art, but refused to take seriously the religious turn. They continued to think of him as the monocled dandy, the inventor of the real *poème en prose*, the man famous for his tireless wit, the poet who told fortunes by horoscope. He was a medley of characterizations: novelist, essayist, pamphleteer, painter, designer, caricaturist, and above all, poet. In the 1860s, long after his death, Max Jacob was called by Charles Le Quintrec, a young poet, also a devout Breton, "notre dernier poete pittoresque."

The prose poems of *Le cornet à dés* (1917) cannot be summarized or paraphrased because they are themselves the paraphrase of some dream, some intuition or memory, which was copied down in its initial incoherences, with its unusual juxtapositions. All worlds are mingled in these poems. The title is appropriate, because from a dice box fall the dice, and each time with a different result, with a different sum. The surreal picture of seven galley ships (*Métempsychose*) can be traced back to its origin in the mind's memory to the seven murdered wives of Bluebeard; a Marathon soldier (*Le soldat de Marathon*), back to a man who has lost his reason; a convert, back to the poet Max Jacob living on the rue Ravignan, in Montmartre, in the first decade of the 20th century.

PICASSO and LITERATURE

In 1964, Brassaï published his *Conversations avec Picasso* in honor of the painter's 83rd birthday. It is in the form of a journal, kept by Brassaï between September 1943 and November 1962. But there are many flashbacks to Picasso's early years in Paris, to the first decade of the century when the artist occupied the small studio in the Bateau-Lavoir, on the rue Ravignan in Montmartre, where he passed through the blue, the rose and the cubist periods, and where he made his first friendships in Paris with Max Jacob, André Salmon and Apollinaire.

The notes Brassaï made after each visit to Picasso's studio (after 1932), or after each meal at the Catalan or the Brasserie Lipp (Picasso's favorite restaurants), or after the meetings at the various cafés (the Flore and the Deux Magots especially) have value for our understanding of Picasso's character, his habits, his methods of work, and his aesthetic theories.

Picasso's career has been a series of revolutionary acts, close in spirit if not in literalness to the revolutionary stimulus of surrealism. He was a revolutionist when, in 1917, he went off to Rome with Cocteau and Diaghilev to paint the sets for the ballet *Parade*.

Picasso's Harlequins and *saltimbanques* belong to the species of *voyou*-poet (Villon and Rimbaud in certain aspects of their poetry, but especially Apollinaire) whose heart is disarmed in the midst of his more cruel brothers. The clown-Harlequin, the type of lonely hero, ever since Watteau painted *Gilles* in the early 18th century, has been continued, and has reached in modern art a unity of tragic attitude and spiritual fervor, whether it be in the poetry of

Verlaine in Stravinsky's *Pétrouchka*, in the paintings of Picasso and Rouault, or in the films of Chaplin.

Picasso's age is best characterized by an enriching and fervent interchange of ideas between poets and painters. Not only do poets write about painters (Apollinaire on cubist painters, Cocteau on Chirico and Picasso, Valéry on Degas, Breton on Matta) but painters engage in the art of writing. Rouault published prose poems and Picasso a play (*Le désir attrapé par la queue*).

Picasso was never closer to dadaists like Tzara and Picabia and to surrealists like Chirico and Miró than when he began modifying abstract architectural cubism by unusual proportions and by half-human, half-inhuman forms that are seen in dreams. He became a prolific fabricator of monstrous forms quite as terrifying as those created by Lautréamont.

Other painters were more literal-minded in their acceptance of surrealism— Max Ernst, André Masson and Chirico, perhaps the greatest, who during the few years of his surrealist fidelity gave a rich documentation on the painter's subconscious. But Picasso's art is the strongest testimonial to the energies and the forces that underlie surrealism. All the various articles of surrealist faith may be exemplified in Picasso: paranoiac-criticism, usually associated with Dali; the art of dislocation; a psychological intuition that involves both eroticism and violence.

It is well known that throughout his very long career, Picasso made no important formal statement about his work. He was often questioned about the intentions and the meanings of his paintings, but he almost always replied curtly in aphorisms, refusals, or jokes. And yet it is because of Picasso especially that all the leading questions on aesthetics were raised once again. He seems to be the leading exponent of *l'ordre nouveau* (Apollinaire's phrase), the leading representative of the generation which, believing in art, dared to lay waste what they called *la vie artistique*.

Picasso was first recognized as a master, as a great painter, by the poets. What is impossible to measure is the degree to which Picasso himself was influenced and changed by the examples he saw constantly around him of the poetic discipline in Jacob, Apollinaire, Cocteau, Eluard. It was a discipline of a lofty nature. For Picasso and Apollinaire purity in art was the deliberate repudiation of anything picturesque or artificially literary. Poets and painters both, inspired perhaps by a famous line of Verlaine, grew to despise the word "literature" and its connotations of arbitrariness and canonical tyranny: "Et tout le reste est littérature."

REVERDY and CUBISM

The style of painting called cubism is visible in a few great works done in Paris between 1907 and 1914, and in several done later by Juan Gris. Picasso, Braque and Fernand Léger were the major painters of those seven years. Many historians today claim that cubism marks a break in the history of art comparable to the break of the Renaissance in its relation to medieval art. It was the moment when modern physics was founded, which led to an increased use of electricity, the radio, the cinema, mass production, mass circulation of newspapers, the automobile, the airplane, the space ship, man's first steps on the surface of the moon.

The cubist painters Picasso, Braque and Gris, and their friends the cubist poets, Apollinaire and Pierre Reverdy (1889–1960) in particular, were sensitive to the consequences of the changes taking place in the world, not only in the aspects of what we call now physiology and sociology but also in the confrontation of imperialism and the socialist international.

Cubism was a break with tradition in the sense that it encouraged a dislocation of forms in order to demonstrate movement and change. It created a new syntax of art capable of accommodating all aspects of the modern experience. The new art forms it led to and encouraged—surrealism, abstract painting, *le nouveau roman*—have justified the cubist claims of creating a transformed world.

Apollinaire and Max Jacob have thus far received greater attention from the critics than has Pierre Reverdy. But the painters have for some time claimed that Reverdy brought to painting a far deeper understanding than Apollinaire revealed in his book *Les Peintres Cubistes*. Reverdy's book *Les Epaves du ciel* was hailed by the surrealists in 1924 as the work of a master.

During the last thirty years of his life, Reverdy lived as a lay associate in the Benedictine monastery of Solesmes, but during the earlier part of his life he was closely associated as a friend and as poet-aesthetician with the cubist and post-cubist painters. His poems, more than those of Jacob and Cocteau, are faithful to the cubist aesthetic. Each of his poems forms a perfect homogeneous and static world quite comparable to the cubist paintings of Picasso and Juan Gris. There is simplicity and even starkness in these poems that are communions between objects and thoughts and acts. Each poem is a reorganization of a still-life. It was Reverdy who announced that Picasso had made up his mind to begin everything all over again: "Picasso décida de tout recommencer."

In the 20s and 30s surrealism was an organized movement, iconoclastic and revolutionary in nature, with its leaders and disciples, its manifestoes and publications and exhibitions. It became international during the years 1919–1939 to such an extent that fourteen countries were represented in its 1938 exhibition. But the surrealists were always concerned with discovering in the past, both near and distant, confirmation for their beliefs and practices. Thus Breton claimed Heraclitus as a surrealist dialectician and Baudelaire as a surrealist moralist.

A literature came into being whose avowed goal was the escape from real or daily life and the creation of an antidote to the insufficiency of "realism." It was a literature in which the hero undertakes not an exploration of the world with which he is familiar but an adventure in a totally exotic land or an investigation of his dream world. The example of Rimbaud in Ethiopia served as a model for the creative artist able to cut loose from all the stultifying bourgeois habits of living. And Lafcadio, the hero of Gide's *Les Caves du Vatican*, whose goal is to commit a gratuitous act, an act having no motivation and no reason, also epitomized much of the new literature. Rimbaud always remained one of the gods of the surrealists, and *Les Caves du Vatican* was the book they preferred to all others of Gide, the only one of his they wholeheartedly accepted.

The new hero is the unadaptable man, the wanderer or the dreamer or the perpetrator of illogical action. He represents what psychologists would define as the schizoid temperament. His method, and even his way of life, is introspection. The great prose masters of this method of introspection—Dostoievsky, Proust and Gide—were heeded and studied by the surrealists who continued their method and pushed it so far that what is introspection in Proust became in surrealist art the dissociation of personality, the splitting apart of the forces of a human character.

The surrealist found himself preoccupied with a contemporary "hamletism" (a word first used by Max Jacob). This hamletism, an excessive analysis and study of self, an effort to probe into the deep restlessness or *inquiétude* of modern man, which results in immobility and inactivity, seems to be a new form of the *mal du siècle*, the romantic malady of the early 19th century. It came into prominence after World War I. In fact dadaism, its most violent expression, originated in 1916 in Zurich before the end of the war. The movement of dada was soon replaced in the early 20s by surrealism, but not before it had expressed its strong negative emphasis on many respectable notions and activities. It rebelled against society, language, religion, intelligence, and especially literature.

The defeatism of the war, felt even after the Armistice of 1918, helps to explain the *inquiétude* of young men in the post-war world—their sense of futility, and their attacks of open remonstrance which find expression in early surrealism.

The new movement was named before the end of the war by Apollinaire. In a letter to Paul Dermée in March 1917, he stated that he preferred to adopt the word *surréalisme* rather than *surnaturalisme*. Apollinaire at this time was the principal god among the living for the first surrealists: Breton, Eluard, Aragon, Péret, Soupault. They also admired Max Jacob, and especially the painters: Picasso, Matisse, Laurencin, le douanier Rousseau, Derain, Braque, Fernand Léger.

The international surrealist exhibition which opened in Paris, in the Galerie Meaght in July 1947, came as a very positive reaffirmation of continued life among the ranks of the surrealists, and as a denial of the charge that the cause of surrealism was extinct. The exhibition was directed by Marcel Duchamp and André Breton. The avowed purpose of the undertaking was to testify to a persisting cohesion among surrealist artists.

In terms of heroes, surrealism has extolled the legends of Lautréamont and Rimbaud, and added to them the examples of three young men who committed suicide. Jacques Vaché, a friend of Breton, died in 1918. He bequeathed the initial hate for literature and scorn for traditional art. By the habits of his life he was the type of mystifying dandy who played on the absurdity of life. In November 1929, Jacques Rigaut, the young secretary of Jacques-Emile Blanche, shot himself. The death of René Crevel, in 1935, was the third in the series. His case was tied up with the relationship between surrealism and communism. After his conversion to communism, he was expelled from the party, with Breton and Eluard, in 1933, but was absolved and reinstated soon afterward.

These three suicides took on for the surrealists the expression of surrealism itself: the gesture of liberation, "of freedom," as Kenneth Burke defines it, "projected into the aesthetic domain." The movement itself is best characterized by its rejection of the human condition of man. The history of French letters from Baudelaire to Vaché and Crevel, from Lautréamont to *Nadja* of André Breton and *Au château d'Argol* of Julien Gracq, might be described as a disposition toward holocaust wherein the hero is damned and sacrificed.

Marinetti's *Manifeste du futurisme*, published in *Le Figaro* in 1909, and the brief movement of dadaism in 1916–19 were preludes to the far more ambitious and affirmative program of surrealism which today, long after the silencing of the obstreperous quarrels, appears as an effort to express those matters, those realities which civilization, in the prudent course of its various routines, disguises or denies. That which comes about in the life of man as the result of chance, and that which in the mind of man is unknowable, are derided by the forces of civilization, but these precisely are matters of important surrealist investigation.

Much of the best French poetry of the past thirty years bears the mark and the influence of surrealism. Such writers as Jean Paulhan, Maurice Blanchot, and Raymond Queneau show distaste for the usual forms of rhetoric, and their preference for bold, spontaneous notations and images can easily be named surrealist. René Char is only one of several poets who continue the surrealist adventure of language as discovery, of language as the means of carrying out some kind of cosmic communion.

In the case of such poets as Henri Michaux and Francis Ponge, as well as Char and Queneau, poetry is the substitute for spirituality. They count among the heirs of surrealism in their constantly expressed need for freedom, in their will to move beyond literary and psychological limitations. They represent surrealism with greater detachment and greater freedom than Eluard, Desnos and Artaud represented it thirty years ago.

One city was able to absorb the movement. Paris was the literal site of most of the activities and the meetings, and it was sung of, especially in the work of Breton and Aragon, as it had never been sung of previously in French literature. The obscure streets, the cafés, the Tour Saint Jacques, the movie houses, the boulevards—all figure in the daring surrealist way of looking at nature and the exterior world. Paris was made into one of the greatest junk collections of all times as well as the site of one of the purest revolutions.

The passage of time has helped to justify the belief that surrealism did formulate and bequeath a body of doctrine on love, on imagination, on the relationship between man and the world. Born in Paris and nurtured by approximately ten men, it spread in all directions and has influenced men everywhere directly or indirectly. In his novel *Paysan de Paris* in 1924, Louis Aragon movingly announced the birth by calling it the newest vertigo given to man, the offspring of frenzy and darkness: "Un vertige de plus est donné à l'homme: le surréalisme, fils de la frénésie et de l'ombre."

On December 10, 1942, Breton delivered a lecture at Yale University in which he exalted the appeal that surrealism has always made to the young. Breton and the early surrealists were all young themselves and affirmed a boundless faith in the type of youthful genius: in Lautréamont,. who died at twenty-four; in Rimbaud, whose writing was completed at twenty; in Chirico, who painted his best canvasses between twenty-three and twenty-eight; in Saint-Just, member of the National Convention, who was guillotined at twenty-seven; in the German writer Novalis who died at thirty; in Seurat who died at thirty-two; in Jarry, whose play *Ubu Roi*, in its first version, was composed when he was fifteen and characterized by Breton as *la grande pièce prophétique et vengeresse des temps modernes*.

In his first *Manifeste du surréalisme* (1924), Breton emphasized the meaning of the word "freedom" as being the basis for surrealism: "Le seul mot de liberté est tout ce qui m'exalte encore." Freedom for the artist, according to Breton, meant first a liberation from rules of art. The artist must express his freedom iconoclastically. In poetry, the leading examples would be: Lautréamont, Rimbaud, Mallarmé in his final poem *Un coup de dés*, Apollinaire—especially in his *poèmes-conversation* of *Calligrammes*. In painting, the examples would be: Van Gogh, Seurat, Rousseau, Matisse, Picasso, Duchamp. These lists varied from year to year with Breton. His life was a series of fervent friendships and violent denunciations of former friends.

From all the writings of Breton, notably the two manifestoes of 1924 and 1930 and the *Situation du surréalisme* of 1942, it is possible to see a five-point program. (1) The importance accorded to dreams and the subconscious life of man. (2) A denial of what is usually considered contradictory or paradoxical in man's experience. (3) A belief in the action of chance (*le hasard*) or "coincidence" which diminishes the antinomy between man and nature. (4) Humor that is visible at the most solemn and even tragic moments of existence. (5) The distinction between the "self" (*soi*) and the "ego" (*le moi*).

Breton's *Nadja* (1928) is divided into two parts: a long preamble of seventy pages, almost half the book, and the story about the character Nadja. The opening sentence, "Qui suis-je?" is answered by Breton when he says he is going to learn a small part of what he has forgotten. But this attempt of memory is to be involuntary. He is going to remember effortlessly what has happened to him, and relate it without commentary and without investigation. The meetings in the story of Breton with the mysterious girl Nadja are fortuitous, resembling an intervention on the part of destiny. She often disappears only to reappear unexpectedly. When they are seated in a café, she draws herself with the features of Mélusine and feels that she is close to that mythical character.

Such occurrences as chance meetings on the street of a man and a woman, as in *Nadja*, became typical sources of a new kind of poetry of incoherences. Surrealism and film-making techniques were able to provide a lyrical transformation of reality—those unpredictable and unusual chance meetings out of which a new meaning of life may be evolved. In such meetings we make up stories about ourselves, as did Nadja, who in her partial state of dementia was probably falsifying many things. But lies, under such conditions, reveal some of the deepest truths about ourselves, truths we are unable to face when we talk with people who know the facts of our biography.

Surrealism is the most honorable form of cheating. The poet jumps from the invisible to the visible, from the angel to man, from Nadja-Mélusine to woman. The uniqueness of the poet, visible in *Nadja*, is his symbol-making power of the savage forces that are in us, and which the social machine suppresses.

PAUL ELUARD (1895–1952)

The surrealist poets Breton, Eluard, Tzara, Soupault continued the tradition of the *voyants* of the 19th century. In the wake of Baudelaire, Rimbaud and Mallarmé, poetry continued to be the effort to find a lost language. Surrealism tried to go beyond the elaborate consciousness of symbolism to the very source of poetic imagination, to the very sleep in which the myths of man are preserved.

Eluard was born in the outskirts of Paris, in Saint-Denis. After studying in Paris between the ages of twelve and sixteen, he spent two years in Switzerland, recovering from an illness. He was mobilized in 1914. The first poems he published in 1917 had been written on a Swiss mountain or in a trench. The permanent themes of his poetry were apparent in his earliest verse: an awareness of the poverty and suffering of the masses, as well as the humble sources of his happiness derived from street scenes, from animals, from the play of light on objects.

In 1918 he met Jean Paulhan, who had by then begun his career as impresario of poets, and he also met the men who were to become the leading surrealists: Breton (this meeting is related in *Nadja*), Aragon, Soupault, Tzara.

Eluard and Breton in particular discovered (or rediscovered) the pure love of woman and sang of this love as ecstatically and vibrantly as any of the earlier French poets. They contributed to a rehabilitation in literature of the role of woman as the carnal and spiritual partner of man. What had once been epic drama and historical recital became in Eluard's poetry cerebral and psychic. The drama of love, for him, was played in the mind. It was lyricism of one moment, a flash of time that is never over, anonymous and universal and hence mythical. The mind appears before itself, filled with the image of woman so resplendent in her nudity that she is all degrees of light: angelic and demonic, unique and universal, carnal and spiritual.

Capitale de la douleur is the collection of Eluard's poetry written between 1919 and 1926. The mystery of the poet's song is that mystery in which love created him and liberated him. In *La Vie Immédiate* (1932) there is a deepening of Eluard's idealism and mythology. The beloved penetrates all beings, and finally the poet identifies her with the universe itself.

During the four years of German occupation, Paul Eluard courageously participated in the Resistance. He showed himself to be a clear-sighted man of action, walking through Paris to distribute tracts and articles and poems that contributed to the spiritual health of the nation. His poems during that period were of Paris, a city unable to resign itself to the enemy's régime, of the masses and the poet's faith in their unwillingness to accept injustice, and of the faces of the condemned. His writing became the poetic chronicle of the new terrorism. His poems were used as propaganda throughout the maquis.

PHILIPPE SOUPAULT (1897–   )

At the age of twenty, in 1917, Soupault met André Breton at one of Apollinaire's Tuesday gatherings at the Café de Flore in Paris. This was the first year of the Dada movement. Between July and November three young poets who soon would call themselves surrealists (Eluard, Picabia and Soupault) published their first collections of poems.

The following year Soupault and Breton, in company with Aragon and Eluard, founded the nucleus of the first surrealist group in Paris. In 1919 Soupault contributed to a dadaist anthology and to the first issues of the surrealist magazine *Littérature*.

In 1921, Soupault was co-author with Breton of the early surrealist book *Les Champs Magnétiques*. This book was not only the first major text of the movement but was also the first example of automatic writing that had the approval of the other surrealists.

In company with Artaud, Soupault was expelled from the surrealist group by Breton, who claimed that Soupault had given too much evidence of interest in traditional literature. And yet Soupault had been one of those who had inaugurated surrealist activities in the early twenties and had helped to make the movement into a kind of laboratory for experimentation with writing and painting. His most successful poems reveal an admiration for Rimbaud and Lautréamont, but his writing is more simple than theirs, the emotions he describes more tenuous, more subdued. In its fluidity and transparency, his poetry is not especially representative of surrealism.

FRANÇOIS MAURIAC (1885–1970)

The boy François Mauriac began his formal studies with the Marianite fathers in a suburb of Bordeaux, where he read Pascal and Racine with special devotion. His first volume of poems, *Les Mains Jointes*, appeared in 1909. After the war, his life was divided between Paris and his estate at Malagar, about fifty kilometers from Bordeaux. This property had a vineyard overlooking the Garonne River, a scene quite accurately described in *Le Noeud de Vipères*. In 1925, the Académie Française awarded the *grand prix du roman* to his *Le Désert de l'Amour*, and in 1933 elected Mauriac to *le fauteuil* of Eugène Brieux. Mauriac's first editorial appeared in *Le Figaro* in 1944, and thus began his career as political writer and commentator. He helped to found *La Table Ronde* in 1948. In 1952 he was given the Nobel prize in recognition of his work as novelist, dramatist, critic and journalist.

Mauriac is the novelist of his province. One river goes through it—the Garonne—and one social class—the bourgeoisie—is described in the novels. Nature is limited to two characteristics: the pine trees of Les Landes (a region near Bordeaux) and the slopes cultivated by the vine-growers. Such is the immutable natural setting of the novels. The houses and the gardens around the houses are very much the same because they belong to the vinegrowers or to the owners of the pine forests. A sudden hailstorm can demolish an entire vineyard. The fires that easily break out in the pine forests represent a constant threat to the families that live in the large houses.

The bourgeoisie with its fixed institutions and habits is the social world of the novels, in which we read of dreams of money and legacies, of family rank and prestige, of the dividing of property, of family jealousies. Mauriac's world is provincial, bourgeois and Christian. He continued to describe this tripartite world during all of his Paris years.

In the third novel, *La Chair et le Sang* (1920), the Mauriac situation and themes began to appear: love and religion joining with class prejudice and an anguish over the emptiness of the world, which is partly neurotic and partly metaphysical.

In *Préséances* (1921), the fourth novel, Mauriac gave his first picture of the closed Bordeaux society, of the bourgeoisie controlling the wine industry, and the portrait of that type of youth isolated from the adult world and suffering from passions that are ill-understood. *Préséances* is not yet the Mauriac novel constructed around a "crisis," but it is a telling analysis of provincial snobbishness and of a certain form of human suffering.

The hero of the fifth novel, Jean Péloueyre (*Le Baiser au lépreux*, 1922) is the subject of Mauriac's first profound study of a human life—it is the story of an ugly-looking boy whose existence is barren and solitary but who, because his family has wealth, is given a beautiful wife, Noémi. With this novel, Mauriac created the form of fiction he later made his own: a tragedy of lust and love and silence, with no trace of oratory, no trace of eloquence.

The study of eroticism, especially as it develops in the life of a young man, is the subject of *Le Fleuve de Feu* (1923), and it becomes the subject of most of the subsequent novels. This study is later to become more explicit in the books of D. H. Lawrence, Henry Miller and Jean Genet, but Mauriac asks questions in his early novels that go far in elucidating the origins and the forcefulness of sexual drives.

Génitrix (1923) marked an advance in the novelist's skill in concreteness. For the first time he used a device he developed and perfected in future writings —a device called in the art of film-making a "flashback," whereby the past is inserted into the present, and whereby the chronological sequence of the narrative is broken up. In *Génitrix*, Félicité Cazenave exploits her triune power of woman, mother and widow. She is the first to be qualified as a "monster" in Mauriac's repertory of characters.

Le Désert de l'Amour (1925) is a study of adolescent love and the incommunicability of passionate love, the strange bewildering law by which men fall in love with beings who do not love them. Before he published his next novel, *Thérèse Desqueyroux* (1927), Mauriac wrote several essays, all of which were concerned with the major themes of his novels: provincial life, Bordeaux, adolescence, and psychological problems obsessing the type of young man who figures in so many of the novels: Raymond in *Le Désert de l'Amour*, Augustin in *Préséances*, Daniel in *Le Fleuve de Feu*.

The major attack on Mauriac's concept of the novel came from Jean-Paul Sartre, in an article written in 1939. Mauriac's main fault, according to Sartre, is that he sees the whole of his universe at all times. His dialogue is always efficacious and moves rapidly ahead, whereas the characters of Dostoievsky and Faulkner do not know what they are to say next, and are thus freer than the creatures of Mauriac. Sartre concluded that God (who knows everything) is not an artist and neither is François Mauriac! Mauriac is a descendent, not from the novelists of the 19th century, Balzac, Flaubert and Zola, but from Pascal and Racine and Baudelaire, writers whose sense of human tragedy is closely allied to a religious interpretation of man's fate.

At the beginning of the century, Charles Péguy stressed the important position the sinner occupies in Christendom ("Le pécheur est aussi de chrétienté"). Mauriac's novels illustrate this same significant and dramatic role of the sinner. When accused of favoring the theme of evil, Mauriac's answer was always the same; that he was interested in the problem of evil and found nothing outrageous in his characters—the newspapers alone furnished sufficient proof that in every city, every day, crimes were committed more strange and more monstrous than those in his novels. As a novelist, he combined in a subtle way the roles of Freudian analyst in his study of the secret disorder of sin, and of theologian in his study of the origin of sin. The typical novels, such as *Le Baiser au lépreux*, *Génitrix*, and *Le Désert de l'Amour*, are inconclusive in the theological sense because the novel, as Mauriac conceived of it, is the story of the peril or the disorder in which the hero finds himself, and the novel stops at the moment the peril may come to an end.

Mauriac's genre was the tragic novel, but a form in which external happenings have little importance. His novels were based upon psychological inquiry and development. On the surface, his characters lead normal lives, but inwardly they are victims of some grave conflict which the novelist projected as a force far more dramatic than any external event could be. This was the basis for Mauriac's succinct delineation of character for the intensity of his tale, for the vigor of his images. If in some instances the dénouement appears weak and unprepared, it is because, as the novelist himself would say, grace is always inexplicable and always fated to appear in a novel as a *deus ex machina*.

GEORGES BERNANOS (1888–1948)

At his death, Bernanos was claimed by the critic André Rousseaux to be the sole contemporary writer upholding the Catholic tradition in France. He was a man of prodigious vitality whose character was marked by opposing traits of violence and tenderness, gaiety and vituperation. He is remembered especially for his passages of invective and strong polemics, and has often been called the pamphleteer of modern France, the successor of Léon Bloy. His work constitutes a testimonial of our time. His books are warnings of many kinds, particularly on the problem of modern man's loss of freedom—political, economic and humanistic. Bernanos' works recall one aspect of French civilization, that associated with the baptistery of Reims and the adventure of the Crusaders. Nothing in his work can be understood unless it is seen from a Christian perspective, as engaging a real man behind a fictional character, and behind him, a nation, and behind it, the entire world.

Like Malraux, Bernanos wrote from an historical viewpoint. He was the first to see in the priest the real hero and martyr of the modern world. In the tradition of Léon Bloy, he assigned to Catholics their real function of worriers and disturbers of the peace, of consciences never at rest. He hurled his priest into all possible dramas of life, sexuality and death (see *Sous le soleil de Satan*, 1926; *Journal d'un curé de campagne*, 1936). The background of his stories is the present period in history when the world does not accept miracles, when the Church refuses saints, and when the individual soul rejects the idea of perfection. Little wonder that Bernanos, as well as Mauriac and Graham Greene, have been difficult sons of the Church.

For Bernanos, the supernatural was not just one element of life reserved for miracles; it represented for him the light of the divine remaining in the most humble creature, the source of every human life and therefore the source of every story. The common vocation of humanity, he felt, was to bring about human perfection by placing it in contact with the divine. The universe of Bernanos, like that of Kierkegaard and Léon Bloy, represented a reaction of a traditional Christian spirit against naturalism. But in this universe of the novelist, God is often manifested as a paradox and as a scandal rather than as a supernatural light.

Every age has created its characteristic type of man; for Greece it was the sage; for Israel the prophet; for the medieval world the saint and the knight; and for the classical age the *honnête homme*. Bernanos believed that the modern age has created a type of man who is mediocre in intelligence and satisfied with himself—the tepid Christian, the complacent priest. This mediocrity he associated with Satanism and judged it to be far more pernicious than earlier, more melodramatic manifestations of the devil's presence. No one stigmatized the middle class more violently than Bernanos, who called it *la canaille bourgeoise* who applauded the conquest of Ethiopia, the Munich pact, the Vichy government.

The structure of *La Joie* (1929) is, even more than *Sous le soleil de Satan*, the expression of a temperament. In it we read what poured from the heart of Bernanos. His particular vision of the world impelled him to write, and he was guided by enthusiasms and indignations. The book is the study of a young girl, Chantal, who finds herself surrounded by a world of strange beings. In their midst, Chantal, invulnerable in her truthfulness, harbors within herself the secret of sanctity. The most striking parts of *La joie* are the long dialogues between Chantal and her father, Chantal and the psychiatrist, Chantal and the priest. The art of these dialogies consists chiefly in two differing and implacably opposed statements on holiness and worldliness.

The last work of Georges Bernanos, written in 1948, was intended to be a film. *Dialogues des Carmélites* was inspired by a work of Gertrude von Le Fort, *Die Letzte am Schofott* (*The Last on the Scaffold*). It was adapted for the stage by Marcelle Tassencourt and Albert Béguin and is, after the dramas of Claudel, the most moving religious play of the century. The play is based upon an historical episode, the guillotining of sixteen Carmelite nuns on July 17, 1794. The supernatural exchange of grace that *Dialogues des Carmélites* illustrates is felt at the moment when Soeur Blanche, who all her life has been unable to overcome an instinctive deep-seated fear, replaces Mère Marie and dominates her fear of death, when the weakest member of the community becomes the strongest. The mingled themes of heroism and holiness that are in Corneille's *Polyeucte* and Racine's *Esther* and Claudel's *L'Annonce faite à Marie* reappear in *Dialogues* with comparable intensity and a similar nobility of language.

The function that Debussy performed for Maeterlinck's *Pelléas et Mélisande* has been carried out by Francis Poulenc, whose opera *Les Carmélites* (1954) closely follows the text of Bernanos. The psychological dilemma of Blanche and the characterizations of the other nuns are consistently developed. The great scenes of the opera are those of the play: the death scene of the prioress in the first act, and the final execution scene.

JULIEN GREEN (1900–   )

Five years before his birth, Julien Green's family moved from Virginia to France. He was born in Paris and lived there until the age of nineteen. His education was completely French, and his family life American. At the age of sixteen, when he was still a pupil at the lycée Janson-de-Sailly, Julien asked his father for permission to see a priest and soon after entered the Catholic Church. When questioned about his American background and affinities, Julien Green has always emphasized the fact that he has been trained predominantly by the culture of France. His language as writer is French; his sensibility and attitudes seem to be as definitely French as those of any other French writer.

In the spring of 1971, Julien Green was made an honorary French citizen by President Pompidou and elected to the Académie Française, to the *fauteuil* of Mauriac.

In 1919, he came to America for the first time and attended the University of Virginia, where he studied Latin, Greek, English and Hebrew for two years. This first direct contact with the country of his parents, the memories of Poe he discovered in Charlottesville, his studies of American writers (especially of Nathaniel Hawthorne), and American university life formed an enriching experience destined to appear in his writings.

The exterior life of Julien Green between 1928 and 1958 is fully narrated in his *Journal*, where we follow his total dedication to the life of a writer, his travels, his deep interest in music and painting, his extensive readings, his friendship with Robert de Saint-Jean, Jacques Maritain, André Gide, and the Dominican priest Père Couturier. Even during the years 1924–39 when Green had lost his faith, his concern with religious matters continued, as well as the exterior aspects of his way of life—his solitude and isolation from the world, his studious serenity, his dignity and meditative thoughtfulness.

The settings he uses for his novels are few in number: the south of the United States for such books as *Mont Cinère* (1926), *Moïra* (1950), and *Chaque homme dans sa nuit* (1960); Paris, and especially the streets at night of Passy, as in *Epaves* (1932); and the small French provincial town, as in *Adrienne Mesurat* (1927) and *Minuit* (1936).

The first books *Mont Cinère*, *Adrienne Mesurat*, *Léviathan* (1929), and the volume of stories *Le Voyageur sur la terre* (1927) stress a certain morbidity of theme and a marked violence in the passions analyzed. An atmosphere of horror and pessimism dominate these early books. The sense of horror is lessened in *L'Autre sommeil* (1931) and *Le Visionnaire* (1934). In these works the introspection of the hero is more intense and more probing. The inner world of the characters, as in *Minuit*, which belongs to this category, becomes so real and tangible that it replaces the exterior world of so-called reality. Such works as *Moïra* and *Chaque homme dans sa nuit* seem to indicate a still further development in the fictional art of the novelist. These are books of more intense tragic struggle in which the conflict between the body and the spirit dominates all else, and the religious problem becomes clearer and more harassing.

In speaking of his method of writing, Green has pointed out that his three plays were all specifically requested, and that the novels came to him of themselves. *Sud* (1953), his first play, was written at the instigation of Louis Jouvet. He composed the first scene without knowing the full subject matter of the play and without knowing to what action the scene would lead. Only later did he realize that the initial scene contained in essence the entire play.

The *Journal*, in its 1961 edition, a large 1200-page single bound volume, shows the writer's progress in his understanding of himself, although the intimate portrait of Julien Green is contained in the novels. The most personal parts of the *Journal* have been deleted and may be published after the writer's death. This is a peaceful work of great literary distinction, the history of a mind in its many encounters with art, religious problems, ideas and friends. All the forms of violence—anger, passion, pride and suffering—are relegated to the novels.

God is at the center of this *Journal*, although Green never adopts the attitude of a righteously religious man. The written communication of this solitary figure, so violent in his novels and so reserved in his *Journal*, is that of a man whose conscience is at all times alert to the dangers that press about him, to the moral dangers so often disguised. His awareness of a diabolical presence in the world is reminiscent of Bernanos, but in the writings of Bernanos the diabolic presence or apparition is histrionic and dramatically revealed. In Green's it is constant and disguised.

According to the novelist's testimony, no plan was followed as he wrote *Moïra*. From day to day, as he wrote, he invented what his characters did and said. In this book, as in *L'Autre sommeil*, written much earlier, the psychology of the hero Joseph Day, a student in a southern university in the United States, is unquestionably patterned on personal psychological traits of Julien Green himself. The hero is on the one hand obsessed by sexual drives, although he has had no sexual experience, and on the other strongly motivated by a religious vocation. Joseph's sexual obsessions are not centered in the girl Moïra, but she bears their brunt when he kills her after she seduces him. He is led to the slaying not of what he desires but of the creature who caused the loss of his purity. The title itself means "fate," and Joseph succumbs to her as to a fascination with his fate.

Green here stresses the theological point so central in Bernanos and Graham Greene, that a man is never fully responsible for his sins; but neither is he completely innocent. *Le Malfaiteur* (1956), Green's tenth novel, was begun in 1937, interrupted in 1938, and finally completed in 1955. One aspect of carnality, as it involves the spiritual life, is the central theme of the novel. It is a stronger and more specific treatment than that found in *Sud*, concerning the love of a woman for a man incapable of loving women.

The novelist's effort is to see the human problem of the protagonist Jean, "the transgressor," in its religious context. The transgression itself, Jean's homosexuality, is never described or analyzed. The reader is told about it in the opening pages. Incidents relating it are only obliquely referred to, but one feels from the beginning of the story to the end the weight of this transgression and its fatality. In the religious context of the book, Jean asks why he is reproached for being what God made him.

In his novel of 1960, *Chaque homme dans sa nuit*, Green has written his most profound work. The title is drawn from a line of Victor Hugo: "Chaque homme dans sa nuit marche vers la lumière." The "night" is the complex of religious problems and anxieties. It is especially that part of the soul where religion and sex meet. Julien Green is aware that the gravity of carnal sin has become almost unintelligible in the modern world. Wisely he places the story of *Chaque homme* in America, where sexuality still has meaning in terms of religion, and where in an atmosphere of Catholic and Protestant tensions, such a drama as he depicts is understandable.

Julien Green stands apart from other contemporary French writers. He is a truly spiritual writer in the sense that his books represent a refusal to accept man's fate. He knows that the education of modern man tends to invalidate and decry the spiritual in man, but his writings form a refusal to negate the attempts of God, in an age of spiritual sloth, to help man recover his lost freedom. If a spiritual victory is not possible, the will to struggle is at least a possible form of victory for today.

HENRY DE MONTHERLANT (1896–   )

Montherlant was born in Paris into a family whose ancestors, from both Brittany and Spain, had been devoted to the ideals of monarchy and the Catholic Church. The word "feudal" has often been used in describing the temperament of this writer, who even today appears aloof from social and political problems, engrossed in the editing of his work and in his reputation of novelist and playwright. He is an isolated figure in French literature. The themes of his novels are intense and tragic, as seen in the story of his school experiences (*La relève du matin*, 1920; *Les Garçons* 1969), sports (*Les Olympiques*, 1924), tauromachy (*Les Bestiaires*, 1926), and the place of woman (*Les Jeunes Filles*, 1930). His novels and plays have uninterruptedly considered a heroic kind of life, a life of action and exaltation.

La Reine Morte (1942) was the first play written during the years Montherlant devoted to the theater. It is built around the incoherence of Ferrante, the aging king of Portugal, a kind of philosopher who is experiencing the horror of his own philosophy. *Le Maître de Santiago* (1947) illustrates the classical origins of Montherlant's style and the type of character he enjoys depicting—the man who isolates himself in a literal and moral asceticism. *Malatesta*, first performed in 1951, is a study of vital energy, anger and impulsiveness in the time of the Italian Renaissance.

To these historical plays, which in part resemble the blood tragedies of the Elizabethan theater, Montherlant has added a few plays in modern dress and setting, such as *Fils de personne* (1943), in which the text is as classically bare as in the others.

The title of the play *La Ville dont le prince est un enfant* is taken from a verse in the book of Ecclesiastes, which condemns a country whose prince is a child. The play, first published in book form in 1951, has as its setting a boys' school in Paris, directed by a religious order. Montherlant classifies *La Ville* with two others—*Le Maître de Santiago* and *Port-Royal*—as his Catholic plays, calling them his three *autos sacramentales*. *La Ville* he specifically calls a tragedy of sacrifice. It is most certainly a key to all his writings.

This particular play is on the theme of sentimental attachments that develop between boys at school, and the role of their spiritual directors. Only one theme is studied in this play, but it is presented with so many different nuances that it seems to be several themes. The text is Montherlant's purest in structure and most human in feeling and pathos. In the final dialogue between the Superior of the Order and Abbé de Pradts, the disciplinary administrator who has manifested an unusual indulgence for the pupil Sandrier, the Abbé articulates the arguments of his heart and the Superior articulates the arguments of a pious theologically sound school principal. The order of the establishment is threatened in the strong attachment of Abbé de Pradts, conflicting with the order of the school itself, superior to the order of friendship or love.

For his eighth play, *Port-Royal*, Montherlant chose an austere subject from the history of Jansenism—a day in August 1664 when the nuns of Port-Royal refused to sign the Formulaire. The principal struggle is between the Archbishop of Paris, whose reasons for condemning the community of Port-Royal are strong and defendable, and the obstinacy of the frail-looking nuns, who oppose the established order. Montherlant's text projects from this struggle a grandeur of pathos which in the dramatic sense has little to do with theology. The nuns' doggedness in the central scene with the Archbishop appears as a blind rebellion. The fight is lost before it is waged, and this fact provides the pathos.

ANDRÉ MALRAUX (1901–   )

The career of André Malraux has undergone a curious and complicated development. Before the war his position was solidly established as one of the leading novelists, whose large social frescoes of *La Condition Humaine* (1933) and *L'Espoir* (1937) had revealed a world torn by the worst catastrophes. But then, in 1948, appeared his work *Psychologie de l'Art* (later issued under the title *Les Voix du Silence*), a work that is far more than art criticism or art history. Malraux is one of the recent men of letters in France to write on art; the lineage is a noble one, comprising such writers as Diderot, Stendhal, Baudelaire, Taine, Alain, Valéry.

Malraux believes that a struggle is at the origin of artistic creation. He is particularly fond of the revolutionaries: Goya, Manet, the medieval sculptors. His long work on the psychology of art, written in an opulent style, is exacting and stimulating. It touches on many problems of literature, as, for example, the emotion of the spectators watching *Oedipus*. Malraux believes that art reveals to us a secret way of possessing the world. He sees the artist as one who creates another universe, who corrects or reorganizes the work of Genesis.

In the first part of *Les Voix*, Malraux elaborates the theory that art is always following one of two beliefs. The first sees man as mastering the world, as dominating the mystery of the world. In this art, Greek and Renaissance, the human figure is triumphant. The second is the belief that the mystery of the world is greater than man and crushes him. The second part of the book deals with that kind of art that contains both beliefs, such as medieval art. In the smiling angel of Reims or *le beau Dieu* of Amiens, Malraux studies the relationship between man and the sacred—and particularly those forms of art that represent a harmony between them.

Throughout this work on art, the reader thinks instinctively of the vast stylized reportings in Malraux' novels: *Les Conquérants* (1928), *La Condition Humaine* and *L'Espoir*. In art as well as in his novels, he prefers the pathetic and the catastrophic. He refers to the arts of all ages and all worlds. The figures scratched in prehistoric cave dwellings cohabit with the works of Braque and Picasso. His work is really on human genius, and he insists on convincing the reader that an artistic creation is the justification of the mystery of our life. He never tires of reiterating the belief that art does not imitate life, but that it imitates art and reveals life.

RAYMOND QUENEAU (1903–   )

As a young writer, Queneau was attracted to surrealism and participated actively in the movement between 1924 and 1929. The experimental quality of his writing is apparent in his poems, which are often built on plays on words and repetitions of key terms (see *Les Ziaux*, 1943). In *Exercices de style* (1948) Queneau presents ninety-nine different versions of the same totally insignificant anecdote. *Les Temps Mêlés* is a collection of three stories written in three different forms: poetry, prose and drama.

Even if Queneau does not rank with the best French novelists of the last thirty years, he remains an outstanding virtuoso of style, a writer who recreates language by means of an abundant use of colloquial speech and slang, and of varied rhetorical devices. In his use of highly stylized slang, Queneau goes farther than even Jean Genet and Ferdinand Céline.

His first novel, *Le Chiendent* (1933), is one of the first books in France to reveal a crisis in the language of fiction. The vision it gives of the world is as barren and desert-like as that found in Sartre and Camus. The slangy monologue of the character Saturnin can be read today as a prophetic caricature of existentialism.

Loin de Rueil (1944) is the novel of a long dream in which the character Jacques l'Aumône, as he watches a cowboy film, carries on a self-identification with each sequence. It is an intriguing example of a novelist's world—half-poetic, half-crazy—a dreamworld of moonlight that recalls Laforgue's *Moralités légendaires* and the paintings of Watteau.

The hero of *Pierrot mon ami* (1942) appears in an amusement park. His antics are reminiscent of Chaplin as he rides in trucks with apes and moves in and out of frustrating love affairs. *Zazie dans le métro* (1959) was an immediate popular success; Zazie is the French Lolita.

Queneau's writing is never an exact transcription of contemporary life and society. He remains a kind of philosopher who once had close affiliation with surrealism, and who has forged a new language based on oratory and *argot*. He was a prophet of existentialism by creating in his novels a sense of the absurd, of the hopelessness and ridiculousness of the modern world.

In nowise has Raymond Queneau reached the vast public of Sartre and Camus, but he has influenced, by reason of his virtuosity and vision, other writers, including the American Henry Miller. In turn, Miller has probably influenced Queneau, or at least encouraged him.

The settings Queneau favors most are the familiar drab settings of a metropolis: movie houses, buses, trains, subways, and the stretches of desolate land around a city. The characters who walk about in these settings are Chaplinesque, phantoms from the *commedia dell'arte*—idlers, poets and clowns. They are looking into the same kind of void that Camus' Meursault (*L'Etranger*) and Sartre's Roquentin (*La Nausée*) look into. For all these new antiheroes, the world has become a no-man's land.

ANTOINE DE SAINT-EXUPÉRY (1900–1944)

During the years following the liberation, 1945–1950, Saint-Exupéry was one of the contemporary writers most deeply revered by French youth. He was often placed with Malraux and Camus as an affirmer of man's heroic actions, as a believer in the ability of man's will to oppose the hostility of the world.

The reputation and the popularity of the aviator-writer had steadily increased during the fifteen years that preceded his death. At the end of the twenties when he began his pioneer flying over the deserts, few Frenchmen realized the importance of these missions, but in the late forties the majority of readers were able to interpret such action as an experience in solitude that encouraged meditation on the meaning of man. They were episodes of risk and tragedy: the establishing of the mail flights south of Buenos Aires and across Patagonia; a crash in Guatemala; a forced landing on the Libyan desert; the final reconnaissance flight over occupied France in July 1944, from which the flier never returned.

No longer considered a major writer, Saint-Exupéry appears today as one of those French moralists whose works are representative of what was noblest in our historical era. In *Terre des hommes* (1939) the themes of action and meditation are closely mingled. The meaning of the earth comes to him from his position in the sky.

During the Vichy regime, he spent two years in New York, unwilling at that time to join the forces of the Free French under General de Gaulle. Saint-Exupéry's meditations on the meaning and the future of France when he was a pilot in a defeated army (*Pilote de Guerre*, 1941) have a significance that is still applicable for many Frenchmen. Long before Jean-Paul Sartre used the word *engagé* to characterize a certain kind of writer, Antoine de Saint-Exupéry illustrated the meaning in his life and his books.

LOUIS-FERDINAND CÉLINE (1894-1961)

When Céline's first novel, *Voyage au bout de la nuit*, was published in 1932, it became one of the most widely read books in Europe, and is still looked upon as a significant modern novel in terms of its influence on sensibility and influence on style. *Guignol's Band* (1944) was similar to the early books in its nihilism, despair and pornography, but it marked a development or change in style that culminated in *Féerie pour une autre fois* (1952).

Guignol's Band was not welcomed in France with the same degree of violent approbation and violent disapproval that had welcomed *Voyage au bout de la nuit*. The obsessive themes of his writing and his characters, largely drawn from pimps and prostitutes, were by then familiar to his readers. The setting of *Guignol's Band* is London, during World War I, and its main action is the life of a young French soldier, Ferdinand, in the underworld, where his hallucinations create the powerful pictures of human degradation that are now in Europe associated with the name of Céline.

He was the first to announce and depict that particular kind of human despair that has become an almost exclusive theme in contemporary literature: the absurdity of human life. We tend to forget how much writers like Sartre and Raymond Queneau and Henry Miller owe to Céline, who first established an agreement between the absurd in man's existence and the obscene in the expression he gives to daily life. The importance of Céline in contemporary literature comes from his having proclaimed a philosophy of man and the world which, for a time at least, dominated other philosophies and other visions.

The scandal his first books created has been greatly attenuated. It coincided with the moment in Europe when the bourgeoisie began to feel its stability threatened by prospects of war and revolution. It was the moment when Malraux replaced Gide for younger French readers, when Saint-Exupéry replaced Duhamel, when Bernanos, for Catholic readers, replaced Mauriac. Céline's first book was the most violently opposed of the period. Its pornography and its antisemitism were especially noted in the denunciations, but the book also contained a violent accusation of a world on the verge of collapse. Those readers who looked upon the book as justified saw it as the prolonged complaint of a man more sensitive than most to the tragedy of his historical period. Only Bernanos, writing from the center of a very different set of values, emitted the same negative cry against his world. Much of the existentialist literature of the forties recalls the books published by Céline in the thirties.

The novels of Céline are like vast poems or lyric structures because of the endless thematic repetitions that characterize his writing. Not since Rabelais has the torrential flow of oral speech been so copied in a literary work. This style of popular speech was taken over from him by Sartre and other writers, but Céline surpasses them all in richness.

JEAN GIONO (1895–1970)

The early novels of Giono (*Colline*, 1928; *Un de Baumugnes*, 1929; *Regain*, 1930) are unique in modern French literature in their celebration of the rural setting of Manosque, the writer's birthplace in Provence, and of the surrounding country and mountain district. Giono grouped these three books as a *Trilogie de Pan*. His subject is pastoral, of an almost primitive type. The early books and those that followed, such as *Le Chant du Monde* (1934), *Que ma joie demeure* (1935), and *Les Vraies Richesses* (1936) are an apology for a return to nature, to a pastoral existence which is sung of lyrically and pantheistically.

In 1940, Giono wrote a commentary on *Moby Dick*. His admiration of the American novel is somewhat explained by the general inadequacies he felt in French realism. What struck him in the Melville story was the totality of the work—what seemed to be the creation of an entire world. Giono called it an example of *le véritable réalisme*.

After the war years, when Giono was accused of collaboration with the Nazis, he began publishing a different type of book, one well-represented by *Le Hussard sur le toit* (1952) whose hero, a young Piedmontese, recalls Stendhal's Fabrice. Like Rousseau and Rimbaud, Giono records in his books a serious dissatisfaction with modern civilization and a protest against man's fate.

LÉON-PAUL FARGUE (1876–1947)

Fargue's earliest poems were appreciated by Mallarmé, who had been Fargue's English teacher at the lycée Rollin in Paris. Fargue himself acknowledged the influence on his work of such poets as Laforgue, Corbière and Lautréamont. His form of writing is markedly independent, an intermediary form between narrative prose and rigorously composed verse.

After the last years of Mallarmé's Tuesday gatherings, Fargue spent his evenings in the literary cafés in Paris, at the *Chat Noir*, for example, in Montmartre, during its richest period: 1895–1910. He was an intimate friend of the composers of those years: Maurice Ravel, Florent Schmitt, Stravinsky, Satie. Some of his poems have been set to music by Ravel, Schmitt, Satie and Auric. His unerring taste in painting helped to introduce Cézanne and other impressionists, and later he became a good friend of Picasso and Braque.

He joined ranks with the surrealists for a while, but never associated with any one group. The literary magazine *Commerce* was founded in 1924, and Fargue became its director. It was distributed by Adrienne Monnier in her bookstore on the rue de l'Odéon, a meeting place for writers where Fargue saw Gide, Valéry and Joyce.

His legend of vagabond poet and noctambulist is well-substantiated in his writings on Paris. Late at night, at Lipp's or the Deux Magots, Fargue appeared at his best—witty, cultivated, ironical, and at the same time mysterious and complicated. Fully half of his writing is devoted to Paris. His pieces on Saint Germain, on the Ile Saint Louis, on the railroad stations and the faubourgs are lyric-realistic prose poems where, behind comic metaphors and concetti, one can sense a deep sadness. Fargue's poetic style is comparable to that developed by Michaux and Audiberti and, to some extent, the style of Giraudoux. The poet's wit and dreams often turned ironical, as they once did with Laforgue.

PIERRE-JEAN JOUVE (1887–   )

Jouve's early poetry, repudiated by him today, was strongly marked by the movement of unanimism. Of all the contemporary French poets, Jouve is perhaps closest to Baudelaire in his concern with the themes of Christian anguish and Christian hope. He is fully aware that his poetry is difficult, and has attempted, in various prefaces to his volumes of verse, to elucidate his art and explain his themes. The preface to *Sueur de Sang* (1933) is a meditation on the meaning he gives to anguish as the foundation of sin and catastrophe.

In addition to his poetry, Jouve has written some penetrating critical studies on Mozart (*Don Juan de Mozart*) and Delacroix, on Baudelaire and on the opera *Wozzeck* of Alban Berg.

JEAN-PAUL SARTRE (1905–   )

Sartre's family, half-Catholic and half-Protestant, came from Le Périgord. He is a cousin of Dr. Albert Schweitzer. His father died when the boy was two, and he was brought up in La Rochelle, after his mother's remarriage in 1916. He completed his schooling in Paris at the lycées of Henri IV and Louis-le-Grand. At the Ecole Normale Supérieure, he passed his *agrégation de philosophie* in 1929. He taught philosophy in Le Havre between 1931 and 1933. In Berlin in the following year, where he served as a teacher in the French Institute, he studied the writings of Hüsserl and Heidegger. Between 1934 and 1939, he was made a prisoner of war by the Germans, and was liberated in 1941. During the Occupation he resumed teaching, first at Neuilly and then at the lycée Condorcet until 1945, the year he founded his magazine *Les Temps Modernes*. He was awarded the Nobel prize in October 1964 and refused it.

Sartre occupied the first place in French literature for approximately twenty years, between 1940 and 1960. He is the leading philosopher of existentialism, using literary forms for the expression of his philosophy. At its inception, as a highly technical philosophy, existentialism annexed the literary genres of novels, plays and essays in order to explain itself to an ever-widening audience.

Sartre belongs to literature in his multiple roles of novelist, dramatist, essayist and polemical writer. His name is often coupled with Voltaire's, and his influence compared with Voltaire's widespread influence in the 18th century. There is a Sartrean "world," recognized as such in many countries of the real world today, and this is the result of a vigorous productive temperament, of an intellect and a sensibility that have redefined some of the eternal problems of humanity.

In all of his writings, Sartre stresses man's solitude, his aloneness, and even, in its extreme form, his alienation. Man's freedom, a power residing in each isolated body, is closely associated with responsibilities, because it is usually defined as that freedom that man may use in assuming some kind of responsibility outside of himself—an autonomous responsibility. These are the familiar existentialist terms and they designate the principal problems upon which Sartre has thus far based most of his writings.

His first novel *La Nausée* (1938) is the diary of Antoine Roquentin (modeled on Sartre himself) in Bouville (modeled on Le Havre). This young scholar is working on an historical biography of an obscure 18th-century character. The book's drama is Roquentin's experience of nausea, a sickness that takes hold of him when objects reveal their absurd existence. Everything seems gratuitous to him.

Le Mur (1939) is a collection of five stories that have already become classics. The title story *Le Mur* studies the attitude of man toward death. *Intimité* is a brilliant illustration of what Sartre means by bad faith (*la mauvaise foi*). It is the study of characters who will not accept themselves for what they are.

The three volumes of the novel *Les Chemins de la liberté* have not been as well-received as other works. *L'Age de raison* (1945) describes the prewar world. *Le Sursis* (1945) describes the week of September 1938 preceding the surrender of Chamberlain and Daladier at Munich. *La Mort dans l'âme* (1949) describes the events of June 1940.

Sartre's philosophical treatise, *L'Etre et le Néant*, was published in 1943. This dialectical work on man was the first book of philosophy since the publications of Henri Bergson to reach a wide audience. It is the basis for an understanding of the philosophical assumptions of all the writings of Sartre, and of existentialism in general.

The term "nothingness" usually has a bad connotation. But in the philosophy of Sartre it refers to the rising up of consciousness above things, a detachment of consciousness in its relationship to matter. Sartre's basic assumption, from which he never deviates, is the belief that because reality is accessible to man only through his consciousness, the sole study of the philosopher is man's consciousness.

The chapters constituting the essay *Qu'est-ce que la littérature?* first appeared as articles in *Les Temps Modernes*, and in book form in 1948. At that time, Sartre was the most discussed writer in France, and probably in Europe. His importance came from the fact that his vision of the world and of man corresponded to many of the fundamental concepts in the modern consciousness.

Sartre propounds that human existence is its own value. It creates its own value. It is not a means, as Christian philosophy is, of discovering transcendental values. The existentialist believes that man is free, and this total freedom, which at first is inseparable from the experience of anguish, is the basis of man's reconciliation with the self.

Sartre never loses sight of what appears to him and to many thinkers as the crisis of modern thought. One of the ways by which this crisis may be averted or repaired would be to restore to literature its full social function. The writer, therefore, according to Sartre, must write for his age at the expense of any preoccupation with the history of the past or with the theology of eternity. The writer is in a "situation." This word, used by Sartre as the title of his volumes of criticism (*Situations* 1947–65), has a specific technical meaning, as used by Marx. The *situation* is the synthesis of all the forces that form and develop the individual man.

In his short study of *Baudelaire* (1947), Sartre has written an existentialist psychoanalysis. The poet is studied as the case history of a man who refused to choose his life in the existentialist sense. The existentialist has to create his own meaning of life, to renew his life and assume it at each instant. Sartre says in his essay that Baudelaire, early in life, made himself into a definitive petrified being in order to escape all responsibility.

When Sartre's long study of Jean Genet was published in 1952, it appeared immediately as one of his most unusual books and one of his most significant. The volume is a philosophical preface, of 600 pages, on Genet's life and on the importance of Genet's writings. *Saint Genet, comédien et martyr* appeared at the peak of Sartre's fame. It is a valuable study for the revelation it provides of Genet's art, for its minute critical examination of Genet's novels, for the philosophical reflections concerning the problem of evil, and for the brilliant way in which Genet's case is used to illustrate existentialism.

Sartre's first play, *Les Mouches*, was first performed and published in 1943. His new treatment of the fable of Orestes seemed to the first public to bear a strong relationship to the moral dilemma created by the Occupation. The new theme of the play is that of Orestes as redeemer. The relationship between Orestes and the people of Argos is a moving dramatic situation in *Les Mouches*, and it is also the source of much of the existentialist philosophy in the play. At the end of the play, by killing Aegisthus and Clytemnestra, Orestes takes on the remorse of the people and frees them from their guilt. The people of Argos represent the old collective power that is enslaved and propagandized. By making his choice, Orestes exists and creates his self.

Huis Clos was first performed in May 1944, just before the Liberation of Paris. Three characters, a man and two women, are in hell, which appears in the form of a livingroom with second empire furniture. This play is Sartre's indictment of the social comedy and the false role that each man plays in it. The most famous utterance in the play, made by Garcin when he says that hell is everyone else—"l'enfer, c'est les autres"—is, in the briefest form possible, Sartre's definition of man's fundamental sin. In social situations we tend to play a part that is not our own. The viscosity of such a social character is the strong metaphor by which Sartre depicts this sin, which will end by making it impossible for man to choose himself, to invent himself freely.

The plays of Sartre have the dynamics of existentialist exercises. In them he tracks down the alibis we make in our daily lives and flails the system of routines by which so much is carried out in history. The fear of standing alone forces us to those routines, exemplified in the plays by fear in the people of Argos (*Les Mouches*), by the static quality of hell (*Huis Clos*), by the goal of security in the bourgeois world (*Les Mains Sales*, 1948).

Into his work Sartre has translated all the anxieties of the past two decades. The personal legend of the man, associated with Paris cafés, has in nowise prevented the work from having a strong repercussion on the European conscience and, to some extent, on the American conscience. The polemical note is audible in every form his writing has taken—in the plays and novels as well as in the essays and the philosophical works.

It was possible at one time, in the forties, to look upon Sartre as a master surrounded by disciples. He no longer has this position, but many writers agree with him on the necessity today for a "committed literature" (*une littérature engagée*). This central concept of responsibility is not unique to Sartre in the 20th century. It is a persistent theme in the work of Péguy, Bernanos and Malraux. Such writers would agree with Sartre that our ways of living and the accomplishments of our life depend solely upon us.

ALBERT CAMUS (1913–1960)

Camus' death in January 1960 in an automobile crash on a familiar summer vacation highway, *route nationale 5*, in the south of France had so many exceptional elements that for many days following, his name seemed to be everywhere in the press.

The absurd accident that caused the instant death of a celebrated writer would suffice to explain the fervor of the journalistic press. But Camus had become much more than a writer in France. He was much more than the author of *L'Etranger*, *La Peste* and *La Chute* for those Frenchmen who felt a national pride in his receiving the Nobel prize two years earlier, at the age of forty-four.

He occupied a privileged place with only two other living writers, Sartre and Malraux—that of leader and inspirer of the younger French intellectuals. The popularity of these three men has fluctuated considerably between 1950 and 1970. At the beginning of the 60s, the name of Camus had less influence on French youth than it did during the years immediately following the Liberation, 1945–1950. But no other French writer had more prestige in France and abroad.

A countless number of Frenchmen and readers outside France had learned to think with Camus, to derive hope and sustenance from his books. He had become a moralist. In the history of French letters the moralists, those writers who stress the purely human values of conduct, occupy the highest and the most original place.

This very position of moralist, in the case of Camus, was looked upon by Sartre as a defect, or as a failure to meet the greater challenge to participate actively in the political events of the moment. Long before the situation in Algeria had become a crisis and a war, Camus had been the first to sound the alarm. When he received the Nobel prize, he said to the king of Sweden, "You are honoring a Frenchman of Algeria."

With the tragedy of his death, it became clear that Camus is a modern hero in every sense—a man whose legend will gradually be formed. His birth in poverty, his revolt against the condition of man and his role of *résistant*, his fame and apotheosis as a writer, his disenchantment and his accidental death coming soon after he had said, "I have done nothing yet, my work lies ahead of me"—these are the elements of a legend.

The simple human facts of his existence have been often rehearsed: his loyalty in friendship; his skill in dancing, swimming, football; his traits of sensualist; his uprightness and intellectual honesty. . . However, the philosophical hypotheses of Camus the thinker have gradually taken precedence over the traits of Camus the man. A generation of readers have meditated on his justification of despair. The way in which Meursault, in *L'Etranger*, looks upon the world was seen to be comparable to a divorce between a man and his life.

Written in 1940, *L'Etranger* was published in 1942, and caused, almost immediately, a marked repercussion. Camus' work then became an effort to reconcile his faith in life with his sense of the absurdity of life. The articles in *Combat*, written after the Liberation, offered as much hope to the French at that time as did the example and the action of General de Gaulle. Camus never denied the repugnance he felt for the world in which he lived, but he never ceased claiming a solidarity with men who suffer in the world.

The reasonableness of his mind was always being baffled by the rapture of his senses, as in the lyric praise of the sun and the sky of Algeria, in his early work of *Noces* (1938), and by the dismay he felt on examining the universe of men. He used to speak of the two possible ways of living in our day—in solitude or in solidarity, and he always avoided advocating either way at the expense of the other.

L'Etranger is the story of a quiet but desperate stoicism. Even if it seems destined now not to occupy a place beside the greatest French novels, it is and will doubtless remain an important document on a form of sensibility in the 20th century.

Throughout the story Meursault acts in accordance with superior physical forces that determine his life. But the physical laws of nature may be harsh on a man and lead ultimately to his destruction. Meursault lives with as much physical comfort as he can find. The great defect in this pattern of comfort and well-being is represented in various manifestations of light, which eventually grow into the blinding force of fate that at the end crush him.

During the night vigil in the nursing home chapel where he stays beside his mother's body, he is made uncomfortable by the strong electric light. The next day he suffers under the strong sunlight during the walk to the cemetery. In part at least, he explains the shooting of the Arab on the beach by the presence of blinding sun in his eyes. During the trial the oppressive heat in the courtroom comes from the sun outside.

The principal action during the second half of the novel is Meursault's slow detachment from everyday life, and a growing awareness of death. He knows that all men are condemned to die, and this thought helps him to accept the legal condemnation of the court.

In the tradition of French fiction, *L'Etranger* is a *récit* rather than a novel. It is thus a condensed abstract kind of novel. In Camus' *récit*, the principal theme is the nudity, the vulnerability of man as events and circumstances force him to an awareness of the absurdity of life. These qualities of simplicity and bareness in the themes are apparent in several key works of French literature, more classifiable as *récits* than *romans*: *Candide* of Voltaire, Constant's *Adolphe*, Gide's *L'Immoraliste*. All of these works, with which Camus' later book *La Chute* (1958) might be grouped, avoid any tendency to cynicism or pathos. In each case, the *récit* stands by itself, independent of the author's commentary or interpretation. This very absence of commentary enhances the book's ambiguities and opens up the actions and attitudes of Meursault to a number of theories. Is he a hedonist? Why did he shoot the Arab? Why does he shoot him five times? Is the story a parable?

The theory of the absurd, expounded in *L'Etranger* and *Le Mythe de Sisyphe* (1943), rests on an awareness of man's mortality, an awareness of the universe as not explicable in human terms. Camus recast, more successfully in his novel *La Peste* (1947) than in his essay *L'Homme Révolté* (1951), the preoccupations of a large number of European thinkers. These men accepted the premise that there is no God and that there are no ultimate values, and they then posed the question of whether there is an ethical code to justify political action.

Camus, in his role of moralist-novelist, or novelist-prophet, gave the world an exemplary figure in Meursault, a man representing the stance and the despair of the new antihero. He is Christ-like in the final scene of his execution: a criminal in the eyes of his society, a redeemer of mankind for some readers of *L'Etranger*. For other readers he is a Pascal without belief in Christ, a Pascal who experiences the wretchedness of man without his greatness. He is rebel against justice, but a Sisyphean rebel who cannot overcome the endlessness of effort. He is, perhaps more than any of these figures, a man alone, a man alienated, a modern man in exile.

JEAN GENET (1910–   )

In 1951, Gallimard published volume two of the *Oeuvres Complètes* of Jean Genet with a minimum of fanfare. The volume included Genet's first two novels: *Notre-Dame-des-Fleurs* and *Miracle de la Rose*, and two poems, *Le Condamné à mort* and *Un chant d'amour*. Volume one was announced as Jean-Paul Sartre's study of *Saint Genet, comédien et martyr*. This was an event in the history of French publishing because heretofore the books of Genet had been sold "under the counter" and consigned to that part of a library called *l'enfer*, where only a few privileged readers could reach them. Gallimard's civic gesture of removing Genet's books from their clandestine existence initiated a movement in publishing that continues today in Paris and New York.

When volume one was published in 1952, many readers came to Genet through Sartre's evaluation and sympathy. The study proposed that Genet be classified among the greatest French writers of the century.

Genet, who is five years younger than Sartre, had boasted that his work is the apology of evil, and Sartre devotes considerable effort to prove that evil is a myth created by the respectable people of a civilization. The wicked commit the deeds the respectable citizens do not dare commit. This theory has some connection with Genet's childhood and adolescence, spent largely in reformatory schools, where an early knowledge and practice of thieving and homosexuality were inevitable.

The episodes of excessive vulgarity in Genet's work never exist for themselves. He is as determined to understand the nature of his impulses and desires, and as detached in his explorations as Sartre is determined in *Saint Genet* to sanctify Genet as actor and martyr. For Sartre the value of man has its basis in the concept of freedom. Through the power of his freedom, man contracts an obligation to life. Genet's existence, especially in its acknowledged homosexuality, illustrates for Sartre the freedom that respectable members of society will never know. Society is in fact protected from this knowledge by the very law courts that condemned and imprisoned Genet. Sartre considers the literary work of Genet the projection, the imaginary picture of his life. His literary genius is identical with his determination to live the drama of his own nature (that is, the exercise of his freedom) up to the ultimate consequence of this drama.

One day the parallels will be studied that exist between Rimbaud's revolt against his condition in the world and Genet's submission to his fate. A world only half-seen by Rimbaud in episodes of *Une saison en enfer* is raucously dramatized in Genet's first novel *Notre-Dame-des Fleurs*. Extravagant in every sense, this late adolescent world of Montmartre, engendered by the early adolescent world in the prisons of Mettray and Fontevrault, is the *légende dorée* of Jean Genet, in which existence is a cult, a ceremony of evil when the male is female. Death in violence obsesses the minds of the tough heroes of Genet (*les durs*: Bulkaen, Pilorge, Harcamone), and martyrdom obsesses the minds of the effeminate (Divine and Notre-Dame-des-Fleurs). The guillotine is the symbol of the male and of his greatest glory.

At every step of the way, Genet has known what he was doing. Hence Sartre's term to designate him *comédien* or actor. And Genet never failed to acknowledge the condition imposed upon him by society when he was young; hence the second term in the title of *martyr*. (This title is taken from a Rotrou play of the 17th century.)

The harshest terms that the world has used in its indictment of Genet— thief, traitor, invert—are used by him in his own writing as his principal themes, as the subject matter of his novels. He began writing in prison with the avowed purpose of composing a new moral order that would explain and allow his mode of life. His nature is essentially religious and one of extreme passivity. The opposite of the revolutionist and the reformer, he is the man who lives outside of the normally constituted society. He has no desire to play a part in it or to triumph over it. During part of 1969–70, he spent time with members of the Black Panther movement in the United States.

The world into which Genet was born, with its laws and institutions, was dominated by the male. This kind of society instinctively tended to exclude and to crush Genet. The virile types he exalts in his writings are traitors and criminals. At a very early age evil became for him synonymous with virility (*mal* and *mâle* have almost the same sound in French). Between the ages of sixteen and thirty, he sought in his reformatories and prisons and bars not a series of transitory adventures, but a way of identifying himself with the individuals whom he met there and admired.

As a baby, Genet was abandoned by his mother and raised in a family not his own. He committed thefts and was sent to a reformatory, from which he escaped and then lived by begging, stealing and prostitution. When he turned to writing, he produced a series of books that are apologies of evil. After society had determined what Jean Genet was, he became something else—a writer and a poet, and hence, according to Sartre's philosophy, practiced his freedom, chose his own life and defined himself.

The concept of sovereignty has always obsessed the imagination of Genet. In *Miracle de la Rose*, his second novel, in those pages in which the character Harcamone is meditating in his cell, the ideal of sovereignty is ascribed to the assassin who is about to be executed. The state of evil is the reverse of the state of holiness for Genet, who plays on the two words because he finds them similar in the sense that the extremes of both are forbidden to an ordinary man and that both are characterized by violence and danger. Genet felt an attraction to the abject in his prison experience, and hence magnified the prison into a palace in which he experienced the sovereignty of evil.

SAMUEL BECKETT (1906–   )

The known facts about Beckett's life are few in number: his Dublin birth of Irish parents, his post as *lecteur d'anglais* at the Ecole Normale Supérieure for two years (1928–30), his friendship with James Joyce in Paris, his year's experience as French teacher in Dublin, his travels in Europe, his return to Paris in

1938, and his life as a writer since that return. Beckett first wrote poems and essays in English (notably one on Proust), and his first novel, *Murphy*, was published in England in 1937. He remained in France during the war. During the years following the Liberation, he wrote directly in French the works with which his name today is associated.

In his trilogy of novels, *Molloy* (1951) preserves the outline of a story. The principal character is a wanderer, a vagabond, but he has a bicycle and he is going to a specified place for a vaguely defined reason. Fragments also make up *Malone meurt* (1951), but the protagonist has become immobile. He is dying and the words are an effort to fill the void into which he is being drawn. *L'Innommable* (1953) is the metamorphosis of the various names, Malone and Mahood especially, into an obscure impersonal survival, a human will which refuses to give over to silence.

The stories or themes initiated in the first two parts of the trilogy continue in *L'Innommable*, but the new emphasis is the problem of the narrator's identity. Who is the "I" who speaks so tirelessly, who is unable not to speak, and who, with a new sense of freedom in words, analyzes his experience of living with an ever-increasing lucidity and self-torture? As his speech becomes more and more liberated, the narrator begins to realize that his entire existence is being threatened by the very speech he is uttering. The speech becomes words which continue articulating themselves without regard for the speaker, with an ever-diminishing human relationship.

The solitary voice of *L'Innommable* struggles against an increasing anonymity and against the implacable imminent confusion of itself with another self. It is the novel of a deeply moving and deeply significant adventure, that of a man who has fallen out of the world and who is unable to die and unable to be reborn with the world.

The theater by its very nature demands that a dramatic text be one that is always immediate for the public. No play among the striking successes of the French avant-garde theater imposed its immediacy more than *En attendant Godot*, written by Beckett in 1952, and first produced by Roger Blin in 1953 in the Théâtre de Babylone, in Paris. It is a work about living, about how we all live, and it succeeds in giving to the public this sense of immediacy without reliance on a traditional plot, stage setting and character analysis. During a performance, we recognize ourselves and those we know in the two tramps who wait for Godot, and in the second couple of servant and master who vainly move about the stage and then move off the stage. The story of *Godot* is composed of fragments of all the stories in which man has attempted to speak of his existence on earth.

The two halves of humanity are in *Godot*: the half that has some degree of hope—Vladimir—and the other half that has almost no hope—Estragon, who worries about his boots and is ready to hang himself. And then we see humanity in another cross section, divided into two other halves: Pozzo, the bully who blusters and does his best to terrify everyone, and Lucky, his slave, on the end of a rope held by Pozzo. Lucky's long speech is a jumble of erudition and history and philosophy delivered in a frenzied way, as if Beckett were telling us this is what happens when civilization becomes corrupt.

The second Beckett play, *Fin de Partie*, was finished in 1956, published in 1957, and produced by Roger Blin that same year in the Studio des Champs-Elysées.

The title of the play is a term used in chess to designate the third and final part of the game. But it designates the end of many things for Beckett, even the end of life itself. The approach to the "end" is indeed the principal theme of all of Beckett's writings.

Two of the characters, Nagg and Nell, live in ashcans, from which they raise the covers from time to time to speak. But most of the dialogue is carried on between their son Hamm, who is paralytic, blind, and confined to a wheelchair, and his male attendant, Clov.

Whereas *Godot* was concerned with the theme of waiting, *Fin de Partie* is on the subject of leaving, on the necessity of reaching the door. We have the impression of watching the end of something—the end, possibly, of the human race. All movement has slowed down. Hamm is paralyzed and confined to his chair. Clov walks with difficulty. Nagg and Nell are legless and occupy little space in their ashcans. The two windows look out onto the sea and the earth, which are without trace of mankind. No affection joins the four characters. Nagg and Nell depend on Hamm for food. Clov, the son-slave, would kill Hamm if he knew the combination to the buffet where the last crackers are stored.

This is the game that man constantly plays and in which he is always checkmated. The fundamental hopelessness of the situation is offset by a steady tone of burlesque and farce. The drama is the lack of meaning which the spectacle of life provides and which is offered to the spectators seated in the theater. In the space of a very few years, Beckett has gained the stature of an international figure. This indictment against civilization is simple and lucid. Similar indictments had been made by Rimbaud, Lautréamont, and Artaud. Beckett's vision of man is comparably grim and absolute, but he has maintained a personal serenity of outlook.

HENRI MICHAUX (1899–   )

Until the age of twenty-one, Michaux lived principally in Brussels where he witnessed the German Occupation between 1914 and 1918. He was born in Namur, in a family of Wallon and Ardennes ancestry. No bond existed between himself and his family. He turned inward, away from the world, and read the mystics and books of travel. The discovery of Lautréamont, when he was twenty-five, was important and initiated his first real acceptance of literature. About this time he met Jules Supervielle who became a close friend, and helped complete the revelation of poetry to Michaux. He met many of the surrealist writers in Paris, but preferred the companionship of painters: Ernst, Klee, Masson. Jean Paulhan was among the first to realize the talent of Michaux and published at Gallimard's his first book in France, *Qui-je-fus* (1927).

His drawings, gouaches and watercolors at first seemed to be contributions to the poems in words. But today they appear more independent, a separate means of expression. Like the poems, they are images fearful of taking on a deliberate form, of renouncing the suggestiveness of their lines. The poem and the gouache are the site of a change or a creation taking place, but they do not necessarily reveal the accomplished metamorphosis, the finished art.

When in 1941 André Gide published a lecture he never delivered, *Découvrons Henri Michaux*, the poet was far from being unknown in France. Today he appears as one of the truly authentic poetic talents who is taking his place beside those writers who investigate the strange and the unusual and who, therefore, transpose or even upset the literary perspective. The relationship that Michaux establishes between the natural and the unbelievable has created a surreal world that has become the familiar world of his poetry.

RENÉ CHAR (1907–   )

René Char was born in Vaucluse, in Provence, and lives today in a town near Avignon, Isle-sur-Sorgue. The Sorgue River starts at the fountain of Vaucluse (immortalized by Petrarch) and flows into the Rhone.

The world of Char's poetry is rural and Mediterranean. All the familiar elements of his native province are in it: crickets and almond trees, olives, grapes, figs, oranges, grass, branches of mimosa. The frequently recurring name of Heraclitus helps to fuse the Greek spirit with the Provençal. The country he describes is sun-flooded, a kingdom of space and dazzling light. Char's love of the land and his solicitude for living growing things are traits of the peasant in him. His manner of considering the objects of his landscape, of undertaking the hardest tasks and facing the gravest risks might be explained by the deep sense of fraternity that characterizes Char's love of man and of the soil. Like most lovers of the land, he has often shown hostility toward modern mechanization and modern forms of exploitation.

About 1930, René Char joined the group of surrealists. Although he soon cut himself off from any strict allegiance to surrealism, he profited from many aspects of the school. From surrealism he learned that revolt against conformity is a natural instinct of the poet, a natural instinct of poetry. Surrealism was a collective experiment that deepened Char's sense of brotherhood. The effort made by Breton, Desnos and Eluard to create out of their poems unusual perspectives and paradoxes by writing at maximum speed and adding image on image affected Char more than the philosophical inquiry—semi-Bergsonian, semi-Freudian—of surrealism.

In the early forties, Char participated in the Resistance movement as captain of the maquis in Provence. His partisan poems are the noblest of the war poems and the most likely to endure. The group *Feuillets d'Hypnos*, dedicated to Albert Camus, and included in *Fureur et Mystère* (1948) best represent the poetry written in France between 1940 and 1944.

Char's war poems, those in *Seuls demeurent* (1945) and *Feuillets d'Hypnos*, were not built solely on noble sentiments but on a rhythmical movement as strong and original as the rhythms of Pascal's prose and Rimbaud's prose poems. Throughout the suggestive statements comprising *Partage formel* (in the volume *Fureur et Mystère*), Char analyzes the basic mysteriousness of all poetry—"Le poème est l'amour réalisé du désir demeuré désir." Heraclitus also was called obscure in his will to effect harmony between opposites. The transformation of time into eternity, associated with the philosopher, has its counterpart in the poet's will to fix in rhythmical language an emotion destined to pass quickly. The strength of the poet grows midway between the state of innocence and knowledge, between love and the death of love:

> Entre innocence et connaissance, amour et néant, le poète étend
> sa santé chaque jour.

The verses of René Char, the aphorisms that abound in his work, and the brief condensed tales that appear in company with the aphorisms, all speak of the nature of poetry. The outside world in which the poet lives is the natural world of constant change, a flowering river of things such as Heraclitus described. But this is the site of risks and provocations. The things he sees there are not poems but they discover their reality in poems. The poetic act is the finding of a form for things that otherwise would never emerge from their abyss or their silence.

The pessimism of Heraclitus was not difficult to discover in *Feuillets d'Hypnos*. The myth of tragedy is man's principal heritage, but it may accompany a lifetime of revolt against this fate. This revolt is the subject matter of some of the leading prose writers of modern France: Malraux, Saint-Exupéry, Camus. It is also the subject matter of Char's poetry. Man's ever-increasing awareness of his fate is equivalent to what Char calls the continuous presence of risk felt by the poet.

SAINT-JOHN PERSE (Alexis Léger, 1887–   )

With the announcement in the late fall of 1960 that Saint-John Perse had been awarded the Nobel prize for literature, the work of a relatively obscure poet became a public concern. The work itself had been previously scrutinized only by that small public devoted to the cause of poetry, although to a wider public the name of Saint-John Perse was known, as were the few biographical details that had often appeared in print: the birth of Alexis Léger on a coral island near Guadeloupe, his education in France, his choice of the diplomatic service in 1914, his sojourn of seven years in China, his high post at the Quai d'Orsay in the Ministry of Foreign Affairs, his refusal to work for the Vichy government, and his arrival in the United States in 1940, where he lived in Washington for seventeen years before returning to France.

From his earliest poems, published under the title *Eloges* in 1910, through *Anabase*, of 1924 (translated by T. S. Eliot in 1930), and *Exil*, published in French in *Poetry* (Chicago) in 1942, and *Amers* (*Seamarks*) of 1957 and *Oiseaux* of 1963, Saint-John Perse has continued to describe and analyze the condition of man in our time, the fate of man at this moment in history. Although this work is quite limited in its proportions, it stands as a work that contains the full mystery of poetic form and utterance.

Poetry today is jealous and watchful of its secret, but this is not new in the history of poetry. It is the ritual secrecy associated with early Orphic poetry. It is comparable to the youthful ambitions and pride of the French Renaissance poets, and to the esoteric theories of the symbolists. Saint-John Perse knows, as all his ancestors among the French poets knew, that man is made to live at peace with nature, that the first function of man is to establish a peaceful relationship between himself and the entire universe.

It is well-known that the early diplomatic career of Saint-John Perse, had he pursued it, would have led him to one of the highest positions in the French government. But he chose the secret destiny of the poet. And even in this vocation, he has always refused to be the professional man of letters. The chronicle of his real life is in his work. It is a personal work, in the deepest sense, and yet it has no trace of the confession. Poetry is the revelation of a man perpetually rehabilitated from the shocks and the clashes of his destiny.

In *Anabase*, in *Vents*, in *Amers*, the poet sought to express the wholeness of man, the integral forces of his life and his memory. Even more than that, he sought to project man ahead into the uncharted and the new, into a future that was impatient to live. There is a dramatic movement everywhere in these poems where man, in his historical and natural environment, is playing the role of his existence.

This poet's work relates the secular and the spiritual efforts of man to see himself as a part of the natural world, to tame the hostile powers of the world, to worship the endlessly renewed beauty of the world, to conjugate his ambitions and dreams with the changes and modifications of time. This became clear in his last long work, *Amers*, a massive ceremonial poem that revealed an extraordinary sensibility to historic man.

The manner of *Amers* is a fuller development of the manner characteristic of the earlier poems. It involves all the diverse activities of man and states them in successive gestures. The world of this poem has the freshness of a new creation. Whatever legendary elements remain are actualized in this poetry, which is always praise, as the title of the first volume, *Eloges*, revealed.

Amers is a poem that moves far beyond the violence of man's history in order to exalt the drama of his fate which is looked upon as a *march*, the march of all humanity. Saint-John Perse himself, in a very brief statement about his poem, calls it the march toward the sea, *la marche vers la mer*. The word sea, *la mer*, is in the title *amers* ("seamarks"), those signs on the land, both natural and man-made, that guide navigators as they approach the coastline. Around the sea the action of the poem will take place.

The sea in this work is both the real sea and a symbol. It is real, as the source of life, and it is symbolic as being the mirror reflecting the destiny of man. The march toward the sea is an image for the quest, for man's eternal search for some experience with the absolute. But this search, as it continues in *Amers*, is exaltation. Man is exalted in his vocation of power and in his desire to know the absolute, to approach the divine. The image of power comes to him from the sea, and from the endless power of words. Covered with foam, the sea resembles a prophetess speaking the most sacred, the most enigmatic words of the poet:

> La Mer elle-même tout écume, comme Sibylle en fleurs sur sa chaise de fer . . .

The work of Saint-John Perse seems to be consecrated to pointing out a way to reconcile man with nature, and hence with himself. In *Anabase* man is seen confronting the burning of the desert sands; in *Vents* (1946) man confronts the violence of the winds, as he confronts the violence of the sea in *Amers*. Not only in *Eloges* but in all the subsequent poems, he praises the sky and sea, the earth and the winds, the snow and the rains. All of creation speaks to this poet, and he speaks to it in the *verset* he uses in the writing of his poetry, and which, in *Exil*, he calls a long sentence forever unintelligible:

> la longue phrase à jamais inintelligible

In his speech at Stockholm, on the occasion of the Nobel prize award, Saint-John Perse emphasized the power of the adventure called poetry and claimed it is not inferior to the great dramatic adventures of science. The poet's purpose is to consecrate the alliance between man and the creation, and he needs the seamarks (*les amers*) to show that the alliance takes place when the land recognizes its relationship of vassal to the sea.

The sea was important in the medieval voyage of Tristan and the quest voyages for the Holy Grail. Many French poets of the 19th and 20th centuries sang of the sea: Hugo in *Oceano Nox*; Baudelaire, whose *Voyage* alludes to the adventure of Ulysses and the voyage taken by the imagination of a child as he pores over maps and prints; Rimbaud, whose *Bateau Ivre* is an answer to Baudelaire's question: "Dites, qu'avez-vous vu?"; Lautréamont, whose sea violence is matched by the sadism of Maldoror; Corbière, the Breton poet, inspired by the sea and who chose the name of Tristan for himself; Valéry, the Mediterranean poet who found in the sea, contemplated from his cemetery at Sète, an incitement to life; Claudel, who like Saint-John Perse frequently crossed the oceans of the world in diplomatic missions, and who analyzed the religious meaning of water in his ode, *L'Esprit et l'Eau*.

In *Amers*, the sea has reminiscences of all of these uses of the sea metaphor. It is celebrated as that place of meeting where all the paths taken by men in every age will converge. It is the one image and the one reality able to sustain all the themes and unite them: the reality of the sea, the limitless power of life that is best transcribed by the sea, the eternity of man in his continuous action, the personal themes of man's solitude and freedom and love, and finally the poet's creation—the image of the poem.

In the love song of *Strophe* (*Etroits sont les vaisseaux*) the most personal, the most intimate experience of man's nature is related in terms of the sea. The beloved, when she speaks, identifies herself with the sea. She is both woman and sea, and the night of love is a sea night. During the violence of passion, the poet, in the power of his language, is recreating the sea and recreating his lover. From the beginning to the end of *Amers*, the sea is the sign of the poet's irrepressible need to create.

EXISTENTIALISM and the FRENCH NOVEL: 1945–1970

During the years immediately following the Liberation, 1945–50, existentialism dominated French intellectual and artistic life. It annexed to its philosophical works the domains of the novel and the theater. It even appropriated a political role and played it alternately in agreement with or in opposition to Marxism.

Jean-Paul Sartre

For Jean-Paul Sartre, the immediate datum is existence when it is felt through the experience of anguish. His philosophy affirms the sovereignty of man's conscience and the presence of the world. He claims that man's existence excludes the existence of God, that man is his own future, that he is what he makes of himself. The older values of good and evil are rejected by Sartre as being erroneously absolute. The new Sartrean value is a man's project and not the good or evil he does.

This philosophy was so compelling that it appeared in the French novel and especially in the writings of Sartre himself, in *La Nausée*, in *Le Mur*, and *Les Chemins de la Liberté*. Albert Camus' awareness of the absurdity of life led him to the idea that man is free to live as he wishes. In *L'Etranger* and *La Peste*, he looks upon human nature as a value that gives to action its meaning and its limitations. The impersonal simple style of Camus, with its clipped, almost monotonous notations, seems today inseparable from the atmosphere of the absurd as it is created and recreated in later novels and plays.

The traditional use of the novel as diversion and entertainment, as an indulgence in sentimentality for the reader, has given way to a new means of communication between intellectuals of several countries. By 1950, the novel had been firmly established as an expression of deep-seated worries, of responsibilities, of moral problems and religious preoccupations that were central to an entire generation. It became international. The French novels were translated immediately into several languages and were read by the same kind of public in several countries who welcomed the books not only as novels but also as instruments of communication.

The new fiction reflects everything, even if it does not comment on everything; it derives from everything as well: from ideas and manners, from politics and science; and it gives back this varied nourishment in the forms of narration and commentary and interpretation.

Up until today, the major French novels have been studies about the inner life of man, analyses of motivations and sentimental reactions. This form is as true of *La Princesse de Clèves* in the 17th century, as it is of *Manon Lescaut* in the 18th, and of Proust and Mauriac and Genet in the 20th. With Proust, and to some degree with the so-called "new novelists," society is questioned more than it is described. In Proust, the immodesty of the novelist's self-revelation is far greater than in Mme de Lafayette, in Laclos, in Balzac and in Zola. Gide spoke of "sincerity" rather than of "immodesty" when he analyzed the modern writer's effort to tell everything about himself. Rousseau's claim in the opening sentence of *Les Confessions* that no one will ever speak as openly or as truthfully about himself as he does, is invalidated by such novelists as Lawrence, Wolfe and Miller outside of France, and by almost all of the major French writers of the past fifty years since *Du côté de chez Swann* appeared in 1913.

Intimacy, and the most secret kind of intimate revelations, have developed within the novel, as the genre itself has developed. This practice has turned the reader into a kind of *voyeur* or vampire. From Rousseau, who announced it blatantly, through Zola, Gide, Mauriac, and today with Nathalie Sarraute, the temptation to write about the most personal secrets of man has become a veritable obsession.

In such a novel as *La Nausée*, the study of a character's conscience is an extraordinary document, and was, in 1938 when it first appeared, quite new. The analysis of Roquentin's conscience is more basic, more personal than any analysis of his sensations or his feelings would be. Sartre gives in this novel a vivid concrete description of a man's memories, of the sense of hollowness, emptiness, indecisiveness and solitude that lie at the very heart of a man's nature. The subject matter of *La Nausée* marks a turning point in the history of the novel. It represents an heroic effort to define a man's destiny.

Albert Camus

More lucidly than Sartre, Albert Camus illustrates in his writing the central paradox of the novel, and of all art, for that matter. Camus believed that art performs simultaneously two functions: that of exalting and that of negating. The novelist, and especially the existentialist novelist, refuses the world as it is and calls upon another kind of world to replace it. This dual action is of course in the word *révolte*, used so often by both Sartre and Camus. The artist attempts to remake a world by depending upon the reality of a world he wants to eradicate. The novel thus brings us back to the origins of revolt, insofar as it tries to give form to a value that is constantly changing because it is involved in the passing of time. The novelist (the artist) attempts to steal from time that which time eventually will demolish. The paradox is stated throughout the writings of Camus, especially in his last two books, the novel *La Chute* (1956) and the collection of stories, *L'Exil et le Royaume* (1957). He shows us man refusing to accept the world as it is, and at the same time refusing to escape from the world. This paradox describes the two extreme forms of the novel, applicable throughout the history of the genre—the depiction of the real world, or what is called realism, and the depiction of man's flight into an imaginary or fantasy world.

Both Sartre and Camus acknowledged the debt they owed the hard realistic American novels of the 30s, whose characters were described solely in terms of their behavior and their exterior actions and reactions. In their writing, however, Sartre and Camus went beyond the limitations of American realism in their effort, precisely, to follow the conscience of their characters and to describe the significance of the world which a man's conscience could give to him.

The protagonist of *La Chute*, Jean-Baptiste Clamence, is the type of man opposite to Camus' early hero Meursault in *L'Etranger*. He is keenly aware of all the modern forms of servitude, willing to "play the game," namely that game of society Meursault would not play. Amsterdam, with its dark stone canals, is the same kind of inferno for Clamence that the real prison was for Meursault at the end of *L'Etranger*. Clamence asks what meaning his life must have if he is not to lie to himself.

If there is a summa in the writings of Camus, it is *La Chute*, the most violent of his books, written with mastery over his craft and involving an expression of ambiguity over man's life on this earth. In the last fifteen or twenty years, such mastery of form and theme has not been achieved except in the cases of Beckett and Genet.

How can this ambiguity be defined? Clamence is a man who multiplies his confessions throughout the book, for this is a story told by one voice in an ill-famed bar in Amsterdam. It is a single voice with a multiplicity of tones —scornful, satiric, proud, complaining, anguished. The book is a story, but it is also an essay, an allegory, a philosophical tale. *La Chute* is ambiguous, and this characteristic is later true of *L'Innommable* of Beckett, of *Miracle de la Rose* of Genet, and of *L'Ecluse* of Jean-Pierre Faye.

Clamence lives in Amsterdam with the knowledge that he is guilty. *La mauvaise conscience* is the theme of his confession, which he slowly unmasks. Camus prolonged the work of Gide and of the more strictly Christian Bernanos by his determination to uncover the truth about man's moral dilemmas and dramas. He denounced as vigorously as Gide and Bernanos the false hopes of modern man. *La Chute* takes its place beside *Les Faux Monnayeurs* of Gide and *Sous le soleil de Satan* of Bernanos as a study of the duplicity inherent in man's character whereby man borrows the ways and the arguments of truth and God.

Samuel Beckett

In 1951, five years earlier than *La Chute*, Samuel Beckett published his novel *Molloy*, which may in time occupy a more important place in the evolution of the French novel. It appeared almost simultaneously with the first books of Nathalie Sarraute and Robbe-Grillet. These writers wanted to purify the novel of elements that did not belong to the genre. Beckett's role in this enterprise is central—quite possibly the major role.

Sartre, in denouncing Mauriac as a type of omniscient novelist, set a new mode with *La Nausée* in which the novelist does not pretend to explain anything. This is the mode of writing that *Molloy* continues. It is sufficient for the character of a novel to describe what he sees and feels. A search for meaning is not apparent in Beckett's work. He discards, denounces and refuses in a peaceful manner. As he demolishes the world existing around man, he builds up in his art of a novelist, a structure in words. His is the novel of language, the kind of novel that Flaubert once said he wished he could write—the novel about nothing (*le livre sur rien.*)

Molloy and all the novels of Beckett are about obsessions that take the place of the characters and events we follow in the traditional kind of novel—"Dire, c'est inventer." In its aphoristic bareness, this sentence from *Molloy* is a kind of motto for Beckett's art and, to some degree, for the art of the new novel. In Gide's novel *Les Faux Monnayeurs*, the narration resembles life in the sense of representing a large number of episodes and themes that begin but do not necessarily continue for long or reach any kind of conclusion. Characters appear, disappear, and reappear as they do in life, without always having a relationship with other characters. Beckett's art is more bare than Gide's; but we find ourselves in the same labyrinthine world in which ways do not lead to a goal, but begin and then merge with other beginning ways.

At the end of his life, James Joyce befriended Beckett, and undoubtedly his influence was great on his friend and exile—like himself—from Ireland. However, in choosing French as his language, Beckett moved in an opposite direction from Joyce, who had enriched the English language with many other languages in order to create a varied and fertile verbal substance. To begin with, French is not as rich as English, and Beckett's French is even more reduced to a basic kind of language. Whereas Beckett is a fervent admirer of Joyce and Proust, his style of writing, in its arch-simplicity, in its lack of poetry, in its monotony and repetitiousness, is the opposite of theirs. Beckett dwells on the infirmities of his characters, on their physical degradation. His sentences come from the movement of physical disintegration that he studies in book after book. He creates first in his characters an obsession with the world about them, and then he seems to undertake very slowly the destruction of that world.

Jean Genet

The same year saw the publication of Beckett's *Molloy*, with its emphasis on man's defeat and failure, on man as an infirm vagabond recalling his life as a long confused emotion in a world that has no meaning, and the first legal publication of Genet's *Miracle de la Rose*, in which a criminal is given the status of an aristocrat, of a sovereign lord.

The theory of alienation is prevalent in contemporary literature, and it has never been orchestrated so richly, with such tragic and sensual poignancy, as in Genet's books. The existences evoked in his novels and plays cannot find their realization. These characters fully understand how estranged, how alienated they are, and they are both obsessed and fascinated by this state.

Genet celebrates those particular manifestations of evil which he knew personally. The central drama is the struggle between the man in authority and the young man to whom he is attracted sexually. Each of the novels is a different world in which the same drama unfolds. *Querelle de Brest* is a ship, with naval officers and sailors; *Pompes funèbres* is the Occupation, with Nazi officers and young Frenchmen of the capital; *Notre-Dame-des-Fleurs* is Montmartre, with its world of male prostitutes and pimps; *Miracle de la Rose* is the prison, with the notorious criminals and their slaves.

Nathalie Sarraute

The term *anti-roman* was invented by Sartre in a preface for Nathalie Sarraute's novel *Portrait d'un inconnu*, first published in 1949, and reprinted by Gallimard in 1957. Mme Sarraute, Alain Robbe-Grillet and Michel Butor are the chief theorists and practitioners of the *nouveau roman*. The movement derives from existentialist theories expressed during the 40s, and possibly from the poems of Francis Ponge, who has devoted his art to the description of objects and who has been praised by both Sartre and Camus. The books of the three novelists are not similar, and often their theories about the art of the novel are so contradictory that it is difficult to think of them as representing a coherent school of writing.

They look upon the new novelists as continuing the work of Joyce and Proust, but in a totally different style. Between the time of Balzac and Proust, the novelist presented in his work types of characters clearly drawn and clearly explained by the psychological life of the characters. Nathalie Sarraute claims that this kind of writing is over, that new domains and new techniques must be discovered by the new novelists. Her ambition is to explore that minute world, that very obscure world in a human being where thought and impulses first form, and which are constantly disappearing and rebeginning. The novelist must look intently (this group of writers has been called *l'école du regard*) at the most minute things: an imperceptible tenseness in a face, the twitching of a muscle, an insignificant object that somehow gives assurance, the minor attacks or innuendos that people inflict upon one another.

The biological term *tropismes*, used by Mme Sarraute as the title of her first book (published in 1938, reprinted in 1957), designates the minute changes in a human being taking place each second—the residue of words spoken, the nuances of sentiments like the shadings of light that come and go, the network of banalities in which a figure is caught. The novelist intervenes in all this to ask questions, to track down motivations, to follow after the dispersal of words and feelings.

Le Planétarium (1959) illustrates Mme Sarraute's skill in organizing a novel around hundreds of details minutely placed together. The stream of consciousness (le monologue intérieur) is used throughout Le Planétarium, an art-form lavishly orchestrated by Virginia Woolf in a much more diffuse way than in Mme Sarraute's novel, whose style is more clipped and precise.

Alain Robbe-Grillet

The novels of Alain Robbe-Grillet are very different from those of Nathalie Sarraute, but the two writers have similar attitudes toward traditional literature. They both know that great novels of the past have been based upon visible reality and have treated political, social and moral issues related·to that reality. Sartre continued that tradition in his littérature engagée. Robbe-Grillet and Sarraute as well as Butor, Simon and Pinget testify to the need to transform the novel and develop technical aspects instigated by the three great revolutionists of the first quarter of the 20th century: Proust, Joyce and Kafka. The school of the nouveau roman claims that the writer moves naturally from the visible to the invisible.

After his first two works, Les Gommes (1953) and Le Voyeur (1955), Robbe-Grillet published an article (Une voix pour le roman futur, La N.R.F. juillet 1956), in which he says that the world for him is neither meaningful (signifiant) nor absurd. It simply is. His third book, La Jalousie (1957), marks a culminating point in his search for his type of novel, in which the world resembles a spectacle from which he as narrator is almost totally eliminated. In this case, the "world" is a banana plantation in the tropics, with a married woman and a friend of the husband and wife who is carrying on a relationship with the wife. All of that is made visible, but the man who is looking at it, and who is the husband and the narrator, is not visible. We see only what he sees, and we soon realize that his glance (son regard) deforms everything. The book's title plays on the two meanings of "jealousy" and "Venetian blind." The same scene, the same spectacle, visible through the blinds, is repeated many times with minute variations, but the suspicions of the jealous husband are never defined. Tragedy is never analyzed as such, yet it is implicit in the very detached descriptions of the scene and in the distance between the man looking and the spectacle he observes.

Dans le labyrinthe (1959), Robbe-Grillet's fourth novel, is more than ever a nightmarish world in which it is difficult to distinguish dreams from reality. A soldier wanders about a city after the moment of the city's defeat. He does not succeed in finding the person to whom he wishes to deliver a package he carries about with him. The title of "labyrinth" is suitable to the wanderings of the soldier along walls, corridors, sidewalks, through doors, the snow and night. This dreamlike labyrinth was already perceptible in the city of *Les Gommes*, in the island of *Le Voyeur*, and in the bungalow of *La Jalousie*. The novelist places us in a void where all the ways lead to an impasse, where time is dislocated, where space is altered, where the world is a closed-in site, suitable as a place for man's obsessions to unfold, and where he lives through a truly Kafkaesque experience.

Michel Butor

Among the best of the postwar novelists, Michel Butor occupies a high place. He is one of those novelists who, by reason of his remarkably controlled language and the seriousness of his literary theory, refuses to allow literature to be considered a diversion. He believes that the authentic work of fiction manifests a new way of being, and this is revealed by the form of the novel. New fictional forms may reveal new things in the world, and new relationships between things and people. In speaking of *Finnegans Wake*, Butor points out that for each reader such a work becomes an instrument of intimate self-knowledge.

The subject matter of Butor's *La Modification* (1957) would be suitable for a conventional psychological novel. A man in Paris takes a train for Rome in order to see his mistress and bring her back with him to Paris. During the trip he changes his mind; his project is no longer valid when he reaches Rome. He has been changed by the places he sees from the train, by his compartment in the train, by Rome, where he is going and which occupies his thoughts. All of these matters physical and mental become the real characters of the novel which force Léon to alter his decision. The reasons for his change of heart are complex, and no reader can be sure of the real reason. This is one of the points of *La Modification*, and indeed of the *nouveau roman*: it is impossible to reach any specific unalterable truth.

Butor's characters are revealed to us by the places where they live, by those places that oppress them. The hero is quite typically a prisoner. In *L'Emploi du temps* (1956), Jacques is a prisoner in the town of Bleston for 365 days. In *La Modification*, Léon is a prisoner for twenty hours in the Paris-Rome express. In Butor's first novel, *Passage de Milan* (1954), all the inhabitants of an apartment house are imprisoned there from seven in the evening until seven o'clock in the morning.

La Jalousie and *La Modification* differ widely in style and manner, but in common they have traits associated today with the *nouveau roman*. The type of hero who was endowed with a civic status and a biography has disappeared from this new type of novel. Subject matter based upon a continuous narrative and anecdotes and episodes has given way to the description of a world where nothing is stable or certain, and where characters, as we know them in the traditional novel, do not exist. The principal character in the *nouveau roman* is no one in particular, but he is a figure whose fantasies become a world in themselves, far more real than the world he is looking at.

Thus the art of Robbe-Grillet and Butor shows an emptiness, a hollowness at the heart of reality. The new structure of these novels demonstrates this experience of emptiness and absence. We are never told, for example, that the husband in *La Jalousie* is jealous, but we may feel this by watching him watch his wife standing beside a man. The function of the *vous* used by Butor in *La Modification* is a form of call or challenge to the reader by which we realize that the language of the novel is that of an inquisition, and the reader is being assumed into the stream of consciousness.

Claude Simon

From book to book, the originality of Claude Simon becomes clearer and stronger. His resemblance to Faulkner has often been pointed out. *Le Vent* (1957) is reminiscent of *Absolom, Absolom!*, and *L'Herbe* (1958) calls to mind *As I Lay Dying*. There are similar stylistic and structural traits in the two writers: long sentences with parentheses, numerous adjectives, a disrupting of chronology. But the fundamental resemblance is in the picture of a universe dominated by fate, where men are powerless in opposing the obscure forces in the world working against them. The symbol of grass growing silently and slowly is life fulfilling its destiny without man having any control over it. The picture of man's defeat in Faulkner is related to a punishment; his is a religious universe where fate means guilt. There is no concept of sin in the world of Claude Simon. The good and the wicked who make up Faulkner's world would have other designations in Simon's world: those clear-minded men who ridicule an absurd world where every human initiative seems grotesque; and the others (*salauds*, as Sartre would call them) who accept the mechanical routine of history and exploit it for personal benefit.

La Route des Flandres (1961) is one of the most adroitly composed books of Claude Simon, in which no one action is uppermost but the reader follows a series of scenes, of pictures, of states of being. No one story or episode is clearly defined. The death of a horse seems to bear a relationship to other developments—with men who are prisoners in Germany, with a jockey's memory of a race, with the owner of a stable. Gradually, by means of minute sketches, a world is composed, and we, the readers, become prisoners of this world.

Jean-Marie Gustave Le Clézio

One of the youngest of the new novelists, Jean-Marie Gustave Le Clézio, published in 1966 his third book, *Le Déluge*, which confirmed the promises of his first novel, *Le Procès-Verbal* (1963) and his collection of stories, *La Fièvre* (1965). *Le Déluge* is an accumulation of pictures, of conversations overheard, of familiar sensations minutely described as the hero François Besson walks through the streets of Nice (never named). The inventory of things, streets, houses, does not have the lyric quality of Camus' writing, and it is not expressed with the pure objectivity that characterizes the art of Sarraute and Robbe-Grillet. This semimetaphysical, half somnolent walker is an intellectualized, gallicized Faulkner or Hemingway character who looks carefully at all the spectacles a city can offer and pushes this experience of observation to its ultimate consequences of murder, of collapse into death, of "flood."

The power of the book is the sentiment of anguish that comes from the spectacle of the most commonplace scenes. It is another example of the metaphysical anguish of being, which—since the novels of Sartre, Camus and Beckett—is the principal problem exposed in a variety of ways in the French novel. It is to be found also in the prose poems of Henri Michaux, in the theater of the absurd, and in the new paintings (Georges Mathieu) and sculptures (Richier).

Le Clézio's sixth book, *Le Livre des fuites* (1969), is another novel on the subject of wanderings and crowded cities. "La ville bouillonne pour rien." And his seventh book, *La Guerre*, of 1970, is a novel about the war of modern society, the innumerable daily acts of aggression in society, and the slow destruction of the natural beauty of today's world. It is a novel about machines, subways, airports and supermarkets.

No literary form reflects more accurately than does the novel the ever-changing structure of society and the ever-changing moral and metaphysical problems of society. During the period between the two wars, novelists were less interested in telling a story than in raising questions in the minds of their readers: moral problems in the novels of Mauriac (*Le Désert de l'Amour*) and Montherlant (*Les Célibataires*), general metaphysical problems concerning the meaning of life in Malraux (*La Condition Humaine*), theological problems concerning man's destiny and salvation in Bernanos (*Sous le soleil de Satan*) and Julien Green (*Léviathan*).

With World War II and the advent of the existentialist writers, there was a fairly distinct break between the novel in which the story element is strong (Zola, Bourget, Anatole France) and the novel with a moral-metaphysical preoccupation. *La Nausée* and *L'Etranger* are not narratives in the traditional sense. They are addressed to the conscience of the reader, whom they ask to examine the reason for man's existence and his actions. The existentialist novel shows man facing the strangeness of his life and his habits, experiencing disgust with himself and with his existence, becoming aware of a fundamental absurdity in his behavior, in the seeming falseness in his earlier religions and philosophies.

Then came, in the 50s, the so-called new novel, which grew out of the remains of the existentialist novel. By the time the Fifth Republic was created, the French novelist had become, especially with the example of Alain Robbe-Grillet, a technocrat of the novels, whose art seems to be a minute inventory of objects, a form that has cut itself off from the pattern of the psychological novel. The new novelists did not find suitable for their books the great social-political themes of *War and Peace*, the personal psychological problems of *A la recherche du temps perdu*, or the theological theme of man's salvation of *Journal d'un curé de campagne*.

When asked what they wrote about, they answered, "about nothing!" Their subject matter has been reduced to a minimum. *Le Planétarium* of Nathalie Sarraute is about the purchase of some chairs and an exchange of apartments. *Le Square* of Marguerite Duras is a conversation between a man and a woman sitting on a public bench. *Le dîner en ville* of Claude Mauriac is a long rather futile conversation around a dinner table in Paris. The theory of commitment, so significant in the existentialist writing of the 40s, has been replaced by the problem of perception in the new novels of the 50s and 60s.

Jean-Pierre Faye

One of the most difficult and perceptive of the new French writers, Jean-Pierre Faye, has quite succinctly expressed his aim in writing as a search for a new expression of the reality of things. He looks upon the traditional psychological language as a code that corresponds to very little today. The novel in the new form given to it by Beckett, Faye and Le Clézio does not represent an effort to dehumanize literature and suppress it, but rather to adapt it to today's world. Rather than describe those psychological motifs that are easily recognizable, these novelists prefer to seize motivations, attractions and repulsions as they occur in their most elementary stage in their characters.

During the period before World War II, the novel had been enriched by the work of three giants—Joyce, who attempted to narrate the entire human experience of a few characters; Proust, who described a world of characters and their environment; and Faulkner, who narrated the history of entire families. By comparison with those books, the world of Beckett's disinherited characters seems a radically changed form of fiction. Of all the experimentalists today, Beckett goes farthest in his determination to abolish strict frontiers between types of writing. His novels are a medley of confessions, dreams, humorous anecdotes, revolting episodes.

The successful French novelists of fifteen or twenty years ago, a Julien Green and a François Mauriac, tended in the 60s to give up the writing of novels for the writing of essays and personal journals. The youthful heroes and the stern matriarchs in the novels of Green and Mauriac have been replaced by the nondescript hero who looks at the world through a keyhole or a blind, who is often suspected of crimes but whose actions are never clear, who keeps close to the walls lining the sidewalks as he crosses the city, who is obsessed by the details of objects such as an ashtray on a café table or a pinball machine, who is often nameless like the characters of Kafka, who follows not the exterior sequence of events, but the chaotic and muddled memories that live on in his mind, memories that relate him to the past and convert his present into his past.

THEATER*

There are three kinds of literary theaters in Paris. The first is the government-subsidized theaters such as the Comédie-Française—official, traditional, maintaining a large classical repertory and cautiously admitting newer plays—and the more recently created Théâtre National Populaire (T.N.P.), whose repertory is smaller and contains more foreign plays. The second type is privately owned, and known by the temperament and characteristics of a director. The avant-garde theater is the third grouping, which during recent years has played an important part in the evolution of the French theater. These are usually small theaters, *théâtres de poche*, where new experimental plays are performed. The plays of Beckett, Ionesco, Genet, Arrabal represent a renaissance of the theater.

The art of certain directors has counted greatly in the evolution of the French theater during the past half-century. André Antoine (1858–1943) was the first of the distinguished line of directors. His Théâtre Libre, founded in 1887, continued for only nine seasons and established the standard type of realistic production which is the basis of the modern French theater. He instituted greater naturalism in speech and acting, and an extreme realism in his care for details and use of real objects on the stage.

The activities, theories and ideals of Jacques Copeau (1897–1949) form the most significant single contribution to the modern French theater. He opened Le Vieux Colombier in 1913. The Copeau productions continued until 1924. He claimed that the task of the *metteur-en-scène* was not to find novel ideas for the production, but to understand and embody the ideas of the playwright.

Copeau's work was continued especially by the four directors of the Cartel, men who revealed similar traits of devotion, labor and imagination. Charles Dullin (1885–1949) founded L'Atelier in 1921. He discovered and trained actors, and was responsible for the first production of such playwrights as Salacrou, Achard, Anouilh and Sartre. Georges Pitoëff (1886–1939) was indefatigable in his apostleship. Georges Baty (1885–1952) sought to diminish the importance of the text, of what he called *Sire, le mot*. Louis Jouvet (1887–1951) created a verbal theater in which the text was given first place. His direction was responsible for the public's following the subtle, complex and ornate thought of Jean Giraudoux.

The devotion of Jean-Louis Barrault (1910–   ) to Claudel is comparable to Jouvet's devotion to Giraudoux. For several years, during the summer, Jean Vilar (1912–71) directed an outdoor theater in Avignon where the façade of

*See also sections on Claudel, Cocteau, Montherlant, existentialism, Sartre, Genet, Beckett.

the Palace of the Popes provided the background. In 1951, Vilar was appointed director of the T.N.P. where he was succeeded in 1963 by Georges Wilson.

The art of such directors, from Copeau to Roger Blin today, helped to form literary taste in the theater. The drama of adultery, or the well-made play, so popular before the First World War, was slow to die, but a few new plays, more sincere and more simple in tone, began attracting attention—plays such as *Martine* (1922) of Jean-Jacques Bernard, and *Le Paquebot Tenacity* (1920) of Vildrac. Jules Romains' *Knock*, with Louis Jouvet, was a success in 1923, probably because it was so far removed from the worn-out theme of adultery in the bourgeois class. During the 30s and 40s, when such professional playwrights as Lenormand (*Le Temps est un songe*, 1919) and Salacrou (*L'Inconnue d'Arras*, 1935) provided new plays, a number of highly esteemed writers, poets, and novelists especially, became known as playwrights and brought the prestige of literary creation to the theater: Giraudoux, Claudel, Cocteau, Montherlant, Gide, Mauriac, Sartre, Julien Green.

The case of Jean Anouilh, who has always been exclusively a playwright, was the exception. Novelists and poets like Claudel, Cocteau and Montherlant wrote their plays in a language that had not been heard for a long time on the stage. Sartre's *Les Mains Sales*, *Dialogues des Carmélites* of Bernanos, and *Bacchus* of Cocteau emphasized political and religious themes that had been absent from the French theater.

These men chose for their plays ambitious, profound and well-tested subjects. They favored classical mythological themes and thus renewed the Greek tradition of Racine's tragedies. Cocteau's *La Machine Infernale* is on the subject of Oedipus, Giraudoux's *La Guerre de Troie n'aura pas lieu* is on Hector and the theme of war, Anouilh's *Antigone* is his interpretation of the Sophocles tragedy, Sartre's *Les Mouches* is the story of Orestes and the problem of man's freedom.

During the Occupation, the theater was prosperous, although there were only three or four exceptional productions: Claudel's *Le Soulier de Satin*, Anouilh's *Antigone* and *La Reine Morte* of Montherlant. After the Occupation, there were signs of transition and change. The work of the Cartel directors was over, and the fate of the French theater fell into the hands of three pupils of Dullin: Barrault, Vilar and André Barsacque.

Since the war, no single playwright in France has occupied the exceptional place held by Giraudoux during the 30s. The possible successor is Jean Anouilh, who has written over twenty full-length plays during a space of thirty years. He is faithful to a familiar antithesis in all of his plays: the men and women who compromise with the world, and the pure in heart who are ultimately defeated. Ionesco is another possible successor. His plays are constantly being revived. In 1970 he was elected to the Académie Française.

The most cherished dream of Antonin Artaud (1895–1948) was to found a new kind of theater which would be a communion between spectators and actors. As in primitive societies, it would be a theater of magic, a mass participation in which the entire culture would find its vitality and its truest expression. He saw signs in France of a new kind of theater, one characterized by freedom, by mystery and the surreal. He found instances of it in Jarry's *Ubu Roi* and Apollinaire's *Les Mamelles de Tirésias*, which he contrasted with the popular plays of Bernstein and François de Curel.

The principal tenet of Artaud's *Le Théâtre et son double* states that reform in the theater must begin with the production itself, with *la mise-en-scène*. The theater is not a direct copy of reality; it is of another kind of dangerous reality. This is what Artaud means by "double" in the title of his book.

In Ionesco's first play, *La Cantatrice Chauve* (1950), he appeared as the playwright refusing one of the principal conventions of the theater—a coherent dialogue carried on between human beings. The same intention is apparent in the plays of Adamov. The principal theme of *Ping-Pong*, for example, seems to be a study of human solitude, or the absence of communication between human beings. In *En attendant Godot*, the two tramps of Beckett stammer bits of confused exasperated dialogue without our ever learning who they are or whom they are waiting for. The first plays of Ionesco, Beckett and Genet introduced a marked change in the mode of composition that invited such terms as "avant-garde," "anti-theater," or "theater of the absurd."

The one-act play has been widely used by the new dramatists: *La dernière bande* of Beckett, *Oraison* of Arrabal, *La Leçon* of Ionesco, *Le professeur Taranne* of Adamov. As the significance of the contemporary play turns from psychology to metaphysics, from an analysis of predictable actions to a questioning of reality and first principles, a fundamental pessimism about man has become evident. These plays often have the brevity and the terrifying concentration of a circus act or a vaudeville stunt.

Ubu Roi, in the presurrealist days, was an attack on the conventions and habits of the theater-going public, and Alfred Jarry, when questioned about his mystifications, used to reply that comprehensible matters would only dull the minds of the spectators—that what was absurd (Jarry was one of the first to use this now overused word) would train the faculties and memory of the audience. Ionesco, in *Victimes du devoir* (1952), outlines this principle when he has his character Nicolas d'Eu explain that there is no longer any such thing as a character who is unified and identifiable.

Whereas the classical French theater, in which major importance was placed on psychological problems, used a minimum of objects in the action of the play, the new theater has stressed the presence of objects in the play's dramaturgy. Cocteau's play *Orphée*, in the middle 1920s, used in a magical way a horse, a window, a mirror. An almost bare tree in *Godot* attracts considerable attention in Beckett's play. The telephone in *Les Bonnes* and a dress are constant preoccupations in Genet's play. Ionesco, more than any other playwright, has utilized objects: the corpse that grows in size in *Amédée*, the coffee cups in *Victimes du devoir*, and a bicycle in *Le Piéton de l'Air*.

In this last play, first performed in 1963, it is obvious that the character Bérenger is Ionesco, speaking about literature and the art of the theater. He doubts whether literature and the theater can comprehend the huge complexity of reality. Bérenger claims that literature has never had the tenseness and the power of life. He recapitulates a thought associated with the dramatic theories of Artaud when he insists that in order to equal life, literature will have to be a thousand times more cruel and terrifying. If the theater is to change, such writers as Jarry, Apollinaire, Artaud and Ionesco would believe that it might incite the spectators to abdicate their usual state of hypnosis or half-somnolence.

The ambition of many of the new creative artists, novelists and painters, as well as dramatists, is to exalt a chaos or labyrinth where they may live through and be seen living through a form of metaphysical anguish which is the mark of the 20th century. The scene in Sartre's novel *La Nausée* in which Roquentin rubs a pebble that is smooth on one side and muddy on the other is one of the earliest where the protagonist experiences a metaphysical anguish he is unable to explain. Between that scene, written in the late 1930s, and the antidramas of Ionesco in the early 1950s, and the films of Alain Resnais in the 1960s, the artists, and especially the dramatists, show us man in situations where his intelligence is unable to cope with his anguish, where he feels surrounded and besieged by an inhuman element. He lives quite literally the drama of the absurd, which is at the same time a drama of mystery and of solitude where he is conscious of the presence of familiar things that have no meaning for him.

The drama of man's endless freedom, defined by the existentialists as a psychological fact, is now, in the new theater, incarnated by characters who no longer look upon language as the means of communication between human beings. Beckett's *clochard* is a choreographic representation of the *outsider*, the everyman of the avant-garde theater. *L'étranger*, the title used by Camus, is merely one name designating the nonconformist. He is the type of amnesiac who has lost contact with the past. Alienation is the fundamental theme of the new plays, and the spectacle of the alienation we watch on the stage is fully calculated to turn the spectator into himself, to force him to an examination of the human condition. The characters of Arrabal, Vauthier, Beckett and Ionesco are, in this sense, our own consciences that have reached a superior degree of sincerity. The plays are testimonials of sincerity, in which the playwright is more concerned with depicting the condition of man's fate than in demonstrating the tragedy of any one individual hero.

The theater is a social art and offers to the men and women of a given generation their own portraits. Ionesco is concerned with man's freedom of spirit, and in order to make his public feel the necessity for this freedom he shows us in his plays the various forms of serfdom in which man habitually lives. We are bound like slaves to slogans, ideologies, verbal mannerisms and manners.

The method of this writing is an exposure on the stage of our anxieties. Ionesco chooses for each play an obsession or a mania, and leads the public to laughter over it. Antitheater is clearly the opposite of the theater of ideology or the theater of commitment (*engagement*) such as Sartre has written. The new theater is a means of penetrating into the vanity of many of the habits that fill our lives.

The parable in Ionesco's *Le Rhinocéros* is on the sacred individuality of man. As the inhabitants of a small provincial town are transformed into rhinoceroses, the protagonist Bérenger alone remains faithful to his vocation of man. He is the last soul in the town to resist the epidemic. He refuses to comply with the collective mania, the standardization of his world.

The familiar mannerisms of Ionesco's art are all in *Le Rhinocéros*: the ritual of the commonplace, the sudden eruption of the fantastic in the most drily banal scene, the meaningless list of words, the repetitions. But Ionesco added a parable and for the first time in his career interested a large public. He lost thereby some of the theatrical purity he had demonstrated in *Les Chaises* and *La Leçon*, in which no didactic element blurred the simple functioning of the infernal machine, of the antilogic of our world.

Roger Blin's production of *Les Nègres* by Jean Genet was the outstanding success of the 1959–60 season. The success came from many sources: from the text itself, one of the strongest Genet has written for the stage; from the *mise-en-scène* of Blin who showed himself sensitive to the poetry and dramatic intention of a difficult text; from the performance of thirteen Blacks who played at being actors with the seriousness and frenzy of children convinced that their game was real.

Les Nègres is a nightly ritual, a kind of mass celebrated before a catafalque. If during the performance one thinks of African ceremonies, of black masses and of certain esoteric-erotic *boîtes-de-nuit* in Paris, one is constantly pulled back to the specific play of Genet, to the poet's creation which transcends all the histrionic types it evokes.

The play is not a satire on colonialism. The revolt of hatred depicted in it is deeper and more universal. The Blacks who speak the opulent language of Genet give expression to a rage that goes far beyond the rage of their race. The oppression from which they suffer is so hostile, so incomprehensible, as to be easily the oppression of mankind. The nightly disappearance of a white woman by a process of magic is one way of exorcism. The play is an incantation, an hallucination. In the earlier play of *Les Bonnes*, Genet studies the curious bond of duplicity between the mistress of the house (Madame) and her two maids. In Sartre's study of the psychology and art of Genet, he analyzes the persistence of this theme in all the writings of Genet. A strangely distorted love joins the saint and the criminal, the guard and the prisoner, the policeman and the thief, the master and the slave, the white and the black. In one sense, the play is about the meaning of theater, about the distinction between a role to be played and a human existence, about the relationship between a ceremony and life.

In *Les Nègres*, the Blacks play the personal drama of Jean Genet. It is the agon between the actor and the martyr. It is the drama of a man who must play the part of a criminal in the very society that has ostracized him because of his crime. The theme of alienation is prevalent in contemporary literature, but it has never been orchestrated so richly, with such tragic and sensual poignancy, as in Genet's novels and plays. The characters fully understand how estranged, how alienated they are, and they are both obsessed and fascinated by this state. Simone de Beauvoir is justified in seeing Genet as a descendent of the *poètes maudits*, and in placing him at the end of a lineage of blasphemers: Lautréamont, Nietzsche, Jarry.

A clue to Genet's dramaturgy is in a letter published in the 1958 edition of *Les Bonnes* where, in six succinct pages, the playwright discusses his total dissatisfaction with the formulas of the contemporary theater. He denounces the stupidity and triviality of actors and directors who seem to base their art of exhibitionism on characterizations that come from their obsessions and dreams. The western play has become a masquerade for Genet. He advocates a theater of ceremony, a return to the conception of the mass, of a theater for initiates, where the high dramatic moment would be comparable to the elevation in the Catholic mass. In becoming a diversion, an entertainment, the modern theater has adulterated the significance of Theater.

The plays of Beckett and Genet have been called antitheater because they fail to express the traditional logic, the traditional explanations of theatrical dialogue. Conventional masks are dropped in this kind of theater, and the spectator comes face to face with the despair of beings who seem inhuman because they appear foreign to themselves. The theater is still, in the new French plays, the site where man's violence is liberated and where the public is purged, at least momentarily, of its own dreams of violence.

CATHOLIC THOUGHT

By its persistence and its vitality, the religious problem has shown an ascendency over all other problems throughout the history of French letters. It is in *Polyeucte*, Corneille's tragedy on sainthood, as well as in *Tartuffe*, Moliere's comedy on religious hypocrisy. Most French writers can be defined by their adherence to religion or by their attack on it. Calvin, at the time of the Renaissance, protested against Rabelais for his "Pagan" naturalism. Pascal, in the 17th century, attacked the *Essais* of Montaigne as the writings of a dangerous sceptic. Later in the century, and within the Church itself, Bossuet rose up against Fénelon and his doctrine of quietism. In the 18th century Voltaire sought the ruin of both Bossuet and Pascal, and in the 19th century Chateaubriand, in his *Génie du Christianisme*, attempted to rehabilitate Bossuet and Pascal and undermine Voltaire. It is quite possible to interpret the history of French literature as an almost uninterrupted controversy carried on between those who believe and those who do not believe.

Contemporary French literature is largely oriented toward criticism. It tends to be, even in its creative aspects, an elaborate accusation of the social order, of institutions and ideas. Both Catholic and non-Catholic critics are less concerned today with the study of the beautiful than with their efforts to make out of criticism a form of meditation.

In a fundamental sense, literary criticism is an explanation of the experience of reading. The new French criticism prefers the work to the author. Charles Du Bos was the first, in the 20th century, to demonstrate an almost exclusive interest in the text. Albert Béguin, another Catholic critic, continued the work of Du Bos, and explored depths in a given literary text of which the author might not have been aware. The Jesuit critic André Blanchet, in his articles on Gide, Malraux, Camus and Sartre, is actually writing a psychoanalysis of contemporary atheism. As a critic, he is a judge of the works, not of the writers.

The essay in the 20th century, in its multiple forms, has often been one of the vital manifestations of the Christian spirit in France. Charles Péguy, many of whose books are long essays, measured by the lyric intensity and duration of his religious views, was a spiritual guide for the first decade of the century. Jacques Rivière, whose essays are brief and brilliant, became a guide for the second decade, for readers whose attention he held by his example of incessant responsibility toward life and art. Charles Du Bos continued this role of critic in the following decade or two.

Charles Du Bos

The work of Du Bos, known by its title of *Approximations*, is characterized by an unusual scrupulosity in his will to understand any work of art he is considering. He lays siege to the life or the book he studying. He remains always a Christian writer believing that a work of art bears a testimonial to some spiritual reality of which the author himself may not always have been conscious.

Du Bos willingly chose subjects of great magnitude: Goethe, Nietzsche, Baudelaire, Claudel, Proust. In the presence of such writers, his receptivity was limitless. He carried on a dialogue with himself in the fashion of an intimate journal. Gide once said to Du Bos that both of them were the type of critic characterized by a love of dialogue and by a dislike of affirmation.

The seven volumes of *Approximations* and the two books on Gide and Mauriac represent a continuous investigation in the combined realms of aesthetics, literature and spirituality. The focus of his work is the study of what he calls the traces of the spiritual in the world of letters. In his early essay on Baudelaire (*Approximations I*), in which he analyzed the poet's humiliation and redemptive suffering, and in the later essay on Claudel (*Approximations VI*), which is the study of the mechanics of conversion, Du Bos gave a form of criticism completely independent of traditional academic patterns. The works of both Péguy and Du Bos, in the final analysis, are personal journals in which writers are discussed—Corneille and Bergson, in the case of Péguy; Joubert and Pascal, in the case of Du Bos—as if they were motifs in the spiritual life of modern man.

Henri Massis

During the twenty-year period between the two wars, French literature was given over to self-examination and self-criticism. Catholic critics especially seemed severe in their analyses and reproaches. Henri Massis, as late as 1941, in his book *Les Idées Restent*, attacked Gide, Proust and Valéry for having alienated French intelligence from its real goal, for having undermined the moral precepts of the nation. During the same years a strong renascence of Catholic literature and a rehabilitation of Catholic thought were taking place. The study of medieval philosophy received a new impetus from the lectures of Etienne Gilson at the Collège de France and from Jacques Maritain at the Institut Catholique in Paris. In the art form of the novel, Catholic sensibility was to play an important part in the work of Bernanos and François Mauriac.

François Mauriac

Ce que je crois (1962), published when Mauriac was seventy-seven years old, is a religious essay, one of several written in the fervor of self-examination, composed in order to discern more clearly the meaning of his religious life. Some of the earlier essays, *Souffrances et bonheur du chrétien*, *Dieu et Mammon*, and the *Journal* 1932–39, analyze spiritual problems of our age. Mauriac's voice is the last of two generations of Catholic writers in France whose work centered about a religious trust and inheritance. Claudel and Péguy were the giants of the first generation. The second generation, writers born in the 1880s, includes Bernanos (1880), Maritain (1882), Du Bos (1882), Mauriac (1885) and Gabriel Marcel (1889).

Jacques Maritain

Early in his career of philosopher, Jacques Maritain's *Art et scolastique* surprised simultaneously two worlds in Paris: the philosophers and the artists. Both worlds realized that the author of this book was a metaphysician who looked upon himself as if he were a contemporary of St. Thomas Aquinas as well as a man who had meditated for a long time on the paintings of Georges Rouault, a revolutionary and totally modern artist. The principal ideas of *Art et scolastique* (first edition 1920) were examined further by Maritain in *Réponse à Jean Cocteau* (1926), in *Frontières de la poésie* (1935), and in *Creative intuition in art and poetry* (1953), first published in English.

Maritain has not only studied the psychology of the modern artist in contrasting it with the spirit of the medieval artisan, but he has also studied countless examples of modern art and the laws that seem to govern these works. These studies have helped him in his understanding of modern man and the tragedies of modern history, in the social and political sense. The exaggeration and the inhumanity of the political state are not without their counterpart in the drama of the modern artist.

In his long career as a writer and thinker, Jacques Maritain has often expressed gratitude for the debt he owes to other writers and to friends—to Henri Bergson, first, who was perhaps the leading master for Maritain in his early years. If Bergson never professed Christianity, he often affirmed his love for Christianity. To Charles Péguy, Maritain owes especially the sense of the temporal vocation of the Christian. The third debt of gratitude is to his godfather Léon Bloy, whose prophetic vocation was continued in Maritain. Bloy spent much of his life in denouncing the lukewarmness, the fears and the prevarications of today's world. In his friendship with Bloy, Maritain sensed especially the man's freedom of spirit and his desire for this freedom to inhabit all men.

Whether he is speaking of Christian philosophy or of modern aesthetics, the accent of Maritain's voice is personal. The purity of his literary style leads one to believe that his nature is that of both a philosopher and a poet. All his life he has been a reader of the poets, and his perceptive comments on the work of Baudelaire, Rimbaud and Cocteau are among the most precious he has bequeathed to future students of French poetry. Maritain knows and accepts the great claims of poetry: that it is the essential language, that it comprises the fullest extent of human expression, that it is the absence of speech as well as the written word.

In 1970, at the age of eighty-nine, Jacques Maritain entered as a novice the order of *Les Petits Frères de Jésus*. After having been a *contestataire* all his life, he chose the rule of obedience for the end of his life.

At this moment (1971) in the history of French letters, pure creativity in the realms of fiction and verse seems to have diminished, and the critic's creativity has developed with boldness and brilliance and taken over first place. It began with Sartre at the close of the war. His key text, "Qu'est-ce que la littérature?" is still being pondered and still being answered. But long before Sartre, it was strong in Péguy, and continued to be strong in writers known primarily for other genres: in Cocteau, in his intermittent flashes of critical insight; in Mauriac, in his analyses of the novelist's art; in Montherlant, in the prefaces to his plays.

With the new French critics, criticism tends to be expressed in terms of a system, of an ideological position. It deprecates the biographical approach to a work of art and represents a return to the text. Charles Du Bos was the instigator of this form of textual analysis which has been continued in the writing of Marcel Raymond, Georges Poulet, Maurice Blanchot, Gaëtan Picon, Jean Starobinski, Jean-Pierre Richard and Jean Rousset.

Another group of critics, in whose writing psychoanalytical analysis is more predominant, has been guided by the example of Gaston Bachelard, Albert Béguin, Charles Mauron and Georges Bataille.

With the goal of criticism clearly announced as the analysis of "structures," it has cut itself off from the historical approach. By studying the internal biology of a work—its organization, its architecture, its phenomenology—the critic hopes to reach its real meaning and to understand the role of the reader as it was defined or implied in the writer's intentions. In abandoning the analysis of all the circumstances that surround a given text—the historical, geographical and literary sources of a text—several of these new critics have engaged upon a subtle internal interpretation.

There is still another group of critics who demonstrate sympathy for a Marxian philosophy of history, but their alliance with the other group is so strong that there is no need to consider them apart: this includes Roland Barthes and Lucien Goldmann, for example.

Each of these critics has his own style, his own obsessions and emphases. What unites them all is a belief that criticism is literature about literature. Despite their many differences of temperament and style, when grouped together these critics do represent a new intellectual climate in France, a new and vigorous approach to an understanding of a work of art.

The new critic is interested in discovering and studying those intentions of a writer that are not immediately perceptible and that were not necessarily known by the author himself. In this kind of search the critic draws extensively on traditional psychoanalysis as it is presented in the work of Freud and Jung.

Charles Mauron's studies of Mallarmé and Racine, and Sartre's studies of Baudelaire and Genet are examples of psychoanalytical criticism in which every detail in a text can be examined as a sign or as a symptom.

Closely related to Sartrean psychoanalysis is Gaston Bachelard's method of analyzing a writer's imagination as it is expressed in his metaphors. Bachelard, whose work antedated Sartre's, sought to discover and study in the recurring metaphors of a writer the mythic significance, the archetypal dream which he believes characterizes and explains a poet's imagination. These archetypal patterns are seen to be related to the four elements: earth, water, fire, air. Bachelard's criticism is a psychoanalysis of matter. The substance (*la matière*) evoked by a poet corresponds to a state of feeling, to a mental state that accounts for the poem or the novel.

As opposed to Mauron and Bachelard, Maurice Blanchot and Georges Poulet have demonstrated in their criticism greater attentiveness to those fully conscious traits in a work which illuminate the intention and the accomplishment of the writer. They do not study the symbols of an author as much as they study the recurring forms or structures of his mind and his writing.

The term "structuralism" as applied to literary criticism has been used to group together such different critics as Barthes and Poulet and the social anthropologist Lévi-Strauss. The basic assumption of this method is the belief that no single element of a work can be understood unless it is seen in its relationship with the entire work, and indeed with all the works of a given author. The structuralist method is a combination of analysis and synthesis, a study in which a detail is seen in a vast perspective.

The goal of this new criticism may be quite complex. It may be more than merely the explication of a sonnet or a novel. It may be the understanding of the entire experience of an author in the light of all his writings. It may even go beyond this in order to illuminate the entire age in which the writer lived. Blanchot's study of Lautréamont, Barthes' study of Michelet, Sartre's long analysis of Genet, Goldmann's Racine, Richard's Mallarmé—these are a few, but eminently noteworthy, of new critical studies in which the aims of the critic are multiple. They are studies in which the structure of a work is related to the structure of a human experience and the structure of a society.

These men have helped to make of criticism an important cultural phenomenon. The dominant question in all their writing is: How is literature to be understood? The new critic tends to distrust and circumvent what is obvious in a work, what is clearly expressed, such as the narrative element if the book is a novel, or the ideology if the book is a play. The moral basis is particularly avoided so that all of the critic's time may be spent on a study of the obscure zones of a writer's sensitivity, of his obsessions. Thus Jean Starobinski, in study-ing Rousseau, tends to pass over the social ideology of the writer in order to devote his attention to Rousseau's personal drama revealed in his relationships with other people.

It has been said that all of modern criticism is "structuralist." By the word "structure," as applied to criticism, is meant not only the visible organization of the work, but the invisible—the inner and psychological architecture of the human experience out of which the writing comes.

In his book *Des Métaphores obsédantes au mythe personnel* (1963), Charles Mauron (who died in 1966) studies Baudelaire, Nerval, Mallarmé and Valéry from the viewpoint of the subconscious of metaphorical analogies. He calls his method *la psychocritique* in order to distinguish it from the "thematic" criticism of Poulet, Richard and Starobinski.

Psychocriticism consists in detecting in a literary work "families" (*familles*) or what Mauron prefers to call "networks" or "clusters" (*réseaux*) of obsessive images. His hypothesis states that those images are signs that come from the writer's subconscious and furnish the principal elements of his style. Mauron insisted that the investigations of the "thematic" critics are radically different from his. In studying the *thèmes structurels* of a work, the critic is still concerned with the consciousness of the writer. He, on the contrary, is concerned with an obsession foreign to the conscious will of the artist where images are less precise, less clear, and are formed by groups of associations (*réseaux d'associa-tions.*)

The new critic has to become a first reader of a work. He has to try to see a work from the angle at which it appears richest and truest: "rechercher le point où l'oeuvre est la plus grande, la plus vraie, la plus riche." In the book from which this quotation is taken, *Lautréamont et Sade* (1949), Blanchot writes a criticism of criticism in order to justify his own method, that of "thematic criticism."

The critic should not be so much concerned with the influence a work has as with the initial movement or impulse that created the work, with the move-ment that formed the creator. Blanchot has a predilection for such a work as *Les Chants de Maldoror*, which he sees as a creation of the self, where a writer is born, where he returns to his origins. Lautréamont is one of a small group of writers to whom Blanchot returns over and over again as authentic artists whose writings are self-creations: Mallarmé, Hölderlin, Kafka, René Char.

"Thematic" is a newer word than "theme" and it is used precisely by the new critics, by Jean-Pierre Richard, for example, to indicate that there are themes in a literary work of whose meaning the author has no absolute knowledge. In this sense, thematic criticism is applicable to Bachelard in his analysis of fire and water, to Poulet in his analysis of the circle, to Starobinski in his analysis of the "eye" of Rousseau.

In Richard's recent book, *Paysage de Chateaubriand* (1967), he undertakes to demonstrate the mechanics of a writer in order to reveal secrets of which the writer himself was not conscious. The real landscape of Chateaubriand, for Richard, is not the scenes of Brittany and America, nor those of Greece and Rome and Jerusalem. All of his work is for this critic the setting of absence: *la mise-en-scène de l'absence*. The real landscape was that of Chateaubriand's soul, the inner landscape, that hollowness and emptiness by which Chateaubriand was defining himself in relationship to the world.

For Roland Barthes, the life of a literary work is measured by the *degree* to which it appears different from the intention of the writer. In the problem of how to read Racine today, Barthes takes sides with the university students who are weary of traditional vocabulary in criticism and platitudinous thought concerning literature. *Essais critiques* (1964) was Barthes' fifth book. During the preceding ten years he had published *Le degré zéro de l'écriture* (1953), *Michelet par lui-même* (1954), *Mythologies* (1957), and *Sur Racine* (1963). In *Essais critiques* he gives studies of some of the newest intellectual discoveries in France: the sociology of Lévi-Strauss, the music of Boulez, the psychoanalysis of Lacan. Barthes notes that today we are leaving the period of "committed literature." In his book of 1966, *Critique et vérité*, he raises such questions as: What is a literary work? What is the meaning of a work?

In the middle 1960s, Claude Lévi-Strauss occupied in French thought the place that Sartre had occupied between 1945 and 1955. Today he is an anthropologist holding the chair of social anthropology at the Collège de France. His ideas have affected the development of literary criticism. The term "structuralism" is closely associated with this scientist.

That aspect of the investigations carried out by Lévi-Strauss which interests the critics the most is the process of decoding a myth—of ferreting out its hidden meaning. This means the deciphering of the filigraine of history, of the motif that had been lost. In such an investigation Lévi-Strauss starts with a fact rather than with an idea, with a reality rather than with a philosophical system.

The principal quarrel involving Lévi-Strauss is over his conception of history. For Sartre, history is carried out by an actor we call "man." He believes that man has the power and the duty to move beyond social structures. The important matter for Sartre is not what has been done to man, but what he has done to what has been done to him ("L'essentiel n'est pas ce que l'on fait de l'homme mais ce qu'il fait de ce qu'on a fait de lui"). Lévi-Strauss answers

Sartre by saying that man seen as the actor of history is an ethnological fact related only to a certain type of society—our own.

In a special issue of *L'Arc*, Sartre groups under the heading of "structuralists" the names of Lévi-Strauss (as ethnologist), Michel Foucault (as philosopher), Althusser (as Marxist) and Jacques Lacan (as psychoanalyst). In the domain of French thought and criticism between 1950 and 1970, something comparable to a reversal of values has taken place that seems to parallel the new movements in literature, in the novel and the theater in particular. Sartre is being looked upon as the last metaphysician. A new generation of scholars has come after him who use a different vocabulary. "Anthropology" has replaced "philosophy," for example. "Structure" is now used instead of "history." One of Sartre's favorite words, "praxis," has been abandoned for "language."

In his book *Les Mots et les Choses* (1966), Michel Foucault is saying that civilizations are discontinuous and that a civilization depends upon its language. He claims that today French civilization is not one that comes at the end of a long Christian, rationalistic, humanistic tradition that started with the essays of Montaigne in the 16th century and ended with the death of Gide in 1951. Each age in French history, according to Foucault, has its own autonomy, its own mentality, its own structure, its own language. Sartre opposed this thesis by claiming that history is continuity and movement, and not a succession of immobilities.

Today's formal literary criticism has become something quite different from the type of judgment, the thoughtful reflective explanation of enjoyment or dislike that traditional criticism represented. The development, in the sense of change, that has taken place in criticism is far more drastic than any development visible in other forms of writing today.

Malraux in his theory of art, Bernanos in his denunciation of the bourgeois spirit, and Camus in his essay on Sisyphus were witnesses to a moment in the history of French criticism when it was impossible for a writer or a critic to look upon a work of art solely as a work of art, solely as an expression of beauty. This critical stance has continued to count for most of the critics who have written since 1950. The most noteworthy mark of contemporary criticism is the desire to be the conscience of literature, to integrate and exceed all the most vital aspects of past critical methods.

    The belief that society is based upon forms of myth and is instinctively reenacting the life-cycle of myth is today in France a vital part of structuralism and hence of that literary criticism associated with structuralism. The expression of mythic literature is not always as overt as it is in *Ulysses* of James Joyce, in *Fragments du Narcisse* of Valéry, or in *Les Chants de Maldoror* of Lautréamont.

It is more difficult to discover the mythical patterns in such works as *Partage de Midi* of Claudel, or *Amers* of Saint-John Perse, or *En attendant Godot* of Samuel Beckett.

Psychoanalysis, with its techniques for bringing to light concealed meanings, is a principal method for discovering the hidden or half-hidden myths in such works. Jung's theory of the collective unconscious, which contends that primitive patterns of life are recorded in the memory of each man, has encouraged the adventurous critic to discover in a given work not only the story of the writer's generation but the story of earlier ages and cultures. The modern critic is propounding, albeit unconsciously at times, that the cohesiveness of society, the unity of man, and the purpose of man are best revealed by literature. Such a claim goes far in explaining why today literary criticism has surpassed other literary forms in France and America.

Never before in the history of literature have literary texts been so carefully scrutinized as they are today by critics who, in the elaboration of their analysis, call upon a number of disciplines and bodies of knowledge. The author of a text is one man, but his text has a multiplicity of meanings. There is an historical meaning to a text, a sociological meaning, a psychology behind the text, a meaning in the text that can only be reached through stylistics. No one method of criticism could possibly exhaust the meanings of a text. Literature is based upon human facts and human activities, and that is why the literary critic of 1971 is necessarily involved in the principal ideological currents of the last ten to twenty years: existentialism, Freudian psychoanalysis, Jungian psychoanalysis, Marxism, structuralism, as well as such continuing disciplines as history, linguistics and literary history.

Modern French criticism offers a painstaking clarification of all that is implicit in a work. This is the natural, and inevitable point at which criticism and philosophy join. Criticism and philosophy cannot avoid an involvement with the ideology of the age in which they are written. The modern critic's determination to consider and explain the total work of a writer is in itself a philosophical tendency. Criticism, like philosophy, always remains to be done. It has endlessly to be done anew, after it undoes what has already been done. The critic and the philosopher reincarnate the now familiar figure of Sisyphus and his rock.

THE YEARS OF CRITICISM
AND STUDENT REVOLT: 1960–1970

At the end of the 1960s a striking analogy became apparent between the student rebellion in France and elsewhere and the so-called avant-garde literature or the avant-garde attitude toward literature. The artist and the student both felt that the major problem of our age is that of communication between men. In May and June of 1968, the students wrote on the walls of the Sorbonne such phrases as "l'imagination au pouvoir" and "Prenez vos désirs pour des réalités." These were new versions of Rimbaud's phrase "changer la vie." They were echoes of surrealist doctrine. Surrealism was in the violence of that May and in the basic claims of the rebels.

The poetic solution to life that the surrealists had taught the generation of the young after World War I was a program that gradually influenced almost all the new art forms in France and abroad. It was an effort to make out of life something that is closer to the dreamworld, something closer to an illumination that cannot always be rationally understood. It was an effort to add to life an element of fantasy, an element of madness. These are all key surrealist words: *rêve, illumination, fantaisie, folie.*

The angry young men of every country today want what the leading spirits of earlier literary movements had wanted. These movements took place first largely in France, and that is perhaps why the angry young Frenchmen see more lucidly today that what they are asking for was asked for by the dadaists in about 1920, the surrealists during the 20s and 30s, and even the Italian futurists.

When a serious stocktaking of the 1960s is made one day in the future, the relationship between the student revolts and the new literature, French literature in particular, will come into clear focus. It was the decade when everything was questioned, when the established values were put to the test, teachings of the Church were questioned and changed, and the goals and the forms of literature were reexamined. The Algerian War in the 50s, the Vietnam War in the 60s, and, before them, the waste and cruelty and enormity of two world wars have provoked in the 20th century a crisis in civilization that may well be more profound than the world crisis at the birth of Christianity, the world crisis of the Renaissance, or the birth and development of industrialism and capitalism in the 19th century.

When a young writer in France today asks why he should try to imitate Racine in the art of poetry or try to write a Balzac novel, he is emphasizing a break with history. In play after play, Ionesco points out the absurdity of human speech, the inadequacy of words in relationship to any human situation. In the two or three major plays of Samuel Beckett, we see the human condition (*l'humaine condition* of Montaigne) reduced to a kind of paralysis, to a minimal life that seems comparable to death.

The impulse to creativity seems to have diminished in the 60s, and the century grew into what had been predicted for some time by astute analysts: an age of criticism. A host of critics and commentators, in France and in the United States, have been asking what has come in the wake of existentialism. The avant-garde is constantly being pushed to the rear by new estimations and new assessments.

Albert Camus still has considerable success in Anglo-Saxon countries. But existentialism, first treated as something corrupt and decadent in the 40s and then discovered as a significant philosophy in about 1950 is today, at the beginning of the 70s, an historical-philosophical movement. In 1964, *Les Mots*, the brief autobiographical work of Sartre, was read with considerable relief. This book indicated that perhaps after all, Sartre was an artist whose aesthetics deserve as much attention as his philosophy and his politics.

Both groups of young and older readers are more and more concerned with the central question: What is literature? They tend to return to the writings of three men in the 19th century who formulated an answer to the question— Baudelaire, Flaubert and Mallarmé. And in the 20th century, they continue to consult the answer to this question as given by Proust, by the surrealists, by Sartre and by Malraux. This question dominates all the others in the new literary magazine in Paris, *Tel Quel*. The title is taken from a sentence of Sartre which speaks of the way in which the world such as it is (*tel quel*) can become eternal. "Il veut . . . que le monde tel qu'il est, passe à l'éternel."

It is not surprising that the creative writers in France of the 50s—Ionesco in his plays and the new novelists Robbe-Grillet, Butor and Sarraute—turned in the 60s to critical writing, to theoretical debate, and even to lecturing. Among the literary giants of the immediate past there are examples of the novel reflecting upon itself, as in the works of Flaubert, Henry James and Marcel Proust. And there are famous examples of the poem reflecting upon itself in the works of Poe, Baudelaire, and Mallarmé. But the 1960s were characterized by an almost monstrous expansion of criticism and scholarship.

Eugène Ionesco published in the 60s three volumes of self-analysis: the first, about how he came to write for the stage (*Notes et Contre-Notes*); the second, about his obsessions, his anguish and his dreams (*Journal en miettes*); and the third, about his preoccupation with death and his political views (*Présent passé, passé présent*). And a man younger than Ionesco, Michel Butor, published in the 60s three volumes of critical essays called *Répertoire*, in which he analyzes in the art of the novelist subconscious intentions and symbolic secrets. An ingenious complexity, a refusal to see matters in any simplified form, characterize this new writing of Ionesco and Butor.

At the beginning of the 60s, soon after the end of the Algerian War, soon after the founding of the new republic, the fifth since 1789, a new atmosphere seemed to exist in France, an atmosphere of restrictions and censorship that contradicted a cherished tradition. Between 1900 and 1939, Paris had been preeminently the city of the arts where the newest and the best in all the arts were made welcome. The French artists made the foreign artists who preferred to live in Paris feel as if they were honorary Parisians: James Joyce from Ireland, Gertrude Stein from America, Picasso and Juan Gris from Spain. During the earlier years of the century, Paris protected and encouraged the greatness of Proust, Valéry, Braque, Matisse. Even during the difficult years of the Occupation, the prestige of Paris in terms of its artistic productions was not diminished. Braque produced some of his finest paintings at that time, Gide published his last significant work, *Thésée*, Malraux his last novel, *Les Noyers de l'Altenburg*, and Aragon some of his best poems. The novelties of those years were the plays and the novels of Sartre and Camus. During the years immediately after the Occupation, Paris continued to be the most hospitable of cities, the most stimulating, the most tolerant of innovations and experiments. Fernand Léger, Le Corbusier, Max Ernst, Chagall, Milhaud are just a few of the major figures who returned to Paris because Paris was the center where their art was encouraged and fortified. The new novelists and the new playwrights flourished during the 50s.

And then something went wrong in the 60s. A new stricture, which lessened at the end of the decade, was placed over the arts. Students became aware of this stricture and it counted to some extent in their revolt of 1968. The liberalism of the Paris of the Third Republic was no longer the same. The Paris that had welcomed Proust, looked upon by many as a subversive writer, that had read *Les Faux-Monnayeurs* of Gide, that had made available Joyce's *Ulysses* and Miller's *Tropic of Cancer*, had become a city where the arts were submitted to authority. Parisians were aware of the close association between the president of the Fifth Republic, General de Gaulle, and a distinguished man of letters, André Malraux, who had served first as minister of information and then as minister of cultural affairs. Examples of control increased. Genet's play, *Les Paravents*, was not at first allowed for fear of public disorder. The film based on Laclos' novel *Les Liaisons Dangereuses* was for a time not allowed to be exported for fear the notion of France would be corrupted in foreign lands. The film based on Diderot's novel *La Religieuse* was banned temporarily in France.

The middle of the decade was a curious moment in the history of French literature and French social history, when the novel seemed to be drying up, when the essay seemed to be proliferating, when the president of the Republic —not only by his political forcefulness but also by his skill as writer—had completely enthralled two outstanding men of letters: Mauriac and Malraux. Etiemble's theory about *le franglais*—that is, the American corrupting the French language—was being taken seriously by some. It was the fear that untranslatable Americanisms would be incorporated into the French language.

The *roman engagé* already seems far away and out of date. And even the *nouveau roman* of the 50s seems to have worn itself out. It is possible that the full force of the cinema will cause an eclipse of the novel. It is certain that cinematographic technique has affected the novel, has tended to reduce drastically the use and the importance of analysis in the novel.

Everything today points to the end of an era and to the beginnings—the tentative, perhaps faltering beginnings of a new era when the patterns and the ideals will be set by the young, when the world will be fashioned by the very special lucidity and recklessness and fearlessness of the young, who feel that everything today has to be reinvented. This is a word associated with the adolescent poet Rimbaud. By "everything" we mean literally that: love, marriage, death, sexuality, the reality of man, and the incessant monologue he carries on with himself about that reality, about his solitude, his fury, the various forms of mysticism that tempt him.

The decade opened auspiciously for poetry with the Nobel prize awarded to Saint-John Perse. For this occasion, the poet wrote a statement about poetry in which he equates the new scientific research with the continuing investigations of poets. Science and poetry are both concerned with mystery. Science, aided by the most delicate and complex instruments, probes the mysteries of the material world, as poetry, aided by unexpected flashes of intuition, probes the spiritual adventure of man as he lives within the world of matter. As the world expands in its physical aspects—three men orbiting the moon Christmas 1968 marked one culminating phase in this expansion—so does the poet testify to the moral infinity of man, to that ever-deepening awareness of how he has lived and why he lives, that we read in the last poems of Saint-John Perse—in *Amers* (1957), in *Chronique* (1960) and in *Oiseaux* (1963).

Whereas the scientist continues to learn more about the physical reaction of matter on matter, so the poet, by the ancient and ever-young processes of analogy and metaphor, continues to learn more about the minute apprehensions, illuminations and impulses of his being. At the very moment in the history of philosophy when philosophers seem to be abandoning the study of metaphysics, the poet, in the role of relay he has played before, has incorporated in his art the practice of metaphysics. The poet cannot be limited to reality as the scientist is. He is more familiar with the ways and the temptations of surrealists. He is committed to a way of life that is also a way of knowledge.

Such a definition would seem to apply to the new poetic work of the 60s, a decade during which three poets died who had made very different but very significant contributions to poetry: Tristan Tzara, in 1963, the founder of dadaism; Jean Cocteau, in 1963 also, who used the word "poetic" in defining whatever kind of writing he published, including poems, films, plays, criticism; and André Breton, in 1966, who by his presence and example had kept alive the meaning of surrealism as a movement long after it had ceased being a movement in a literal sense. Two critics who died in the same decade, Gaston Bachelard and Charles Mauron, should be named here because of their studies into the mysteries of the language of poets, of those who celebrated water and dreams (*L'Eau et les Rêves* of Bachelard), and of that poet who, more than any other French poet, explained the incantatory effect of poetry and the power of poetic imagery: *Introduction à la psychanalyse de Mallarmé* by Mauron.

Four of the older poets published new important collections: Pierre Emmanuel, with *Evangéliaire* of 1961; René Char, with *La Parole en Archipel* of 1962; Francis Ponge, with *Le Grand Recueil* of 1963; and Jean Grosjean, with *Apocalypse* of 1966. And then, three of the younger poets: Alain Bosquet, with *Maître objet* of 1962; Jean-Pierre Faye, with *Couleurs pliées* of 1964; and Marc Alyn, with *Nuit majeure* of 1968.

Apollinaire, in his type of *poème-collage*, emulated Braque and Picasso in their cubistic forms. The surrealist poems of Robert Desnos, automatic texts written in a somnambulistic passivity, represented a new use of the subconscious. Jouve and his disciple Pierre Emmanuel and still younger poets like Robert Sabatier and Alain Bosquet continued to redefine poetry and experiment with the enigmas of language and the derangements of the senses that had been transmitted to them by Rimbaud. By now, the youngest poets, Marc Alyn, Charles Le Quintrec have moved beyond the eras of existentialism and absurdism, but they still express the anguish and the bewilderment of their age.

The poems of Char and Philippe Jacottet do not have the autonomous completed form of Mallarmé's sonnets. Even the prose poems of Rimbaud have an inner coherent structure, an almost narrative form that attaches them to a traditional formal poetry. The newer poems remain more faithful to their psychic origins, to the original experience from which they derive. The verbal richness of Char and the verbal bareness of André du Bouchet are equally difficult poetic forms for the noninitiate in modern poetry. The concern of these men is not the discovery of words to designate objects in the world and sentiments in the heart of a man; it is rather an effort to liberate objects, by means of words, from their familiar setting, and sentiments from the prison of a body and from the prison of time.

One of the major themes in contemporary French poetry is the effort on the part of the poets to understand the reasons that compel a man to write poetry. The dazzling explanation of poetic creation given by Rimbaud on certain pages of *Une Saison en Enfer* and by Saint-John Perse in certain passages of *Amers* are continued and explored in the work of Jouve, Emmanuel and Grosjean. The meaning given to the poetic experience designates the spiritual climate of a decade. The confidences of poets often equate or even transcend the thought of philosophers.

The cult of humility is one of the marks of the new poetry. To everything that is, the poet is attentive. His attentiveness is as moving and as fluid as are all the elements in the world to which he is attentive. These elements come and go in the metamorphoses of the seasons. Death in the poems, for example, of Jean Cocteau, is one of these elements—as familiar and accessible as those elements that can be called parts of life.

Poetry remains today, for those who practice it with the highest skill, the attempt to elucidate the mystery of man in his relationship with nature, with other men, and with himself. At one time, and not very long ago, poetry was accused of being obscure. Such an accusation is no longer valid. Poetry is illumination, even if its function is to explore the most hidden, the most obscure mysteries of man's being.

Ways of approaching the subject of poetry vary in time and with time, and these constitute schools and movements. Today's poet is best characterized by an absence of any need to justify or to explain his art. For a hundred years, especially in France, beginning with Baudelaire in the middle of the 19th century and ending with the death of Valéry in the middle of the 20th century, poetry was vibrantly justified and explained. Another poetic age has begun now in which the poet is the recipient of a long period of poetics, of poetic pedagogy, and when he is at last free to play a more receptive role. He writes and sings poetry because it is irresistible. At the present moment in French letters, when the work of poets is being examined more minutely than ever before—Poulet examining Mallarmé, Goldmann and Barthes examining Racine—the poets themselves of the decade, Bosquet, Jaccotet, Bonnefoy, and others, remain resolutely isolated from one another, each distinct in his writing, each determined to think the universe for himself.

There is almost no trace of love poetry in the 60s. The subject of solitude, but a philosophical kind of solitude, as analyzed by Sartre in *La Nausée*, makes of the new poems minute dramas in which the poet, not as a self-pitier but as a lucid analyst and philosopher, sings of doubts and contradictions and mis-understandings that often testify to the same kind of courage found in the plays of Beckett and Arrabal. Such a poem as *Oiseaux* of Saint-John Perse, the most established and celebrated French poet of the 60s, and such a poem as *Nuit majeure* of Marc Alyn, one of the youngest of today's poets, celebrate universes that are beyond our vision, and light years that tax our mental and moral limitations.

BIBLIOGRAPHY

Most of the texts mentioned in this history are easily available in one or more of the following series:

1. Bibliothèque de la Pléiade (Gallimard)
2. Classiques Garnier
3. Classiques and Nouveaux Classiques Larousse
4. Collection l'Intégrale, Le Seuil
5. Livre de Poche

GENERAL HISTORIES OF FRENCH LITERATURE

Brereton, Geoffrey, *A Short History of French Literature*. Penguin, 1954.
Collection Lagarde et Michard. Textes et littérature, 6 vol., Bordas.
Littérature Française, 2 vol. Larousse, 1967. Under the direction of Antoine Adam, Georges Lerminier, Edouard Morot-Sir.

MIDDLE AGES

Bédier, J., *Les légendes épiques*. Champion, 1908–13.
Cohen, G., *Le Théâtre en France au moyen âge*, 2 vols. Rieder, 1928–31.
Gilson, E., *La philosophie au moyen âge*. Payot, 1930.

LEWIS, C. S., *The Allegory of Love.* Oxford, 1936.
LOOMIS, R. S., *The Arthurian Tradition and Chrétien de Troyes.* Columbia University Press, 1949.
MÂLE, E., *L'Art religieux au 13e siècle.* Colin, 1931.
SAULNIER, V. L., *La littérature du moyen âge.* Presses universitaires de France (P.U.F.), 1943.
SICILIANO, *Villon et les thèmes poétiques du moyen âge.* Colin, 1934.
The Poems of Villon, French-English ed., transl. Galway Kinnell. New American Library, 1965.

RENAISSANCE

BREMOND, H., *Histoire littéraire du sentiment religieux,* 11 vols. Bloud et Gay, 1916.
FEBVRE, L., *Le problème de l'incroyance au 16e siècle.* Albin Michel, 1942.
GADOFFRE, G., *Ronsard par lui-même.* Seuil, 1960.
JOURDA, P., *Marguerite d'Angoulême.* Champion, 1930.
MOREAU, P., *Montaigne.* Hatier, 1939.
PLATTARD, J., *La vie et l'oeuvre de Rabelais.* Boivin, 1939.
SAULNIER, V. L., *La littérature française de la Renaissance.* P.U.F., 1969.
——, *Maurice Scève,* 2 vols. Klincksieck, 1948.
SEZNEC, J., *La survivance des dieux antiques.* London: Warburg Institute, 1940.
TETEL, M., *Rabelais.* Twayne, 1967.
VIANEY, J., *Le pétrarquisme en France.* Montpellier; Coulet, 1909.
VILLEY, P., *Marot et Rabelais.* Champion, 1923.
——, *Montaigne.* Rieder, 1933.

SEVENTEENTH CENTURY

BARTHES, R., *Sur Racine.* Seuil, 1963.
BENICHOU, P., *Morales du Grand Siècle.* Gallimard, 1948.
BRAY, R., *Formation de la doctrine classique en France.* Univ. de Paris, 1927.
——, *Molière homme de théâtre.* Mercure de France, 1954.
DOUBROVSKY, J., *Corneille et la dialectique du héros.* Gallimard, 1964.
MAULNIER, T., *Racine.* Gallimard, 1936.

MAY, G., *Tragédie cornélienne, tragédie racinienne.* Univ. of Illinois, 1948.
MESNARD, J., *Pascal.* Hatier, 1951.
PEYRE, H., *Le classicisme français.* Maison Française de New York: 1942.
ROUSSET, J., *La littérature de l'âge baroque en France.* Corti, 1954.
SAULNIER, V. L., *La littérature française du siècle classique.* P.U.F., 1958.
TURNELL, M., *The Classical Moment.* New Directions, 1946.

EIGHTEENTH CENTURY

GUYOT, C., *Diderot par lui-même.* Seuil, 1958.
HAZARD, P., *La pensée européenne au 18e siècle,* 3 vols. Boivin, 1946.
MORNET, D., *Rousseau.* Hatier, 1950.
POMEAU, R., *Beaumarchais.* Hatier, 1957.
———, *Voltaire par lui-même.* Seuil, 1955.
SAULNIER, V. L., *La littérature française du siècle philosophique.* P.U.F., 1969.
STAROBINSKI, J., *J. J. Rousseau, la transparence et l'obstacle.* Plon, 1957.
TORREY, N., *The Spirit of Voltaire.* Russell and Russell, 1968.

NINETEENTH CENTURY

BACHELARD, G., *Lautréamont.* Corti, 1940.
BARDÈCHE, M., *Balzac romancier.* Plon, 1940.
BÉGUIN, A., *Balzac visionnaire.* Skira, 1945.
———, *Gérard de Nerval.* Corti, 1945.
———, *L'Ame romantique et le rêve.* Corti, 1946.
BLUM, L., *Stendhal et le beylisme.* Albin Michel, 1912.
CASTEX, P. G., *Vigny.* Hatier, 1952.
FOWLIE, W., *Mallarmé.* U. of Chicago Press, 1962.
———, *Rimbaud: A Critical Study.* U. of Chicago Press, 1965.
———, *Stendhal.* Macmillan, 1969.
JASINSKI, R., *Théophile Gautier, les années romantiques.* Vuibert, 1929.
MAUROIS, A., *Chateaubriand.* Grasset, 1938.
MONDOR, H., *Vie de Mallarmé.* Gallimard, 1941.

RAYMOND, M., *De Baudelaire au surréalisme.* Corréa, 1940.
RUFF, M., *Baudelaire.* Hatier, 1966.
——, *Rimbaud.* Hatier, 1968.
SAULNIER, V. L., *La littérature française du siècle romantique.* P.U.F., 1960.
STEEGMULLER, F., *Flaubert and Madame Bovary.* Viking, 1939.
THIBAUDET, A., *Histoire de la littérature française de 1789 à nos jours.* Gallimard, 1938.
TURNELL, M., *The Novel in France.* New Directions, 1950.

TWENTIETH CENTURY

CORMEAU, N., *L'Art de François Mauriac.* Grasset, 1951.
CRUICKSHANK, J., *The Novelist As Philosopher.* Oxford, 1962. (on Queneau, Sartre, Beckett, Camus, Robbe-Grillet, etc.)
ESSLIN, M., *The Theater of the Absurd.* Doubleday-Anchor, 1961.
FOWLIE, W., *Age of Surrealism.* Indiana Univ. Press, 1960.
——, *André Gide: His Life and Art.* Macmillan, 1965.
——, *Claudel.* Bowes and Bowes, 1957.
——, *Climate of Violence: the French Literary Tradition from Baudelaire to the Present.* Macmillan, 1967.
——, *Dionysus in Paris: A Guide to Contemporary French Theater.* Meridian, 1960.
——, *The French Critic.* U. of S. Illinois, 1968.
——, *A Guide to Contemporary French Literature.* Meridian, 1957.
——, *Jean Cocteau: The History of a Poet's Age.* Univ. of Indiana Press, 1966.
——, *A Reading of Proust.* Anchor-Doubleday, 1964.
GUICHARNAUD, J., *Modern French Theater.* Yale Univ. Press, 1967.
LEVI-STRAUSS, C., *Tristes Tropiques.* Plon, 1958.
PEYRE, H., *French Novelists Today.* Oxford, 1967.
PIAGET, J., *Le Structuralisme.* P.U.F., 1968.
PICON, G., *André Malraux.* Gallimard, 1946.
O'DONNELL, D., *Maria Cross.* Oxford, 1953. (on Catholic writers)
SHATTUCK, R., *The Banquet Years.* Harcourt Brace, 1955.

INDEX OF AUTHORS